Trade Policy Review

Turkey
2012

World Trade Organization
Geneva, March 2012

WTO/GATT TRADE POLICY REVIEWS CURRENTLY AVAILABLE

Albania	2010
Antigua and Barbuda	2001
Angola	2006
Argentina	1999, 2007
Armania	2010
Australia	1989, 1994, 1998, 2002, 2007, 2011
Austria	1992
Bahrain	2000, 2007
Bangladesh	1992, 2000, 2006
Barbados	2002, 2008
Belize	2010
Belize and Suriname	2004
Benin	1997
Benin, Burkina Faso and Mali	2004, 2010
Bolivia	1993, 1999, 2005
Brazil	1992, 1995, 2000, 2004, 2009
Brunei Darussalam	2001, 2008
Bulgaria	2003
Burundi	2003
Cambodia	2011
Cameroon	1995, 2001
Cameroon and Gabon	2007
Canada	1990, 1992, 1994, 1996, 1998, 2000, 2003, 2007, 2011
Central African Republic	2007
Chad	2007
Chile	1991, 1997, 2003, 2009
China	2006, 2008, 2010
Colombia	1990, 1996, 2006
Congo	2006, 2010
Costa Rica	1995, 2001, 2007
Côte d'Ivoire	1995
Croatia	2010
Cyprus	1997
Czech Republic	1996, 2001
Djibouti	2006
Dominica	2001
Dominican Republic	1996, 2002, 2008
East African Community	2006
Ecuador	2005, 2011
Egypt	1992, 1999, 2005
El Salvador	1996, 2003, 2010
European Communities (European Union)	1991, 1993, 1995, 1997, 2000, 2002, 2004, 2007, 2009, 2011
Fiji	1997, 2009
Finland	1997
Gabon	2001
Gambia	2004, 2010
Georgia	2009
Ghana	1992, 2001, 2008
Grenada	2001
Guatemala	2002, 2009
Guinea	1999, 2005, 2011
Guyana	2003, 2009
Haiti	2003
Honduras	2003, 2010
Hong Kong, China	1990, 1994, 1998, 2002, 2006, 2010
Hungary	1991, 1998
Iceland	1994, 2000, 2006
India	1993, 1998, 2002, 2007, 2011
Indonesia	1995, 1998, 2003, 2007
Israel	1995, 1999, 2006
Jamaica	1998, 2005, 2011
Japan	1992, 1995, 1998, 2000, 2002, 2005, 2007, 2009, 2011
Jordan	2008
Kenya	1993, 2000
Kyrgyz Republic	2006
Liechtenstein	2000, 2004
Macao, China	1994, 2001, 2007
Madagascar	2001, 2008
Malawi	2002, 2010
Malaysia	1993, 1997, 2001, 2006, 2010
Maldives	2003, 2009
Mauritania	2002, 2011
Mauritius	1995, 2001, 2008
Mexico	1993, 1997, 2002, 2008
Mongolia	2005
Morocco	1990, 1996, 2003, 2009
Mozambique	2001, 2009
Nepal	2012
New Zealand	1990, 1996, 2003, 2009
Nicaragua	1999, 2006
Niger/Senegal	2003, 2009
Nigeria	1991, 1998, 2005, 2011
Norway	1991, 1996, 2000, 2004, 2008
Oman	2008
Pakistan	1995, 2002, 2008
Panama	2007
Papua New Guinea	1999, 2010
Paraguay	1997, 2005, 2011
Peru	1994, 2000, 2007
Philippines	1993, 1999, 2005, 2012
Poland	1992, 2000
Qatar	2005
Republic of Korea	1992, 1996, 2000, 2004, 2008
Romania	1992, 1999, 2005
Rwanda	2004
Saint Kitts and Nevis	2001
Saint Lucia	2001
Saint Vincent and the Grenadines	2001
Separate Customs Territory of Taiwan, Penghu, Kinmen, and Matsu	2006, 2010
Sierra Leone	2005
Singapore	1992, 1996, 2000, 2004, 2008
Slovak Republic	1995, 2001
Slovenia	2002
Solomon Islands	1998, 2009
Southern African Customs Union	1998, 2003, 2009
Sri Lanka	1995, 2004, 2010
Sweden	1995
Switzerland and Liechtenstein	1991, 1996, 2000, 2004, 2008
Tanzania	2000
Thailand	1991, 1995, 1999, 2003, 2007, 2011
The Kingdom of Saudi Arabia	2012
The State of Kuwait	2012
Togo	1999, 2006
Trinidad & Tobago	1998, 2005, 2012
Tunisia	1994, 2005
Turkey	1994, 1998, 2003, 2007, 2012
Uganda	1995, 2001
United Arab Emirates	2006, 2012
United States	1990, 1992, 1994, 1996, 1999, 2001, 2004, 2006, 2008, 2010
Uruguay	1992, 1998, 2006
Venezuela	1996, 2002
Zambia	1996, 2002, 2009
Zimbabwe	1995, 2011

Co-Published by the World Trade Organization and Bernan Press. Printed in the U.S.A.

ISBN 13: 978-1-59888-569-9
ISSN: 1556-2050

All reports are available in English, French, and Spanish.

For more information, please contact:

WTO PUBLICATIONS
Centre William Rappard
Rue de Lausanne 154
1211 Geneva 21, Switzerland
Telephone: (41 22) 739 5208, 5308
Fax: (41 22) 739 5792
Email: publications@wto.org
www.wto.org

BERNAN PRESS, a wholly owned subsidiary of
The Rowman & Littlefield Publishing Group, Inc.
4501 Forbes Boulevard, Suite 200
Lanham, MD 20706, U.S.A.
Telephone: (301) 459-7666 (Washington, D.C. area)
(800) 865-3457 (toll-free)
Email:customercare@bernan.com
www.bernan.com

PREFACE

The Trade Policy Review Mechanism (TPRM) was first established on a trial basis by the GATT CONTRACTING PARTIES in April 1989. The Mechanism became a permanent feature of the World Trade Organization under the Marrakesh Agreement which established the WTO in January 1995.

The objectives of the TPRM are to contribute to improved adherence by all WTO Members to rules, disciplines and commitments made under the Multilateral Trade Agreements and, where applicable, the Plurilateral Trade Agreements, and hence to the smoother functioning of the multilateral trading system, by achieving greater transparency in, and understanding of, the trade policies and practices of Members. Accordingly, the review mechanism enables the regular collective appreciation and evaluation of the full range of individual Members' trade policies and practices and their impact on the functioning of the multilateral trading system. It is not intended to serve as a basis for the enforcement of specific obligations under the Agreements or for dispute settlement procedures, or to impose new policy commitments on Members.

The assessment carried out under the TPRM takes place, to the extent relevant, against the background of the wider economic and developmental needs, policies and objectives of the Member concerned, as well as its external environment. However, the function of the review mechanism is to examine the impact of a Member's trade policies and practices on the multilateral trading system.

Under the TPRM, the trade policies of all Members are subject to periodic review. The four largest trading entities in terms of world market share, counting the European Union as one, are reviewed every two years, the 16 next largest trading entities every four years, and other Members every six years; a longer period may be fixed for least-developed countries.

The reviews are conducted by the Trade Policy Review Body (TPRB) on the basis of two documents: a policy statement by the Member under review and a comprehensive report drawn up by the WTO Secretariat on its own responsibility.

TABLE OF CONTENTS

Note: The documents that comprise this publication are available online at: http://www.wto.org/english/tratop_e/tpr_e/tp_rep_e.htm.

PART A

CONCLUDING REMARKS BY THE CHAIRPERSON

OF THE TRADE POLICY REVIEW BODY,

H.E. MR. MARIO MATUS

AT THE TRADE POLICY REVIEW

OF TURKEY

21 AND 23 FEBRUARY 2012

CONCLUDING REMARKS BY THE CHAIRPERSON

1. This fifth Trade Policy Review of the Republic of Turkey has been an excellent opportunity for us all to improve our understanding of Turkey's trade and trade-related policies and practices and how they have evolved since the previous review in 2007. We are grateful for the active participation of the Turkish delegation headed by H.E. Mr. Cemalettin Damlaci, Deputy Undersecretary at the Ministry of Economy. I would also like to thank the discussant, H.E. Ambassador István Major of Hungary, and Members of the TPRB for contributing to our fruitful exchange of views.

2. Members commended Turkey for its impressive recovery from the global financial crisis, having capitalized on structural reforms undertaken in response to past crises. Noting that Turkey has set ambitious targets for its economy by 2023, to be achieved with the development of an export-oriented production structure, Members sought more information on how Turkey intended to attain its goals.

3. Members appreciated Turkey's active participation in the WTO and its commitment to a strong and effective multilateral trading system. Although the dominance of the EU has become less pronounced in Turkey's foreign trade over the last four years, Turkey is closely linked to the EU through the customs union, and Turkey's negotiations to ultimately become an EU Member. Many questions were raised about Turkey's participation in preferential trade agreements and on-going negotiations to expand the network of trade preferences even further. Turkey's GSP scheme, whereby Turkey extends preferences unilaterally to other developing countries, and in particular LDCs, was highlighted and appreciated.

4. Although Members found that Turkey had relied on macroeconomic measures to exit successfully from the shocks caused by the global financial crisis, some evidence of recent trade restrictive measures was also highlighted and examined. Areas for further reform were also identified. Action on these fronts would enhance the competitiveness of the Turkish economy and contribute to sustained economic growth, to the benefit of Turkey and its trading partners. In particular, Turkey might give consideration to the following points:

- **Tariffs:** The gap between Turkey's applied tariffs and its commitments within the WTO framework is considerable. While Members would expect significant efforts from Turkey to reduce this gap in the future, Turkey should also be careful not to exploit this "policy space" to the detriment of its trading partners in the interim.

- **Trade remedies**: Turkey has become a major user of anti-dumping and safeguard measures. I note the slowdown in new anti-dumping investigations as a positive sign, but also that some concerns were raised about recent decisions to extend certain safeguard measures and whether these decisions had complied with all the requirements of the WTO.

- **TBT and SPS:** Turkey was encouraged to improve its procedures for the publication and notification of draft technical regulations and conformity assessment procedures. Turkey was urged to ensure that its SPS measures not be maintained without scientific evidence nor be more trade-restrictive than necessary.

- **Government procurement:** Some Members encouraged Turkey to remove the existing price preference for domestic suppliers in public procurement and consider accession to the Government Procurement Agreement at the earliest possible stage.

- **Intellectual property:** Several Members noted that the protection of intellectual property had improved in Turkey, and encouraged the authorities to continue their efforts to ensure more effective enforcement of IPRs.

- **Agriculture:** Some delegations noted that Turkey's agricultural sector has become less market oriented with increasing levels of subsidies, and a shift towards more trade-distorting forms of support. Enhanced transparency in the market interventions of state-owned enterprises was called for. Turkey should also keep Members regularly informed by providing accurate and timely notifications on domestic support and export subsidies to the WTO.

5. This successfully concludes our fifth Review of the Republic of Turkey. The large number of advance questions and the many interventions by Members indicate the important role of Turkey in the multilateral trading system. Turkey's recent economic performance is a success story which we would all like to see continued in the years to come.

PART B

REPORT BY THE WTO SECRETARIAT

This report was drafted by Mr. Cato Adrian, Mr. Thomas Friedheim, and Mrs. Vesile Kulacoglu.

CONTENTS

CHARTS

TABLES

APPENDIX TABLES

SUMMARY

1. Like so many other countries across the world, Turkey felt the impact of the global financial crisis in 2008 and 2009, with a precipitous decline in exports accompanied by a loss of domestic demand. However, Turkey was able to capitalize on structural reforms undertaken in the aftermath of severe domestic economic crises in 1999 and 2001. The reforms included market liberalization to promote private sector growth, privatization, agricultural reform, banking system strengthening, fiscal discipline, tight monetary policy with inflation targeting, and a floating exchange rate regime. Thus, in responding to the recent crisis, a robust banking sector and a good fiscal position allowed the Government to provide fiscal stimulus to restore growth. The economic decline proved short-lived and the subsequent rebound has been strong.

2. Turkey's real GDP grew by 9% in 2010, and a further 7.5% increase has been projected for 2011. Unemployment, which rose from just over 10% in 2006 and 2007 to 14% in 2010, has been returning towards pre-crisis levels at a relatively rapid pace. Annual inflation, which ran at close to 70% in the late 1990s and in 2001, has been brought down to 10% or less since 2004. Turkey's current account deficit, which widened to the equivalent of 6.5% of GDP in 2010, appears to pose the main challenge to continued rapid economic expansion. Although the financing of the deficit has not been a major issue so far, the recent crisis has highlighted the effects of rapid changes in business and investor sentiment.

3. The European Union remains Turkey's most important trading partner and investor. The EU accounted for nearly 70% of total FDI inflows into Turkey during 2005-10. Nearly 40% of its imports come from the EU, and just over 50% of exports go to the EU. However, the dominance of the EU in Turkey's foreign trade has declined markedly over the last five years, reflecting a notable shift in Turkish exports towards growth markets in its neighbourhood, in North Africa, certain CIS countries, and in Asia.

4. Turkey's overall framework for the formulation and implementation of trade policy has remained broadly unchanged since its last Trade Policy Review. However, following a reorganization of ministries and certain public institutions in 2011, key functions in relation to Turkey's foreign trade policies now rest with the Ministry of Economy (formerly the Undersecretariat of the Prime Ministry for Foreign Trade), in cooperation and coordination with other ministries and authorities. The Ministry of Economy regularly seeks inputs from the private sector and NGOs in the formulation and review of Turkey's trade policies. A WTO-DDA Coordination Committee has been established for follow-up on DDA-related issues and to determine Turkey's strategy in multilateral negotiations. Turkey attaches great importance to the successful conclusion of the DDA, and has taken major initiatives to support LDCs in their efforts to eradicate poverty.

5. The Customs Union between Turkey and the EU, which entered into force on 1 January 1996, and the negotiations for accession to the EU, which began in October 2005, have remained cornerstones for Turkey's trade policies as Turkey's commitments give rise to on-going work to align its legislation with the EU *acquis*, as well as efforts to harmonize trade preferences exchanged with other trading partners. Turkey has a free-trade agreement with EFTA, and is part of the Euro-Mediterranean Partnership. At present, Turkey has 16 bilateral FTAs in force, having concluded 7 bilateral FTA negotiations since its last Trade Policy Review. Moreover, Turkey is currently engaged in negotiations with 13 partners, and has initiated the launch of negotiations with an additional 10 trading partners. Turkey also participates in the Economic Cooperation Organization (ECO), Developing-8 (D-8), the Organization of Islamic Cooperation (OIC), and the Black Sea Economic Cooperation (BSEC). As noted in previous TPRs, Turkey's participation in regional and bilateral trade agreements has contributed to improving competition in the economy, but has added

complexity to its trade regime and potentially detracted efforts away from multilateral efforts to open its economy further.

6. Turkey relies on internal taxes on goods and services to raise government revenue, rather than trade taxes such as customs duties. In 2010, internal taxes – principally VAT levied on imports and exports, and the Special Consumption Tax – accounted for almost 58% of the Turkish Government's tax revenue, or over 44% of total government revenues. By contrast, customs duties represented no more than 1% of total government revenue in 2010.

7. Turkey's VAT and the Special Consumption Tax make no distinction between imported and domestically produced goods, in principle. However, as the Special Consumption Tax on alcoholic beverages varies considerably depending on the type of product, the tax system has the potential to favour the consumption of some products relative to others. The VAT is imposed at the general rate of 18%, but reduced rates (8% and 1%) are applied on some goods and services, and certain types of transactions are tax exempt.

8. Turkey applies the Customs Union common external tariff (CET) to industrial goods, and its applied MFN tariffs for non-agricultural products are low, on average 5%. However, this relative openness is not reflected in Turkey's WTO commitments as it has left 66.5% of its non-agricultural tariff lines unbound, and the simple average on the tariff lines where Turkey has binding commitments is 17.4%. The import regime for industrial goods is *de facto* even more open than the CET indicates, as the Customs Union and free-trade agreements provide duty-free access for many of Turkey's most important trading partners. In addition, Turkey has the possibility to open tariff-rate quotas for non-agricultural goods, the Investment Encouragement Programme provides for duty and tax concessions on imports, exporters benefit from an inward-processing scheme, and a "suspension list" enables manufacturers to import certain raw materials and intermediary inputs at low or duty-exempt rates.

9. Although legal provisions allow the Turkish Government to increase applied MFN rates when these are deemed insufficient to provide "adequate" protection to domestic industries, Turkey's MFN import tariffs have not changed significantly overall since 2007. However, Turkey is an important user of anti-dumping measures, with 118 duty measures in force as of August 2011, compared to 93 at the end of 2007, and 27 at the end of 2002. Turkey imposed its first countervailing duty measure in 2009, and has initiated investigations and extended safeguard measures pursuant to the Agreement on Safeguards on a number of products since 2007. Furthermore, following an investigation launched in January 2011, Turkey has raised its MFN tariffs on a wide range of textiles and clothing goods.

10. Turkey prohibits or restricts imports of various goods to protect health and safety, ensure compliance with domestic legislation or international obligations, for reasons of national security, environmental protection, etc. Textiles and clothing products became subject to registration to monitor their importation on 1 January 2010. More generally, Turkey has implemented an import surveillance system since 2004. The system is price-based for some products.

11. Turkey has modified its Investment Encouragement Programme since the last TPR. The programme now follows a three-pillar approach based on regional and sectoral implementation, large-scale investments contributing to international competitiveness, and a general investment encouragement mechanism. A new Law on Monitoring and Supervision of State Aids entered into force in October 2010. Although state ownership remains important, notably in certain banks, transport companies, public utilities, energy and mining enterprises, and agricultural marketing boards, Turkey has continued its privatization programme launched in 1984. Over the last four years, the sale of electricity distribution companies, port operation rights, petrochemical, and tobacco

enterprises, and a further stake in Türk Telekom, has raised significant revenue, and further privatization plans are advancing for sugar processors, roads, and bridges. Turkey has made some progress in the fight against abuse of intellectual property rights during the last four years. The agriculture sector accounted for 8.4% of Turkey's GDP in 2010. Turkey ranks among the largest agricultural producers in the world. Its main traditional exports include hazelnuts, fruit and vegetables, and oriental tobacco. Except for the industrial component of processed agricultural products, trade in agricultural commodities is not subject to the Customs Union CET. Turkey has occasionally adjusted tariffs on selected agricultural products to respond to domestic supply and demand conditions. It has some latitude in this regard, given the considerable gap between applied and bound MFN tariffs (on average 48% versus 72%). The average applied import duty is effectively lower, as Turkey maintains numerous tariff-rate quotas under preferential agreements, and may open tariff-rate quotas unilaterally from time to time to facilitate imports.

12. Turkey has not provided agriculture support notifications to the WTO since 2002. Based on the available information, the value of support to agricultural producers in Turkey appears to have been increasing recently. The market-oriented Agricultural Reform Implementation Project was phased out in 2008. Moreover, with the termination of a direct income support scheme in 2009, an increasing portion of the support is now extended in the form of deficiency payments and other instruments, such as area-based payments. Turkey's market price support has increased in recent years, due mainly to higher domestic prices rather than lower world market prices. The resulting losses for state-owned enterprises trading in commodities such as grains and sugar have been offset by transfers from the Turkish Treasury. Sixteen product groups are eligible to receive export subsidies.

13. Although agriculture and manufacturing remain important, the Turkish economy is now dominated by services. The tourism industry is a major earner of foreign exchange, and the Government provides incentives and other types of assistance to develop the sector further. Other important sectors in terms of output, employment, and foreign trade are financial services, transportation, telecommunications, wholesale and retail trade, and an outward-oriented construction industry. With rapidly rising energy consumption, Turkey commenced reforms in the energy sector in 2001. The process, including privatizations, has advanced considerably in electricity distribution, where the current strategy foresees that all consumers, including households, should be able to choose their suppliers by 2015. The reform efforts have been less successful in natural gas, where the state-owned enterprise BOTAŞ continues to dominate imports and the wholesale of natural gas. Turkey is targeting an increasing share of renewable energy sources to meet its growing demand for energy.

14. The recent economic crisis has highlighted the benefits of the economic reforms undertaken by Turkey since 2001 and the value in maintaining and continuing these reforms. On the trade side, Turkey's partners would benefit from increased transparency and predictability in their access to the Turkish market through the conclusion of multilateral trade negotiations leading to more extensive tariff binding commitments for industrial goods, lower bound rates on agricultural and manufactured products, simplification and rationalization of the tariff regime, and further services commitments. At the same time, Turkey's trading partners can foster a positive trade climate by ensuring that their markets remain open to Turkey.

I. ECONOMIC ENVIRONMENT

(1) MAJOR FEATURES OF THE ECONOMY

1. The Republic of Turkey covers an area of just over 784,000 square kilometres (including lakes) with a population of nearly 73 million (2010).[1] Around 76% of the inhabitants live in urban areas; the largest cities being Istanbul (12.6 million), Ankara (4.7 million), and Izmir (3.7 million). Some 4 million Turks live abroad.[2] The population growth has been declining steadily in recent years, and currently averages 1.3% per annum. Over 26% are in the 0-14 year age group, and life expectancy at birth is 74.3 years at present. In 2010, Turkey ranked 83rd among 169 countries with comparable data on the Human Development Index.[3]

2. Services, employing nearly 50% of the labour force in Turkey, constitute the largest share of Turkey's GDP (60%), followed by manufacturing (16%), and agriculture (more than 8%). Tourism is a major earner of foreign exchange for Turkey. The manufacturing sector is outward oriented, and Turkey is a major world producer and exporter of several agricultural commodities. The agriculture sector remains an important source of employment in Turkey's rural areas, providing work for around 6 million people.

3. As half of Turkey's population is under the age of 29, the labour market needs to absorb 1 million new entrants every year. The female participation rate in employment remains low. While 72.9% of the male population within the working age are employed, the rate for women is 30.3%.

4. Turkey introduced the new Turkish lira on 1 January 2005, removing six zeros from the old currency. The word "new" was struck with effect from 1 January 2009, and the official name is the Turkish lira (TL). Turkey accepted the obligations of Article VIII of the IMF Articles of Agreement on 22 March 1990, and moved from a crawling peg to a floating exchange rate system on 22 February 2001.

(2) RECENT ECONOMIC DEVELOPMENTS

5. After a highly volatile performance in 1990s, the Turkish economy experienced its most severe recession since the 1940s in 2001. Significant structural reforms were introduced in response to the 2001 crisis, and Turkey subsequently entered an unusually long period of sustained growth and economic stability.[4] A strong appreciation of the Turkish lira in 2006 had a dampening effect on economic growth in 2007, but the economy was still expanding until the arrival of the global financial crisis in mid 2008.

6. Initially, the unprecedented decline in foreign demand prompted a free fall in Turkey's exports, in turn affecting output and investment. The loss of business and consumer confidence

---

[1] The population data is based on the "Address Based Population Registration System" as of 31 December 2010.

[2] The migration of workers began with the conclusion of an agreement with the Federal Republic of Germany in October 1961, followed by similar agreements with other European countries in the first half of the 1960s. Turkish workers increasingly picked up jobs in the Middle East from the mid 1970s, and after 1990 also in the Russian Federation.

[3] UNDP online information, "Human Development Index". Viewed at: hdrstats.undp.org/en/countries/profiles/TUR.html

[4] The reforms included fiscal discipline; tight monetary policy with inflation targeting; a floating exchange-rate regime; a strengthened banking system; public sector reform; privatization; and market liberalization. For details, see WTO (2003).

amplified the shock. Turkey's GDP fell by nearly 5% in real terms between 2008 and 2009 (Table I.1). Although the unemployment rate increased from 11% to 14%, the rise was mitigated by employment support measures and wage adjustments.[5]

Table I.1
Main economic indicators, 2006-10

	2006	2007	2008	2009	2010
Miscellaneous					
GDP (TL billion)	758.4	843.2	950.5	952.6	1,103.7
GDP (US$ billion)	526.4	648.8	742.1	616.7	734.9
Real GDP growth rate (%)	6.9	4.7	0.7	-4.8	9
Population, total ('000)[a]	69,395	70,215	71,095	72,050	73,003
GDP per capita (US$)[b]	7,583	9,234	10,440	8,578	10,043
Unemployment, total (% of total labour force)	10.2	10.3	11.0	14.0	11.9
Consumer price index (end of period; % change)	9.7	8.4	10.1	6.5	6.4
Monetary sector					
Nominal growth of M2 broad money (%)	23.4	15.4	27.5	12.9	19.0
Money and quasi money (M2) as % of GDP	39.2	40.7	46.0	51.9	53.3
Average nominal treasury bill interest rate (%)	18.1	18.4	19.2	11.6	8.1
GDP by economic activities at current prices			(%)		
Agriculture	8.3	7.6	7.6	8.3	8.4
Industry	20.1	20.0	19.8	19.1	19.2
Mining and quarrying	1.2	1.2	1.4	1.5	1.4
Manufacturing	17.2	16.8	16.2	15.2	15.5
Electricity	1.8	1.9	2.2	2.4	2.3
Services	58.3	60.3	61.0	61.1	59.9
Other[c]	13.2	12.1	11.7	11.5	12.5
Government finance			(% of GDP)		
Public sector primary balance	4.7	3.1	1.6	-1.0	-0.8[d]
Public sector borrowing requirement	1.9	-0.1	-1.6	-5.1	-2.3[d]
Net debt of public sector	34.0	29.5	28.2	32.5	28.8
National accounts			(% of GDP)		
Private consumption	70.5	71.3	69.8	71.5	71.3
Public consumption	12.3	12.8	12.8	14.7	14.3
Gross fixed capital formation	22.3	21.4	19.9	16.9	18.7
Change in inventories	-0.2	-0.4	1.9	-1.9	1.2
XGS / GDP (%)	22.7	22.3	23.9	23.3	21.1
MGS/ GDP (%)	27.6	27.5	28.3	24.4	26.6
Memorandum					
Current account balance (US$ billion)	-32.2	-38.4	-42.0	-14.0	-47.7
Gross external debt (% of GDP; end of period)[e]	39.5	38.5	37.8	43.5	39.4
Gross external debt (US$ billion)[e]	207.7	249.5	280.4	268.4	289.4
Gross foreign reserves (US$ billion)	..	76.2	74.0	73.8[d]	81.3[f]
Official net foreign reserves (US$ billion)	63.3	76.4	74.2	74.8	86.0

Table I.1 (cont'd)

[5] While the number of workers in industry declined from 2008 to 2009, agricultural employment increased. Employment increased in all sectors in 2010.

	2006	2007	2008	2009	2010
Trade in goods and services (% of GDP)	49.9	49.3	52.1	47.6	48.0
Inward FDI stock (% of GDP)	18.1	23.6	10.8	22.8	24.7
Outward FDI stock (% of GDP)	1.7	1.9	2.4	3.6	2.9

.. Not available.

a Mid-Year Population, Turkstat.
b 2011 Annual Programme, Ministry of Development.
c Including net taxes (taxes minus subsidies).
d Preliminary.
e Provisional due to revisions in foreign debt data, figures may change retrospectively.
f Projection.

Source: CBRT Electronic Data Delivery System. Viewed at: http://evds.tcmb.gov.tr/yeni/cbt-uk.html; Turkstat, Undersecretariat of Turkish Treasury; and IMF (2010), *Turkey: Staff Report for the 2010 Article IV Consultation and Post-Program Monitoring – Supplementary Information; Staff Report; Informational Annex; and Public Information Notice on the Executive Board Discussion*, IMF Country Report No. 10/278. Viewed at: http://www.imf.org/ external/pubs/ft/scr/2010/cr10278.pdf.

7. The banking sector proved robust, and the financial position of the Turkish Government allowed for discretionary stimulus of the economy. Turkey's economic recovery, led by growth in private consumption and a rebound in exports, began in the second quarter of 2009 and continued through 2010.[6] Real GDP is estimated to have risen by 9% in 2010, and a 7.5% increase has been projected for 2011.

8. Identified as a source of macroeconomic imbalances in the past, Turkey's fiscal position improved markedly from 1999 onwards. The public sector primary balance was consistently in surplus from 2000 through 2008 and the overall balance, although in deficit, was kept below 2% of GDP from 2005 through 2008. As a consequence, net public sector debt, which had stood at 61.5% of GDP in 2002, had fallen to 34% in 2006 and had dropped further (to 28.2%) by 2008. Although the Government's fiscal position deteriorated as a result of the global crisis, the primary and overall deficits were contained, and Turkey has been able to recover from the downturn with net public sector debt remaining at less than 35% of GDP.

9. Turkey's gross external debt also declined steadily during the last decade, from a level equivalent to 56.2% of GDP in 2001 to less than 40% in 2008. While Turkey's gross external debt increased from US$250 billion in 2007 to US$290 billion in 2010, the level of external debt remains around 40% of GDP. During the financial crisis, long-term capital inflows dried up and were replaced by short-term funding and portfolio investments, i.e. non-resident purchases of government debt securities and short-term loans and deposits from foreign banks to Turkish banks. Longer-term capital appears to be returning to Turkey along with the economic recovery, but the crisis highlighted the challenges posed by rapid changes in business and investor sentiment.

10. The inflation-targeting framework pursued by the Central Bank of Turkey since 2001 has been successful in driving down annual consumer price inflation from 29.7% in 2002 to 10% or less since 2004. Movements year-to-year are influenced by fluctuations in energy prices, the strength of domestic demand, and developments in the real effective exchange rate of the Turkish lira. Using 2003 as the basis, the lira appreciated by nearly 20% until the end of 2007, then went into a decline, which took the (CPI-based) real effective exchange rate close to the 2003 level in the early days of the

[6] Turkey's GDP fell nearly 14% (peak-to-trough) during the crisis; the steepest decline in the OECD area. The subsequent recovery has also been the most pronounced among OECD countries (OECD, 2010b).

financial crisis. A steady appreciation of 10% from early 2009 until the end of 2010 has been followed by a significant decline in 2011.

(3) TRADE PERFORMANCE

11. Turkey's current account has not been in surplus since 2001, and the deficit rose steadily until 2008, primarily due to a widening gap between the value of exports and imports of merchandise. A significant contraction of imports in 2009 reduced the current account deficit to US$14 billion for the year, but the subsequent economic recovery has once again been accompanied by a growing deficit, equal to 6.5% of Turkey's GDP in 2010.

12. The contraction in foreign demand brought a 22.6% decline in Turkey's exports of goods from 2008 to 2009. Nevertheless, Turkey's exports rose threefold in U.S. dollar terms between 2002 and 2010. Turkey is still predominantly an exporter of manufactured goods, in particular automotive products, textiles and clothing, iron and steel, and chemicals. However, the overall share of manufactures in Turkey's exports has declined from a peak of 84% in 2004 to 78.3% at present (Table AI.1 and Chart I.1).[7] Exports of agricultural products, mostly food, have been rising over the last three years and represent around 11% of Turkey's exports at present, the same share as in 2002.

13. The European Union, led by Germany, the United Kingdom, Italy, and France, remains the principal market for Turkish goods. However, the EU share in Turkey's exports declined by nearly 10 percentage points (from 60.1% to 50.8%) from 2006 to 2010, reflecting a successful shift in Turkish export sales to neighbouring countries (Iraq, Iran, Syria and Azerbaijan) as well as to growth markets in the Middle East, North Africa, certain CIS countries, and Asia since 2008 (Table AI.2 and Chart I.2).

14. Turkey's merchandise imports exceeded US$200 billion in 2008, representing a five-fold increase in seven years. Following a 30% fall in 2009, imports were back at US$186 billion in 2010. The structure of Turkey's imports has largely remained unchanged over the last five years, the principal items being machinery and transport equipment (29%), fuels (21%), chemicals (14%), and a broad range of consumer goods (Table AI.3). However, Turkey's imports reflect a significant degree of intra-industry trade whereby intermediate goods are imported, processed and sold for export, notably in motor vehicles and accessories, iron and steel, and machinery.

15. Although imports from the United States, China, India, and Kazakhstan have risen significantly since 2006, the EU (primarily Germany, Italy and France) continues to be the main source of Turkey's imports (Table AI.4 and Chart I.2). In 2010, the Russian Federation, Germany, China, the United States, and Italy all provided goods worth more than US$10 billion to Turkey.

16. On a bilateral basis, Turkey ran a surplus in its trade with countries such as Iraq, the United Kingdom, the UAE, and Egypt in 2010. By contrast, substantial deficits were recorded with the Russian Federation (US$17 billion), China (US$15 billion), the United States (US$8.6 billion), and Germany (US$6 billion). Turkey's merchandise trade is sensitive to movements in foreign exchange rates. Due to importation of fuels, and trade with countries in East Asia, Turkey's imports are mainly denominated in U.S. dollars (over 60%). On the other hand, exports of manufactures to traditional markets result in nearly 50% of Turkey's exports being settled in euros.

[7] Textiles and clothing, which accounted for 40% of Turkey's merchandise exports in 1995, and 26% in 2005, currently holds a share of 19%. The share has been rising slightly over the last three years.

Chart I.1
Composition of merchandise trade, 2006 and 2010

Per cent

2006 **2010**

(a) Exports, including re-exports (f.o.b.)

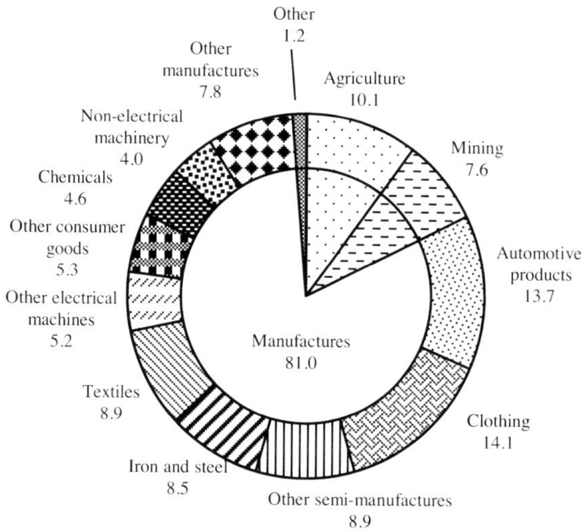

Total: US$85.5 billion

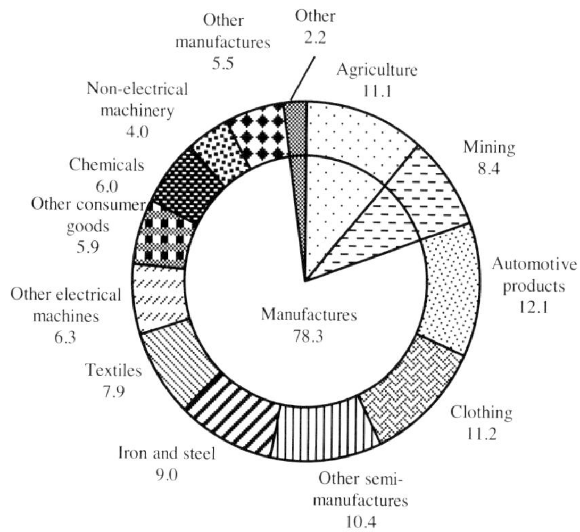

Total: US$113.9 billion

(b) Imports (c.i.f.)

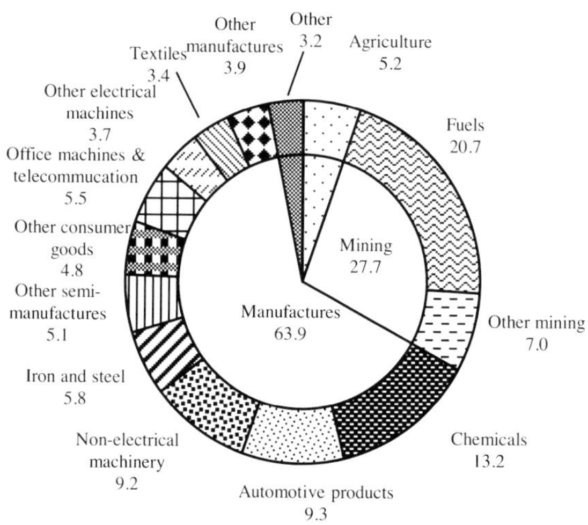

Total: US$139.6 billion

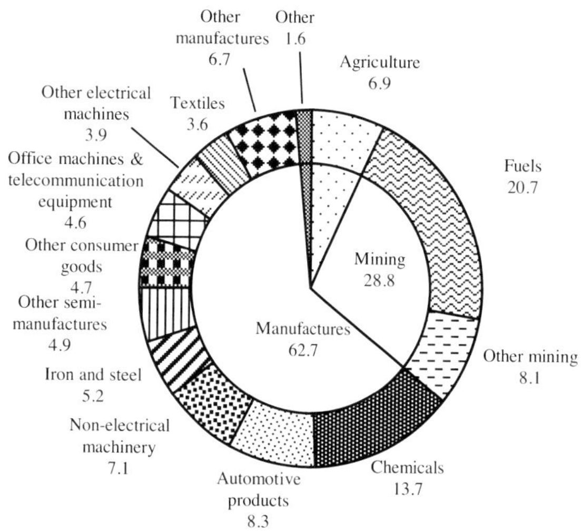

Total: US$185.5 billion

Source: **UNSD, Comtrade database (SITC Rev.3) and data provided by the Turkish authorities.**

Chart I.2
Direction of merchandise trade, 2006 and 2010

Per cent

2006 **2010**

(a) Exports, including re-exports (f.o.b.)

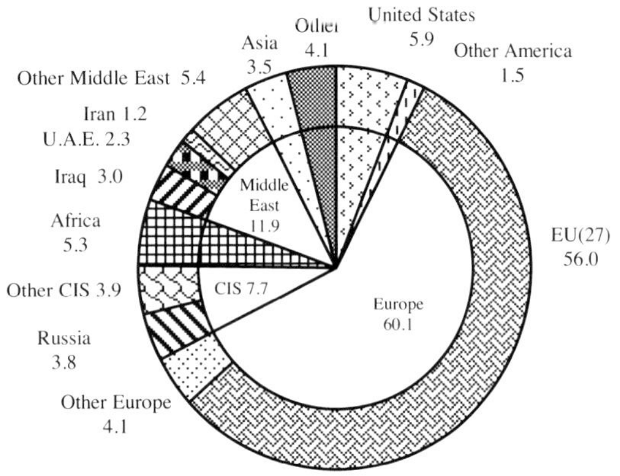

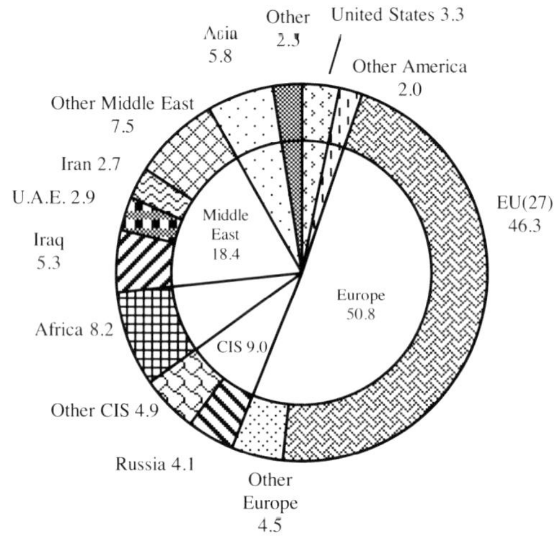

Total: US$85.5 billion

Total: US$113.9 billion

(b) Imports (c.i.f.)

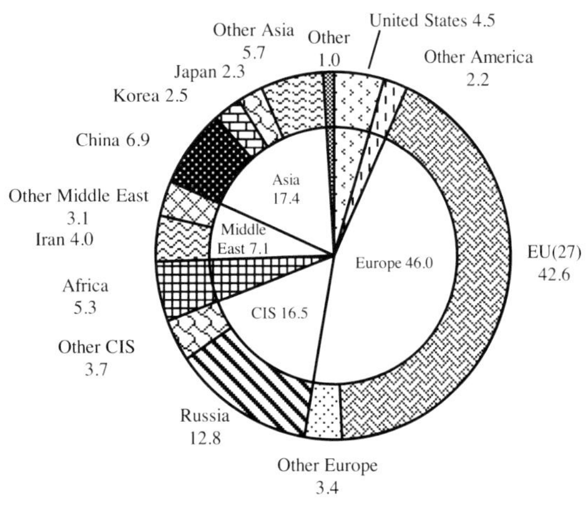

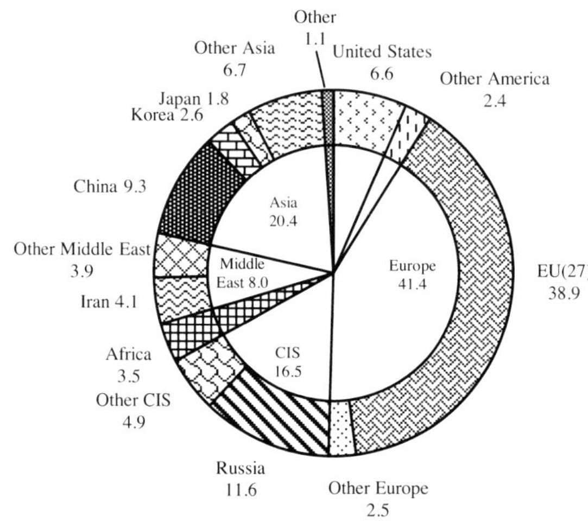

Total: US$139.6 billion

Total: US$185.5 billion

***Source*: UNSD, Comtrade database (SITC Rev.3) and data provided by the Turkish authorities.**

17. Turkey continues to be a net exporter of services due to its significant surplus in travel services, averaging US$16 billion per year from 2006 to 2010. Turkey is normally also a net exporter of construction and transportation services, and a net importer of insurance, banking and other business services (Table I.2). Worker remittances, which were providing foreign exchange worth approximately US$5 billion each year to Turkey in the late 1990s, now amount to less than US$1 billion annually.

Table I.2
Balance of payments, 2006-10
(US$ billion)

	2006	2007	2008	2009	2010
Current account	-32.2	-38.4	-42.0	-14.0	-47.7
Goods	-41.1	-46.9	-53.0	-24.9	-56.4
Exports	93.6	115.4	140.8	109.6	120.9
Imports	-134.7	-162.2	-193.8	-134.5	-177.3
Services	13.6	13.3	17.3	16.7	14.6
Credit	25.5	28.9	35.1	33.5	34.1
Debit	-12.0	-15.6	-17.8	-16.7	-19.4
Transportation (net)	0.3	-0.4	-0.2	1.3	0.7
Travel (net)	14.1	15.2	18.4	17.1	16.0
Construction services (net)	0.9	0.8	1.0	1.1	0.9
Insurance services (net)	-0.6	-0.9	-0.7	-0.5	-0.5
Financial services (net)	-0.2	-0.2	-0.1	-0.4	-0.2
Other business services (net)	-0.4	-0.8	-1.0	-1.3	-1.3
Government services (net)	-0.9	-0.7	-0.8	-0.8	-0.9
Other services (net)	0.5	0.4	0.7	0.3	0.0
Income	-6.7	-7.1	-8.4	-8.2	-7.3
Credit	4.4	6.4	6.9	5.2	4.5
Debit	-11.1	-13.5	-15.3	-13.4	-11.8
Current transfers	1.9	2.2	2.1	2.3	1.4
Official transfers	0.6	0.8	0.7	1.2	0.6
Workers remittances	1.1	1.2	1.4	0.9	0.9
Capital and financial account	32.1	36.7	37.3	8.9	43.0
Capital account	0.0	0.0	-0.1	0.0	-0.1
Financial account	32.1	36.7	37.3	9.0	43.1
Direct investment	19.3	19.9	17.0	6.9	7.8
Abroad	-0.9	-2.1	-2.5	-1.6	-1.5
In Turkey	20.2	22.0	19.5	8.4	9.3
Portfolio investment	7.4	0.8	-5.0	0.2	16.1
Assets	-4.0	-1.9	-1.2	-2.7	-3.5
Liabilities	11.4	2.8	-3.8	2.9	19.6
Other investment	11.5	23.9	24.3	2.0	32.0
Assets	-13.5	-5.0	-12.1	11.0	7.0
Liabilities	25.0	28.9	36.4	-9.0	24.9
Reserve assets	-6.1	-8.0	1.1	-0.1	-12.8
Net errors and omissions	0.2	1.8	4.7	5.1	4.7

Source: CBRT online information. Viewed at: http://www.tcmb.gov.tr.

(4) OUTLOOK

18. According to the Turkish Government's Medium-Term Programme for 2012-14, the main objectives are to sustain growth, increase employment, improve public balances, and reduce the current account deficit to increase Turkey's welfare level. The programme is accompanied by a Medium-Term Fiscal Plan setting specific targets for the central government budget.[8] Public expenditures are to be reviewed carefully to maximize the resources available for economic growth led by the private sector. The fiscal plan foresees a steady improvement in the public sector primary balance to reach a surplus of 1.5% in 2014, with the public sector borrowing requirement declining to 0.4% of GDP.[9]

19. The programme and fiscal plan are based on macroeconomic indicators suggesting that the Turkish economy should expand by 4.5%, 4%, and 5% in real terms over the next three years, led by rising output in services and in manufacturing industries. The annual consumer price inflation is expected to average around 6% on a declining trend. The current account deficit is projected to fall from 8% of GDP in 2012 to 7.5% in 2013, and 7% in 2014.

20. Over the medium and longer term, Turkey intends to focus on infrastructure investments supporting efficiency and productivity, notably investments in education, health, research and development, transportation, energy, the provision of drinking water, and the development of information and communication technologies. Priority is also given to projects to reduce regional imbalances.

21. With a GDP of more than US$750 billion, Turkey is currently the 17th largest economy in the world. In 2009, Turkey ranked 22nd among the world's exporters of merchandise and 14th amongst exporters of services. For imports, Turkey's ranking was 24th (merchandise) and 26th (services).[10] The government of Turkey has set ambitious targets for 2023, marking the 100th anniversary of the establishment of the Turkish Republic. The 2023 Export Strategy provides a general framework for the objectives. The Ministry of Economy, the Ministry of Development, and the Turkish Exporters Assembly are preparing detailed roadmaps.[11] Amongst its goals, Turkey is aspiring to be among the world's top ten economies, with a GDP per capita of more than US$25,000, as well as to reach exports worth US$500 billion annually.

[8] The three-year Medium-Term Fiscal Plan has been prepared by the Ministry of Finance and finalized by the High Planning Council.

[9] Data for the first months of 2011 indicate that the Government is ahead of its targets due to rapidly rising tax receipts, while the growth in expenditures is being contained.

[10] WTO (2009). Turkey's position is calculated treating the European Union as one entity and excluding intra-EU trade. Turkey's standing remained the same as in 2005 except for services imports, where Turkey slipped two places.

[11] The Turkish Grand National Assembly approved the Long-Term Development Strategy (2001-2023) and the 8th Five-Year Development Plan (2001-05) on 27 June 2000. The Long-Term Development Strategy, which set the target for Turkey to enter the world's top ten economies, is the main guide for the economic and social transformation. The objective is retained in the Ninth Development Plan. Targets are prioritized and incorporated in three-year medium-term programmes and annual programmes. Related governmental organizations prepare, coordinate, and implement sectoral strategies considered to be roadmaps for the specified targets.

II. TRADE AND INVESTMENT REGIMES

(1) GENERAL FRAMEWORK

1. The 1982 Constitution asserts that Turkey is a secular and democratic republic governed by the rule of law, with an independent judiciary and fundamental human rights for all citizens. The Constitution may be amended by referendum or a qualified majority vote (2/3) in the Turkish Parliament, known as the Turkish Grand National Assembly (TGNA).[1] The single-chamber TGNA consists of 550 members elected by popular vote every five years on the basis of proportional representation.[2] The Constitutional Court is at the top of the judiciary, followed by the High Court of Cassation, Council of State, Court of Accounts, High Military Court of Appeals, and Military High Administrative Court.

2. The President, elected by popular vote for a five-year term, has broad supervisory powers.[3] He appoints (and may dismiss) the Prime Minister and other ministers, on the advice of the Prime Minister. The present Cabinet consists of the Prime Minister, four Deputy Prime Ministers, and 21 Ministers.

3. Turkey's overall framework for the formulation and implementation of trade policy has remained broadly unchanged since the last TPR of Turkey. However, following a reorganization of the institutional structures of ministries and certain public institutions initiated in June 2011, the titles of the relevant institutions and their portfolios have been adjusted in recent months.[4] The Ministry of Economy (formerly the Undersecretariat of the Prime Ministry for Foreign Trade) formulates, administers, and coordinates Turkey's foreign trade policies. Depending on the nature of the issue, the Ministry may consult with other ministries and agencies such as the ministries of Foreign Affairs; Science, Industry and Technology; Finance; Food, Agriculture and Livestock; Health; Culture and Tourism; Energy and Natural Resources; Environment and Urbanism; Development; Customs and Trade; the Undersecretariat of Treasury; the Central Bank of Turkey; the Turkish Patent Institute; the Competition Authority; the Public Procurement Authority; the Banking Regulation and Supervision Agency (BRSA); the Information and Communication Technologies Authority; the Energy Market Regulatory Authority; the Sugar Authority; the Tobacco and Alcohol Market Regulatory Authority; the Public Procurement Agency; and the Export Credit Bank of Turkey (Turk Eximbank). A number of independent regulatory institutions with responsibilities in goods- and services-related matters are listed in Table II.1. The Ministry of Economy, through the Directorate-General of Incentives Implementation and Foreign Investment, is responsible for state aids provided to investments and matters related to foreign direct investment in Turkey (section (4) below).

4. The Ministry of Economy conducts periodic reviews and assessments of trade policies. In this context, the export and import regimes and legislation on standardization are reviewed annually and updated as necessary. The private sector and NGOs provide inputs to trade policy formulation by communicating their views to the Ministry of Economy either directly or through the Union of Chambers and Commodity Exchanges of Turkey (TOBB), the Turkish Exporters Assembly (TIM), the Turkish Businessmen's and Industrialists' Association (TUSIAD), the Independent Businessmen's and Industrialists' Association (MUSIAD), and the Foreign Economic Relations Board (DEIK), as

[1] Only members of the TGNA may propose amendments to the Constitution.

[2] A party must obtain minimum 10% of the votes cast at the national level to participate in the distribution of parliamentary seats.

[3] The President may be re-elected, but only once, for a second five-year term. Until 2007, the President of Turkey was elected by Parliament for a single seven-year term.

[4] Decree Law No. 637, published in *Official Gazette* No. 27958 (bis), 8 June 2011.

well as individual and local chambers of commerce, and exporters' associations.[5] Consultation is sometimes held with universities and research institutes, such as the Economic Development Foundation (IKV), the Economic Policy Research Foundation of Turkey (TEPAV) and the Foreign Trade Association of Turkey (TURKTRADE).[6]

Table II.1
Independent regulatory institutions, 2011

Institution	Law No./Year	Sectors	Task
Capital Market Board	2499/1981	Capital markets	Regulating and supervising the capital markets and protecting the rights and interests of investors
Radio and Television Supreme Council	6112/2011	Radio, television, and on-demand media services	Regulating and supervising radio, television, and on-demand media services
Competition Authority	4054/1994	Goods and services markets (all sectors)	Prohibiting agreements, decisions, and concerted practices that restrict competition, and any abuse of dominant position by one or more undertakings; controlling mergers and acquisitions; establishing a competition culture as part of its competition advocacy role
Banking Regulation and Supervision Agency	4389/1999 (Banks Act No. 4389 was superseded by Banking Law No. 5411/2005)	Banking	Protecting the rights and interests of depositors; laying down principles regarding the establishment, management, operation, acquisition, merger, liquidation, and supervision of banks in order to ensure efficient operation of the credit system with due regard to the requisites of economic development, and confidence and stability in the financial market
Information and Communication Technologies Authority	4502/2000 5809/2008	Telecommunications	Constituting a dynamic and strong market based on fair competition; contributing to the sectoral policy-making process; taking measures to protect consumer rights; ensuring efficient and productive use of scarce resources in the sector, such as frequency and numbers
Electronic Signature Law	5070/2004	Information technology	Defining the principles for the legal and technical aspects and application of electronic signatures
Energy Market Regulatory Authority	4628/2001 4646/2001 5015/2003 5307/2005	Electric energy Natural gas Petroleum Liquefied petroleum gas (LPG)	Constituting a financially strong, stable, and transparent energy market operating under private law in a competitive environment to provide adequate, refined, continuous, and environment-friendly electricity and natural gas; ensuring independent regulation and supervision in the market; regulate the guidance, surveillance and supervision activities in the delivery of petroleum and LPG, to ensure the transparent, non-discriminatory, and stable supply from domestic and foreign resources to consumers, directly or after processing in a cost-effective manner
Sugar Authority	4634/2001	Sugar, starch-based sweeteners	Regulating the sugar regime through establishment of procedures and principles regarding sugar production, and the conditions and methods of marketing
Tobacco and Alcohol Market Regulatory Authority	4733/2002 (Amended by Law No. 5752/2008)	Tobacco, tobacco products, alcohol and alcoholic beverages	Regulating the procedures and principles regarding production, domestic and external purchase and sale of tobacco, tobacco products, alcohol, and alcoholic beverages
Public Procurement Authority	4734/2002	All public institutions	Determining the procedures and principles to be applied in public procurements; examining the complaints concerning all public procurements

Source: Information provided by the Turkish authorities.

[5] The views of the private sector, including NGOs, are customarily taken into consideration throughout the process (although this is not legally required).

[6] The former Export Promotion Centre (IGEME) has been integrated into the Ministry of Economy.

5. The hierarchy of legal instruments in Turkey comprises the Constitution, laws, decrees, regulations, implementing regulations, Council of Ministers' decisions, and other administrative Acts such as circulars. In general, policies are formulated and implemented by means of laws.[7] The main legislation relating to international trade is the Foreign Trade Regulations Law (No. 2976 of 1984). International agreements duly put into effect in Turkey, including the WTO Agreements, carry the force of law. Thus, their provisions would apply in the case of any inconsistency between them and domestic law, which would consequently have to be amended to reflect Turkey's international commitments. The WTO Agreements, and Turkey's current and future trade relations with the European Union, are the main factors influencing the Turkish trading system.

6. The main pieces of trade-related legislation in Turkey are listed in Table AII.1. The present Turkish Commercial Code (No. 6762), in force since 1957, stipulates that trading companies may take the form of a collective, commandite, joint-stock, or limited liability company, or be a cooperative. All companies established according to the Commercial Code are regarded as Turkish companies. A new Commercial Code (No. 6102), published in the *Official Gazette* on 14 February 2011, will enter into force on 1 July 2012. Secondary legislation to implement the new Commercial Code is in preparation. The new Code also regulates the establishment of branches of foreign companies.[8] The establishment of representative offices is regulated in the Foreign Direct Investment Law (No. 4875).

(2) POLICY OBJECTIVES

7. Since it entered into force on 1 January 1996, the Customs Union with the EU has been the main factor shaping Turkey's foreign trade policy. The EU opened accession negotiations with Turkey in October 2005. Guidance on reform priorities is provided through the Accession Partnership, adopted in February 2008. Turkey's (third) National Programme was promulgated on 31 December 2008 to achieve the objectives identified in the Accession Partnership. On 15 March 2010, the Turkish Council of Ministers adopted an action plan for 2010-11 outlining legislation to be enacted and studies to be carried out on the various chapters of the accession negotiations.[9]

8. At the national level, Turkey's Long-Term Development Strategy (2001-2023), prepared by the Ministry of Development, envisages the development of an export-oriented, technology-intensive production structure, with emphasis on high-value-added products and services. Export-oriented activities, particularly of small and medium-sized enterprises, are to be supported, *inter alia,* by providing credit, guarantees, and insurance through Turk Eximbank; harmonization of foreign

---

[7] The relevant minister presents the draft law to the Council of Ministers, which forwards the adopted draft to Parliament for approval. Draft laws may also be proposed by members of the Turkish Grand National Assembly. Bills are forwarded for assessment to the standing sub-commissions of the TGNA; if approved, they are forwarded to the President for signature. Laws enter into force upon publication in the *Official Gazette*. Decisions with respect to policy proposals may also be made by means of Council of Minister decrees, which must be published in the *Official Gazette*. The import and export regimes, safeguard measures, and surveillance of imports are all being implemented through decrees.

[8] Until now, the establishment of a branch of a foreign company has been regulated by a temporary law of 30 December 1914, requiring permission from the former Ministry of Industry and Trade. The temporary law has been repealed through Law No. 6103 of 2011. The new legislation will enter into force on the same day as the new Commercial Code, i.e. 1 July 2012.

[9] Turkey adopted its first National Programme to transpose the EU *acquis* on 19 March 2001, setting out the procedures and a programme for implementing actions in priority areas. The second National Programme was launched in 2003 and a third National Programme in 2008. In addition, Turkey announced a Programme for Alignment with the EU *acquis* 2007-2013 on 17 April 2007.

investment legislation with EU norms; reduced bureaucratic procedures for exporters; and improved basic infrastructure.

9. Turkey has also embarked on a branding strategy aimed at improving the image of Turkish products around the world, and providing strategic support to Turkish firms and exporters' and producers' unions. Turkey does not have an export strategy plan at present. However, a long-term export strategy document (Export Strategy for 2023) is being prepared.

10. The main objective of Turkey's Ninth Development Plan (2007-13) is to increase competitiveness, *inter alia*, by improving the business environment, reducing the informal economy, increasing the quality and effectiveness of public services, fostering regional development, and modernizing the energy and transportation infrastructure. Turkey is also examining various strategies for improving its information and communication technology infrastructure, as a means to enhance productivity.

(3) TRADE AGREEMENTS AND ARRANGEMENTS

(i) WTO

11. Turkey became an original Member of the WTO on 26 March 1995, having been a contracting party to the GATT since 1951. Turkey accords MFN treatment (or better) to all other Members of the WTO, except Armenia.[10] Turkey is not a signatory to any of the plurilateral agreements resulting from the Uruguay Round, but participates as an observer in the Committees on Government Procurement and Trade in Civil Aircraft. Turkey is a party to the Information Technology Agreement (ITA), having signed the Ministerial Declaration on Trade in Information Technology Products at the Singapore Ministerial Conference. Turkey's most recent WTO notifications are listed in Table II.2.

Table II.2
Selected notifications to the WTO, January 2011 to 8 November 2011

Requirement	Subject	Most recent notification	Date
GATT 1994			
Article XXIV:7(a) - (Free-trade areas)	Regional trade agreement - Turkey and EFTA states	WT/REG86/N/1/Add.7	02.09.11
		WT/REG86/N/1/Add.6	21.07.11
		WT/REG86/N/1/Add.4	04.05.11
	Regional trade agreement - Turkey and Jordan	WT/REG294/N/1	08.03.11
	Regional trade agreement - Turkey and Chile	WT/REG293/N/1	25.02.11
Anti-dumping - Implementation of Article VI of the GATT 1994			
Article 16.4	Report (ad hoc)	G/ADP/N/219/Rev.1	26.10.11
Article 16.4	Report (semi-annual)	G/ADP/N/216/TUR	12.09.11
Article 16.5	Competent authority	G/ADP/N/14/Add.32	14.10.11
Agreement on Import Licensing procedures			
Articles 1.4(a) and 8.2(b)	Changes in laws, regulations, and procedures	G/LIC/N/1/TUR/9	03.10.11
Article 7.4	Replies to the questionnaire on import licensing procedures	G/LIC/N/3/TUR/11	03.10.11

Table II.2 (cont'd)

[10] Turkey invoked Article XIII of the Marrakesh Agreement establishing the WTO as Armenia's WTO accession negotiations were being wrapped up in 2002 (see document WT/L/501, 3 December 2002).

Requirement	Subject	Most recent notification	Date
Safeguards			
Article 12.1(a)	Polyethylene terephthalate	G/SG/N/11/TUR/16	24.06.11
Articles 12.1(b) and 12.1(c)		G/SG/N/10/TUR/13	24.06.11
		G/SG/N/8/TUR/13	24.06.11
		G/SG/N/6/TUR/16	28.03.11
Articles 12.1(a), 12.4, and 9 footnote 2	Spectacle frames (extension)	G/SG/N/14/TUR/5, G/SG/N/11/TUR/14, G/SG/N/7/TUR/8	15.04.11
Articles 12.1(b) and 12.1(c)		G/SG/N/11/TUR/8/Suppl.1, G/SG/N/10/TUR/8/Suppl.1, G/SG/N/8/TUR/8/Suppl.1	08.11.11
Articles 12.1(a), 12.4, and 9 footnote 2	Travel goods, handbags and similar containers (extension)	G/SG/N/14/TUR/6, G/SG/N/11/TUR/15, G/SG/N/7/TUR/9	08.04.11
Articles 12.1(b) and 12.1(c)		G/SG/N/11/TUR/9/Supp.1, G/SG/N/10/TUR/9/Suppl.1, G/SG/N/8/TUR/9/Suppl.1	08.11.11
Articles 12.1(a), 12.4, and 9 footnote 2	Cotton yarn (extension)	G/SG/N/11/TUR/17 and Corr.1, G/SG/N/7/TUR/10, G/SG/N/6/TUR/14/Suppl.1	24.06.11
Articles 12.1(a), 12.4, and 9 footnote 2	Certain electrical appliances (extension)	G/SG/N/11/TUR/11/Suppl.1, G/SG/N/7/TUR/11, G/SG/N/6/TUR/13/Suppl.1	08.11.11
Sanitary and phytosanitary measures			
Article 7, Annex B	Regulation on plant quarantine	G/SPS/N/TUR/23	08.11.11
	Regulation implementing feed hygiene	G/SPS/N/TUR/22	04.11.11
	Regulation implementing on the planning on the market and use of feed	G/SPS/N/TUR/21	04.11.11
	Regulation implementing the methods of sampling and analysis for official control of foodstuffs	G/SPS/N/TUR/20	04.11.11
	Regulation on import controls of food of plant origin and feed	G/SPS/N/TUR/19	07.09.11
	Draft regulation	G/SPS/N/TUR/18	26.07.11
	Draft regulation	G/SPS/N/TUR/17	25.05.11
	Regulation on pre-notification and veterinary checks for entry of live animals and animal products into the country	G/SPS/N/TUR/16	16.05.11
	Regulation laying down specific rules for the official controls on foods of animal origin	G/SPS/N/TUR/15	19.04.11
	Regulation on the official controls of food and feed	G/SPS/N/TUR/14	19.04.11
	Regulation on food hygiene	G/SPS/N/TUR/13	19.04.11
	Regulation on specific hygiene	G/SPS/N/TUR/12	19.04.11
	Rules for food of animal origin		
Subsidies and countervailing measures			
Article 25.11	Semi-annual report	G/SCM/N/228/Add.1	19.10.11
Article 25.12	Competent authority	G/SCM/N/18/Add.32	14.10.11
Technical barriers to trade			
Article 2.9.2	Regulation on import controls of food of plant origin and feed	G/TBT/N/TUR/6	31.08.11

Source: WTO documents.

12. Turkey attaches great importance to the successful conclusion of the Doha Development Agenda (DDA), as an opportunity to establish a more competitive and fairer international trading system. Turkey expects the negotiations to lead to a balanced outcome that takes into account the developmental concerns of WTO Members. A WTO-DDA Coordination Committee, headed by the Ministry of Economy with the participation of public and private sectors and NGOs (and academicians, as necessary), has been established to follow up issues related to the DDA and to determine Turkey's strategy in multilateral negotiations. Turkey generally takes the EU negotiation position into consideration in the DDA, particularly with respect to non-agricultural products, as these are fully covered under the Customs Union between Turkey and the EU.

13. As a member of the G-20, a candidate country to the European Union, and an emerging economy, Turkey has taken major initiatives to support LDCs in their efforts to eradicate poverty. Turkey hosted the United Nations Ministerial Conference on LDCs in 2007, and the 4th United Nations Conference on Least Developed Countries was held in Istanbul in May 2011.[11] Turkey has also put LDC-related topics high on the agenda of the international community. Turkey has pledged to make US$200 million available annually from 2012, for technical cooperation programmes, projects, and scholarships. Turkey's investments in LDCs amount to nearly US$2 billion at present, and the Turkish Government aims to increase this to US$5 billion by 2015, and US$12 billion by 2020. As a donor to the Enhanced Integrated Framework, Turkey notes that numerous development projects have been implemented successfully in 23 partner countries through programme coordinating offices of the Turkish Cooperation and Development Agency (TIKA).[12]

14. Turkey has been involved in several cases under the WTO Dispute Settlement Mechanism to date, acting as complainant in two cases and as respondent in eight cases (Table II.3). Since its last Review, Turkey has not participated in any new case as a complainant or respondent. However, it has reserved its third-party rights in a number of disputes involving other WTO Members.[13]

[11] The Istanbul Programme of Action, agreed at the 2011 Conference, is a detailed document aiming at the ultimate eradication of extreme poverty and hunger in LDCs.

[12] The TIKA is engaged in development assistance projects in more than 100 countries worldwide.

[13] In addition to the nine disputes enumerated in WTO (2007), Turkey has requested third-party participation in (i) China - measures affecting the protection and enforcement of intellectual property rights (DS362); (ii) Colombia - indicative prices and restrictions on ports of entry (DS366); (iii) EU - tariff treatment of certain information technology products (DS375, DS376, DS377); (iv) United States - definitive anti-dumping and countervailing duties on certain products from China (DS379); (v) United States - measures concerning the importation, marketing and sale of tuna and tuna products (DS381); (vi) certain measures affecting imports of poultry from China (DS392); (vii) China - measures related to the exportation of various raw materials (DS394, DS395; DS398); (viii) EU - definitive anti-dumping measures on certain iron or steel fasteners from China (DS397); (ix) United States - measures affecting imports of certain passenger vehicle and light truck tyres from China (DS399); (x) EU - anti-dumping measures on certain footwear from China (DS405); (xi) United States - measures affecting the production and sale of clove cigarettes (DS406); and (xii) Dominican Republic - safeguard measures on imports of polypropylene bags and tubular fabric (DS415, DS416, DS417, DS418).

Table II.3
WTO dispute settlement cases involving Turkey as respondent or complainant, 1995-2011

Dispute	Raised by/against	Actions	Outcome
Restrictions on imports of textile and clothing products	Hong Kong, China/Turkey	Consultations requested on 12 February 1996, under GATT Articles XI, XIII, and XXIV as well as WTO ATC Article 2 (WT/DS29/1)	Pending consultation
Restrictions on imports of textile and clothing products	India/Turkey	Consultation requested on 21 March 1996, under GATT Articles XI, XIII, and XXIV as well as WTO ATC Article 2 (WT/DS34/1). Establishment of panel requested on 2 February 1998 (WT/DS34/2). DSB agreed to establish a panel on 13 March 1998 (WT/DSB/M/43). Panel report adopted on 19 November 1999 (WT/DS34/11). Appellate Body Report adopted on 19 November 1999 (WT/DS34/11)	Notification of mutually agreed solution on 6 July 2001 (WT/DS34/14)
Taxation of foreign film revenues	United States/Turkey	Consultation requested on 12 June 1996, under GATT Article III (WT/DS43/1). Establishment of a panel requested on 10 January 1997 (WT/DS43/2). DSB agreed to establish a panel on 25 February 1997 (WT/DS/M/29)	Notification of mutually agreed solution on 24 July 1997 (WT/DS43/3)
Restrictions on imports of textile and clothing products	Thailand/Turkey	Consultation requested on 20 June 1996, under GATT Articles I, II, XI, XIII, and XXIV as well as WTO ATC Article 2 (WT/DS47/1)	Pending consultation
Anti-dumping duty on steel and iron pipe fittings	Brazil/Turkey	Consultation requested on 9 October 2000, under GATT Article XXIII and Article 17 of the Anti-Dumping Agreement (WT/DS208/1)	Pending consultation
Certain import procedures for fresh fruit	Ecuador/Turkey	Consultation requested on 31 August 2001, under GATT Article XXII, Article 11 of the SPS Agreement, Article 6 of the Import Licensing Agreement, Article 19 of the Agreement on Agriculture, and GATS Article XXII (WT/DS237/1). Establishment of panel requested on 13 June 2002 (WT/DS237/3). DSB agreed to establish a panel on 29 July 2002 (WT/DSB/M/130)	Notification of mutually agreed solution on 29 November 2002 (WT/DS237/4)
Import ban on pet food from Hungary	Hungary/Turkey	Consultation requested on 3 May 2002, under GATT Article XXIII, Article II of the SPS Agreement, and Article 19 of the Agreement on Agriculture (WT/DS256/1)	Pending consultation
Measures affecting the importation of rice	United States/Turkey	Consultation requested on 2 November 2005, under GATT Articles III, XI:1 and Article 2.1 of the TRIMs Agreement, Article 4.2 of the Agriculture Agreement (WT/DS334/1), and various Articles of the Import Licensing Agreement (WT/DS334/). Establishment of panel requested on 6 February 2006 (WT/DS334/4). DSB agreed to establish a panel on 17 March 2006 (WT/DS334/5/Rev.1)	Panel report issued to the parties on 8 June 2007; circulated to all Members in September 2007
Definitive anti-dumping measures on steel rebar from Turkey	Turkey/Egypt	Consultation requested on 6 November 2000, under GATT Article XXIII and Article 17.3 of the Anti-Dumping Agreement (WT/DS211/1) Establishment of a panel requested on 3 May 2001 (WT/DS211/2) and 11 May 2001 (WT/DS211/2/Corr.1). DSB agreed to establish a panel on 20 June 2001 (WT/DSB/M/106). Panel report adopted on 1 October 2002 (WT/DS211/5)	Parties notified in meeting of 29 August 2003 that the matter would no longer be pursued with the DSB. Egypt revoked the measure on 3 August 2004
Definitive anti-dumping measures on blanketing from Turkey	Turkey/South Africa	Consultation requested on 9 April 2003, under GATT Article XXIII and Article 17 of the Anti-Dumping Agreement (WT/DS288/1)	Panel has not been established, complaint not withdrawn. No mutually agreed solution notified

Source: WTO Secretariat.

(ii) Regional agreements

(a) Customs Union with the European Union

15. Turkey signed an Association Agreement to promote trade and economic relations with the EU in 1963. The timetable for the formation of a customs union was laid down by an additional protocol in 1973. The EU had unilaterally eliminated all customs duties and equivalent measures on the specified products when the trade-related provisions of the Interim Agreement of the Protocol entered into force in September 1971, whereas Turkey was accorded a transition period of 22 years.

16. The Customs Union between Turkey and the EU entered into force on 1 January 1996 according to the Decision No. 1/95 of the Turkey-EU Association Council.[14] The Customs Union provides for a common external tariff (CET) for the products covered, and foresees that Turkey will align its trade-related legislation with the EU *acquis* in several areas essential for market access, e.g. with respect to product standards.[15] The Customs Union covers all industrial products as well as the industrial component of processed agricultural goods, TRIPS, and competition policy, but does not extend to agricultural commodities, services, or government procurement.[16] Unlike members of the European Economic Area, Turkey may be subject to anti-dumping and countervailing measures taken by the EU. Trade in agricultural products is regulated according to Decision No. 1/98 of the Association Council, amended by Decision No. 2/2006 to take into account the EU enlargement in 2004.[17] A free-trade area has existed since 1996 between Turkey and the EU for products covered by the European Coal and Steel Community.

17. Turkey was granted the status of candidate country for EU membership at the Helsinki European Council in 1999. Subject to the fulfilment of certain conditions, EU member states endorsed "enlarging and deepening" the Customs Union and opening accession negotiations with Turkey at the Copenhagen European Council in December 2002. Negotiations began on 3 October 2005. By September 2011, 13 negotiation chapters had been opened, and one of them provisionally completed.[18]

(b) Free-trade agreement with the European Free Trade Association (EFTA)

18. The free-trade agreement between Turkey and EFTA is based on an asymmetrical model similar to Turkey's Customs Union with the EU. The agreement covers industrial products (within HS Chapters 25 to 97), fish and marine products, processed agricultural goods[19], intellectual property, competition rules, state aid, and anti-dumping.[20] The agreement entered into force on 1 April 1992, from which date EFTA states abolished all customs duties and charges of equivalent effect on non-agricultural imports from Turkey, except for textiles and apparel goods, for which EFTA countries eliminated the import duties on 1 January 1996.[21] Turkey has granted non-agricultural

[14] The Association Council is the main decision-making body of the association.

[15] Until 1 January 2001, Turkey was allowed to maintain import duty rates above the CET for certain "sensitive" products, i.e. at the outset 290 items at the HS 12-digit level.

[16] Negotiations addressing services and government procurement were launched in 2000, but are now part of Turkey's accession process.

[17] Free movement of agricultural goods is an agreed common objective, but no firm timetable has been set for the integration of agriculture into the Customs Union.

[18] EU (2011).

[19] Except for items such as mannitol, sorbitol, casein, egg and milk albumin, and dextrin.

[20] For trade in agricultural goods, Turkey has concluded bilateral agreements with individual EFTA countries.

[21] EFTA comprises Switzerland, Norway, Iceland, and Liechtenstein. For Iceland, the FTA with Turkey entered into force in September 1992.

imports from EFTA states the same customs duty treatment as imports from the EU since 1 January 1993, and provides duty-free treatment for fish and marine products. Trade in processed agricultural products follows the same system as that applied to Turkey's trade with the EU.

19. Turkey and EFTA states supervise the functioning and implementation of the agreement in a Joint Committee. At its ninth meeting, on 2-3 December 2009, a protocol was added on the mutual recognition of conformity assessment of products. It was also agreed to examine the possibility of extending the free-trade agreement to cover trade in services.

(c) Euro-Mediterranean partnership

20. In November 1995, the Euro-Mediterranean Conference of Ministers of Foreign Affairs marked the starting point of the Euro-Mediterranean Partnership, a framework to be based on three pillars (political and security cooperation, economic and financial partnership, and a social, human and cultural agenda). In the context of the Partnership and as part of the creation of a Euro-Mediterranean Free-Trade Area, Turkey has concluded bilateral free-trade agreements with Egypt, Israel, Morocco, Tunisia, Palestinian Authority, Jordan, Syria, and Lebanon (section (iii) below).[22]

(d) Economic Cooperation Organization

21. Together with Iran and Pakistan, Turkey formed the Economic Cooperation Organization (ECO) in 1985. The ECO was expanded to include Afghanistan, Azerbaijan, Kazakhstan, Kyrgyz Republic, Tajikistan, Turkmenistan, and Uzbekistan in 1992. The stated purpose of the ECO is to foster sustainable socio-economic development, and cooperation projects have been launched in priority areas such as energy, trade, transportation, agriculture, and drug control.

22. ECO members signed a framework agreement to enhance trade relations between them in March 2000. Afghanistan, Iran, Pakistan, Tajikistan, and Turkey concluded the ECO Trade Agreement (ECOTA) in July 2003. The ECOTA has binding provisions on, *inter alia*, state monopolies, state aid, the protection of intellectual property rights, dumping and anti-dumping measures, and the elimination of quantitative restrictions to trade. Tariffs are to be reduced by no less than 10% per year to a maximum of 15% within eight years of the entry into force of the ECOTA. Following the completion of the ratification process by Iran, the ECOTA entered into force on 24 April 2008. It is expected to become fully operational after the exchange of lists.

(e) Developing-8 (D-8)

23. Developing-8 (D-8) is an organization for development cooperation between Bangladesh, Egypt, Indonesia, Iran, Malaysia, Nigeria, Pakistan, and Turkey. The establishment of the D-8 was announced through the Istanbul Declaration of Summit of Heads of State/Government on 15 June 1997. The aim of the D-8 Organization for Economic Cooperation is to improve the member states' position in the world economy, diversify and create new opportunities in trade relations, enhance their participation in decision-making at the international level, and to improve the standards of living of their populations.

[22] The Euro-Mediterranean Partnership comprises the current 27 members of the EU together with Algeria, Egypt, Israel, Jordan, Lebanon, Morocco, Palestinian Authority, Syria, Tunisia, and Turkey. Libya has held observer status since 1999. The original aim was to achieve the Euro-Mediterranean Free-Trade Area by 2010.

24. The members of the D-8 signed a preferential trade agreement (PTA) to enhance economic and trade integration in 2006. The agreement aims at promoting and expanding trade through tariff reductions and the elimination of non-tariff barriers (NTBs). The tariff reductions and NTB-related clauses are to apply to goods covering 8% of the HS tariff lines with tariff rates above 10% for each contracting member. Tariffs above 25% are to be reduced to 25%; tariffs below 25%, but above 15% are to be cut to 15%, and a tariff of 10% will apply to tariffs in the 10-15% range. LDCs will reduce their tariffs in eight annual instalments, other countries in four instalments. The PTA obtained legal force between Turkey, Malaysia, Iran, and Nigeria on 25 August 2011, following the completion of their internal ratification processes. The D-8 PTA is expected to become fully operational after the completion of the exchange of tariff concession lists.

(f) The Organization of Islamic Cooperation (OIC)

25. The Organization of Islamic Co-operation (OIC), formerly the Organization of the Islamic Conference, is an inter-governmental organization with 57 member states spread across four continents.[23] The OIC aims at strengthening intra-Islamic economic and trade cooperation and deepening economic integration, leading to the establishment of an Islamic Common Market. As a first step, Framework Agreement on Trade Preferential System among the Member States of the OIC (TPS/OIC) entered into force in 2002. The framework agreement sets out the general rules and principles for the negotiations to establish the TPS/OIC. The negotiations on the modalities for tariff reductions and the timetable were completed, and the Protocol on Preferential Tariff Scheme for TPS/OIC (PRETAS) was adopted in 2005, and entered into force in February 2010. The tariff reduction commitments of the PRETAS are to apply to 7% of the HS tariff lines with tariff rates above 10% for each contracting member. Tariffs above 25% are to be cut to 25%, and tariffs of 15% and 10% will apply to tariffs previously in the (respective) 15-25% and 10-15% range. The PRETAS also covers non-tariff barriers, anti-dumping and safeguard measures, and other trade-related issues. Negotiations on rules of origin were completed in 2007. The rules entered into force on 9 August 2011. However, for the TPS/OIC to become fully operational, at least ten OIC members must complete the signature and ratification of the three legal instruments of the agreement, and submit their tariff concession lists. So far, only five members (including Turkey) have completed the process.

(g) Black Sea Economic Cooperation (BSEC)

26. The BSEC declaration, signed on 25 June 1992 by Albania, Armenia, Azerbaijan, Bulgaria, Georgia, Greece, Moldova, Romania, the Russian Federation, Turkey, and Ukraine, was aimed at improving and diversifying their economic and trade relations. The BSEC provides for cooperation in various areas, including banking and finance; and the exchange of economic and statistical data on energy, transport, telecommunications, trade and industry, agriculture and agri-industry, environmental protection, tourism, and science and technology. The Black Sea Trade and Development Bank became operational in 1999. Although a declaration of intent to form a BSEC free-trade area was adopted in 1997, the BSEC has not provided a framework for the exchange of preferential tariff concessions. As noted in the declaration, the progressive establishment of such an area will have to take into account each member's existing and future links with the EU.

(iii) Bilateral free-trade agreements

27. Turkey's free-trade and association agreements contain a standard model based on the preferences each party has exchanged with the EU. Trade in industrial goods is fully liberalized at the

[23] The decision to establish the organization was taken at a summit in Rabat on 25 September 1969.

end of a transitional period, whereas mutual concessions are exchanged on selected agricultural and processed agricultural goods. Since its last Review, Turkey has finalized negotiations with Montenegro, Serbia, Georgia, Chile, Jordan, Lebanon, and Mauritius. Turkey has 16 FTAs in force at present.[24] Details of the agreements concluded, and earlier agreements remaining in force, are provided in Table II.4.[25]

Table II.4
Bilateral trade agreements, 2011

Country	Date of agreement	Entry into force	Major Turkish exports and imports covered by the agreement
EFTA	10.12.1991	01.04.1992	Phased reduction of tariffs on industrial goods; complete elimination on industrial goods by 1 January 1999
Israel	14.03.1996	01.05.1997	Phased reduction of tariffs on industrial goods; complete elimination on industrial goods on 1 January 2000
Macedonia (FYR)	07.09.1999	01.09.2000	Phased reduction of tariffs on industrial goods; complete elimination on industrial goods by 1 January 2008
Croatia	13.03.2002	01.07.2003	Phased reduction of tariffs on industrial goods; complete elimination on industrial goods by 1 January 2007
Bosnia-Herzegovina	03.07.2002	01.07.2003	Phased reduction of tariffs on industrial goods; complete elimination on industrial goods by 1 January 2007
Palestinian Authority	20.07.2004	01.06.2005	Phased reduction of tariffs on industrial goods; complete elimination on industrial goods by 1 June 2015
Tunisia	25.11.2004	01.07.2005	Phased reduction of tariffs on industrial goods; complete elimination on industrial goods by 1 July 2014
Morocco	07.04.2004	01.01.2006	Phased reduction of tariffs on industrial goods; complete elimination on industrial goods by 1 January 2015
Syria	22.12.2004	01.01.2007	Phased reduction of tariffs on industrial goods; complete elimination on industrial goods by 1 January 2019
Egypt	27.12.2005	01.03.2007	Phased reduction of tariffs on industrial goods; complete elimination on industrial goods by 1 January 2020
Albania	22.12.2006	01.05.2008	Phased reduction of tariffs on industrial goods; complete elimination on industrial goods by 1 January 2013
Montenegro	26.11.2008	01.03.2010	Phased reduction of tariffs on industrial goods; complete elimination on industrial goods by 1 January 2015
Serbia	01.06.2009	01.09.2010	Phased reduction of tariffs on industrial goods; complete elimination on industrial goods by 1 January 2015
Georgia	21.11.2007	01.11.2008	Full elimination of tariffs on industrial goods by 1 November 2008
Chile	14.07.2009	01.03.2011	Phased reduction of tariffs on industrial goods; complete elimination on industrial goods by 1 January 2015
Jordan	01.12.2009	01.03.2011	Phased reduction of tariffs on most industrial goods; elimination on industrial goods by 1 January 2018
Lebanon[a]	24.10.2010	..	Phased reduction of tariffs on most industrial goods; elimination on industrial goods by 1 January 2020
Mauritius[b]	09.09.2011	..	Phased reduction of tariffs on most industrial goods, elimination on industrial goods by 1 January 2022

.. Not available.

a The Turkey-Lebanon FTA was signed on 24 November 2010 and will enter into force once the internal ratification procedures have been completed in both countries.

b The Turkey-Mauritius FTA was signed on 9 September 2011 and will enter into force once the internal ratification procedures have been completed in both countries.

Source: Information provided by the Turkish authorities.

---

[24] The ratification processes have commenced for the FTAs with Lebanon and Mauritius; the FTAs are expected to enter into force in 2012.

[25] Turkey's free-trade agreements with Bulgaria, Czech Republic, Estonia, Hungary, Latvia, Lithuania, Poland, Romania, Slovak Republic, and Slovenia expired in the context of EU enlargement.

28. Turkey is currently engaged in negotiations with the Faroe Islands, the Gulf Cooperation Council, MERCOSUR, Ukraine, Moldova, Colombia, Ecuador, Libya, Seychelles, Korea, Cameroon, Democratic Republic of Congo, and Malaysia. Turkey has initiated the launch of negotiations with: Mexico; the South African Customs Union (SACU); Algeria; ASEAN countries; Indonesia; India; the Africa, Caribbean and Pacific (ACP) countries; Canada; Peru; and Central America. Moreover, exploratory talks with the CARICOM Secretariat were held in 2009. To date, Mexico, SACU, and Algeria have not responded to Turkey's invitation to engage in FTA negotiations.

(iv) Other preferential trade arrangements

29. Pursuant to Article 16 of Decision No. 1/95 of the Turkey-EU Association Council, Turkey has been moving to align its Generalized System of Preferences (GSP) Scheme with that of the EU. Preferences are granted on selected non-agricultural goods, including raw materials and semi-finished goods, depending on the level of "sensitivity". Duties are fully eliminated on non-sensitive products, while duty reductions apply on the more sensitive items.[26] Duties are eliminated for least developed countries in line with the EU Everything But Arms Initiative, and Turkey grants additional preferences to specific countries under the Special Incentives Arrangements for Sustainable Development and Good Governance. Beneficiaries under Turkey's GSP scheme are announced annually in the Annexes to its import regime.[27] As of 2010, Turkey's GSP regime mirrors that of the EU in terms of product coverage, geographical coverage (except for Armenia), and duty-reduction rates. Turkey has not yet adopted the amendments to the EU GSP scheme, notably regarding rules of origin, which entered into force on 1 January 2011.

30. Turkish exports are granted preferential treatment under the GSP schemes of Canada, Japan, New Zealand, the Russian Federation, and the United States. In the Russian Federation, imports from Turkey are subject to a tariff reduction of 25% of the general rate except for products on a negative list.[28] The United States extends GSP treatment to 3,400 products of Turkish origin at the HS 8-digit level. Turkey exported 734 products (HS 8-digit) to the United States under its GSP programme in 2010.[29]

(4) INVESTMENT REGIME

31. Turkey enacted the Decree on Improving the Investment Environment in Turkey on 11 December 2001 as part of a national strategy to increase domestic and foreign investments. The Decree established the Coordination Council for the Improvement of the Investment Environment and technical subcommittees to identify and remove remaining barriers to private investment. Legislation to ensure the registration of investments in one day, and reduce the number of required documents, was approved by Parliament on 11 June 2003 and published in the *Official Gazette* on 17 June 2003. Additional steps to improve the business and investment climate include the adoption of the Foreign Direct Investment Law No. 4875 in 2003, and the establishment of the Turkish Investment Support and Promotion Agency in 2006.

---

[26] The preference generally amounts to a 3.5 percentage point reduction in the MFN tariff rate, except where the EU GSP scheme allows for larger preferential reductions (then these higher reductions apply), and for HS Chapters 50-63, where the cuts equal 20% of the MFN duty rate.

[27] Iraq was recently added to Turkey's list of beneficiaries.

[28] Due to their Customs Union with the Russian Federation, Kazakhstan and Belarus also follow a common approach on GSP.

[29] Like all other exporters eligible for GSP treatment in the United States, Turkey is subject to provisions such as the "competitive need limitation" and the "*de minimis* waiver". Turkish exports to the United States under GSP amounted to US$644.5 million in 2009 and US$793 million in 2010.

32. Turkey has been a member of the International Centre for Settlement of Investment Disputes and the Multilateral Investment Guarantee Agency since 1987. Turkey joined the Convention on the Recognition and Enforcement of Foreign Arbitral Awards, and the European Convention on International Commercial Arbitration in 1991. The Law on International Arbitration No. 4686, enacted in July 2001, provides for international arbitration to resolve conflicts from public service concession contracts involving any foreign element. Turkey has signed 82 bilateral agreements for the promotion and protection of foreign direct investment; 73 are in force.

33. Key elements of the 2003 Foreign Direct Investment Law included the freedom to invest, the reassurance of existing guarantees of foreign investors' rights in one document, the adoption of international standards in defining a "foreign investor" and "foreign direct investment", and a policy shift from ex-ante control to investment promotion and facilitation with minimal ex-post monitoring.[30] The Law guarantees national treatment and investor rights.

34. All companies established according to the Turkish Commercial Code are regarded as Turkish companies, with equal rights and responsibilities as stated in the Constitution and in other laws. The rights include national treatment, guarantee against expropriation without compensation, transfer of proceeds, the right to expatriate personnel, and access to international arbitration or any other means of dispute settlement.

35. A 100% foreign owned company may operate in nearly all sectors of the Turkish economy. Remaining restrictions on foreign ownership are laid down in legislation regulating specific activities (Table II.5). Under recent liberalization in the area of broadcasting, the limitation on foreign equity participation in a media service provider was raised from 25% to 50% in March 2011. Other restrictions have remained unchanged since Turkey's last Trade Policy Review. Thus, foreign equity participation may not exceed 49% in aviation and in maritime services provided under concession agreements, and foreigners may not obtain a fishing licence in Turkey. Special permission under specific laws is required to provide accounting, auditing, and bookkeeping services; for the establishment of private employment offices; and for investments in the financial sector, petroleum, mining, electricity, and education services. Acquisition of real estate by foreigners remains restricted, or subject to reciprocity provisions. In accordance with the Land Registry Law No. 2644, foreigners purchasing land plots between 2.5 and 30 hectares need permission from the Council of Ministers. Foreigners may not purchase land exceeding 30 hectares.[31]

---

[30] The Law abolished all former screening and approval procedures, and share transfer requirements. The term foreign investor was broadened to include Turks living abroad as well as international organizations.

[31] In early 2008, the Constitutional Court suspended provisions in the Foreign Direct Investment Law and the Title Deed Law, which had allowed the purchase of land by foreign individuals, foreign trade corporations (i.e. established abroad under foreign law), or foreign capital companies (i.e. established in Turkey). The Turkish Government subsequently passed new legislation to permit foreign acquisition of land. According to this legislation, foreign natural persons may acquire real estate for residence and business purposes, subject to reciprocity and compliance with legal restrictions. The properties must be separated and registered (for business or residence) in implemented development plans or localized development plans. The total area acquired by foreign individuals may not exceed 10% of the land within implemented development plans or localized development plans, or 2.5 hectares for each individual property. As information on foreign land ownership is not readily available, this may cause problems and legal challenges for individual investors seeking to purchase land in Turkey. Pursuant to Article 36 of the Land Registry Law, foreign capital companies established in Turkey and registered in the Turkish Commercial Registries are legally accepted as Turkish companies regardless of the citizenship of their shareholders. Foreign capital companies may thus acquire real estate to conduct the business activities listed in the articles of association of the company, except in military

Table II.5
Foreign direct investment restrictions, 2011

Sectors	Legal source	Restriction
Broadcasting	Law on Establishment of Radio and Television Enterprises and Their Media Services Law No. 6112; 15 February 2011	The proportion of total direct foreign capital in a media service provider may not exceed 50% of the paid-in capital.
Aviation	Civil Aviation Law No. 2920 SHY-6A (Regulation on Commercial Air Transport Operations) SHY-22 (Regulation on Airport Groundhandling)	No more than 49% equity participation by foreigners. Licences to operate airlines are only granted to locally incorporated companies whose management is under the control of Turkish citizens and the majority of voting shares are owned by Turkish citizens. Airlines, of which the majority of shares are controlled by foreigners, are not permitted to carry passengers from one national airport to another. To obtain groundhandling services licences (A and C Group Licences), the majority authorized administration and representation of the company must be Turkish. The contract of such a company has to guarantee that the votes of its majority shareholders belong to Turkish nationals.
Maritime transportation	Cabotage Act No. 815, Turkish Commercial Code No. 6762 (to be replaced by Turkish Commercial Code No. 6102 on 1 July 2012)	No more than 49% equity participation by foreigners. Cabotage is reserved to national flag carriers. Registration of commercial ships is granted only to locally incorporated companies whose management is under the control of Turkish citizens, and majority of voting shares are owned by Turkish citizens.
Port services	Cabotage Act No. 815, Turkish Commercial Code No. 6762 (to be replaced by Turkish Commercial Code No. 6102 on 1 July 2012), Privatization Law No. 4046, and Law No. 5189 of 16 June 2004	Port services are provided under concession agreements.
Fishing	Fishing Law No. 1380, Bylaw on Fishing Products No. 6710, Turkish Commercial Code No. 6762	Foreigners may not obtain a fishing licence. Vessels owned by foreigners also may not register as fishing vessels in Turkey, unless owned by Turkish nationals or by companies of which majority of voting shares are owned by Turkish citizens.
Accounting, auditing and book-keeping services	Law No. 3568 on Accountancy, Financial Advisory and Certified Financial Advisory Services, 1989	Special permission required. Foreign financial advisors who are citizens of countries that have officially codified the principles of the profession of financial advisory may, under reciprocal conditions, be authorized by approval of the Prime Minister upon the proposal of the Ministry of Finance, provided that these persons have the qualifications required for Turkish financial advisors and have rights to perform similar services in their own countries.
Financial sector	Banking Law No. 5411, Bank Cards and Credit Cards Law No. 5464, Decree Law No. 90 on Linding Activities, Capital Market Law No. 2499, amended by Laws No. 3794 and 4487 and the relevant Communiqués; Financial Leasing Law No. 3226; Insurance Law No. 5684	Special permission required. Permission to establish a bank, which has to be founded in the form of a joint-stock company, or to open the first branch of a foreign bank in Turkey, shall be given by the Banking Regulation and Supervision Board. Only intermediary institutions (including banks) established in Turkey and authorized by the Capital Market Board may perform securities activities; however, banks may not trade in the Istanbul Stock Exchange (ISE) equities market. Mutual funds may be founded only by authorized banks, insurance companies, non-bank securities intermediaries; and pension funds by private pension companies established in Turkey. Portfolio management and investment advisory services may be performed by non-bank securities intermediaries, non-deposit taking banks and portfolio management companies established in Turkey.

Table II.5 (cont'd)

zones (military forbidden zones, military security zones, and strategic zones), which require permission from the Turkish military authorities, or in special security zones (subject to permission by the province governorship).

Sectors	Legal source	Restriction
		An insurance company or reinsurance company that is to operate in Turkey must be established as a joint-stock company or a cooperative. Foreign insurance and reinsurance companies may also operate in Turkey by opening branches, provided that they have not been prohibited in their country of operation. Following establishment, insurance and reinsurance companies must obtain an operational licence from the Undersecretariat of Treasury; a separate licence is issued for each insurance branch. Other than specific exceptions, cross-border supply of insurance services is prohibited. Foreign commercial presence or presence of foreign natural persons regarding services auxiliary to insurance is permitted only for consultancy and risk-management services.
Petroleum	Petroleum Law No. 6326 and Petroleum Market Law No. 5015	Special permission required. Foreign enterprises may invest in marketing and sales activities without restriction. They may invest in upstream activities including exploration and exploitation activities may be conducted under a licence granted by the General Directorate of Petroleum Affairs providing that they are not controlled or owned by a foreign State (this restriction may be lifted by the Council of Ministers). Petroleum-related activities may be carried out through locally incorporated stock companies or Turkish branches of stock companies incorporated abroad. Downstream market activities including, refining, transportation through pipelines and storage may be conducted under a licence granted by the Energy Market Regulatory Authority.
Mining	Mining Law No. 3213	Foreigners may invest in the mining subsector only through local branches (Chapter II(4)). However, exploration and exploitation of boron are reserved for the Government. For uranium and thorium, the public sector may explore and exploit these minerals without selling. On the contrary selling of these radioactive minerals may be permitted by the Cabinet Council.
Real-estate trading	Land Registry Law No. 2644	Foreign trade corporations (trade companies established in foreign countries according to their own law) and foreign real persons in Turkey may acquire land. In the acquisition of land by foreign real persons the "principle of reciprocity" applies. Acquisition of real estate by foreign trade corporations in Turkey is subject to the provisions of special laws. Foreign real persons may acquire real estate in Turkey with some legal restrictions. Acquisition of real estate by foreign real persons should be for residence or business purposes and separated and registered for these purposes in the implemented or localized development plans.
Electricity	Electricity Market Law No. 4628	The total market share of any real or private entity, either directly or via controlling the generation companies, may not exceed 20% of the total installed capacity. This threshold is applied as 10% for wholesale of electricity under same conditions. Within the context of privatization activities foreign real persons and legal entities may not have a market share that will enable them controling power in the electricity generation, transmission, and distribution subsectors. In 2010, electricity served by private distribution companies increased to approximately 46% of the total market.
Education	Law No. 5580 on Private Education Institutions Legislation on Foundations	Foreign real or legal persons may not set up education institutions unless all students are foreigners. International private education institutions may be set up by real or legal persons upon authorization of the Council of Ministers. For tertiary education institutions, the majority in the administrative bodies must be Turkish nationals.
Private employment offices	Law No. 4904	According to the amendment made in 2007 by Law No. 4904, only Turkish citizens may establish, administer or act on behalf of a private employment agency. If a foreign company wishes to establish an agency in Turkey, the agency must be represented by a Turkish citizen. According to some changes in this Law in 2008, the obligation of being a Turkish citizen in order to establish, administer and represent an agency has been removed; foreigners may now establish private employment agencies.

Source: Information provided by the Turkish authorities.

36. The OECD FDI regulatory restrictiveness index (designed to capture equity restrictions, screening and prior approval, measures regarding foreign key personnel, and other operational

restrictions) gives Turkey an overall score below the OECD average (Table II.6).[32] According to the 2010 data, aside from real estate (which is considered "closed"), FDI restrictions apply in media, transport, and business services. All other sectors covered by the index are "open". However, the index does not consider actual enforcement of statutory restrictions, which is difficult to assess.[33]

Table II.6
Turkey's FDI regulatory restrictiveness index[a], 2010

	Turkey	OECD average	Non-OECD average
Agriculture and forestry	0.000	0.128	0.227
Fishing	0.000	0.320	0.333
Mining	0.000	0.122	0.209
Manufacturing[b]	0.000	0.030	0.059
Electricity	0.000	0.123	0.125
Construction	0.000	0.053	0.055
Distribution[c]	0.000	0.029	0.120
Hotels and restaurants	0.000	0.030	0.077
Transport	0.208	0.227	0.289
Media	0.250	0.180	0.316
Telecom	0.000	0.092	0.174
Financial services[d]	0.000	0.053	0.132
Business services	0.125	0.067	0.167
Real estate	1.000	0.283	0.277
Total	0.072	0.095	0.157

a 1 = closed; 0 = open.
b Average scores for 5 manufacturing sectors.
c Average scores for retail and wholesale distribution.
d Average scores for banking, insurance, and other finance.

Source: OECD (2010), *OECD's FDI restrictiveness Index: 2010 update*. Viewed at: http://www.oecd.org/dataoecd/32/19/45563285.pdf.

37. Investment incentives, such as import duty exemptions and subsidized credits, are available to domestic and foreign investors alike. Turkish residents wishing to invest abroad are free to export capital in cash, by bank transfer or in kind in accordance with Turkey's Customs Regulations.[34]

38. Turkey's FDI inflows, which rose markedly from 2004 onwards, in part due to privatizations of state-owned companies, appear to have been affected by the global financial crisis (Table II.7). After a steep decline from 2007 to 2008, the stock of inward FDI peaked in 2010, and is currently back at the pre-crisis level relative to Turkey's GDP. According to UNCTAD's Inward FDI Performance Index, Turkey ranked 108th in 2010, down from 94st in 2008 and 71st in 2006.[35] Turkey's FDI outflows peaked in 2008, but the FDI outward stock has continued to rise, and stood at almost US$22 billion in 2009, up from about US$6 billion in 2002-03. According to UNCTAD's outward FDI Performance Index, Turkey ranked 77th out of 125 economies for the period 2005-07.

[32] In 2006, Turkey's score was somewhat above the OECD average. A comparison of the 2006 and 2010 results in absolute values is not strictly appropriate due to changes in the methodology (OECD, 2010b).

[33] According to EU (2011), Turkey's licensing procedures are relatively lengthy. For example, 25 different procedures are still needed in order to build a warehouse. Market exit is difficult too, as closing a business still takes 3.3 years on average.

[34] An authorization requirement from the Undersecretariat of Treasury for outward investment exceeding US$5 million was abolished at the end of 2006.

[35] UNCTAD (2011).

Table II.7
Foreign direct investment, 1995-2010
(US$ million)

	1995-2005[a]	2006	2007	2008	2009	2010
FDI inflows	2,188	20,185	22,047	19,504	8,411	9,278
FDI inward stock	33,511	95,076	154,020	80,225	140,493	181,590
FDI inward stock (% of GDP)	10.2	18.1	23.6	10.8	22.8	24.7
FDI outflows	484	924	2,106	2,549	1,553	1,464
FDI outward stock	5,935	8,866	12,210	17,846	22,250	21,570
FDI outward stock (% of GDP)	2.0	1.7	1.9	2.4	3.6	2.9

a Annual average (2000-05 average for inward and outward FDI stock).

Source: The Central Bank of Turkey.

39. The peak in FDI inflows in 2007 and the subsequent decline can to a large extent be ascribed to the financial services sector, where FDI amounted to US$1.6 billion in 2010 down from over US$11 billion in 2007, due to the acquisitions of various banks by foreign investors. Although FDI by sector may vary substantially year-to-year, FDI into Turkey is predominantly in services (financial intermediation, communications, energy supply, and distribution services) and in manufacturing. Although FDI in agriculture, hunting, fishing and forestry has been increasing since 2008, the share in total FDI inflows is still negligible, averaging 0.4% over the period 2005-10, compared with services (80%), manufacturing (18%), and mining and quarrying (1.4%). The European Union, led by the Netherlands, Austria, France, Belgium, Greece, and Germany, continues to be by far the largest investor in Turkey, representing nearly 70% of total FDI inflows during 2005-10.[36]

40. Turkey's outward FDI, which averaged US$2 billion during 2005-10, is primarily directed towards services (45.5%), notably financial intermediation (21%); manufacturing (35%); and mining and quarrying (18.5%). During this period, nearly 60% of Turkish overseas investments went to five countries; Azerbaijan, the Netherlands, Germany, Malta, and Luxemburg.

[36] In the first six months of 2011, FDI inflows into Turkey amounted to US$9.1 billion, primarily in the financial sector, energy, and manufacturing. EU investors, led by Austria and Spain, accounted for more than 90% of these investments.

III. TRADE POLICIES AND PRACTICES BY MEASURE

(1) MEASURES DIRECTLY AFFECTING IMPORTS

(i) Import procedures and requirements

1. Customs Law No. 4458 (as amended), together with its Regulations constitutes the basic legal framework for customs matters.[1] Over the years, Turkey has been taking steps to gradually align its customs legislation with the *acquis communautaire* of the EU. Since its last TPR, Turkey has redrafted the implementing provisions of the Customs Law. In addition, the tasks of the new Ministry of Customs and Trade were published in June 2011, following the government reorganization.[2] On the administrative and operational side, Turkey has concluded an agreement with Greece to build a second border-crossing bridge; signed a protocol with Georgia on the circulation of passengers, vehicles, and goods at three-border-crossing points and agreed minutes regarding the exchange of data; inaugurated new premised at the Hamzabeyli Border Gate; reopened the Çobanbey Railroad Border Gate (closed in 1980); and engaged in cooperation with Syria and Iran on the joint operation of border crossings.

2. Under the GIMOP (Customs Modernization Project), the Ministry of Customs and Trade has been implementing several programmes to make the customs administration more effective and efficient. The GÜMSİS (Project of Security Systems at Customs Border Posts) programme was launched in 2001 to monitor and prevent illegal trafficking of goods, vehicles, and travelers. Further modules have been integrated under the GÜMSİS umbrella, including a vehicle and container inspection (x-ray) system, a nuclear detection system, a GPS-based transit-vehicle-tracking system, and a licence-plate scanning system. In 2002, BILGE (a computer software package) was introduced to carry out all real-time customs formalities. BILGE includes subsystems for summary declarations, warehouse management, tariffs, and accounting.

3. The format of the Turkish customs declaration has been aligned with the single administrative document (SAD) used for customs procedures in the EU. In order to benefit from preferential rates of customs duty during customs clearance, EUR.1 or EUR.MED movement certificates are required for imports from non-EU countries with which Turkey has free-trade agreements, and from EU member states for imports of agricultural goods, and coal and steel products. The Customs Authority may grant permission to simplify formalities and procedures, including by waiving some of the documentation requirements. The use of a clearing agent is not compulsory, and the use of customs brokers is not obligatory.

4. A summary declaration, normally effected using BILGE, must be presented at the customs office by the end of the working day following the arrival of goods at Customs.[3] The original

[1] Customs Law No. 4458 replaced Customs Law No. 1615/1972 in February 2000. The main changes in the framework are detailed in WTO (2003).

[2] The new Customs Regulation was published in the *Official Gazette* No. 27369 on 7 October 2009, and the Decree as Law on the Organization and Tasks of the Ministry of Customs and Trade No. 640 in the *Official Gazette* No. 27958 on 8 June 2011. Other recent customs-related legislation includes the Law Amending the Customs Law and Certain Laws and Decree Laws No. 5911 (*Official Gazette* No. 27281, 7 July 2009), and the Decree of the Council of Ministers No. 2009/15481 on Implementation of some Clauses of the Customs Code No. 4458 (*Official Gazette* No. 27369, 7 October 2009).

[3] The transition to a pre-arrival declaration system is in progress. The legislative amendments have been completed, and the new system is expected to become technically operational during 2012.

manifest or bill of lading must be attached to the summary declaration.[4] Import clearance is normally completed with 24 hours, provided all the required documentation is in order, irrespective of the mode of transport.

5. The importers are responsible for customs clearance. Merchandise arriving by road, railway, or air transport should be cleared within 20 days, for importations via maritime transport the requirement is 45 days. The deadline may be extended at the request of the importer. Unless administrative or judicial proceedings have been invoked regarding the imported goods, failure to clear merchandise through Customs within the stipulated deadlines may lead to confiscation and disposal at auction. The declarant may reserve the right to apply the free circulation procedure until publication of the auction date, against payment of a fine of 1% of the c.i.f. value of the goods in question.

6. Certain goods may only be imported through specialized customs offices. Motor vehicles, tractors, motorcycles and their spare parts and accessories must be cleared at the Yesilkoy, Gebze, Izmit or Mersin customs directorates; textile products must pass through the Customs directorate at Halkali, Atatürk Havaliman, Sabiha Gökçen Airport, Gemlik, Mersin, Izmir, Denizli, Ankara, Kayseri or Gaziantep; fertilizer may be imported through the customs administration at Derince, Mersin, Samsun, Izmir, Aliaga, Dikili, Kapikule station, Tekirdag, Bandirma, Gemlik, Iskenderun, Ambarli, Haydarpasa or Antalya; and some solvents and petrochemical products must be cleared by the Gebze Petrochemical Customs Directorate. Exceptional circumstances, whereby goods may be imported through other customs directorates, are defined in the legislation setting up the specialized customs directorates.

7. Any natural or legal person with a tax number is eligible to undertake imports, without any certification requirements.[5] The importation of certain products requires an import licence (section (vii) below).

8. Effective 1 January 2010, textiles and clothing products became subject to registration, to monitor imports of these goods.[6] Registration, which takes place prior to import, includes a certified exporter registry form. Information to be provided includes the company's legal title, address, number of employees, total sales, international quality certificates, and a listing of other destinations for the company's exports.[7] Applications for registration may be submitted via the internet or XML-based software. The exporter registry form is certified by the competent authorities, e.g. the Chambers of Commerce, Turkish public notaries, or a Turkish Consulate General.[8] The form should be submitted once; updates or renewals may be effected through the internet. Exporters are reminded to renew their certificates via e-mail. The product coverage of this surveillance measure is provided in Table AIII.1.

[4] The Ministry of Customs and Trade may allow the use of another internationally approved commercial or official document containing the details necessary for the identification of goods.

[5] Partnerships formed by persons entitled by law to undertake legal acts, although not endowed with legal personality status, may also engage in importation.

[6] Communiqué No. 2010/1, published in the *Official Gazette* No. 27449 (bis 2) on 31 December 2009.

[7] Enterprises may enter "commercial secret" where they believe the response would reveal business-sensitive information.

[8] Consular certification is not required provided Turkey has an apostille agreement pursuant to the 1961 Hague Convention in force with the exporting country.

(ii) Ordinary customs duties

(a) Bound and applied MFN duties, statutory tariffs

9. Turkey's tariff is based on the 2007 Harmonized Commodity Description and Coding System (HS) and comprises 16,448 tariff lines. Turkey's Customs Tariff is implemented at the 12 level, where the first 6 digits indicate the Harmonized System nomenclature, the 7th and 8th digits correspond to the combined nomenclature of the EU, and the 9th and 10th digits are used to display subheadings created for taxation. The purpose of the last two digits is to collect statistical data.

10. As a result of the Uruguay Round, Turkey bound all agriculture tariff lines and 33.5% of its tariff lines for industrial products.[9] Turkey's simple average bound rate is close to 72% for agricultural products, compared with 17.4% on its non-agricultural bound tariff lines (Table III.1). Turkey's final bound rates range from zero to 225% on agricultural goods and from zero to 82% on non-agricultural items.[10] The incidence of tariff bindings in non-agricultural sectors is not uniform (Chart III.1). While Turkey has bound more than 60% of the tariff lines for machinery, precision equipment, chemicals, transport equipment, and plastics and rubber, no tariff lines are bound for products falling within HS Chapters 26, 36, 60, 64, 67, 75, 78, 83, 89, 93 and 97.

11. Turkey's applied tariff consists predominantly of *ad valorem* rates, which apply to 98.3% of tariff lines. Specific, compound, mixed, and variable duties affect some 278 tariff lines at the 12 digit level (Table AIII.2).[11] Specific duties are levied on certain alcoholic beverages, salt, and cinematographic films. Mixed duties apply to items such as carpets, glass and glassware products, and watches.[12] The compound duties affect mainly processed agricultural products such as yoghurt and pasta. Variable duties apply to items such as dairy spreads, sugar confectionery, chocolate, malt, cereals, and prepared potatoes. The compound and variable duties are linked to the implementation of Turkey's customs union commitments with the EU, where the Turkish lira equivalents of the components expressed in euros are to be paid into the Mass Housing Fund, which is applied to Annexes III and IV of the Turkish Import Regime. Turkey does not have seasonal tariffs.

12. Turkey's implementation of the Customs Union Decision, and thus the common external tariff on industrial products, yields a marked difference between the tariff protection afforded to agricultural production versus manufacturing industries. Whereas the simple average applied MFN tariff amounted to 12.2% overall in 2011, the average was 47.9% for agricultural goods and only 4.1% for products within HS Chapters 25 to 97 (Table III.2). The tariff peaks are also markedly higher in the agriculture sector compared with other economic activities. Whilst the average MFN tariff on meat and dairy products exceeds 100%, and is close to 100% on meat and fish preparations, only textiles and clothing items face average tariffs above 10% among the non-agricultural tariff lines (Table AIII.3). Duty-free items represent 23.2% of all tariff lines and include products under the Information Technology Agreement, pharmaceutical products, pulp of wood, some cement, and

[9] The calculations in this section are based on data for 2011 provided by the Turkish authorities, comprising 16,448 tariff lines in total. In WTO (2007), the calculations were made on the basis of 18,253 tariff lines at the HS 12-digit level, resulting in an incidence of bindings of 46.3% of all tariff lines and around 36% for non-agricultural products.

[10] Turkey reduced its bound tariffs in equal annual instalments between 1995 and 2004. GATT 1994, Schedule XXXVII.

[11] While 57 of these tariff lines are unbound, Turkey has only bound 4 tariff lines subject to non-*ad valorem* rates of duty at specific rates; the majority of the lines are bound at *ad valorem* rates (Table AIII.2).

[12] The incidence of mixed duties has declined somewhat since 2007 as mixed rates have been replaced by *ad valorem* duties ranging from 9% to 15% on certain flat-rolled products of iron and non-alloy steel.

products of animal origin. Although Turkey is not a signatory to the plurilateral Agreement on Trade in Civil Aircraft, it provides duty-free treatment to a large number of items for use in civil aircraft (List VI to the 2010 Customs Tariff).

Table III.1
Structure of MFN tariffs in Turkey, 2011
(Per cent)

		2011	Final bound[a]
1.	Bound tariff lines (% of all tariff lines)	51.9	51.9
2.	Duty-free tariff lines (% of all tariff lines)	23.2	3.0
3.	Tariff quotas (% of all tariff lines)	..	..
4.	Non-*ad valorem* tariffs (% of all tariff lines)	1.7	0.2
5.	Non-*ad valorem* tariffs with no AVEs (% of all tariff lines)	0.3	0.2
6.	Simple average tariff rate	12.2	36.9
	Agricultural products (WTO definition)	47.9	71.9
	Non-agricultural products (WTO definition)	5.0	17.4
	Agriculture, hunting, forestry and fishing (ISIC 1)	26.0	45.8
	Mining and quarrying (ISIC 2)	0.2	8.6
	Manufacturing (ISIC 3)	11.6	36.1
7.	Simple average rate of dutiable lines only	15.9	n.a.
8.	Domestic tariff "spikes" (% of all tariff lines)[b]	9.1	3.7
9.	International tariff "peaks" (% of all tariff lines)[c]	14.6	33.0
10.	Overall standard deviation of applied rates	27.1	44.1
11.	"Nuisance" applied rates (% of all tariff lines)[d]	6.7	0.0

.. Not available.
n.a. Not applicable.

a Final bound rates are based on the 2006 tariff schedule in HS02 nomenclature. Calculations on bound averages are based on 6,347 bound tariff lines (including partially bound).
b Domestic tariff spikes are defined as those exceeding three times the overall simple average applied rate (indicator 6).
c International tariff peaks are defined as those exceeding 15%.
d Nuisance rates are those greater than zero, but less than or equal to 2%.

Note: 2011 tariff is based on HS07 nomenclature consisting of 16,448 tariff lines (at 12-digit tariff line level).
Calculations include AVEs provided by the authorities for non-*ad valorem* rates. In case of unavailability of AVEs, the *ad valorem* part is used for compound rates.

Source: WTO Secretariat calculations, based on data provided by the Turkish authorities.

13. Law No. 474 on Customs Tariff Schedule allows the Government to increase the applied MFN rates when these are deemed insufficient to provide "adequate" protection to domestic industries.[13] The Law sets the so-called statutory tariff, which is different from the applied MFN tariff adopted annually by the Council of Ministers.[14] Under the Law, the Government may replace applied MFN rates by 150% of the corresponding rates of the statutory tariff to ensure higher protection to local industries. However, according to the Turkish authorities, the statutory tariff is only applied for tariff lines that are unbound in the WTO framework or fall outside of the scope of the Customs Union Decision. For bound tariff lines or lines covered by the Customs Union, any increases in the applied MFN rate will be capped by Turkey's commitment levels.[15]

---

[13] Law No. 474, published in the *Official Gazette* of 25 May 1964 and amended by Law No. 4217, published in the *Official Gazette* of 8 December 1996.

[14] The Import Regime Decree is issued annually and amended only in exceptional circumstances.

[15] Article 2 of Law No. 474 authorizes the Council of Ministers to increase or decrease the statutory tariff rates and states that provisions of international agreements signed by Turkey must be respected. The Decisions of the Council of Ministers are published in the *Official Gazette*.

Chart III.1
Share of bound tariff lines, by non-agricultural goods

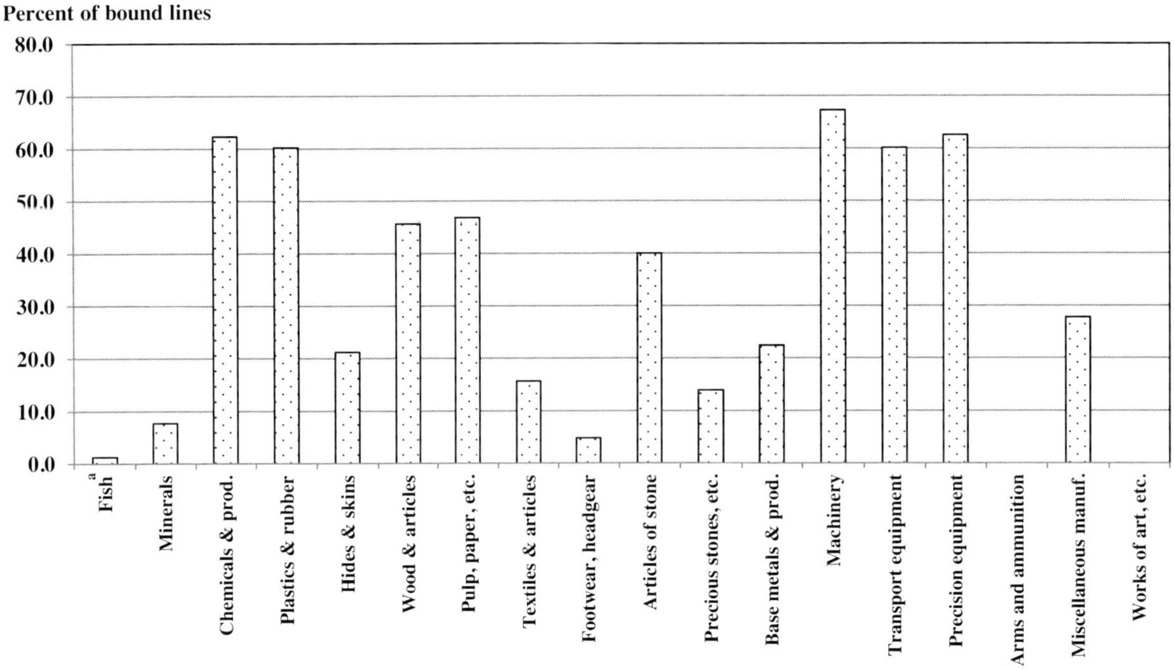

a HS chapter 03.

Note: Share of bound lines (including partially bound) are calculated based on the 2006 tariff schedule in HS02 nomenclature.
Source: WTO Secretariat estimates, based on WTO IDB and CTS databases.

Table III.2
Summary analysis of MFN tariff, 2011

Analysis	No. of lines[a]	Applied 2011 rates				Imports 2010[a] (US$ million)
		Simple avg. tariff (%)	Range tariff (%)	Standard deviation (%)	CV	
Total	16,448	12.2	0-225	27.1	2.2	185,541
HS 01-24	2,936	49.2	0-225	48.8	1.0	7,683
HS25-97	13,512	4.1	0-37.9	3.8	0.9	165,185
By WTO definition						
Agriculture	2,742	47.9	0-225	51.3	1.1	9,721
Live animals and products thereof	398	105.9	0-225	71.4	0.7	584
Dairy products	178	115.8	8.3-180	60.9	0.5	115
Coffee and tea, cocoa, sugar, etc.	423	39.1	0-145	33.5	0.9	1,172
Cut flowers and plants	119	10.6	0-46.8	14.9	1.4	92
Fruit and vegetables	600	41.0	0-145.8	22.6	0.6	672
Grains	65	52.3	0-130	45.0	0.9	1,057
Oil seeds, fats, oils and their products	250	20.1	0-50	15.9	0.8	2,755
Beverages and spirits	302	46.8	0-70	27.7	0.6	162
Tobacco	28	38.8	10-74.9	22.3	0.6	368
Other agricultural products	379	6.4	0-46.8	8.5	1.3	2,742
Non-agriculture	13,706	5.0	0-81.9	7.1	1.4	163,148
Fish and fishery products	393	35.0	0-81.9	18.0	0.5	242

Table III.2 (cont'd)

Analysis	No. of lines[a]	Applied 2011 rates: Simple avg. tariff (%)	Range tariff (%)	Standard deviation (%)	CV	Imports 2010[a] (US$ million)
Mineral products, precious stones and precious metals	847	2.6	0-21.12	3.0	1.2	11,893
Metals	1,856	4.2	0-22.4	5.1	1.2	26,980
Chemicals and photographic supplies	3,132	4.7	0-37.9	2.6	0.5	24,607
Leather, rubber, footwear and travel goods	458	4.1	0-17	4.2	1.0	3,471
Wood, pulp, paper and furniture	793	0.8	0-10	1.9	2.4	5,290
Textiles and clothing	2,372	7.9	0-12	3.0	0.4	10,905
Transport equipment	422	5.2	0-22	4.8	0.9	17,969
Non-electric machinery	1,450	1.6	0-9.7	1.4	0.9	21,368
Electric machinery	838	2.4	0-14	2.7	1.1	14,137
Non agricultural articles n.e.s.	1,040	2.4	0-13.9	1.9	0.8	5,659
Petroleum	105	3.4	0-4.7	1.0	0.3	20,626
By ISIC sector[b]						
Agriculture, hunting, forestry and fishing	855	26.0	0-150	32.0	1.2	6,170
Mining	191	0.2	0-11.68	1.1	5.9	14,249
Manufacturing	15,401	11.6	0-225	26.7	2.3	152,429
By stage of processing						
Raw materials	1,667	18.8	0-150	27.0	1.4	26,129
Semi-processed products	5,943	6.5	0-135	11.0	1.7	53,377
Fully-processed products	8,838	14.8	0-225	33.3	2.3	93,362

a The total of imports is higher than the sum of sub-items, as certain imports, to the value of US$12,672.8 million are not classified in the Harmonized System.

b International Standard Industrial Classification (Rev.2). Electricity, gas and water are excluded (1 tariff line).

Note: CV = coefficient of variation.
Calculations include AVEs provided by the authorities for non-*ad valorem* rates. In case of unavailability of AVEs, the *ad valorem* part is used for compound rates.

Source: WTO Secretariat calculations, based on data provided by the Turkish authorities; imports data from UNSD, Comtrade database.

14. Significant differences between bound and applied rates leave Turkey some flexibility to increase its MFN duties on a number of agricultural goods (Chart III.2). The gap between bound and applied duties on industrial products, combined with a relatively low incidence of tariff bindings, provides significant scope for Turkey to increase its duties on non-agricultural products within the WTO framework. However, unilateral increases by Turkey would run contrary to the Customs Union Decision.

15. Overall, Turkey's applied MFN rates have not changed significantly since 2007.[16] Among recent changes, Turkey reduced its MFN tariffs on live bovine animals for breeding (HS 010290) from 20% to zero effective 28 October 2010; from 30% to 15% for live bovine animals for slaughter; from 225% to 30% on certain sheep meat (HS 0204) on 22 December 2010; and from 130% to zero on wheat, oat and buckwheat (HS 1001, 1004 and 1008) for the period 25 February to 1 May 2011. However, the MFN import duty was increased to 75% on certain meat (HS 0201 and 0202) on 2 July 2011, and the MFN duty was increased by 20% or 30% on some textile and apparel products on 15 September 2011.[17]

[16] According to the Turkish authorities, the simple average MFN tariff for agricultural and fish products varied between 58.5% and 60.5% from 2007 to 2011.

[17] According to the WTO Report on G-20 Trade Measures (mid-October 2010 to April 2011), Turkey imposed the higher duties on textiles and clothing goods provisionally from 22 July 2011.

Chart III.2
Bound and applied duties on agricultural products, by HS 2-digit, 2011

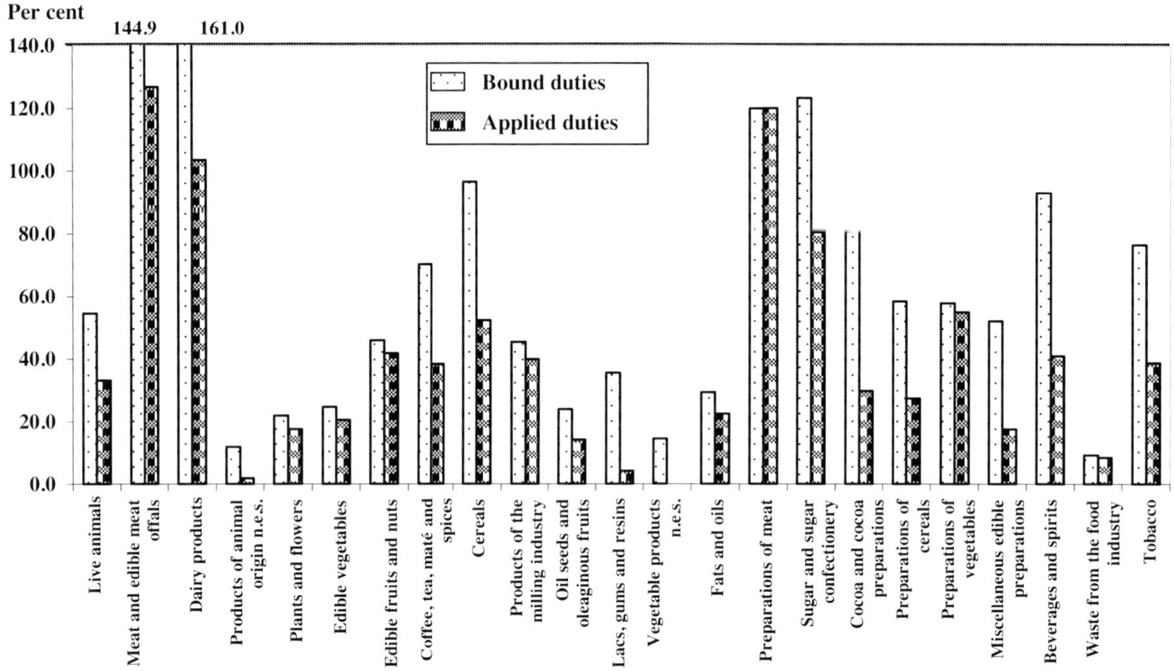

Source: WTO Secretariat estimates, based on data provided by the Turkish authorities and WTO CTS database.

(b) Tariff preferences

16. Commensurate with its commitments under the Customs Union Decision, Turkey has been aligning its preferences to third countries, including the GSP Scheme, with the EU trade regime. This is leading to progressive elimination of all or virtually all tariffs on products falling within HS Chapters 25 to 97, and selective liberalization of certain agricultural commodities and processed agricultural products (Tables III.3 and AIII.4). The tariff preferences on agricultural goods are generally implemented through tariff-rate quotas (section (iv) below).

Table III.3
Tariff averages, 2011
(Per cent)

	HS 01-97	HS 01-24	HS 25-97	WTO agriculture	WTO non-agriculture
MFN	12.2	49.2	4.1	47.9	5.0
GSP	10.0	47.5	1.9	46.0	2.9
Serbia	8.8	49.2	0.0	47.8	1.0
Tunisia	8.8	49.2	0.0	47.8	1.0
Syria	8.8	49.2	0.0	47.8	1.0
Morocco	8.8	49.2	0.0	47.8	1.0
West Bank and the Gaza Strip	8.8	49.2	0.0	47.8	1.0
Kosovo	8.8	49.2	0.0	47.8	1.0
Croatia	8.8	49.1	0.0	47.7	1.0
Israel	8.8	49.2	0.0	48.0[a]	1.0
Countries benefiting from special incentive arrangements	8.7	46.8	0.4	45.2	1.4
Albania	8.7	48.6	0.0	47.1	1.0
LDC	8.6	46.7	0.4	45.0	1.4
Macedonia (FYR)	8.6	47.8	0.0	46.3	1.0
Egypt	8.5	47.5	0.0	47.8	0.7
EU	8.2	48.4	0.0	47.4	0.9
Georgia	7.7	43.3	0.0	41.4	1.0
EFTA	7.4	43.8	0.0	47.4	0.0
Bosnia-Herzegovina	0.9	5.0	0.0	5.3	0.0

a The average on preferential agreements may be higher than the MFN average as in some cases there is no information on AVEs or the *ad valorem* part of non-*ad valorem* duties.

Note: Calculations include AVEs provided by the authorities for non-*ad valorem* rates. In case of unavailability of AVEs, the *ad valorem* part is used for compound rates.

Source: WTO Secretariat calculations, based on data provided by the Turkish authorities.

(iii) Other duties and charges (ODCs)

17. For all tariff line items in its Goods Schedule, Turkey has bound "other charges and duties" (Article II.1(b) of the GATT) at non-zero rates for all items except those marked "free". The possible ODCs could amount to 15% of the customs duty as a "municipality share", in addition to taxes of 4% for goods arriving by maritime transport (transportation infrastructure fee) or 3% by road, rail or air transport.

18. At present, Turkey applies a Mass Housing Fund (MHF) levy on imported fish and fish products falling within HS Chapters 2, 3, 15, 16 and 23. The levy is differentiated according to imports from the EU, EFTA member states, and other countries, and ranges from zero to 35% *ad valorem*. Turkey has not bound its tariffs for fish and fish products, but imports from EFTA member states enter free from import duty and the MHF levy under the Turkey-EFTA Free Trade Agreement.

(iv) Tariff-rate quotas and tariff exemptions

19. Turkey does not have tariff quota commitments listed in its Goods Schedule. However, it occasionally opens MFN tariff quotas unilaterally.[18] Quota allocations are made on a "first come, first served" or "past performance" basis. The in-quota tariff rates are differentiated between duty-free and reduced MFN rate. In addition, preferential tariff-rate quotas are administered on numerous agricultural and processed agricultural products (Table AIII.5). On non-agricultural products, Turkey opened preferential tariff-rate quotas for acrylonitryl and compressors on 1 January 2011. Allocations of the 12-month TRQs are made on a "past performance" and "production capacity" basis. Approximately 90% of the TRQ for compressors has been utilized and 100% for acrylonitryl.

20. The Investment Encouragement Programme (IEP) provides for duty and tax concessions on imports. In addition, exporters benefit from the inward-processing scheme. Imports of certain products for disabled persons or certain public administrations, financial leasing, projects financed by donors, and some temporary imports are eligible for tariff concessions. All imports by the Ministry of Defence in the context of the North Atlantic Treaty Organization are exempt from the payment of customs duties (Table III.4).

21. The IEP aims, *inter alia,* to reduce regional disparities and promote small and medium-sized enterprises. In principle, all investment projects are eligible.[19] Project applications are subject to assessment by the Ministry of Economy. Investment projects, which are granted an Investment Encouragement Certificate benefit from customs duty exemptions on all machinery and equipment to be used in the production process. Exemption from VAT is provided pursuant to Law No. 3065 of 25 October 1984. Domestic and foreign investors benefit from equal terms and conditions. Foreign exchange earning activities are exempt from stamp duty and charges pursuant to Laws Nos. 488 and 492.

22. The inward processing scheme allows Turkish manufacturers/exporters to import materials free of duty and other commercial policy measures. Goods imported under this scheme are intended for re-export from the customs territory of Turkey in the form of "compensating products", i.e. all goods obtained from processing operations. Normally, the manufacturer/exporter will request the suspension of import duty and VAT until export of the finished product, but the duties and VAT may also be paid and subsequently reimbursed under the drawback system.

23. The "suspension list" (List V in Turkey's Customs Tariff) enables manufacturers to import certain raw materials and intermediary inputs, i.e. chemical raw materials and inputs for the electronics industry, at low or duty-exempt rates. Moreover, tariff-rate quotas may be opened for products with insufficient production capacities within the Customs Union.[20]

---

[18] The United States requested consultations with Turkey in November 2005 regarding certain measures affecting the importation of rice (WTO document DS334). The Panel found, *inter alia,* that Turkey's requirement that importers purchase domestic rice in order to be allowed to import rice under the tariff-rate quotas was inconsistent with GATT Article III:4, but did not make a recommendation as the measure was no longer in force and Turkey had declared its intention not to reintroduce the measure. Turkey's tariff-rate quota for rice was abolished on 31 July 2006.

[19] Investments not supported, or supported conditionally, under the General Investment Encouragement System are listed in Annex IV of WTO document G/SCM/N/186/TUR, March 2010.

[20] Turkey has prepared the suspension list in co-operation with the EU. However, any Turkish requests for the opening of tariff-rate quotas would only be applicable within Turkey.

Table III.4
Key features of concessional entry schemes, 2011

Scheme	Eligibility	Incentives
Investment encouragement programme	Feasible investment projects deemed by the Undersecretariat of Treasury to reduce regional imbalances within the country, create new employment opportunities, and increase competitiveness while using technologies with greater value added	Exemption from customs and fund levies for imported machinery and equipment on the Machinery and Equipment list approved by the Undersecretariat of the Treasury[a] VAT exemption for imported and locally purchased machinery and equipment on the list
Inward processing regime		
(a) Conditional exemption for imports (suspension system)	Any exporter	Intended for goods to be re-exported; suspension of duty and VAT on raw materials, auxiliary materials, semi-finished and finished products, packaging materials
(b) Use of equivalent goods	Any exporter	Suspension of customs duties and VAT on imported inputs after export of compensating products
(c) Repayment of duties collected on imports	Any exporter	Refund of customs duty and VAT paid on imported inputs, after export of goods with imported inputs, based on a drawback method
NATO	North Atlantic Treaty Organization	0% on all imports
Defence	Ministry of National Defence or by public institutions on behalf of the Ministry	0% on all imports
Donations	State administrations; certain items to be used mainly for the public interest, approved by relevant ministries	..
	Vehicles produced especially for disabled persons	..
Financial leasing	Vessels, air carriers, medical equipment, and high-tech products	Total or partial relief from import duties up to the date the leasing contract is over; VAT reductions
	Movable and unmovable property	Suspension of all customs duties and exemption of duties, charges, and fees for the leasing contract up to the date the leasing contract is over
Temporary imports	Any importer; certain commercial or personal items	Total or partial relief from import duties on temporary use in Turkey for 6 to 12 months without any change except normal depreciation due to their use
Project credit (donor)	Project evaluation criteria of Turk Eximbank	Terms and conditions of the project loan are in accordance with the provisions of the OECD Consensus
Encouragement of tourism	..	..
Private (special) laws regarding exemptions	..	..

.. Not available.

a Goods imported at 20% duty: passenger vehicles, buses (excluding double-decker buses), tractors (excluding tractors conforming to Euro-1 or Euro-2 norms and having environment-friendly engines), trailers (except refrigerated trailers), televisions, videos, mini-refrigerators, furniture, import of yachts (including motorboats), trucks, (excluding off-road truck types and rock-type dump trucks that are not allowed on highways), mixers, and trans-mixers.
Goods imported at 18% duty: expansion or new investments for a minimum capacity of 100,000 units per year of firms that will manufacture automobiles considered as new models for a period of ten years after the date of their first production worldwide.
Goods imported at 10% duty: raw materials, intermediary goods, and operating materials to be imported for operational needs.
Goods imported at 5% duty: construction material.

Note: No performance requirements are in place under these schemes.

Source: WTO Secretariat, based on information provided by the Turkish authorities.

(v) Fees and charges for services rendered

24. All shipments requiring formal clearance by the Turkish customs authorities are subject to an ordino fee of US$100 per customs declaration, and a stamp duty, set at TL 40.10 for 2011. Charges for printed documents used by the customs administration are enumerated in Table III.5. Customs

clearance outside of normal opening hours incurs additional charges. The fee for overtime is set at TL 5.50 per hour for export transactions and TL 13.20 per hour for all other operations.[21] Costs for analyses or examinations carried out in customs laboratories or outsourced units are borne by the declarants (Customs Act No. 4458, Article 66, subparagraph 4, amended by the Act of 18 June 2009 and Act No. 5911).[22] Consignments valued at €75 or less do not require formal clearance by Customs.

Table III.5
Fees and charges

Name of account	Parcel/Pcs	Annex no.	Price
Customs summary declaration form	1,000	9	
Certificate of customs status		65	
Application for customs procedure with economic impact (application for authorization to operate customs warehouses) inward processing control sheet (outward processing control sheet)		55	
Auth. for customs procedure with economic impact (control sheet for auth. to operate customs warehouses) inward processing auth. (outward processing auth. control sheet)		56	
Verbal declaration for temporary importation		57	
Inf 2 (outward processing triangular traffic)		64	1.70
Inf 9 information sheet (inward processing)		47	
Identification and assessment sheet for goods consigned to EU from free zones		67	
Application for return or removal		77	
Container tracking form at entry	2,000		
Container tracking form at exit	2,000		
Application for ending customs transactions of goods that violate intellectual and industrial property rights		19	
Customs declaration in quadruplicate	500	20.2	
Continuation sheet in quadruplicate	500	20.4	
T S document (control sheet)		36-36,1	
T S simplified procedure (control sheet)		36.2-3	
Loading list T 5		36.4-5	
Inf 1 information sheet		50	
Inf 5 (inward processing / triangular traffic)		49	2.20
Inf 6 (information sheet for temporary importation)		61	
Inf 1 information sheet (inward processing)		51	
Inf 6 form (customs warehouses / handling in free zones)		41	
Temporary import declaration and undertaking for vehicles leaving the Turkish customs territory (83/A)		68	
Temporary import declaration and undertaking for non-commercial goods consigned from the Turkish customs territory (83/B)			

Table III.5 (cont'd)

[21] According to Article 3.1 of Communiqué No. 74, customs personnel receive an allowance for overtime work and work carried out on official holidays. Based on Article 122.1.a of the Council of Ministers' Decision No. 2009/15481, the allowance is TL 5 per hour for export transactions and TL 12 for other transactions. Trucks carrying Turkish licence plates are charged an overtime fee of TL 12 per truck for export transactions and TL 19 for other transactions (Article 122.1.b). The fee is also charged to trucks with foreign licence plates taking goods into Turkey. However, depending on the time of the transaction and the mutuality principle, the fee may not be collected from trucks with foreign licence plates transiting through Turkey.

[22] Payments for laboratory analyses and examinations are recorded as revenue in a fund entitled Working Capital regarding the Fees Charged for the Analyses Conducted at Customs Laboratories and the Goods Disposed under the Customs Legislation; operating expenses for tools, materials, supplies, software, training and the like are charged against this fund. Laboratory analysis fees were published in the Customs Regulations of 7 October 2009, Enclosure 24.

Name of account	Parcel/Pcs	Annex no.	Price
Customs declaration in octoplicate	250	20.1	
Continuation sheet in octoplicate	250	20.3	3.30
Inf 4 information sheet			
Laboratory analysis report		30	
Laboratory analysis continuation report			
Second analysis report		82	5.50
Certificate of authorization for processing under customs control		53	
Application for binding tariff information		1	

Source: Information provided by the Turkish authorities.

25. An importer may appoint a customs broker to handle formal clearance procedures. Goods that fail to pass customs clearance within 45 days (from the date on which the summary declaration is lodged for goods carried by sea) or 20 days (goods transported by modes other than sea) are disposed of. The Customs Office may extend this period for justified reasons. An additional 30 days to complete the procedure may be granted against a supplementary fee of 1% of the value of the shipment.

26. Turkey began full implementation of a strip-stamp requirement for alcoholic beverages and tobacco products in November 2007. The special stamp contains an activated code to be applied on each product.[23] For imported goods, the codified label may be affixed (i) at production sites abroad before the products are shipped to Turkey, (ii) in customs areas for alcoholic beverages and tobacco products in Turkey, or (iii) at facilities operated by an authorized company in the provinces of Istanbul, Izmir, or Mersin. The price for the strip stamps is the same for imported and domestically produced goods, except for beer, where the price difference is due to the cost of the stamp paper. The Turkish authorities are considering various options to eliminate the price difference.

(vi) Application of internal taxes

27. The Special Consumption Tax (SCT) was introduced on 1 August 2002, replacing 16 selective taxes on oil products, motor vehicles, alcoholic beverages and tobacco products, and various luxury goods. The SCT is levied on imports as well as domestic production, and published in the form of four lists. The SCT is primarily collected on imports when goods are cleared through Customs, and for domestically produced goods when these are delivered to the customers. The petroleum products covered by the SCT and the corresponding tax rates are enumerated in Table AIII.6. Air conditioners, refrigerators, freezers, record and cassette players, and television receivers are subject to SCT at a rate of 6.7% *ad valorem*; for caviar, furs, precious stones, cosmetics, mobile phones, crystal chandeliers, and revolvers the SCT amounts to 20% *ad valorem*. The tax rates on motor vehicles and other transport equipment range from 1% for certain buses to 84% for certain vehicles under 3.5 tonnes (Table III.6).

[23] The requirement is not applied to alcoholic beverages in packaging of 5cl or less. The strip stamp has not been applied to wine during the aging process since 1 January 2010.

Table III.6
Excise duties or special consumption tax on motor vehicles, 2011

HS Code	Product description	Tax rate (%)
8701.20	Tractors for semi-trailers	4
87.02	Motor vehicles for transport of 10 persons and more (including driver)	
	Autobus	1
	Midibus	4
	Minibus	9
87.03	Motor cars and other motor vehicles principally designed for the transport of persons (other than those of heading No. 87.02), including station wagons and racing cars.[a]	
	Those with maximum load capacity of 850 kg or less, and with piston displacement of less than 2,000 cc	10
	Those with maximum load capacity of more than 850 kg, and with piston displacement of less than 2,800 cc	10
	Only those with electric motor	10
	Of a cylinder capacity not exceeding 3,200 cm^3, having 9 seats including driver	10
	Only those with electric motor	10
	Others	
	Of a cylinder capacity not exceeding 1,600 cm^3	37
	Of a cylinder capacity exceeding 1,600 cm^3 but not exceeding 2,000 cm^3	60
	Of a cylinder capacity exceeding 2,000 cm^3	84
	Only those with electric motor	
	Of a motor power not exceeding 85 kW	3
	Of a motor power exceeding 85 kW but not exceeding 120 kW	7
	Of a motor power exceeding 120 kW	15
8703.10.11.00.00	Vehicles specially designed for traveling on snow, vehicles with compression ignition, internal combustion reciprocating piston engine/diesel and semi-diesel) or vehicles with spark-ignition internal combustion reciprocating piston engine	6.7
8703.10.18.00.00	Others Golf cars similar vehicles	6.7
87.04	Motor vehicles for the transport of goods[b]	
	Of cylinder capacity not exceeding 3,000 cm^3	10
	Of cylinder capacity exceeding 3,000 cm^3 but not exceeding 4,000 cm^3	52
	Of cylinder capacity exceeding 4,000 cm^3	75
	Only those with electric motor	
	Of a motor power not exceeding 85 kW	10
	Of a motor power exceeding 85 kW but not exceeding 120 kW	52
	Of a motor power exceeding 120 kW	75
	Of load limit under 620 kg and having box truck Only those with electric motor	10
	Others	10
	Others Only those with electric motor	4 4
87.05	Special purpose motor vehicles, other than those principally designed for the transport of persons or goods (for example, breakdown lorries, fire fighting vehicles, concrete-mixer lorries, road sweeper lorries, spraying lorries, mobile workshops, mobile radiological units) (excluding fire fighting vehicles) Those only subject to recording and registration, excluding fire fighting vehicles	4
87.09	Works trucks, self-propelled, not fitted with lifting or handing equipment, of the type used in factories, warehouses, dock areas or airports for short distance transport of goods; tractors of the type used on railway the components and parts of these vehicles	4
87.11	Motorcycles (including mopeds) and cycles fitted with an auxiliary motor, with or without side-cars; side cars (except side cars) (except only those with electric motor) Of a cylinder capacity not exceeding 250 cm^3 Of a cylinder capacity exceeding 250 cm^3	 8 37
8711.90.00.00.00	Others (only those with electric motor) Of a motor power not exceeding 20 kW Of a motor power exceeding 20 kW	 3 37

Table III.6 (cont'd)

HS Code	Product description	Tax rate (%)
88.02	Other aircraft (for example, helicopters, aeroplanes); spacecraft (including satellites) and spacecraft launch vehicles and vehicles under orbit	0.5
	(Only helicopters and aeroplanes) (except military aircrafts, special helicopters and aeroplanes for pesticide and fire extinguishing use)	
8901.10.10.00.11	Cruise-ships not exceeding 18 gross tonnage	6.7
8901.10.90.00.11	Passenger ships and cruise ships	6.7
89.03	Yachts and other vessels for pleasure or sports; rowing boats and canoes (except inflatable, rowing boats, and canoes not exceeding 100 kg	8

a Only passenger cars, station wagons, racing cars, off-road vehicles, etc. (including cash-carrying vehicles), motorhomes, and motor vehicles that run on electricity, gas, solar energy etc. Except for motor vehicles such as ambulances, prisoner vehicles, funeral vehicles, fire department lead-vehicles that are manufactured for special purpose; compression-ignition piston engine (diesel and semi-diesel) and spark-ignition piston combustion vehicles that have been designed to be driven on snow, others (golf cars etc. vehicles).

Of motor vehicles (except all wheel-driven passenger cars, station wagons, race cars and off-road vehicles) of less than 3.5 tonnes weight, which are used for carriage of goods, and the passenger capacity (passenger capacity is calculating by multiplying the number of passenger, including the driver, by 70 kg. When making this calculation, the fixed appliance for mounting of seats will be taken into consideration as if they were the seats) of which is less than 50% of the maximum load capacity (the total load weight, including the driver and the passengers, that a vehicle can safely carry).

b Those only subject to recording and registration.

Those with maximum load capacity of 4,700 kilograms or less, and with other seats by the driver or those with side windows other than that of the driver (except trucks without box and with piston displacement of 3,200 cc or less).

Source: Information provided by the Turkish authorities.

28. The SCT applicable to alcoholic beverages and tobacco products has undergone some notable changes since the last Review of Turkey. Minimum tax levels on alcohol products, expressed in *ad valorem* equivalents, were eliminated in 2009.[24] Since then, all alcoholic beverages have been subject to specific rates of SCT only, except for beer, where the tax rate is the higher of 63% *ad valorem* or TL 0.44 per litre of pure alcohol. The specific rates were increased by 10% across-the-board in late 2009 and raised a further 30% in October 2010.[25] The rates of SCT vary considerably depending on the type of beverage (Table III.7).

29. Revenue from SCT levied on raw tobacco and tobacco products is channelled into the Tobacco Fund. The tax rates applicable in 2011 are set out in Table III.8. A Tobacco Fund levy on processed tobacco was abolished as of 1 January 2010.[26] Imported raw tobacco, including tobacco used in domestically produced cigarettes, is subject to a Tobacco Fund levy of US$2,250 per tonne.[27]

30. Turkey applies VAT on the supply and import of goods and many types of services. The general rate of VAT has been set at 18% since 15 May 2001. Special VAT rates apply to List I and List II items, notably to basic foodstuffs, books and similar publications (8%), and to raw cotton and dried hazelnuts (1%). On imports, VAT is calculated on the import price inclusive of customs duties and SCT, if applicable. VAT is not levied on exports, goods imported in accordance with an investment incentive certificate, goods in transit, or purchases by embassies and diplomatic staff, etc.

[24] Cabinet Decree No. 2009/14882 of 14 April 2009.

[25] Cabinet Decree No. 2009/15725 of 29 December 2009 and Cabinet Decree No. 2010/973 of 25 October 2010.

[26] Cabinet Decree No. 2009/15685, published in the *Official Gazette* No. 27447 on 29 December 2009.

[27] The levy was reduced from US$3,000 to the present level through Cabinet Decree No. 27801 of 30 December 2010.

Table III.7
Excise duties on alcoholic beverages, 2011

HS Code	Product description	Tax rate (%)	Tax rate (specific amount in TL)
2202.10.00.00.13	Cola soda pops	25	-
2203.00	Beers produced from malt	63	0.44
22.04	Wine of fresh grapes (including fortified wines); grape must (other than that of heading No. 20.09) (except 2204.10 sparkling wine and 2204.30 other grape musts)	0	2.44
2204.10	Sparkling wines	0	16.12
22.05	Vermouth and other wines of fresh grapes (flavored with plants or aromatic substances) (except 2205.10.10.00.00, 2205.10.90.00.12)	0	22.10
2205.10.10.00.00	Whose alcoholic strength by volume is 18% or less	0	17.55
2206.00	Other fermented drinks (such as apple wine, pear wine, honey wine), mixed fermented drinks not in any other part of the tariff, and blends of fermented drinks with non-alcoholic drinks	0	2.44
2205.10.90.00.12	Whose alcoholic strength by volume is 22% or more	0	85.80
2207.20	Other alcoholic drinks with any degree of alcohol content, which are produced with denatured ethyl alcohol or by alcohol that is obtained by distillation (except for denatured ethyl alcohol of any degree)	0	85.80
22.08	Undenatured ethyl alcohol of less that 80%; distilled alcoholic drinks, liqueurs and other alcoholic drinks (2208.90.91; 2208.90.99) except for undenatured ethyl alcohol of less than 80% (except 2208.20, 2208.50, 2208.60, 2208.70 and 2208.90)	0	85.80
2208.20	Grape wine or alcoholic drinks that are obtained by distilling grape marcs	0	71.50
2208,50	Gin and Geneva	0	57.20
2208.60	Vodka (except 2208.60.91.00.00, 2208.60.99.00.00)	0	57.20
2208.60.91.00.00	Those in containers of less than 2 litres (with alcohol content of more than 45.4%)	0	85.80
2208.60.99.00.00	Those in containers of more than 2 liters (with alcohol content of more than 45.4%)	0	85.80
2208.70	Liqueurs	0	78.65
2208.90	Others (except 2208.90.48.00.11 and 2208.90.71.00.11)	0	85.80
2208.90.48.00.11	Raki (in containers of 2 litres or less)	0	51.48
2208.90.71.00.11	Raki (in containers of more than 2 litres)	0	51.48

Source: Information provided by the Turkish authorities.

Table III.8
Excise duties on tobacco products, 2011

HS Code	Product description	Tax rate (%)	Minimum specific amount (TL)
2402.10.00.00.11	Cigars that contain tobacco	30	0.1325
2402.10.00.00.12	Cheroots	30	0.1325
2402.10.00.00.19	Cigarillos	30	0.1325
2402.20	Cigarettes that contain tobacco	63	0.1325
2402.90.00.00.00	Others		
	Cigars, cheroots and cigarillos made of ingredients deemed as a tobacco	30	0.1325
	Cigarettes made of ingredients deemed as a tobacco	63	0.1325
2403.10	Smoking tobacco (whether or not containing tobacco substitutes in any proportion) (except 2403.10.10.00.19 and 2403.10.90.00.19)	63	0.1325
2403.10.10.00.19	Others (in immediate packing of a net content not exceeding 500 g)	63	0.0342
2403.10.90.00.19	Others (in immediate packing of a net content exceeding 500 g)	63	0.0342
2403.99.10.00.00	Snuff and chewing tobacco	63	0.1325

Source: Information provided by the Turkish authorities.

31. A reduced VAT rate of 8% for contract manufacturing for textile and ready-to-wear works, and for services provided in private care houses and rest homes entered into effect on 1 June 2007, and for restaurant services on January 2008. The reduced VAT rate of 8% has been in effect since 2007, on similar accommodation services offered by hotels, motels, pensions, and holiday villages, as well as toothbrushes, contact lenses, spectacle lenses for glasses, certain excavators, knitting machines, etc.

32. Transactions effected by banks and insurance companies are exempt from VAT under Article 17 of Law No. 3065. Thus, banks and insurers cannot recover VAT paid on their inputs. However, a Banking and Insurance Transaction Tax (BITT) is levied at 5% on certain operations, e.g. on interest income and commissions. Transactions involving liquidity bills issued by the Central Bank of Turkey and money-market trading transactions between banks and subsidiaries are subject to 1% BITT.[28] The BITT on foreign exchange transactions has been at zero since 1 May 2008 under Cabinet Decree No. 2008/13459.

33. Internal taxes make an important contribution to Turkey's public finances. The TL 59.4 billion raised by the Special Consumption Tax in 2010 accounted for 24% of the Government's tax revenue, and 18.5% of total budget revenues, in that year. Similarly, the share of VAT in total tax receipts was 30% (TL 38.6 billion collected on domestically produced goods and TL 36.2 billion on imports). The Government also received TL 3.7 billion from the Banking and Insurance Transaction Tax, TL 4.1 billion from a special tax on communication services, and TL 0.64 billion from a tax on gambling in 2010. By comparison, government revenue from customs duties totalled TL 3.2 billion.

(vii) Import prohibitions, restrictions, and licensing

34. Turkey prohibits the import of ten items by broad product category (Table III.9). The product coverage remains unchanged since 2003. Turkey justifies these restrictions under the general exceptions and security exceptions provided by GATT Articles XX and XXI, i.e. the necessity to protect public morals or human, animal or plant life or health; compliance with domestic legislation or international obligations; or for reasons of national security.

35. Various goods are subject to licensing (Table III.10). Licensing is employed, for example, to enforce compliance with international conventions (material for the manufacture of chemical weapons, CITES); for reasons of national security or public safety (explosives, radioactive substances, fertilizer, maps and related items); or to ensure that the imported goods are used for the stated purpose (items for use in civil aircraft, liquefied petroleum gases). Certificates issued by the Ministry of Science, Industry and Technology for machine tools, various electrical household appliances, computers, transport equipment, telecommunications equipment, cameras, and health-related goods enforce a requirement on the distributors to provide adequate after-sales service and maintain sufficient stocks of spare parts and accessories. Imported motor vehicles are also subject to approval by the Ministry of Science, Industry and Technology, pursuant to Communiqué No. 10/7, to ensure that the vehicles are suitable for Turkish highways. An eligibility certificate, issued by the Turkish Sugar Authority (without any import restriction), is required for the importation of certain sugar substitutes.

[28] The BITT on sale and repo of domestically issued corporate bonds was reduced from 5% to 1% in late 2010 to develop the corporate debt market.

Table III.9
Import prohibitions, 2011

Description	Invocation of WTO Article	Domestic/international legislation
Narcotics, hashish and prepared opium (2 items)[a]	Health, IA[b] (Article XX:b, h)	Law No. 2313 on the Control of Narcotics, and the International Agreement on Narcotics Goods (1961)
Ozone depleting substances (1 item)[a, c]	Environment (Article XX:b, d)	Copenhagen Amendment to Montreal Protocol on Substances that Deplete the Ozone Layer, Import Regime No. 2011/14
Colouring matter (1 item)	Health (Article XX:b)	Law No. 1593 on the Protection of Public Health; Regulation on Special Conditions of Foodstuffs and Supplies and Objects Concerning Public Health; Import Regime Communiqué No. 2007/15 Add II (List)
Scheduled chemical weapons in I and II of the Convention (4 items)[c]	Environment (Article XX:b, d)	The Convention on the Prohibition of the Development, Production, Stockpiling and Use of Chemical Weapons and their Destruction; Import Regime Communiqué No. 2011/17 (List I)
Measurement instruments not conforming to Turkish legal norms (non-metric or double standard) (6 items)	Compliance with domestic law (Article XX:d)	Law No. 3516 on Standards and Accords
Arms and ammunition, propellant powders, prepared explosives, fuses, caps igniters detonators[a] (3 items)	Security (Article XXI:b(i),(ii))	Law on Firearms (No. 6136 of 1953); Import Regime Communiqué No. 2011/2[d]
Gambling instruments (except for specified tourism purposes)[a] (1 item)	Public morals (Article XX:a)	Law No. 1072 on Gambling Instruments like Roulette, Tilt, and Pinball
Products making illegal use of a trade mark (all industrial products)	Compliance with domestic law; IA[b] (Article XX:d,h) Public morals (Article XX:a)	Paris Convention 1883 annexed to the Law of 1930 on Accession to 1925 Hague Agreement on International Industrial Property (1925); Statutory Decree No. 556 on the Protection of Trademarks Customs Law (No. 4458 of 1999)
Soil, leaf, stem, straw, and natural manure used for agricultural purpose (excluding turf and perlites cultivated in culture environment)	Health (Article XX:b)	Regulation on Agricultural Quarantine
Spawn of silk-worm	..	Law No. 859 on Cultivation and Sale of Silk-worm and Silk-worm Spawn

.. Not available.

a Prohibited except when imported by authorized government bodies.
b IA: Undertaken in pursuance of obligations under intergovernmental commodity agreements.
c Imports prohibited only from non-members of the international agreements.
d Following an amendment to related legislation, private companies are also authorized to import products within the scope of Import Regime Communiqué No. 2011/2.

Source: WTO Secretariat, based on information provided by the Turkish authorities.

36. Imports of old, second-hand, renovated, faulty and obsolete goods are subject to permission by the Ministry of Economy.[29] Measuring and weighing instruments to be released for free circulation in Turkey are subject to control by the Directorate General of Measures and Standards (Ministry of Science, Industry and Technology); and carrying materials comprising cinematographic and musical works are subject to registration by the Directorate of Copyright and Cinema with the aim of combating piracy. Restrictions arising from Turkey's SPS regulations are discussed below (section (3)(iii)).

[29] According to the Turkish authorities, most goods may be imported freely provided they are not more than ten years old.

Table III.10
Imports requiring a licence, 2011

Description	Reason for licence
Radioactivity-related items (11 items) Uranium ores, isotopes, nuclear reactors, X-rays	Imports only permitted on approval by the Turkish Atomic Energy Authority: to ensure patient security against the probable harmful effects of radioactivity
Telecommunications, machinery, and related items (74 items) Electrical apparatus for line telegraphy, telephone answering machines, radar, transmission, reception apparatus, air-conditioning machines, household-type electrical refrigerators, clothes dryers, instantaneous gas water heaters, sewing machines of household types, machine-tools for drilling etc., vacuum cleaners, some photocopying machines, certain motor vehicles	Imports only permitted with a certificate issued by the Ministry of Science, Industry and Technology to the effect that after-sale services such as maintenance and repair are warranted on a regional basis and that maintenance service technicians and spare-part stocks are sufficient: to ensure that imports are in conformity with the national telecommunication network and to protect consumers
Motor vehicles (7 items) The road tractors for semi-trailers (8701.20), motor vehicles for the transportation of ten or more persons (87.02), motor cars and other motor vehicles principally designed for the transport of persons (including racing cars and station wagons) (87.03), motor vehicles for transport of goods (87.04), special-purpose motor vehicles other than those designed for the transport of persons or goods (87.05), motorcycles (including mopeds) and cycles fitted with an auxiliary motor, with or without side cars (87.11), trailers and semi-trailers (87.16)	Imports only permitted with a pro forma invoice certified by the Ministry of Science, Industry and Technology: to ensure the suitability of imported vehicles for highways
Fertilizers (5 items) Animal or vegetable fertilizers, and mineral or chemical fertilizers	Imports only permitted on approval by the Ministry of Food, Agriculture and Livestock: to avoid damage to health of humans, animals or to the lifecycle of plants
Banknotes and related items (1 item) Banknotes, securities	Article 3/a of Decree No. 32 on Protection of the Value of the Turkish Currency "Imports of Turkish currency and instruments denominated in Turkish currency shall be free." Article 4/a of the aforementioned Decree "Importation of foreign exchange to Turkey is free" Imports of banknotes are free: to ensure the continuation of administrative order related to precious documents, e.g. shares, bonds
Explosives and related items (14 items) Technical ammonium nitrate, prepared explosives, some fuses, fireworks, some astronomical instruments	Imports only permitted on approval by the General Directorate of Security in the Ministry of Interior: to ensure national security and public safety
Products affecting worker health (12 items), benzene	Imports only permitted on approval by the Institute of Workers' Health and Security in the Ministry of Works and Social Security: to protect workers' health
Civil aircraft related items (81 items) A wide range of items of a kind used on civil aircraft	Imports only permitted on approval by the General Directorate of Civil Aviation in the Ministry of Transportation: to prevent the use of imported goods in areas other than civil aviation
Maps related items (2 items) Maps and hydrographic or similar charts of all kinds, and digital maps and map information recorded on magnetic or optical media	Imports only permitted on approval by the General Command of Cartography in the Ministry of Defence, and the General Command of Naval Forces: national security
Items related to the manufacture of chemical weapons (22 items) A wide range of chemical products used in the production of weapons	Imports only permitted on approval by the Ministry of Economy: to comply with the Convention on the Prohibition of Chemical Weapons
Some sugar substitutes (11 items) Aspartam, saccharin	Eligibility certificate, issued by the Turkish Sugar Authority without any import restriction, is required for imports of certain sugar substitutes. Control of these products at the import stage is by Ministry of Food, Agriculture and Livestock
Endangered species of wild fauna and flora	Imports only permitted on approval by the Ministry of Food, Agriculture and Livestock or the Ministry of Forestry and Water Affairs: to comply with the Convention on International Trade in Endangered Species of Wild Fauna and Flora (CITES)
Energy Electricity and natural gas	Imports are allowed only be companies licensed by EMRA: to ensure effective operations in market activities and to comply with relevant EU Directives
Petroleum and liquefied petroleum gas	Imports are allowed only by companies licensed by EMRA: to prevent the unorthodox use of those items out of purpose and to ensure fuel quality

Source: WTO Secretariat, based on information provided by the Turkish authorities; and WTO document G/LIC/N/3/TUR/10, 7 September 2010.

37. In 2003, Turkey implemented a Certificate of Conformity for Importation requirement for alcoholic beverages, i.e. spirits, wine, and beer. The certificate was abolished and replaced by a Notification System for Alcoholic Beverages in February 2008, which is supervised by the Tobacco and Alcohol Market Regulatory Authority.

38. Harmonizing its import policy with the EU, Turkey has been applying import quotas on certain textile and clothing products since 1 January 1996.[30] If the exporting country agrees to a bilateral understanding, the quota is balanced in response to needs. At present, Turkey applies quotas to textile and clothing products from Belarus and the Democratic People's Republic of Korea, with which an agreement has not been reached, under the single checking system. Quota restrictions applied to China, Montenegro, Uzbekistan, and Turkmenistan have been abolished.

(viii) Customs valuation

39. Turkey's basic provisions on customs valuation are contained in Customs Law No. 4458, Articles 23 to 31. As stipulated in the Agreement on Implementation of Article VII of the GATT 1994, the primary basis for custom value is the transaction value, i.e. the price actually paid or payable for goods sold for export to Turkey adjusted, as necessary, in accordance with the provisions of Article 8 of the Agreement. The hierarchy of alternate valuation methods follows the sequential order laid down in the Agreement. However, utilizing the flexibility accorded to developing countries in Annex III, paragraph 3, Turkey has reserved the right, indefinitely, not to reverse the deductive and computed value methods at the request of the importer.[31] The Interpretative Notes to the Agreement are incorporated in Turkey's legislation through the basic provisions of Customs Law No. 4458 and Articles 43 through 57, and Annexes 8 and 9, of the Customs Regulation.

40. Simplified procedures are available, at the request of the importer, to determine the customs value of perishable goods.[32] Turkey implements the provisions of the Decision on the Treatment of Interest Charges in the Customs Value of Goods through Article 28 (c) and Article 28, paragraph 2 of the Customs Law and Article 52 of the Customs Regulation. The Decision on the Valuation of Carrier Media Bearing Software for Data-Processing Equipment has been included in the Customs Law (Article 29) and the Customs Regulation (Article 54). Turkey has applied these decisions since February 2000, i.e. when the Customs Law entered into force.[33]

41. The right of appeal of decisions by the customs authorities is governed by Title XII (Articles 242-1 and 243-1) of the Customs Law. Any person may appeal decisions regarding customs duties, fines, and administrative measures to a superior authority or to the same authority that took the decision if no superior authority exists. For tax issues, the final decisions of a regional directorate or the Ministry of Customs and Trade may be challenged in the tax courts.

(ix) Rules of origin

42. The basic legal provisions on Turkey's non-preferential rules of origin are set out in Customs Law No. 4458, Articles 17 to 21. Pursuant to the Customs Union Decision, Turkey has been applying the same rules of origin as the EU to third countries since 1 January 1996.

---

[30] WTO document WT/REG22/7, 24 November 1997.
[31] WTO document G/VAL/2/Rev.15, 21 October 2002.
[32] Article 45 of the Implementing Regulation of Customs Law No. 4458.
[33] WTO document G/VAL/N/3/TUR/1, 21 September 2004.

43. Turkey's preferential trade agreements set out preferential rules of origin, normally based on a wholly obtained or substantial transformation criterion, with scope for cumulation. Turkey has been part of the Pan-European Origin Cumulation System since 1 January 1999. The arrangement allows the use of any material from any country within the zone (EU, EFTA, and Turkey) to produce a good whilst retaining preferential origin. This diagonal cumulation system has been extended to the Faroe Islands and to Mediterranean countries participating in the Euro-Mediterranean partnership through the Barcelona Declaration of 2004. Thus, the Pan-Euro-Mediterranean Cumulation System operates on the same principle.[34] The application of diagonal cumulation requires the implementation of identical rules of origin among the parties. Turkey is still conducting an internal evaluation regarding the adoption of the EU's new GSP legislation, which includes revised rules of origin.

44. According to Customs Law No. 4458, economic operators may request advance assessments (BTI-Binding Tariff Information) for the determination of import and export taxes, the calculation of duty drawback and import-export payments within the context of Turkey's agricultural policy, or for the use of certificates providing tariff or origin information submitted for the purpose of customs clearance. The assessments are issued by the Ministry of Customs and Trade and authorized customs directorates and may be valid for six years, provided the information submitted by the applicant is accurate and complete, and the declared goods correspond exactly to the description in the BTI. The assessments may cease to be valid if changes are made in the Turkish Customs Tariff Nomenclature and the information no longer conforms with it, or amendments incompatible with the BTI are made in the Harmonized System Nomenclature and its Explanatory Notes by the WCO. Such changes are to be published in the *Official Journal*, and the holder of the BTI must be notified. However, an operator who has concluded binding contracts for the purchase or sale of goods for which he has a BTI may continue to use it for another six months following the date of publication or notification (or until the end of the validity period for relevant certificates).

(x) Anti-dumping, countervailing duty, and safeguard regimes

(a) Anti-dumping and countervailing measures

45. The legislative framework for the imposition of anti-dumping and countervailing measures has remained unchanged since Turkey last Trade Policies Review. Turkey revised its legislation in 1999 to conform to the relevant WTO Agreements and its Customs Union obligations. At present, the framework consists of Law No. 4412/1999 on the Prevention of Unfair Competition in Imports; Decree No. 13482/1999 on the Prevention of Unfair Competition in Imports, amended by Decree No. 9840/2005; and the Regulation on the Prevention of Unfair Competition in Imports, amended in 2002 and 2006. The provisions of the WTO Agreement on Subsidies and Countervailing Measures and the Agreement on Implementation of Article VI of the GATT 1994 (Anti-Dumping Agreement) would be observed in case of any inconsistency between domestic legislation and Turkey's multilateral obligations.

46. The Directorate General of the Ministry of Economy is in charge of preliminary examination, upon complaint or *ex officio*.[35] Should the Directorate General conclude that an investigation is

[34] Like the EU, which publishes entry dates for Pan-Euro-Mediterranean rules of origin protocols in its *Official Journal*, the Ministry of Customs and Trade publishes a "notice" in the Turkish *Official Gazette* informing economic operators of the date of entry into force of Pan-Euro-Med origin protocols with partner countries. The last notice was published in *Official Gazette* No. 27875 on 15 March 2011.

[35] A complaint made "by or on behalf of the domestic industry" must fulfil the requirements laid down in Article 5.4 of the WTO Anti-Dumping Agreement. Examinations must be completed within 45 days, and decisions to initiate an investigation must be published in the *Official Gazette*. The Turkish authorities may

justified, it will formalize a recommendation to this effect to the Board of Evaluation of Unfair Competition in Importation which, if it concurs, will authorize the Directorate General to carry out the investigation. The Board, headed by the Director General or the Deputy-Director General of Imports, comprises representatives of the Ministry of Food, Agriculture and Livestock; the Ministry of Science, Industry and Technology; the Ministry of Development; the Ministry of Customs and Trade; the Union of Chambers and Commodity Exchanges of Turkey; the Union of Chambers of Agriculture; and the relevant head of department in the Directorate General of Imports.[36] The Board may make proposals in the course of an investigation, evaluates the results, and submits decisions on the imposition of provisional and/or definitive measures to the State Minister in charge of foreign trade affairs, for approval. Provisional measures may be imposed no earlier than 60 days from the initiation of an investigation, and their duration is limited to 4 months.[37] Definitive measures remain in force for five years from the date of imposition or from the conclusion of the most recent review covering both dumping and injury.

47. Use of anti-dumping measures has been rising over the years in Turkey. As of August 2011, Turkey had 118 anti-dumping duty measures in force, compared with 93 at the end of 2007, and 27 at the end of 2002.[38] China (47) is the main exporter affected by these measures, followed by Indonesia (10), India and Chinese Taipei (8 each), and Thailand and Malaysia (7 each). Anti-dumping duties affect mostly textile and clothing items, base metal products, plastics and rubber articles, and a range of other manufactured goods such as lighters and pencils (Tables III.11 and III.12). The duties are either expressed in *ad valorem* rates or in specific terms (US$/unit).

48. Until 2008, Turkey had never initiated or imposed a countervailing measure. However, on 22 March 2009, PET films originating in India became subject to countervailing duties ranging from 4.25% to 21.61%.

(b) Safeguard measures

49. Turkey's legal framework for the imposition of safeguard measures consists of Decree No. 2004/7305 (published in the *Official Gazette* No. 25476 on 29 May 2004), amended by Decree No. 2007/12850 (*Official Gazette* No. 26721, 5 December 2007), and the Regulation on Safeguard Measures for Imports (*Official Gazette* No. 25486, 8 June 2004). The amendment to the Decree, issued after Turkey's last Review, aims at more effective application of safeguard measures, specifically by extending the scope to imports of parts or components of a product subject to a safeguard measure, or parts or components incorporating the value added to be safeguarded by the imposed measure.

---

decide to initiate an investigation *ex officio* if the affected industry is fragmented with an exceptionally large number of producers, provided sufficient evidence exists to indicate dumping, injury, and a causal link. According to the authorities, no *ex officio* investigations have been initiated.

[36] The Directorate General acts as the secretariat of the Board.

[37] However, pursuant to Article 12 of the Law, provisional measures may be extended to a period not exceeding six months at the request of exporters with a significant share of the exports of the products to Turkey.

[38] Of these 118 anti-dumping duties, 14 were anti-circumvention measures taken against 10 trading partners in 6 product groups. Anti-circumvention provisions were incorporated in Turkey's legislation through Decree No. 9840/2005.

Table III.11
Definitive anti-dumping measures in force, August 2011

Country/Customs territory and product	Communiqué	Imposition of final measure	Duty (as % of c.i.f. or specific)
Brazil			
Fittings	2006/23	07.09.2006	20.2%-23.75% (c.i.f.) or US$400/tonne
Bulgaria			
Fittings	2006/24	07.09.2006	US$400/tonne
Mono ethylene glycol (MEG)	2010/11	02.05.2010	20%
Canada			
Oriented strand board (OSB)	2008/34	18.12.2008	14.93%
China, P.R			
Pre finished engineered laminated flooring	2006/17	08.07.2006	35%
Wall type split air conditioners	2006/20	26.07.2006	25%
Fittings	2006/23	07.09.2006	US$800/tonne
Granite	2006/25	14.09.2006	US$90/tonne
Plywood consisting solely of sheets of wood (up to 6 mm thickness)	2006/28	20.10.2006	US$240/m^3
V. belts	2007/4	31.03.2007	US$5.04/kg
Woven fabrics of synthetic and artificial staple fibres	2007/10	19.06.2007	87%
Refractory bricks of chromite, magnesite or chrome magnesite; other articles-containing magnesite, dolomite or chromite	2007/11	01.09.2007	US$145/tonne
Wall clocks (battery, accumulator or main powered)	2007/17	24.10.2007	US$2.10/piece
Parts of lighter	2008/16	01.05.2008	US$0.02/piece
Pocket lighters, gas fueled, non-refillable	2008/16	01.05.2008	US$0.05/piece
Pocket lighters, gas fueled, refillable with electrical ignition system & parts of lighters	2008/16	01.05.2008	US$0.05/piece
Laminated flooring	2008/24	30.07.2008	US$1.60-2.40/m2
Woven fabrics of synthetic filament yarn	2008/25	01.08.2008	70.44%
Blankets & long pile fabrics of synthetic fibres and others of man-made fibres for blankets	2008/27	01.08.2008	US$4/kg
Textured yarn of nylon or other polyamides, measuring per single yarn more than 50 tex	2008/31	05.09.2008	37.40%
Aluminium offset printing plates	2008/32	15.11.2008	US$2.65/kg
Tarpaulin made of polyethylene/polypropylene	2008/33	15.11.2008	US$1.06/kg
Pencils with leads of graphite, etc.	2008/35	18.12.2008	US$3.16/144 pieces
Hook and loop	2008/36	18.12.2008	US$3.86/kg
Polyester textured yarn	2008/41	31.12.2008	US$268-351/tonne
Yarn of man-made or synthetic or artificial staple fibres	2009/1	12.01.2009	US$0.49-0.80/kg
Certain finished or semi-finished artificial leather	2009/12	18.04.2009	US$1.9/kg
Knives for electromechanical domestic kitchen appliances	2009/17	18.06.2009	US$20.85/kg
Cylindrical door locks (excluding electromechanicals) & other door locks (excluding electromechanicals) & only cylinder and case for door locks	2009/21	30.07.2009	US$0.74-1.77/piece
Stud-link of iron or steel & welded link chain of iron or steel	2009/25	25.07.2009	US$1,069/tonne
Bicycle tyres and bicycle tubes	2009/29	05.08.2009	33%-50%
Motorcycle tyres and motorcycle tubes	2009/30	05.08.2009	37%-100%
Certain types of new pneumatic tires, of rubber	2011/8	21.06.2011	60%
Polyester synthetic staple	2009/33	05.10.2009	US$0.21/kg
Ball point pens	2009/35	12.11.2009	US$0.066/piece
Certain tube or pipe fittings of iron or steel	2010/2	22.01.2010	US$663/tonne
Certain made-up textile articles and fabrics made of artificial or synthetics fibres	2010/8	11.04.2010	US$70.44/kg
Glass lid/cover	2010/12	23.05.2010	US$0.91/kg

Table III.11 (cont'd)

Country/Customs territory and product	Communiqué	Imposition of final measure	Duty (as % of c.i.f. or specific)
Articulated link chain and parts thereof	2010/13	23.05.2010	US$1200/tonne
Baby carriages	2010/14	23.05.2010	US$12/piece
Fan coil	2010/16	31.05.2010	0.3427%
Hinges of base metal & hat-racks, hat-pegs, brackets and similar fixtures of base metal & base metal mountings, fittings and similar articles suitable for furniture	2010/18	20.07.2010	US$1.64-0.75/kg
Metalized yarn	2010/21	21.07.2010	US$2.2/kg
Ropes and cables (including locked coil ropes)	2010/22	21.07.2010	US$1/kg
Refillable pocket flint lighters	2010/27	31.10.2010	US$0.05/piece
Textile fabrics, impregnated with polyurethane-leather & textile fabrics, impregnated with polyurethane-others & textile fabrics, impregnated, coated, covered, or laminated with polyurethane – leather substitute	2010/28	31.10.2010	US$1-2.2/kg
Slide fasteners	2010/29	30.10.2010	US$3/kg
Glass fibre reinforcement materials	2011/1	31.12.2010	20.2%-23.75% (c.i.f.)
Tools for drilling & tools for milling	2011/2	31.12.2010	US$6-10/kg
Pentaerythritol	2011/6	03.05.2010	US$270/tonne
Skid chain or motor vehicles of iron or steel	2011/7	03.05.2011	US$1,500/tonne
Core wire of base metal	2011/16	28.07.2011	21.12%-28.87%
Chinese Taipei			
Polyester textured yarn	2006/31	21.12.2006	9.9-28.6%
Hook and loop	2008/36	18.12.2008	US$1.83/kg
Polyester synthetic staple	2009/13	18.04.2004	6.4%-20.1%
Bicycle tyres and bicycle tubes	2010/20	17.07.2010	30%-40%
Motorcycle tyres and motorcycle tubes	2010/20	17.07.2010	6%-21%
Metalized yarn	2010/21	21.07.2010	US$2.2/kg
Saudi Arabia			
Polyester synthetic staple	2007/13	01.09.2007	US$0,11/kg
Mono ethylene glycol	2010/11	02.05.2010	4%-20%
Germany			
Polyvinyl chloride	2009/18	25.06.2009	US$25-45/tonne
Hong Kong, China			
Glass lid/cover	2010/12	23.05.2010	US$0.91/kg
India			
Fittings	2006/24	07.09.2006	US$305-400/tonne
Polyester textured yarn	2006/31	21.12.2006	6.8-20.3%
V-belts	2007/4	31.03.2007	US$3.5/kg
Yarn of manmade or synthetic or artificial staple fibres	2009/1	12.01.2009	US$0.29-0.39/kg
Polyester synthetic staple	2009/13	18.04.2009	16,5%-23,9%
Bicycle tyres and bicycle tubes	2009/29	05.08.2009	20%;64%
Metalized yarn	2010/21	21.07.2010	US$2.2/kg

Table III.11 (cont'd)

Country/Customs territory and product	Communiqué	Imposition of final measure	Duty (as % of c.i.f. or specific)
Indonesia			
Pre finished engineered laminated flooring	2006/17	08.07.2006	25%
Fittings	2006/24	07.09.2006	US$253-400/tonne
Polyester synthetic staple fibres	2006/26	08.09.2006	6.2%-12%
Polyester textured yarn	2008/41	31.12.2008	US$48-240/tonne
Yarn of man-made or synthetic or artificial staple fibres	2009/1	12.01.2009	US$0-0.40/kg
Bicycle tyres & bicycle tubes	2009/27	01.08.2009	17.8%;29.6%-33%
Motorcycle tyres & motorcycle tubes	2009/28	01.08.2009	0%;19.6%-29%
Glass lid/cover	2010/12	23.05.2010	US$0.14-0.50/kg
Italy			
Polyvinyl chloride	2009/18	25.06.2009	US$25-45/tonne
Korea, Rep. of			
Polyester flat yarns	2006/12	18.05.2006	5.2%-10.9%
Polyester synthetic staple fibres	2006/26	08.09.2006	10% (c.i.f.)
Polyester textured yarn	2006/31	21.12.2006	33.7% (c.i.f.)
Woven fabrics of synthetic filament yarn	2008/25	01.08.2008	14.64%-40%
Metallized yarn	2010/21	21.07.2010	US$2.2/kg
Kuwait			
Mono ethylene glycol (meg)	2010/11	02.05.2010	6%-20%
Malaysia			
Woven fabrics of synthetic filament yarn	2008/25	01.08.2008	7.76%-15.93%
Polyester textured yarn	2008/41	31.12.2008	US$276/tonne
Vulcanized rubber thread and cord	2009/14	18.06.2009	11.6%-16.9%
Bicycle tyres and bicycle tubes	2009/27	1.08.2009	29.6%-33%; 5.6-33%
Motorcycle tyres and motorcycle tubes	2009/28	01.08.2009	19.6%-29.6%;19.6%-29.6
Romania			
Polyvinyl chloride	2009/18	25.06.2009	US$25-45/tonne
Russian Federation			
Cooper wire rod	2011/14	09.11.2005	3%
Ropes and cables (including locked coil ropes)	2010/22	21.07.2010	US$0.5/kg
Sri Lanka			
Bicycle tyres	2010/20	17.07.2010	50%
Bicycle tubes	2010/20	17.07.2010	44%
Thailand			
Fittings	2006/24	07.09.2006	US$147-400/tonne
Woven fabrics of synthetic filament yarn	2008/25	1.08.2008	8.67%-30.93%
Polyester textured yarn	2008/41	31.12.2008	US$198-300/tonne
Polyester synthetic staple fibres	2009/13	18.04.2009	15.8%-22%
Bicycle tyres and bicycle tubes	2009/29	05.08.2009	100%;100%
Motorcycle tyres and motorcycle tubes	2009/30	05.08.2009	68%;100%

Table III.11 (cont'd)

Country/Customs territory and product	Communiqué	Imposition of final measure	Duty (as % of c.i.f. or specific)
Ukraine			
Wire of refined copper	2011/14	08.06.2006	6.9%
United States			
Oriented strand board (OSB)	2008/34	18.12.2008	24.10%
Polyvinyl chloride	2009/18	25.06.2009	US$45/tonne
Viet Nam			
V-belts	2007/4	31.03.2007	US$4.55/kg
Tarpaulin made of polyethylene/polypropylene	2008/33	15.11.2008	US$1.16/kg
Bicycle tyres	2010/20	17.07.2010	30%
Bicycle tubes	2010/20	17.07.2010	44%
Motorcycle tyres	2010/20	17.07.2010	29%
Motorcycle tubes	2010/20	17.07.2010	49%

Source: Information provided by the Turkish authorities.

Table III.12
Definitive anti-circumvention measures in force, May 2011

Country/ Customs territory and product	Communiqué	Imposition of final measure	Duty
China, P. R.			
Standard wire, ropes and cables	2006/32	30 December 2006	US$1/kg
Chinese Taipei			
Hinges of base metal & hat- racks, hat- pegs, brackets and similar fixtures of base metal & base mountings, fittings and similar articles suitable for furniture	2008/29	27 August 2008	US$1.64/kg US$1.64/kg US$0.75/kg
Indonesia			
Hinges of base metal & hat- racks, hat- pegs, brackets and similar fixtures of base metal & base mountings, fittings and similar articles suitable for furniture	2008/29	27 August 2008	US$1.64/kg US$1.64/kg US$0.75/kg
Only wall-type split air-conditioners & only outdoor unit of wall-type split air-conditioners (except for outdoor unit of VRF systems) & only indoor unit of wall-type split air-conditioners	2011/3	31 January 2011	25%
Korea, Rep. of			
Woven fabrics of synthetic filament yarn	2008/25	01 August 2008	14.64%-40%
Malaysia			
Hinges of base metal & hat- racks, hat- pegs, brackets and similar fixtures of base metal & base mountings, fittings and similar articles suitable for furniture	2008/29	27 August 2008	US$1.64/kg US$1.64/kg US$0.75/kg
Only wall-type split air-conditioners & only outdoor unit of wall-type split air-conditioners (except for outdoor unit of VRF systems) & only indoor unit of wall-type split air-conditioners	2009/6	28 February 2009	0-25%
Pakistan			
Only wall-type split air-conditioners & only outdoor unit of wall-type split air-conditioners (except for outdoor unit of VRF systems) & only indoor unit of wall-type split air-conditioners	2011/3	31 January 2011	25%

Table III.12 (cont'd)

Country/ Customs territory and product	Communiqué	Imposition of final measure	Duty
Russian Federation			
Standard wire, ropes and cables	2006/32	30 December 2006	US$0.5/kg
Thailand			
Pencils with leads of graphite and pencils with leads of crayons encased in a rigid sheath	2007/5	14 April 2007	US$3.16/144 piece
Philippines			
Only wall-type split air-conditioners & only outdoor unit of wall-type split air-conditioners (except for outdoor unit of VRF systems) & only indoor unit of wall-type split air-conditioners	2011/3	31 January 2011	25%
Woven fabrics of synthetic filament yarn	2006/30	18 November.2006	70.44%
Viet Nam			
Only wall-type split air-conditioners & only outdoor unit of wall-type split air-conditioners (except for outdoor unit of VRF systems) & only indoor unit of wall-type split air-conditioners	2011/3	31 January 2011	25%
Pocket lighters, gas fueled, non-refillable & refillable pocket flint lighters & pocket lighters, gas fueled, refillable with electrical ignition system & parts of lighters	2008/17	28 April 2008	US$0.05/piece US$0.05/piece US$0.05/piece US$0.02/piece

Source: Information provided by the Turkish authorities.

50. The authority to propose, apply, and monitor safeguard measures rests with the Ministry of Economy. The Board for the Evaluation of Safeguard Measures for Imports decides, *inter alia,* whether to initiate an investigation; to adopt, review, extend, modify or abolish any provisional or definitive safeguard measure; and to determine the form, extent, and duration of such measures. The duration of a safeguard measure, including any provisional measure, may not exceed four years unless the measure is extended. The total period of application of a safeguard measure must not exceed ten years.

51. Since its last Review, Turkey has extended the safeguard measures initially imposed in 2006 on imports from all countries of steam irons, vacuum cleaners, footwear, and motorcycles (2007). In new cases, Turkey imposed definitive safeguard measures on all imports of certain electrical appliances and cotton yarn in 2008, and on matches in 2009 (Table III.13). On the other hand, safeguards on activated earths and clays, certain voltmeters, ammeters, and salt were not extended when they lapsed in 2008 and 2009. Among the most recent developments, Turkey conducted a safeguard investigation against imports of polyethylene terephthalate, and the measure will enter into effect upon publication of approval by the Cabinet of Ministers, after all legal procedures have been completed. Turkey has also initiated investigations to extend its safeguard measures on imports of spectacle frames; travel goods, handbags and similar containers; and cotton yarn. Provisional safeguard measures are in force while the investigations continue.[39]

[39] Concerning cotton yarn, a request has been made, pursuant to Article 13.1(b) of the Agreement on Safeguards, that the Committee on Safeguards should determine whether Turkey has complied with the procedural requirements of the Agreement in connection with the safeguard measure (see WTO document G/SG/W/221, 8 November 2011).

Table III.13
Definitive safeguard measures in force, 2011

Product	Date of imposition of definitive measure
Certain electrical appliances	10/8/2008
Cotton yarn	11/8/2008
Matches	6/12/2009
Vacuum cleaners	13/2/2010
Steam smoothing irons	13/2/2010
Motorcycles	13/2/2010
Footwear	13/2/2010

Source: Information provided by the Turkish authorities.

52. Turkey has implemented an import surveillance system based on Council of Ministers' Decision No. 2004/7304[40]; the Ministry of Economy issues a Surveillance Document. The purpose of the system is to monitor and collect specific data. For certain products, the surveillance system is price-based; thus, only products imported at prices below certain c.i.f. values are being monitored.

(2) MEASURES DIRECTLY AFFECTING EXPORTS

(i) Export procedures and requirements

53. Registration and documentation requirements for exporters are similar to those applicable to importers (section (1)(i) above). In addition, exporters must register with the Exporters Union and their local Chamber of Commerce. A fee ranging from 0.02% to 0.1% of the f.o.b. value of exports is charged as a service commission. The level of the fee is set by the general assemblies of the respective organizations, i.e. by the exporters themselves.

54. Registration requirements remain in force for (i) exports of goods eligible for premium deduction under the Support and Price Stabilization Fund (SPSF); (ii) goods paid for by the SPSF; (iii) exports within the framework of special accounts for the payment of instalments on credits for the conduct of barter trade; (iv) exports under the Natural Gas Agreement between Turkey and the Russian Federation; (v) exports of goods under restrictions applicable to countries that are implementing quantitative restrictions on Turkish exports (no such cases at present); (vi) exports to countries subject to UN economic sanctions resolutions; (vii) goods certified under the "Fundamentals and Implementation of Organic Farming" regulation; (viii) export of goods covered by the Vienna Agreement regarding the protection of the ozone layer, as well as the related protocols and amendments; (ix) exports of unprocessed olive oil and processed bulk or barrelled olive oil, liquorice root, raw meerschaum, and sample pipe; and (x) exports of unprocessed olives in bags, sacks or boxes, livestock, bulk conic pepper, raw olive (unfermented), scrap of copper and zinc, marble, gherkin, and cement. Registration is on a case-by-case basis at the time of each export transaction. The Ministry of Customs and Trade may authorize exporters who fulfil certain conditions to issue invoice declarations and EUR-MED invoice declarations.

55. The Ministry of Customs and Trade may authorize exporters of goods destined to the EU market and covered by the Customs Union Decision to issue movement certificates (A.TR) without submitting them to the relevant authorities for endorsement. Such authorization may be granted to exporters making frequent consignments, provided the exporters have not been involved in any serious or repeated offence against customs or tax legislation, and that they maintain records that can be checked by the customs authorities.

[40] The Decision was published in the *Official Gazette* No. 25476, 29 May 2004.

(ii) Export taxes, fees, and charges

56. Turkey applied export taxes on raw skins (at a rate of US$0.5 per kg), unshelled hazelnuts (US$0.04 per kg), and shelled hazelnuts (US$0.08 per kg). The revenue from these taxes is channelled into the Support and Price Stabilization Fund.

(iii) Export restrictions

57. Turkey prohibits exports of 12 items (by broad category, mostly agricultural goods) for environmental, health or cultural reasons (Table III.14). An export prohibition on angora goats was replaced by export licensing in September 2009. At present, licences are required for exports of 24 categories of products (Table III.15), including certain agricultural and fish items. Licensing is also used to enforce obligations under international agreements and conventions, notably for narcotics, hazardous wastes, nuclear and missile technology, and dual-use goods and technologies.[41] Electricity may only be exported by enterprises holding wholesale licences. In addition, approval from the Ministry of Energy and Natural Resources is required for exports of electricity to countries with which interconnections are not based on a synchronous parallel operating regime. Petroleum products (petrol, diesel, and LPG) may only be exported by licenced refineries and distributors.

58. The Ministry of Economy issued a revised Communiqué of Foreign Trade in Endangered Species of Wild Fauna and Flora in February 2011, under which the Ministry of Forestry and Water Affairs issues CITES certificates for exports and re-exports of each specie listed in the Communiqué. Exporters of endangered species of wild fauna and flora must attach the certificates, valid for six months, to their customs declaration forms.

59. The Decree on the Regime of Technical Regulations and Standardization for Foreign Trade empowers the Government to make agricultural goods for export subject to quality control, and to determine the type of quality control applicable to such goods. The products are exported with control certificates issued by the regional branches of the Ministry of Economy, indicating conformity with established standards. Some 150 agricultural products (at the HS 12-digit level), including citrus fruit, apples, groundnuts, certain edible oils, dried apricots, dried figs, and some hazelnuts, are subject to compulsory export controls for quality purposes.

[41] Turkey is a party to the Wassenaar Arrangement on export controls for conventional arms and dual use goods and technologies. Member states, including Turkey, maintain export controls for the goods and technologies specified in the control lists annexed to the Arrangement according to their national legislation. However, Turkey also follows closely the EU export control regime governed by Regulation No. 428/2009 and the list of controlled dual-use items in the Annexes to this Regulation.

Table III.14
Export prohibitions, 2011

Description of item	Invocation of WTO Article	Domestic/International law
All game and wild animals (except species on the list of "exports requiring a licence", alive or meat and/or pieces and garments thereof (Ch. 1 and 2)[a]	Environment (Article XX:g)	Decision of the Council of Ministers (No. 234 of 8 March 1990)
Natural flower bulbs (1 item)	Environment (Article XX:g)	Export Regime Decree (No. 7623 of 22 December 1995)
Tobacco seeds and tobacco seedlings		Implementing Regulation on Methods and Essentials Concerning Tobacco Production and Processing and Internal and External Trade (Official Gazette dated 10/07/2010, numbered 27637) based on the Law No. 4733, dated 09/01/2002 (amended by Law No. 5752 dated 15/04/2008)
Dates "Phoenix the ophrasti crenter" (1 item)	Environment (Article XX:g)	Export Regime Decree (No. 7623 of 22 December 1995)
Indian hemp (1 item)[a]	Health (Article XX:b)	Law on the Controls of Narcotics (No. 2313 of 24 June 1933)
Pterocarya carpinifolia (1 item)	Environment (Article XX:g)	Export Regime Decree (No. 7623 of 22 December 1995)
Liquidamber orientalis (1 item)	Environment (Article XX:g)	Export Regime Decree (No. 7623 of 22 December 1995)
Plants of olive, fig (except species certificated domestically that are registered and published in the National Species List), hazelnut, pistachio, and grapevine (sultanas seedless)	Environment (Article XX:g)	Export Regime Decree (No. 7623 of 22 December 1995)
Walnut, mulberry, cherry, pear, plum, badger, ash, elm, and lime in logs, in timber, in plank, and in sketch (Ch. 44)[a]	Environment (Article XX:g)	Decision of the Council of Ministers (No. 8186 of 24 April 1974)
Wood	Environment (Article XX:g)	Export Regime Decree (No. 7623 of 22 December 1995)
Antiques and archaeological works (1 item)[a]	National treasures (Article XX:f)	Law on Ancient Works of Art (No. 2863 of 21 July 1983)
Sahlep (powder and of all sorts)	..	Export Regime Decree (No. 7623 of 22 December 1995)

.. Not available.

a Export prohibited in 1993.

Source: WTO Secretariat, based on information provided by the Turkish authorities.

Table III.15
Exports requiring a licence, 2011

Description of items	Authority responsible	Legal basis
Angora goats (1 item)	Ministry of Food, Agriculture and Livestock	Law on the Amelioration of Animals (No. 4631 of 10 March 2001)
Opium and poppy seeds	Ministry of Health	Law No. 2313 of 24 June 1933
Addictive and psychotropic substances	Ministry of Health	Law No. 2313 of 24 June 1933; Addictive substances stated in the Psychotropic Agreement dated 1961, revised in 1972; Psychotropic Agreement dated 1971; and UN Agreement (dated 1988) to prohibit addictive substances
Products subject to Basel Convention on the Control of Transboundary Movements of Hazardous Wastes and their Disposal	Ministry of Forestry and Water Affairs	Decree No. 94/5419 of 7 March 1994

Table III.15 (cont'd)

Description of items	Authority responsible	Legal basis
Living or non-living boars, wolves, jackals, foxes, martens, badgers, snakes, turtles, lizards, and identifiable parts of and clothing produced from them	Ministry of Forestry and Water Affairs	Decree No. 645 regarding the Organization and Functions of the Ministry of Forestry and Water Affairs
Fertilizers (excluding chemical fertilizers)	Ministry of Food, Agriculture and Livestock	Decrees No. 2/1771 of 27 December 1924; and No. 6/4090 of 19 December 1964
Seeds (except forest-tree seeds)	Ministry of Food, Agriculture and Livestock	Law No. 5553, of 31 October 2006, and Communiqué No. 96/31 of 19 September 1996
Fishing products subject to "prohibition derived from the principles of fishery" (including leeches)	Ministry of Food, Agriculture and Livestock	Law No. 1380 of 22 March 1971 (as amended by Law No. 3288 of 28 May 1986)
Racehorses	Ministry of Food, Agriculture and Livestock	Law on the Amelioration of Animals (No. 4631 of 10 March 2001)
Feeds covered by the Feed Law	Ministry of Food, Agriculture and Livestock	Law No. 1734 of 29 May 1973
Pharmaceuticals for veterinary purposes	Ministry of Food, Agriculture and Livestock	Law No. 3490
Export of natural flower bulbs subject to quota or any other kind restrictions	Ministry of Food, Agriculture and Livestock	Decree No. 95/7623 of 22 December 1995
Live animals kept for stud	Ministry of Food, Agriculture and Livestock	Law on the Amelioration of Animals (No. 4631 of 10 March 2001)
Natural mushrooms (only exports to EU countries)	Ministry of Food, Agriculture and Livestock	Decree No. 95/7623 of 22 December 1995
Live tuna fish (Thynus thunnus)	Ministry of Food, Agriculture and Livestock	Decree No. 95/7623 of 22 December 1995
Substances listed in the annexes to the Wassenaar Arrangement and the Australian Group	Ministry of Economy	Wassenaar Arrangement list for Dual-use Goods and Technologies and in the Australian Group Chemical Precursors
Sugar	The Turkish Sugar Authority	Decree No. 2007/9 of 17 August 2007
Technology and equipment used for nuclear purposes	Turkish Atomic Energy Authority	Reg. No. 26642 of 13 September 2007
Goods covered by the Missile Technology Controlling Regime	Ministry of National Defence	Decree No. 5201of 29 June 2004
Tobacco leaf and tobacco waste	Tobacco and Alcohol Market Regulatory Authority	Law No. 4733 of 9 January 2002
Implements of war that are subject to control, military exploders and spare parts and related technologies	Ministry of National Defence	Law No. 5201 of 2 July 2007
Forest tree seeds and other breeding materials	Ministry of Forestry and Water Affairs	Decree No. 645 regarding the Organization and Functions of the Ministry of Forestry and Water Affairs
Olive tree sapling (species certificated domestically which are registered and published in the National Species List)	Ministry of Food, Agriculture and Livestock	Export Regime Decree (No. 7623 of 22 December 1995)
Explosive materials within the context of Regulatory Statute 87/12028	Ministry of Internal Affairs	Law No. 6551 of 18 May 1955, Regulatory Statute 87/12028 and 2001/2443

Source: Information provided by the Turkish authorities.

(iv) Export subsidies, finance, assistance, and promotion

60. Exporters benefit from duty and tax concessions (see sections (1)(iv) and (vi)). Exporters of 16 agricultural commodities or processed agricultural products are eligible for export subsidies under

the Export Subsidy Programme for Agricultural Products[42], established to develop Turkey's export potential in processed agricultural products (Chapter IV, Table AIV.2). This programme is financed from the Support and Price Stabilization Fund.

61. The Turk Eximbank, a state-owned bank established in 1987, is the only official export credit agency in Turkey. The Bank operates a number of export credit, guarantee, and insurance schemes. The main objectives of the Bank are to increase the volume of Turkish exports, develop new export markets, increase the share of Turkish exporters in international trade, diversify exports of goods and services, and support Turkish exporters, investors, and overseas contractors. Turk Eximbank presents its annual programmes to the Supreme Advisory and Credit Guidance Committee, chaired by the State Minister in charge of the Bank's activities.[43] The Committee sets upper limits for credits, guarantees, and insurance transactions to be effected by the Turk Eximbank, either as a gross amount or by country, sector, and programme. The Bank funds its activities mostly by borrowing from commercial banks or tapping the international financial markets, or through capital injections from the Turkish Treasury. Turk Eximbank provided in total US$8.9 billion in export financing support and pure cover in 2010, representing financial support to almost 8% of Turkey's exports in that year.

62. Turk Eximbank supports exporters, companies engaging in foreign-currency-earning services, and overseas investors and contractors with short-, medium-, and long-term export credit programmes (Table AIII.7). Moreover, export receivables are discounted to promote sales and deferred payment conditions, and to increase export volume. Short-term financial assistance is made available to exporters at the pre- and post-shipment stages with a term up to 540 days for loans in Turkish lira or foreign currency. Credits are allocated through the commercial banks in Turkey or directly by Turk Eximbank. In 2010, 55% of Turk Eximbank's short-term credits were extended via intermediary commercial banks and 45% were provided directly.[44] At the end of 2010, short-term export credit facilities accounted for 97% of Turk Eximbank's total loan portfolio.

63. Turk Eximbank's medium- and long-term financial support programmes have been developed mainly for the export of capital goods and turnkey investment projects to be undertaken by Turkish and Turkey-based contractors. The majority of these programmes involve extending financing facilities to buyers outside of Turkey for the purchase of Turkish goods and/or services. Depending on the risk classification of the type of loan or the country of the borrower, a sovereign guarantee or reputable bank guarantee in favour of Turk Eximbank has been a pre-requisite for many medium- and long-term financial operations, e.g. project finance loans.

64. Insurance against commercial and political risks is also offered by Turk Eximbank (Table III.16). Commercial risk-based losses are indemnified by the Bank from its own resources while political risks, in principle, are backed by the Government. However, Turk Eximbank has never submitted any indemnification request for political losses to the Turkish Treasury. Moreover, short-term political risks have also been ceded to a reinsurance panel (within certain country limits) since 2000. Premium rates for insurance programmes range from 0.08% to 4% (comprehensive for commercial and political risks), or from 0.02% to 4% for political risks only, and vary according to

---

[42] Implemented through Decrees Nos. 2008/1 and 2009/1 of the Money-Credit and Coordination Council for the years 2008 and 2009.

[43] Turk Eximbank, which is wholly state-owned, is under the responsibility of the Prime Ministry or such other State Ministry nominated by the Prime Minister.

[44] The commercial banks are responsible for the default risk of borrowers for the credits allocated through them. The commercial banks are allowed a margin of up to 1% per annum for credits denominated in Turkish lira, and 0.5% per annum for credits in foreign currency. A collateral and/or bank guarantee is required for credits allocated by Turk Eximbank directly to the client.

the risk category of the buyer's country, the payment term, and the status of the buyer (private, public or sovereign).

Table III.16
Key features of the export insurance programmes, 2011

Programme	Coverage
Short-Term Export Credit Insurance Programme	Up to 90% of losses incurred as a result of commercial and political risks on shipments made by an exporter within one year, with payments deferred up to 360 days. Comprehensive cover is available, including pre-shipment period (180 days maximum); post-shipment cover is compulsory where applicable. Premium rates vary according to, *inter alia*, the risk category of the buyer's country, the legal status of the buyer, and the relevant payment term and maturity.
Specific Export Credit Insurance Post-shipment Political Risk Programme	Cover against political risks in the post-shipment period for receivables from sales on credit terms relating to the export of capital and semi-capital goods with at least 60% domestic content. Cover is available up to 90% with 15% of the contract value to be paid in advance. Premium rates are specifically calculated taking into account the above-mentioned criteria.
Specific Export Credit Insurance Comprehensive Post-Shipment Risk Programme	Same as Specific Export Credit Insurance Post-shipment Political Risk, except that both political and commercial risks are covered.
Insurance Programme for Unfair Calling of Bonds	Cover applies to bid bonds, advance payment and performance bond for Turkish contractors in order to eliminate the risk of unfair calling of bonds. Bonds are issued by a bank in favour of the public buyer based in the borrowing countries for projects undertaken by Turkish contractors or subcontractors. Turk Eximbank is responsible for identifying the Turkish contractor, where a call is made under the bond by reason of events or circumstances beyond the contractor's control.

Source: WTO Secretariat, based on information provided by the Turkish authorities.

65. Pursuant to Article 12 of the Customs Union Decision, Turkey has been harmonizing its legislation with that of the EU with respect to officially supported export credits. Within this framework, the OECD Consensus principles on officially supported credits with a repayment term of two or more years have been adopted. Turk Eximbank is a full member of the Berne Union (the international association of export credit insurers), and represents Turkey in the Group on Export Credits and Credit Guarantees (ECG) and in the Participants Group (PG) of the OECD Trade Committee.[45]

66. KOSGEB, a public agency for the development of SMEs, was established in 1990 as a non-profit organization affiliated to the Ministry of Science, Industry and Technology. KOSGEB is financed under the general budget. KOSGEB assists SMEs in, *inter alia,* cofinancing business trips abroad (up to 50% of the costs, maximum TL 10,000), creating own brands, and providing export promotion credits. KOSGEB also provides business-matching models to SMEs, and a database to bring together local and foreign SMEs. Business-matching opportunities are assessed by a qualified operator company.

67. Further to Decree Law No. 637 concerning the Organization and Duties of the Ministry of Economy, published in June 2011, the former Export Promotion Centre (IGEME) has been abolished and incorporated into the Ministry of Economy.

[45] Turkey has been a member of the ECG since April 1998, and an observer of PG since November 2006.

(3) MEASURES AFFECTING PRODUCTION AND TRADE

(i) Subsidies

68. Turkey's Investment Encouragement Programme (IEP), which is the only support programme targeting investment, has been subject to some modifications during the review period.[46] The current legal framework is contained in the Decree Concerning State Encouragements to Investments to define the purpose, scope, incentives, regional classification, eligibility criteria and other basic implementation rules.[47] The IEP now follows a three-pillar approach, focusing on regional and sectoral implementation, large-scale investments contributing to international competitiveness employing high technologies and R&D activities, and a general investment encouragement mechanism. For regional and sectoral support, Turkey is divided into four regions, and the incentives provided are linked to the nature of the investment and the development status of the region where the investment is located.[48]

69. Minimum investment levels range from TL 50 million to TL 1 billion for large-scale investments, and minimum investments, differentiated by region and sector, have been established for regions I to IV. The general investment encouragement mechanism covers investments that do not fall within the scope of regional support or large investments, but are above the specified minimum amounts. However, the general mechanism excludes investments in certain specified activities, and specific conditions must be fulfilled for investments in some other agricultural and services-related activities.[49]

70. The IEP is implemented by the Ministry of Economy, which issues Investment Encouragement Certificates that allow investors to benefit from the incentives listed in the certificates. Customs duty and VAT exemptions are available for all investments under the IEP. In addition, regional support and incentives for large investments include reductions in corporate or income tax, budget funding of the social security premium to be paid by the employer, and land allocation.[50] Investments in regions III and IV, in research and development, or in environmental projects may also benefit from interest support.[51]

71. Pursuant to Communiqué No. 2008/1 and in the context of Law No. 5084 on Encouragement of Investments and Employment and Amendment of Certain Laws[52], Turkey will continue to provide energy support until 31 December 2012, i.e. subsidized electricity to enterprises located in provinces with a (2001) GDP per capita of US$1,500 or less, or a negative socio-economic development index

---

[46] The General Investment Encouragement Programme and the Aids Granted to Small and Medium-sized Enterprises Investments were merged to form the IEP in 2006.

[47] Decree No. 2009/15199 of 14 July 2009, published in the *Official Gazette* on 16 July 2009.

[48] The regional demarcation is based on the NUTS2 classification (Nomenclature of Territorial Units for Statistics), an instrument providing a single uniform breakdown of territorial units for the production of regional statistics in the European Union. The regions and supported sectors are listed in Annexes I and II of WTO document G/SCM/N/186/TUR.

[49] Investments that are not supported or are supported conditionally under the general investment encouragement system are listed in Annex IV of WTO document G/SCM/N/186/TUR.

[50] Until the end of 2010, enterprises involved in the production of textiles and clothing or leather and leather products could also be granted support if they relocated from regions I and II to region IV, provided they employed at least 50 persons after the move.

[51] The support is granted for a maximum of five years, and the maximum subsidy or subsidized rate of interest depends on the region, type of investment, and whether the loan is granted in Turkish lira or foreign currency.

[52] Amended by Law No. 5350 of 12 May 2005 and Law No. 5615 of 28 March 2007.

(for 2003) according to the State Planning Organization.[53] Enterprises must have at least 10 to 30 employees, depending on the sector or date of application, or operate in manufacturing, mining, tourism accommodation, education or heath, or specified agricultural activities.[54]

72. Under Ministerial Council Resolution on State Aids Related to Exports (No. 6401 of 27 December 1994), Turkey has established 11 state-aid programmes, some of which target SMEs (Table III.17). Additional support programmes are the organized industrial zones (OIZs), industrial zones, the small-scale industrial estates scheme, KOSGEB, and technology development zones.

Table III.17
Key features of the state aid programmes, 2011

Programme	Aim and beneficiaries	Support	Implementing institutions
Research and development projects	To support companies conducting R&D projects, regardless of size; all industrial companies and firms that produce software	Soft loan for capital support (to be paid back in US$ with Libor plus interest) for two years	Turkish Technology Development Foundation
		- SME Project Support Programme - R&D, Innovation and Industrial Practice Support Programme	KOSGEB
Environmental protection activities	To support expenses of SMEs during certification of quality assurance, environmental management systems, and CE marking; all SMEs manufacturing and software companies	50% of the relevant certification expenses	Exporters' Unions
		- Thematic Project Support Programme	KOSGEB
Participation in international fairs and exhibitions	To increase participation in fairs abroad; companies, sectoral foreign trade companies, producers/manufacturers organizations	50% of participation fees (in the case of national participation); 50% of the rental cost of empty stand, and 50% of transportation costs (in the case of individual participation)	Exporters' Unions
		- Business Matching Support	KOSGEB
Organizing domestic fairs with international participation[a]	To promote international fairs organized in Turkey and to foster international participation; companies that organize international fairs in Turkey	50% of promotional activities; 50% of transportation expenses of representatives of foreign companies; and 50% of expenses regarding activities during the fair	Exporters' Unions
		- Foreign Business Trip Support - Business Matching Support	KOSGEB
Market research projects	To increase awareness of companies about new markets; companies, sectoral foreign trade companies, producers/ manufacturers organizations	Buying market research projects, reports, and statistics; financial assistance for companies participating in trade missions abroad, and for becoming members of B2B websites so as to market their products abroad	Export Promotion Centre
		- Foreign Business Trip Support - Business Matching Support	KOSGEB

Table III.17 (cont'd)

[53] The provinces are listed in Annex V of WTO document G/SCM/N/186/TUR.

[54] The base rate of the subsidy, which is 20% of the electricity cost, may be augmented by the overall number of employees or newly hired labour, but may not exceed 50% of the price for electricity to enterprises operating in organized industrial zones or industrial zones, or 40% for enterprises located elsewhere.

Programme	Aim and beneficiaries	Support	Implementing institutions
Operating stores abroad	To promote companies operating stores abroad; companies, and sectoral foreign trade companies	50% of the advertisement, rent, office inventory and decoration expenditures of companies operating a store abroad	Exporters' Unions
Encouraging employment in sectoral foreign trade companies	To promote employment; sectoral foreign trade companies	75% of the pre-tax salary for one manager and two staff with professional experience, for one year	Ministry of Economy
Competitiveness	Institution of collaborations (exporter unions, chamber of commerce, organized industrial zones, sectoral associations, sectoral foreign trade companies) are given support for project based common activities for their members	Analysis, sector analysis in terms of creating shared vision, road map for the project members); Training, counselling and advisory activities for companies; International marketing and sales activities; Employment of coordinator/manager (for managing the project and organizing project based common activities); 75% of training costs for programmes up to six months; 75% of consultancy services costs up to one year	Export Promotion Centre
Encouraging designers	To promote designers' companies activities abroad	50% of consultancy fees, rental fees, advertisement, certification expenses and fees for the registration of trade marks	Exporters' Unions and Ministry of Economy
Technical consultancy activities abroad	To encourage technical consultancy companies to operate abroad	At least 50% of rental fees, advertisement, market research projects, fair and conference participation fees, feasibility studies and agreement expenditures	Ministry of Economy
Promoting Turkish trade marks and improving the image of Turkish goods	To support brand creation and positioning activities, companies, and sectoral foreign trade companies	50% of consultancy fees, rental fees, advertisement, certification expenses and fees for the registration of trade marks	Exporters' Unions and Ministry of Economy

a The fair must be organized at least three years in advance, a minimum of 100 companies is required (25 of which must be foreign), and a fair cannot be supported more than twice.

Source: Information provided by the Turkish authorities.

73. The OIZs offer subsidized industrial plots; infrastructure, including transportation and communication facilities; and subsidized credits. Some 93 OIZs have been established since the start-up in 1962. Credit granted during 2006-10 amounted to US$268.5 million. Industrial zones are established by the Council of Ministers pursuant to the Industrial Zones Law.[55] The Ministry of Science, Industry and Technology develops proposals to establish industrial zones, and funds the acquisition of land and the preparation of infrastructure. Dating back to 1965, the small-scale industrial estates scheme provides credit for the construction of modern workshops with sanitary conditions. Main activities in the estates are car-repair workshops, metal manufacturing, and wood-working industries. Between 2006 and 2010, Turkey established 35 new OIZs and 47 small estates.

[55] Law No. 4737, published in the *Official Gazette* of 19 January 2002.

74. KOSGEB, which focuses on the development of SMEs, provides services related to production, marketing, and quality control, as well as support programmes such as the SME Project, the Thematic Project, Cooperation-Collaboration, R&D, Innovation and Industrial Practice, Entrepreneurship, and General and Emerging Companies Market SME. Technology development zones have been established to promote the development of technology and software and related R&D capabilities through cooperation between universities, research institutions, and the business community.[56] Financial support is made available for land procurement, infrastructure, the construction of administrative buildings, etc. Income and corporate tax exemptions have been granted until the end of 2023. Researchers, software engineers, and R&D personnel working in the zone(s) are also exempt from all types of tax until the end of 2013. Turkey has established 43 technology development zones.

75. The Law on Monitoring and Supervision of State Aids, which entered into force on 23 October 2010, sets the framework for ensuring the compatibility of state aids with the related provisions of agreements and decisions between Turkey and the EU. A State Aids Monitoring and Supervision Board is responsible for the monitoring, supervision, and evaluation of compatibility. The Board will, as necessary, provide notifications to the European Commission and other related authorities, having collected relevant information from the aid-granting authorities. The General Directorate of State Aids acts as secretariat for the Board.

(ii) Technical barriers to trade, standards, and certification

76. Decision No. 1/95 of the Turkey-EU Association Council, which establishes the Customs Union between Turkey and the EU, also calls for Turkey to adopt EU instruments required to eliminate all technical barriers to trade in particular products.[57] Accordingly, in 2002, Turkey adopted the Law No. 4703 on the Preparation and Implementation of Technical Legislation on Products and four implementing regulations[58] The Turkish authorities are planning to amend the framework law and the implementing regulations due to changes in the EU horizontal legislation in 2008 and 2010.

77. The Ministry of Economy is responsible for the implementation of the Agreement on Technical Barriers to Trade in Turkey.[59] Turkey has established two National TBT Enquiry Points; the Directorate General of Product Safety and Inspection (under the the Ministry of Economy) for technical regulations and conformity assessment procedures, and the Turkish Standards Institution (TSE) for standards. The Directorate General maintains a website to facilitate access to TBT

[56] Technology Development Zones Law No. 4691 was approved by the Grand National Assembly of Turkey on 26 June 2001.

[57] Viewed at: http://eur-lex.europa.eu/LexUriServ/LexUriServ.do?uri=CELEX:21996D0213(01):EN:HTML.

[58] Law No. 4703 was published in *Official Gazette* No. 24459, 11 July 2001. The implementing regulations are (i) the Regulation on the Notification of the Technical Legislation and Standards between Turkey and the EC (*Official Gazette* No. 24715, 3 April 2002); (ii) the Regulation on the Affixing and Use of the EC Conformity Marking on Products, (iii) the Regulation on Conformity Assessment Bodies and Notified Bodies, and (iv) Regulation Relating to the Market Surveillance and Inspection of Products. The last three regulations were published in the *Official Gazette* No. 24643, 17 January 2002 and entered into force on 11 January 2002. For a description of the main provisions of the 2002 legislation see WTO (2003).

[59] Turkey notified its measures taken for the implementation and administration of the TBT Agreement, in 1997 (WTO document G/TBT/2/Add.33). The implementing Regulation on the Implementation of the Notifications Foreseen in the TBT Agreement, which also provided the legal basis for the creation of the National Enquiry Point, was published in the *Official Gazette* No. 22965, 15 April 1997.

notifications, and to obtain opinions from the different stakeholders on implementation of measures and market access challenges.[60]

(a) Standards

78. The Turkish Standards Institution (TSE) has been developing and implementing standards for all types of material and products manufactured in Turkey (or imported) since 1960. The TSE is a full member of the International Organization for Standardization (ISO) and the International Electrotechnical Commission (IEC). At the European level, the TSE is an affiliate member of the European Committee for Standardization (CEN) and the European Committee for Electrotechnical Standardization (CENELEC).[61] Turkey is also a member of the International Telecommunications Union (ITU), although this is managed by the Ministry of Transport, Maritime and Communications.

79. TSE accepted the TBT Code of Good Practice for the Preparation, Adoption and Application of Standards in 1995.[62] The TSE publishes an annual work programme.[63] A (minimum) two-month comment period is provided for draft standards, taking into account the content and specificity of the draft. At present, Turkey has 33,097 standards, by definition voluntary. According to the Turkish authorities, the TSE has adopted almost 99% of CEN and CENELEC standards into Turkish standards. Manufacturers that follow Turkish standards aligned with European product standards are presumed to be in conformity with the requirements of the associated EU Directives, and equivalent Turkish technical regulations.

(b) Technical regulations

80. The Regime for Technical Regulations and Standardization for Foreign Trade, in force since 1995 and amended by Decree No. 9454/2005, provides the national framework for Turkey's technical regulations and conformity assessment procedures.[64] The regime is transitional and revised annually in the light of progress in the transposition of EU legislation into Turkey's legal system. The technical regulations impose product requirements and specifications on imported and domestically produced goods, including requirements related to health and safety, environmental aspects, and labelling.

81. According to the Turkish authorities, Turkey has transposed around 82% of the sector-specific EU directives into Turkish technical regulations, including 222 technical regulations and the adoption of 24 "new approach" Directives covering products such as radio and telecommunication terminal equipment, batteries and accumulators, toys, personal protective equipment, construction products, medical devices, gas appliances, civil explosives, and lifts. The transposed Directives cover approximately 70% of manufactured goods imported into Turkey, and impose various technical product requirements and specifications.[65] Conformity assessment controls for these products are implemented through annual Communiqués.[66] Other Communiqués relate to product groups

---

[60] Viewed at: http://www.teknikengel.gov.tr.

[61] The TSE applied for full membership in CEN and CENELEC in 2010 and expects to complete the process by the end of 2011.

[62] See WTO document G/TBT/CS/N/35, 15 April 1996.

[63] Viewed at: http://www.standardsinfo.net/info/docs_wto/SCD_Update_EN.pdf; and http://www.tse.org.tr/TSEIntWeb/Standard/Versiyon/IsProgrami.aspx?Durum=EN

[64] The regime consists of Decree No. 96/7794, a Regulation, and Communiqués.

[65] US Commercial Service online information, "Doing Business in Turkey: 2011 Country Commercial Guide for US Companies". Viewed at: http://export.gov/turkey/doingbusinessinturkey/index.asp

[66] Communiqués on Standardization for Foreign Trade Nos. 2011/8, 2011/9, 2011/14, 2011/16, 2011/29, and 2011/39.

controlled by other legislation or subject to import rules or prohibitions, for example controlled or prohibited wastes, narcotics, chemical products, solid fuels, pharmaceuticals, and controlled or prohibited scrap metal.[67]

82. Technical regulations are prepared by Ministries and/or relevant public authorities and published in the *Official Gazette*. The Ministry of Economy oversees the process. It is responsible for the harmonization of horizontal Turkish technical regulations with EU technical legislation, and serves as the contact point for notifications to the European Commission of draft technical legislation transposing EU legislation.[68] Following consultations and amendments, the confirmed Turkish legislation is published in the Turkish *Official Gazette*.[69]

83. All technical regulations and conformity assessment procedures published and put into force by Ministries and other public authorities are published in the *Official Gazette*, which may be accessed via the Internet free of charge. Turkey does not publish notices of draft technical regulations and conformity assessment procedures; it has not notified to the WTO draft technical legislation that is being harmonized with EU legislation, as this legislation would already have been notified. However, given the growing importance of transparency at the international level, Turkey is reconsidering this policy, and the national TBT enquiry point is urging ministries and other public institutions to notify their technical regulations. Upon request, Turkey will provide the full text of draft measures (in English, if possible, otherwise in Turkish). Turkey generally allows a 60-day comment period.

84. The Communiqués on Standardization for Foreign Trade are revised annually to take account of issues arising from the implementation process or proposals and opinions gathered from the public and private sectors. In urgent situations, a Communiqué may also be amended in the course of the year. Modifications to the regime may include the elimination of technical regulations or conformity assessment procedures.[70]

85. Turkey's legislation for marking, labelling, and packaging, largely unchanged since 2007, is primarily based on three technical regulations: on marking, labelling and packaging of materials and products supplied packaged into the market (TS 4331), on the labelling of textile products (TS 1418), and on the marking by colours or alphanumeric system for electro-technical purposes (TS 6429). Clearly legible and visible labels displaying price, place of production, and distinctive characteristics must be affixed on retail goods, their packaging or their containers.[71] Where it is not possible to affix

[67] Communiqués on Standardization for Foreign Trade Nos. 2011/1 to 7, 2011/17, 2011/20, and 2011/23.

[68] Turkey participates in an EU-wide notification system for technical regulations, under Directive 98/34/EC. Turkey joined the system in 2002, provided its first notification in 2004, and has so far notified 36 national technical regulations.

[69] For "new approach" legislation, the European Commission and Turkey sign a statement confirming that the Turkish technical regulation and EU Directive are fully aligned.

[70] Since 2007, Turkey has abolished communiqués concerning imports of liquid fuels and cosmetics and detergents, reworked a communiqué on imports of hazardous waste and metal scrap into two separate communiqués, thereby eliminating the conformity assessment for imported metal scrap (except for customs checks for radiation contamination), and reduced significantly the number of products subject to inspection at Customs (see in particular Communiqués Nos. 2011/1 and 2011/9).

[71] Except for a few products, operating, user, and maintenance instruction manuals must be in Turkish and accompany each industrial product. Where goods and services offered to consumers may constitute a threat to the consumer's physical or mental health or the environment, it is obligatory to include information and warnings concerning this threat in a clearly legible and visible manner on the good or in the attached users' guides.

such labels on particular goods, clearly visible and accessible lists containing this information must be prepared and displayed. The same marking, labelling, and packaging requirements apply to domestic and imported products.

86. The Decree on Labelling and Packing referring to Law No. 1262 regulates the marking, packaging, and labelling of pharmaceuticals; and the Decree referring to the Law No. 3977 regulates the marking, packaging, and labelling of cosmetics. Tobacco products and alcoholic beverages must be affixed with strip-stamps with security markings designed to provide tax security, under Communiqué No. 1 on Tracking and Tracing System Related to Tobacco Products and Alcoholic Beverages pursuant to Article 257 (repeated) of the Tax Procedural Law No. 213.

(c) Conformity assessment procedures

87. Turkey's conformity assessment procedures vary according to whether the product is covered by transposed EU Directives, and the risk level of the product. All products covered by the EU's new approach Directives must carry the CE mark. For some products, the CE mark is obtained from bodies designated by the relevant public authorities and notified to the European Commission by the Ministry of Economy.[72] Other products are accompanied by a supplier's declaration of conformity (i.e. with the requirements of the CE mark). Products not covered by the new approach Directives must meet the requirements of the relevant Turkish technical regulations for market access.

88. High-risk products, and other products listed in the annexes of the Communiqués on Standardization for Foreign Trade, are required to meet additional testing. Certification and conformity assessment procedures are performed by the Ministry of Environment and Urbanization on environment-related products such as hazardous wastes, solid fuels, and metal scrap, and by the Ministry of Health on medical products, pharmaceuticals, and narcotic drugs. For a number of imported goods, the Ministries of Health; Food Agriculture and Livestock (MFAL); or Environment and Urbanization issue "control certificates".[73] The Ministry of Economy has appointed the TSE to carry out conformity assessment on imported industrial goods such as machinery, LVD, EMC, fittings, and piston rings.[74] The TSE also oversees industrial metrology and calibration, and laboratory services for conformity assessment and certification.[75] While high-risk products from the EU bearing a CE mark are not subject to the inspection and documentation requirements of the Communiqués on Standardization for Foreign Trade, imports from third countries are.[76] Import controls on products covered by other EU Directives are performed by product inspectors in the provincial offices of the Ministry of Economy. A new Turkish Product Safety System was launched in late 2010 to facilitate electronic risk-based export and import controls of goods.

---

[72] In all, 18 Turkish conformity assessment/certification bodies have been appointed as notified bodies to perform conformity assessment procedures against the requirements of 13 EU new approach directives.

[73] See Communiqués on Standardization for Foreign Trade Nos. 2011/5, 2011/6, 2011/17 and 2011/20. Control certificates are issued for products such as pharmaceuticals, certain medicines, organic chemicals, vaccines, chemicals, forestry materials, foodstuff, live animals and plants, grains and plant seeds, animal products, veterinary products, and hormones. The MFAL applies risk-analysis methods in controlling, *inter alia,* imported animals, plants, foodstuffs, seeds, and veterinary products.

[74] See Communiqués on Standardization for Foreign Trade Nos. 2011/1 and 2011/9.

[75] The scope of inspection services and the exact mode of operation by the TSE are set out annually in legislation issued by UFT: currently UFT Communiqué No. 2011/1.

[76] U.S. Commercial Service online information. Viewed at: http://export.gov/turkey/doing businessinturkey/index.asp

89. The TSE carries out certification services related to TS-EN-ISO 9001:2000; TS-EN-ISO 14001; TS 13001 (HACCP); and TS 18001 (OHSAS).[77] As of August 2007, the TSE had issued more than 52,000 products/services certificates.[78] The TSE is also involved in quality and system certification, and trains and certifies personnel in quality, environment, health, and safety. Mutual recognition of testing procedures is assured by agreements between Turkey and EU member states. The TSE joined the IEC System for Conformity Testing and Certification of Electrical Equipment (the IEC-EE CB Scheme) to ensure mutual recognition of results of tests performed in conformity with IEC standards on safety of electrical appliances in 1998, and the TSE became a signatory to various mutual recognition arrangements under the Low Voltage Directive (LVD) in 1999.

90. The Turkish Accreditation Agency (TURKAK), established in 2000, is responsible for accrediting domestic and foreign conformity assessment bodies and ensuring that they carry out laboratory, certification, and inspection services in accordance with international standards.[79] TURKAK is a full member of the European cooperation for Accreditation (EcA), the International Accreditation Forum (IAF), and the International Laboratory Accreditation Cooperation (ILAC). The Conformity Assessment Association (UDDer), established in 2006, brings together 65 Turkish stakeholders to support the development of conformity assessment activities in Turkey, including their recognition at national and international levels. Under Law No. 1705, the General Directorate of Measures and Standards of the Ministry of Science, Industry and Technology (MSIT) is responsible for quality control systems concerning legal metrology, establishment of calibration systems of test laboratories, and operating private laboratories in accordance with the Measurement and Calibration Law No. 3516 of 1989.

91. All products, imported or domestically produced, are subject to market surveillance activities, carried out by 10 public authorities.[80] The Ministry of Economy handles coordination between the authorities through the Market Surveillance Coordination Board. The Ministry prepares annual reports including information and statistics on the market surveillance activities.

92. Since 2007, Turkey has provided six notifications of technical regulations and conformity assessment procedures relating to measures for construction products, fertilizer, olive oil, foodstuff, and animal feed. In addition, a Turkey-Ukraine memorandum on Intent for Cooperation in the sphere of Technical Regulations, Standardization, Metrology, Conformity Assessment and Consumer Protection was notified to the WTO by Ukraine.[81] Turkey has also concluded various other

[77] Hazard Analysis and Critical Control Points is a systematic preventive approach to, *inter alia*, identify potential hazards. The Occupational Health and Safety Management System is an international occupational health and safety system specification. Certificates under the scope of TS-EN-ISO 9000 and TS-EN-ISO 14001 standards have been granted to 3,091 and 303 companies, respectively.

[78] Imports for own needs by producers with such certificates are exempted from inspection, as are imported inputs destined for use in manufactured products certified by the TSE.

[79] Turkey has almost 5,000 public and private laboratories, and 120 certification bodies. As of 30 September 2011, TURKAK had accredited 357 testing laboratories, 67 calibration laboratories, 3 medical laboratories, 72 inspection bodies, 53 quality management system certification bodies, 39 environment management system certification bodies, 16 food safety management system certification bodies, 5 medical devices management system certification bodies, information safety management system certification bodies, 27 product certification bodies, and 16 personnel management system certification bodies.

[80] The market surveillance authorities are the Ministries of Science, Industry and Technology; Customs and Trade; Labour and Social Security; Health; Food, Agriculture and Livestock; and Environment and Urban Planning; the Undersecretariat of the Prime Ministry for Maritime Affairs; the Energy Market Regulatory Authority; the Tobacco and Alcohol Market Regulatory Authority; and the Information and Communication Technologies Authority.

[81] WTO document G/TBT/10.7/N/89, 1 October 2008.

cooperation agreements, for example with China, EFTA member states, Israel, Bulgaria, Iran, and Lebanon on standardization, metrology, and conformity assessment.

93. Four specific trade concerns have been raised against Turkey in the TBT Committee since 2007.[82] Common features among the concerns have been the lack of transparency in the development and implementation of measures, incomplete and untimely notification to the WTO, and the insufficient time provided to adapt to the relevant requirements.[83]

(iii) Sanitary and phytosanitary measures

94. Turkey is a full member of the World Organization for Animal Health (OIE), the International Plant Protection Convention (IPPC), and the Codex Alimentarius Commission, and is harmonizing its legislation with the international standards set by these institutions.[84] Turkey's SPS legislation is primarily based on Law No. 5996 on Veterinary Services, Plant Health, Food and Feed (2010), which amalgamated a number of previous laws in this area; the Sanitary Law No. 1593 of 1930; the Fishery Law No. 1380, as amended by Law No. 3288 of 1986; the Turkish Food Codex Regulation (1997), currently under revision; and the Law on Agricultural Quarantine.[85] Turkey adopted a Biosafety Law and a related GMO Regulation in 2010, regulating all aspects of agricultural biotechnology in Turkey, and requiring food and feed products containing GMOs to be labeled as such.[86] Turkey continues to transpose the EU *acquis* into its food-related legislation.

95. Turkey makes no distinction between domestically produced and imported goods in its application of health and sanitary controls. Imports of agricultural products and foodstuffs require a control certificate issued by the Ministry of Food, Agriculture and Livestock (MFAL)[87]; the Ministry of Health issues control certificates for imported pharmaceutical products, drugs, certain consumable medical products, cosmetics, and detergents; and imported forestry materials require a control certificate issued by the Ministry of Environment and Urbanization in coordination with MFAL.[88] Lists of the products subject to control certificates are published annually. The related communiqué is prepared under the coordination of MFAL and the Ministry of Economy.

96. Depending on the type of product, the application to the relevant ministry for a control certificate should be accompanied by a pro forma invoice, a health certificate, a certificate of analysis, a formula or list of contents of the product, a pedigree certificate, and a radiation analysis report. The documents must be obtained from and/or approved by the relevant authorities in the producer country,

---

[82] The concerns relate to Turkey's product-tracking system for tobacco products and alcoholic beverages, inspections of imported medical equipment, documentation requirements for medical devices, and its GMP system for pharmaceuticals.

[83] See WTO documents G/TBT/M/42, 43, 47, 50, 51, 52, and 53. Meanwhile, Turkey has raised specific trade concerns with respect to three measures, and exercised its rights as a third party to two disputes related to the TBT Agreement (tuna products and clove cigarettes).

[84] For an extensive summary of Turkey's laws, regulations, and requirements see USDA Foreign Agriculture Service (2011).

[85] According to the Law on Agricultural Quarantine, live animals entering Turkey must be kept under quarantine for 21 days, and veterinary tests undertaken in the exporting country may be carried out again in Turkey.

[86] Following a proposal from the Biosafety Board, the GMO threshold level for labeling has been set at 0.9% for the approved genes.

[87] Annex VI of the Communiqué on the Standardization in Foreign Trade presents a List A for "products subject to control certificates", and a List B for "other products".

[88] In some cases, the certificate may be waived if the importer assures the authorities that the products are destined for specified purposes or for the manufacturer's own use.

and be in original language together with a translation into Turkish.[89] For live animals and certain animal products, the importer or those in charge of the shipment should obtain prior permission (i.e. before importation) from the competent authority. Certificates and other relevant documents should be presented during the controls at the point of entry or customs area where the actual importation takes place. Veterinary checks include verification of documents, identity controls, and physical checks. Control documents for non-animal-origin food and feed do not need to be submitted to the customs authorities in the course of importation.[90] The period of validity of control certificates ranges from four to twelve months, depending on the product.

97. Turkey has signed cooperation agreements to prevent animal diseases from entering the country through trade in and transit of live animals and animal products, veterinary medications, fodder, and other products that may affect animal health.[91] Moreover, bilateral agreements on a product-by-product basis have been signed with Belgium, France, Germany, Italy, the Netherlands, New Zealand, the United Kingdom, and the United States in relation to the use of sanitary and phytosanitary certificates.

98. Turkey faced its first avian influenza (AI) outbreak in October 2005, and further outbreaks followed in 2006 during which some 2.5 million birds were culled. No new human or bird cases of avian influenza have been reported in Turkey since April 2008. Vaccination campaigns against new strains of foot-and-mouth disease have been implemented effectively, and continued for other diseases such as brucellosis, sheep and goat plague, anthrax, sheep and goat pox, bluetongue, and Newcastle disease and rabies.

99. For the implementation of the Agreement on the Application of Sanitary and Phytosanitary Measures, Turkey's National Enquiry Point and Notification Authority is the General Directorate of Food and Control of the MFAL.[92] Turkey notifies new SPS measures affecting trade through the WTO, and a period of six months is foreseen before entry into force of the relevant regulations.

100. Since its last TPR in 2007, Turkey has provided 23 SPS-related notifications to the WTO, either as regular notifications or addenda or corrigenda to previous notifications.[93] One specific trade concern has been raised in the SPS Committee in relation to Turkey's new legislation on biosafety.[94] Turkey has exercised its third-party rights with respect to one recent dispute related to the SPS Agreement.[95]

---

[89] For food and food-contact materials, only health certificates must be obtained and/or approved by the relevant authorities in the producer country.

[90] Instead, the MFAL sends official letters to the relevant customs office specifying conformity or non-conformity.

[91] Turkey has signed cooperation agreements with Algeria, Bulgaria, Germany, Iran, the Netherlands, Syria, and Tunisia. Negotiations continue with Albania, Azerbaijan, Croatia, Czech Republic, Georgia, Kuwait, FYROM, the Russian Federation, Slovakia, and Ukraine.

[92] The Authority was previously the General Directorate of the Protection and Control of the Ministry of Agriculture and Rural Affairs.

[93] Turkey also publishes notices of SPS measures in its *Official Gazette*, and all SPS-related measures in force in Turkey are available at the GDFC website (http://www.gkgm.gov.tr/).

[94] See WTO documents G/SPS/R/59, paras. 30-33; G/SPS/R/61, paras. 34-36; and G/SPS/R/62 paras 59-61. In the past, concerns have been raised in relation to an import ban on livestock (1998), a ban on pet food imports related to transmissible spongiform encephalopathy (2000), and control certificates for banana imports (2001).

[95] WTO document DS392; "United States – Certain Measures Affecting Imports of Poultry from China".

(iv) Free zones, special economic areas

101. Free Zones Law No. 3218 of 15 June 1985 and the Free Zones Regulation of 1993 constitute the basic legal framework for the operation of Turkey's 19 free zones. The legislation is designed, *inter alia,* to promote foreign direct investment and joint ventures in export-oriented enterprises, provide easy access to imported raw materials and equipment on favourable terms, and to increase employment. Free zones are also targeted at regional development. The foundation and operation of the free zones are generally undertaken through a mix of government and private partnership (often within the framework of build-operate-transfer schemes, such as in the Aegean, Kocaeli, Adana-Yumurtalik, and Samsun free zones). Investors may construct their own premises in the free zones, but office space, workshops and warehouses are also available for rent. An operating licence is valid for maximum 15 years for tenant users (30 years for users building their own facilities). If the operating licence is for production, the validity term is extended to 20 and 45 years for tenant users and investors, respectively.

102. Financial incentives available to free-zone companies include exemption from payment of customs duties and fees; exemption from corporate, income, and value-added taxes; free repatriation of profits; 100% repatriation of capital without prior permission; and absence of foreign exchange restrictions. New arrangements for tax incentives in the free zones were introduced under Law No. 5084 of 29 January 2004 on the Encouragement of Investments and Employment. Pursuant to Law No. 5084, all exemptions except those already accorded to established firms were to be terminated by 31 December 2008. However, according to Law No. 5810 of 12 November 2008 (amending Law No. 3218) only free-zone users operating under a production licence may be exempted from income and corporate taxes. This exemption applies until the end of the taxation period of the year in which Turkey becomes a full member of the EU.[96]

103. Enterprises established in the free zones are active in a wide range of areas, including high-technology products, leather goods, and storage facilities. All industrial, commercial and service operations deemed appropriate by the Supreme Planning Board may be conducted in the Free Zones, under Article 10 of the Free Zones Regulation. Offshore banking and insurance business is not allowed. Customs broker activities may be conducted by acquiring either an activity licence or an entry permit document.[97] Entry into the zones of firearms and ammunition, radioactive substances, and dangerous and toxic wastes is prohibited (Article 32 of the Regulation). Inflammables, explosives, combustibles, fire-inducing substances or materials dangerous to other substances may only be brought into the zones with a special arrangement or facility for that purpose. The movement in and out of the zones of narcotic substances, psychotropic substances, and related chemical substances and their preparations are subject to national and international legislation implemented by the Ministry of Health.

104. Although foreign investors benefit from the same incentives as Turkish investors, and no limitation exists on foreign capital participation in investments in the free zones, most enterprises established in the zones are of Turkish origin. At the end of 2010, the free zones comprised 2,532 enterprises, of which 470 were foreign owned.[98] Sales from the free zones to the Turkish market outweigh sales to other countries (Table III.18). Sales into the domestic customs territory are

[96] Free zone users obtaining an operating licence other than for production after 6 February 2004 do not benefit from income and corporate tax exemptions. For tenants holding an operating licence on that date, the corporate tax exemption has remained applicable for the period of validity of the operating licence, whereas income tax on wages became payable as from 2009.

[97] Based on Article 50 of the Free Zones Implementation Regulation, modified on 22 April 2010.

[98] The corresponding number of operating licences was 3,235 and 598, respectively.

subject to Turkey's MFN import regime, including the payment of import duties and taxes.[99] Deliveries from the domestic market into the free zones constitute roughly one quarter of the "import" value of the zones. The domestic suppliers are not eligible for incentives applicable in the free zones.

Table III.18
Free zones trade, 2007-10
(US$ million and %)

	2007		2008		2009		2010	
	US$	%	US$	%	US$	%	US$	%
Free zones to domestic market	7,917	32,22	7,262	29,55	5,174	29,14	5,291	28,49
Domestic market to free zones	3,045	12,39	3,195	13	2,177	12,26	2,295	12,36
Other countries to free zones	8,300	33,78	8,248	33,56	5,493	30,93	6,626	35,67
Free zones to other countries	5,311	21,61	5,873	23,90	4,914	27,67	4,361	23,47
Total	24,573	100	24,578	100	17,757	100	18,572	100

Source: Information provided by the Turkish authorities.

(v) Transit

105. The basic provisions on customs formalities related to goods in transit are laid down in Articles 84 to 92 of the Customs Law. As a general rule, goods in transit are not examined by the customs administration at the point of entry. When deemed necessary, the consignments may be sealed or escorted by customs officials. In case of suspicion or denunciation, goods in transit may be inspected; if the principal so desires, he, his representative or the transporter should be present. The Ministry of Customs and Trade is authorized to adopt regulations regarding the examination of goods in transit and transit periods, transit routes, checkpoints or halting places for goods carried overland. Transit periods, transit routes, checkpoints or halting places are set out in the TIR Regulation. Competent regional directorates of the Ministry of Economy are entitled to authorize the transit of goods subject to import prohibition. Goods in transit are subject to customs fees for services rendered (e.g. for loading, unloading, sealing or warehousing).

(vi) Countertrade and barter

106. Turkey currently has no specific regulation on barter or countertrade as "Communiqué No. 4/2006 on Exportation Made through Counter-Purchase or Barter" was abolished through Communiqué No. 10/2008. Such practices must therefore be conducted pursuant to the Export Regulation.

107. Civil offset practices are managed by the Ministry of Economy and regulated by Communiqué No 6/2007. Two civil aviation offset projects, initiated in 1998 and 2000, were completed in 2008 and 2010, respectively.

(vii) Government procurement

108. Turkey's basic legislation on government procurement – the Public Procurement Law (PPL) No. 4734 of 2002 and the Public Procurement Contracts Law No. 4735 of 2002 – entered into force on 1 January 2003. The laws have been supplemented by the (i) Regulation on Implementation of Services Procurements; (ii) Regulation on Implementation of Goods Procurements; (iii) Regulation on

[99] Holders of operating licences issued before 6 February 2004 also pay a 0.1% (c.i.f. value) to 0.9% (f.o.b. value) fee on goods brought into the zone from aboard and/or sold from the zone into Turkey. The fee is not applied on operating licences issued currently.

Implementation of Works Procurements; (iv) Regulation on Implementation of Consultancy Services Procurements; (v) Regulation on Implementation of Electronic Procurement; and (vi) the Regulation on Administrative Applications against Procurements.

109. The Public Procurement Law (PPL) has been amended on several occasions, most notably in December 2008 through Law No. 5812, to align Turkey's public procurement legislation with the EU *acquis*. Modelled on EU Directives, Law No. 5812 introduced several new instruments such as prior notice; the availability of framework agreements for all contracting authorities; a standstill period (between the award decision and the conclusion of a contract); e-procurement provisions including electronic auctions, shorter time-limits for electronic publication of procurement notices, electronic availability of tender documents and procurement notices, and the establishment of an Electronic Public Procurement Platform (EPPP); simplified procedures involving shorter time-limits and reduced administrative burdens for potential suppliers; and tighter review procedures.[100]

110. The tendering procedures set out in the PPL are (i) open tenders, whereby all tenderers may submit bids, and notices are published not less than 40 days prior to the launch of the tendering process; (ii) restricted tenders, where the contracting entity invites tenders from selected bidders after an open-ended pre-qualification process[101]; and (iii) negotiated tenders, applied under certain conditions.[102] Direct procurement may be used in limited circumstances, for example when only one supplier exists or the procurement does not exceed TL 38,144 for contracting entities within metropolitan municipalities, or TL 12,709 for other contracting entities.[103]

111. The contracting officer must notify the results of the bid evaluation to all who have submitted tenders. If the awarded bidder does not take the contract, it is offered to the second most advantageous bid. The Public Procurement Contracts Law stipulates principles and procedures for the issuance and implementation of contracts awarded pursuant to the PPL, including required content, limitations to carrying-over, and cancellation provisions.

112. In accordance with the PPL (Article 53), the Public Procurement Authority (PPA) was established to ensure effective implementation of the legislation and proper application of the rules and procedures during tender proceedings. The Authority is administratively and financially autonomous, with a link to the Ministry of Finance. The PPA consists of a presidency, the Public Procurement Board (PPB), and service units.[104] The PPB is the main decision-making body of the Authority, examining complaints and, as necessary, taking corrective action including the

[100] Since 1 January 2007, notices relating to procurements covered by the PPL have not been published in hard copy, but posted on the electronic Public Procurement Bulletin, where contracting entities also advertise their tender decisions following the signing of the contract. Procurement notices, tender documents, and contract award decisions can be viewed by those concerned at the EPPP. As of 1 August 2011, the EPPP had more than 260,000 registered users, including over 22,000 registered contracting entities and some 17,000 registered tenderers.

[101] Pre-qualification notices are published not less than 14 days in advance of the deadline for the pre-qualification application, and a letter of invitation to tender is sent to all pre-qualified candidates at least 40 days prior to submission.

[102] Negotiated tenders are conducted in a two-stage process, with initial proposals covering aspects such as technical details and the means to fulfil the requirements of the contract, followed by the presentation of final offers, including the tender price. Negotiated tenders may be used, for example, when open or restricted tenders have been unsuccessful (i.e. no bids) or when technical or financial parameters have been found impossible to define.

[103] Publication of a tender notice is not required for direct procurements.

[104] The ten members of the PPB are appointed by the Council of Ministers and serve for a single, non-renewable five-year term.

determination of remedies, cancellation of tender decisions, or termination of tender proceedings.[105] The PPA changed its internal organization on 16 July 2008 to separate clearly its advisory and review functions so as to minimize the potential for conflicts of interest.

113. The Public Procurement Law covers most public entities and institutions governed by public law, under public control or using public funds (Articles 1 and 2). A separate section (Articles 48-52) regulates the procurement of consultancy services. Outside the scope of the PPL are procurements of some goods and services of certain public institutions (e.g. operators in the telecom, transport, energy, and water subsectors[106]); procurement related to defence, security, and intelligence needs; procurement carried out through foreign financing pursuant to international agreements; purchases of goods and services for research and development projects; procurement related to agriculture and livestock; purchases from the State Supply Office (DMO)[107]; and procurement by public entities abroad, e.g. embassies and consulates. The thresholds and monetary limits specified in the PPL are updated annually by the PPA according to the evolution of the Index of Wholesale Prices.[108]

114. A 15% price preference may be granted to domestic tenderers pursuant to Article 63 of the PPL. The preference is not applicable to joint ventures between Turkish and foreign companies.[109] The tenderers must present a certificate of origin, issued by the chamber of commerce in the area where the goods have been produced, to benefit from the preference margin.[110]

115. Although open and restricted tenders are the main procedures used, some concerns have been expressed that Turkey's public procurement policies are being undermined by resort to exceptions to the regulatory framework.[111] In 2010, 27% of public procurement contracts, representing 13% of the overall contract value, were not subject to the tender procedures stipulated in the PPL. Furthermore, the price preference clause was applied to 22% of the overall contract value (above the PPL threshold).

---

[105] For procurements carried out within the scope of Law No. 4734, complaints are addressed to the contracting entities and appeals forwarded to the PPA. The complaint and appeal applications are mandatory administrative paths to be exhausted before filing a lawsuit.

[106] For public banks, construction tenders fall within the scope of the PPL, while other procurements may be covered by the Banking Act No. 4603.

[107] Procurement by the DMO is covered by the PPL. The DMO was a central procuring entity, selling and reselling goods to other public institutions, before the enactment of Law No. 4734. All public institutions covered by the PPL are required to purchase from the DMO items such as paper and cardboard products, stationery and office materials, office machines and tools, furnishings, lighting and heating apparatus, cleaning equipment, vehicles and accessories, and other office stocks. The items available are announced by the DMO at the beginning of each year.

[108] Based on the index of the previous year, new revised values become effective on 1 February each year. In 2011, the thresholds above which foreigners were entitled to participate in tenders were TL 699,270 for goods and services to entities operating under the general or annexed budget (TL 1,165,451 for other entities within the scope of the PPL), and TL 25.64021 million for construction for administrations covered by the PPL. In case of emergency, the thresholds may be further updated upon a proposal by the PPA and approval by the Council of Ministers.

[109] Foreign-owned companies incorporated under Turkish law may qualify as domestic bidders.

[110] The chamber of commerce will require certain documents such as the industrial certificate of registration issued by MSIT or the food certificate of registration from MFAL.

[111] EU (2010) and USTR (2011). According to the European Commission, Turkey will need to revise its legislation to reduce the frequency of use of alternative procurement procedures.

116. Turkey has been participating as an observer in the WTO Committee on Government Procurement since June 1996.[112] As an observer, Turkey has been following the negotiations to revise the Agreement on Government Procurement.

(viii) State trading, state-owned enterprises, and privatization

117. Turkey's privatization programme, which began in 1984, is reducing the influence of the public sector in the Turkish economy. However, the State remains an important owner of banks, transportation companies, public utilities, energy and mining enterprises, and processors of certain agricultural commodities (Table III.19). Many of these operate under monopolistic conditions or hold exclusive rights, and their losses trigger budgetary transfers.

118. The privatization programme is carried out in accordance with Privatization Law No. 4046 of November 1994, as amended. The Privatization Administration (a temporary organization with a staff of approximately 250 civil servants) acts as the executive agency, while the Privatization High Council (four designated ministers acting under the presidency of the Prime Minister) is the decision-making body. The Privatization Administration may work with other relevant ministries and authorities in the privatization of specific public enterprises. The Competition Authority monitors privatizations, and its authorization is required for certain types of transactions before they become legally effective.[113]

119. Privatizations, which frequently involve ex-ante restructuring, are conducted through a variety of methods, including (i) asset sale or sale of shares (block sale and/or public offer); (ii) sale or transfer of operational rights; (iii) leasing; (iv) establishment of property rights other than ownership; and (v) a profit sharing model and other legal provisions depending on the nature of the business.[114] Assets are valued using at least two of the several valuation methods before they are put forward for tendering. The Tender Commission, which conducts the tender, may opt for public auction, closed bidding, closed bidding among designated bidders, or bargaining.[115] Once the Privatization High Council has approved the transaction, the Privatization Administration contacts the successful bidder to finalize the contract, the payment conditions, and the transfer of the assets. The Privatization High Council has established a "golden share" for five enterprises deemed to be of strategic importance: Turkish Airlines (THY); Turk Telekom; PETKIM (petrochemicals); ERDEMIR (iron and steel); and TUPRAS (petroleum refining).

[112] WTO document GPA/M/2, 23 July 1996.

[113] The broad merger-control provisions of Law on the Protection of Competition No. 4054 are also applicable to privatizations conducted by the State. For further details see WTO (2007).

[114] Public-private partnership is being developed as a financing model for future investments, for example for the construction of hospitals, highways and motorways, high-speed trains, and other infrastructure projects.

[115] The bids/bidders are evaluated on price and non-price commitments, as well as other relevant criteria, such as financial strength or sector experience. Tenders may be cancelled if no bids are received. Tenders have also been halted by the Council of State due to non-compliance with existing laws and regulations.

Table III.19
Selected public enterprises, 2011

Public enterprises	Activity	State ownership (%)	Related law
Manufacturing			
MKEK	Machinery and chemicals	100.00	Decree Law No. 233
DMO	Office supplies	100.00	Decree Law No. 233
SUMER HOLDING	Textiles	100.00	Law No. 4046
Mining			
ETI MADEN ISLETMELERI	Mining industry	100.00	Decree Law No. 233
TTK	Hard coal mining	100.00	Decree Law No. 233
TKI	Lignite mining	100.00	Decree Law No. 233
KBI	Copper	100.00	Law No. 4046
Electricity			
TEIAS	Electricity transmission	100.00	Decree Law No. 233
EUAS	Electricity generation	100.00	Decree Law No. 233
TETAS	Electricity contracting & wholesale	100.00	Decree Law No. 233
TEDAS	Asset owner of electricity distribution & retail sale	100.00	Decree Law No. 4046
TEMSAN	Electromechanic equipment	Subsidiary	Decree Law No. 233
YENIKÖY ELEKTRIK ÜRETIM	Electricity generation	100.00	Decree Law No. 233
KEMERKÖY ELEKTRIK ÜRETIM	Electricity generation	100.00	Decree Law No. 233
Petroleum			
TPAO	Crude oil exploration and production	100.00	Decree Law No. 233
BOTAS	Crude oil and natural gas transportation and natural gas import, transportation, distribution and sale	100.00	Decree Law No. 233
Agriculture			
TSFAS	Sugar processing	100.00	Law No. 4046
TMO	Trade of grain and other products	100.00	Decree Law No. 233
CAYKUR	Tea processing	100.00	Decree Law No. 233
TTA	Leaf, tobacco and salt	100.00	Law No. 4046
EBK	Meat, fish processing	100.00	Decree Law No. 233
Transportation			
TCDD	Railway services	100.00	Decree Law No. 233
TUDEMSAS	Railway transportation equipment	Subsidiary	Decree Law No. 233
TULOMSAS	Railway transportation equipment	Subsidiary	Decree Law No. 233
TUVASAS	Railway transportation equipment	Subsidiary	Decree Law No. 233
DHMI	Airports administration	100.00	Decree Law No. 233
KIYEM	Coast security	100.00	Decree Law No. 233
TDI	Seaports administration	100.00	Law No. 4046
THY	Airlines	49.12	Law No. 4046
Communication			
PTT	Post, telegraph	100.00	Decree Law No. 233
TURK TELEKOM	Telecommunication	31.68	Laws Nos. 4046 and 406
TURKSAT	Satellite communication and cable TV	100.00	Law No. 406
Banking			
TC ZIRAAT BANKASI	Banking (agricultural support credits)	100.00	Laws Nos. 4603 and 5411
T. HALKBANKASI A.S.	Banking	75.02	Law No. 4603 and 5411
T.KALKINMA.BANKASI A.S.	Banking (development)	99.08	Laws Nos. 4456 and 5411
T. IHRACAT KREDI BANKASI A.S. (T. EXIMBANK)	Banking (export credit)	100.00	Laws Nos. 3332 and 5411
T. VAKIFLAR BANKASI T.A.O.	Banking	58.45	Laws Nos. 6219 and 5411

Source: Information provided by the Turkish authorities.

120. Since 1986, Turkey has raised more than US$42 billion through privatizations carried out by the Privatization Administration.[116] The most significant transactions completed since 2003 are listed in Table III.20.[117] The Government has privatized all its cement manufacturing enterprises; a food chain store (GIMA); producers of animal feed, milk, and dairy products; the majority of the meat, fish and poultry processing companies; wood processing enterprises; a number of seaports; all shipyards; Turkish cargo lines; all refineries; a petrochemical processing company; the iron and steel industry; two commercial banks (Etibank and Sümerbank); and all textile manufacturing units owned by Sümerbank. The privatization of 19 electricity distribution companies began in 2008 and continued in 2010 and 2011. Nine power generation plants were sold in 2008, and the transfer of operating rights for 52 small and medium sized hydro-electric power stations was completed in 2010. The final tender of a 56.09% stake in DOĞUSAN A.Ş. (a manufacturer of concrete perlit tiles) has been finalized, technically.[118]

121. The Privatization Administration is planning to privatize 24 sugar processors by 2014. The companies have been grouped in six portfolios; tender announcements for three of these portfolios should be issued before the end of 2011. Preparations are advancing for the privatization of the two Bosphorous bridges, seven toll motorways, the Ankara and Izmir ring roads, and the service units operated by the Turkish Highways General Directorate. A first attempt to privatize the national lottery, in 2009, was unsuccessful. Technical studies to launch a re-tender are continuing.

122. The Turkish Red Crescent is the only state-trading enterprise that continues to be notified to the WTO by Turkey.[119] The non-profit, humanitarian aid organization holds exclusive rights to import certain drugs used in the fight against malaria and syphilis, i.e. cinchona bark, potassium iodide, alkaloids of cinchona and their derivatives (quinidine), and primaquine diphosphate. TEKEL, a former tobacco and alcohol state monopoly, was stripped of its exclusive import rights in 2001, and subsequently privatized.[120]

[116] Including privatizations conducted by other governmental institutions, Turkey's net proceeds from privatizations had reached US$53.5 billion at end-June 2011. The revenue from privatizations, dividends, and other financial income from enterprises in the privatization portfolio are channelled into the Privatization Fund. Costs relating to the privatization process, restructuring, operational losses, etc. are charged against the fund. Surplus cash is transferred to the Treasury pursuant to Article 10 of Law No. 4046. In 2010, the transfer to the Treasury amounted to US$1,714 million.

[117] The single most important transaction has been the privatization of Türk Telekom, when 55% of the company raised US$6.55 billion in a block sale to Ojer Telekomünikasyon A.Ş (a consortium led by Saud Oger and Telecom Italia) in 2005. A further 15% of the shares was sold in a public offering to local and foreign investors in late 2008, resulting in net proceeds of more than US$1.9 billion. No decision has yet been taken regarding the sale of the State's remaining stake of 31.68%.

[118] DOĞUSAN A.Ş. is listed on the Istanbul Stock Exchange, and the company's shares (43.91%) are tradeable there.

[119] The latest notification was circulated in WTO document G/STR/N/13/TUR, 21 June 2010.

[120] See WTO (2003) and WTO (2007).

Table III.20
Privatization, 2003-10

Privatized company	Sector	Year	Method of privatization	Amount (US$ million)
BURSAGAZ	Gas distribution	2004	Block sale	120
TEKEL (Turkish State monopoly)	Alcoholic beverages	2004	Block sale	292
TUGSAS-IGSAS	Gas distribution	2004	Block sale	100.5
THY	Airline transport	2004	23% PO	191.2
ETİ ALUMINIUM	Mining	2005	100% Block sale	305
TURK TELEKOM	Telecommunications	2005	55% Block sale	6,550
ISTANBUL HILTON OTEL	Tourism	2005	Asset sale	255
TUPRAS	Refining	2005	14% ISE	454
PETKIM	Petrochemicals	2005	34% ISE	274
TUPRAS	Refining	2006	51% Block sale	4,140
ERDEMIR	Iron & steel	2006	46% Block sale	2,770
BASAK INSURANCE COMPANY	Insurance	2006	100% Block sale	268
BUYUK EFES OTEL	Tourism	2006	100% Block sale	121.5
BUYUK TARABYA	Tourism	2006	100% Block sale	145.3
THY	Airline transport	2006	28.75% PO	207.8
HALKBANK	Banking	2007	25% IPO	1,839[a]
MERSIN PORT	Port operation	2007	36 years of concession	755[b]
GENERAL DIRECTORATE OF STATE HIGHWAYS (1st Levent Real Estate)	Real estate	2007	Asset sale	800
MOTOR VEHICLE INSPECTION STATION	Service	2007	20 years (concession)	614[c]
TURK TELEKOM	Telecommunications	2008	15% ISE	1,911
TEKELTURKISH TOBACCO	Tobacco products	2008	Asset sale	1,720
PETKIM	Petrochemical	2008	51% Block sale	2,040
ANKARA NATURAL ELECTRIC PRODUCTION	Electricity generation	2008	Sale of shares based in TOR	510
TEDAS BASKENT	Electricity distribution	2009	Sale of shares based in TOR	1,200
TEDAS SAKARYA	Electricity distribution	2009	Sale of shares based in TOR	600
TEDAS MERAM	Electricity distribution	2009	Sale of shares based in TOR	440
SAMSUN PORT	Port operation	2010	36 years (concession)	125.2
BANDIRMA PORT	Port operation	2010	36 years (concession)	175.5
TEDAŞ OSMANGAZİ	Electricity distribution	2010	Sale of shares based in TOR	485
TEDAŞ ÇAMLIBEL	Electricity distribution	2010	Sale of shares based in TOR	258.5
TEDAŞ ULUDAĞ	Electricity distribution	2010	Sale of shares based in TOR	940
TEDAŞ YESILIRMAK	Electricity distribution	2010	Sale of shares based in TOR	441.5
TEDAŞ FIRAT	Electricity distribution	2010	Sale of shares based in TOR	230.2
Total of all implementations (1986-2010)				**41,720**

a Approximately US$1.2 billion represents the portion allotted to foreign investors as of the transaction date.
b 40% of the amount represents foreign direct investment by the Port of Singapore Authority as of the transaction date.
c 30% of the amount represents foreign direct investment by the German enterprise TUV-SUD as of the transaction date.

Note: PO = Public offer; ISE = Istanbul Stock Exchange; IPO = Initial public offer; TOR = Transfer of operational rights.

Source: Prime Ministry (2010), *Privatization Administration - Annual Report 2010.* Viewed at: www.oib.gov.tr/2011/dosyalar/oib_faaliyet%202010_ING.pdf.

(ix) Competition policy

123. The Law on the Protection of Competition No. 4054, promulgated in 1994 and last amended in 2008, remains the principal legal basis for the promotion and enforcement of competitive

conditions in goods and services markets.[121] The Competition Authority, led by a seven-member Competition Board, has been responsible for the implementation and enforcement of the law since 1997.[122] Secondary legislation, mainly in the form of regulations, is prepared by the Authority and issued by the Board.[123]

124. Turkey's competition legislation addresses three principal issues: anti-competitive agreements, concerted practices, and decisions; abuse of dominant position; and mergers and acquisitions distorting the competitive structure of the market. Agreements distorting, restricting or preventing competition are in principle prohibited, unless the Competition Board grants an exemption (or block exemption). The Board may also grant negative clearance, thereby confirming that an agreement, decision, practice or proposed merger or acquisition transaction is not deemed contrary to the competition rules. Any practice affecting the Turkish market is within the scope of the law, including agreements concluded outside Turkey (the effects doctrine). Except for certain types of merger in banking, which are outside the scope of the Law, all sectors are covered.[124]

125. Pursuant to Articles 27(g) and 30(f) of the Law, the Competition Authority may provide opinions on draft legislation and administrative practices of other agencies and institutions. Thus, comments were made on a draft amendment to the bylaw on raw material and sugar prices in 2009, and on draft amendments to the Act on the Electricity Market, a draft bylaw by the Tobacco and Alcohol Market Regulatory Authority on the sale and display of tobacco products and alcoholic beverages, and on the tender specifications of the Turkish Football Federation in 2010.

126. In October 2009, the Competition Authority signed a protocol with the Public Procurement Agency to build a cooperation framework between the two agencies, aiming notably to deal effectively with bid rigging and to make public tenders more competitive.[125] Efforts to conclude agreements with the Energy Market Regulatory Authority and the Information and Communication Technologies Authority are ongoing. The Authority has been working closely with the Privatization Administration on the privatization of many state-owned enterprises.

127. The number of files concluded by the Competition Authority rose steadily between 2000 and 2008 (Table III.21).

---

[121] The Law was amended in 2008 through Law No. 5728. A bill to amend the Law, *inter alia,* introducing a *de minimis* rule and making mergers and acquisitions subject to a "significant lessening of competition" test, was submitted to the Grand National Assembly of Turkey in July 2008. This bill could not be enacted in the previous legislative period and therefore became invalid. The Government or members of the Grand National Assembly may renew the bill. The Competition Authority will try to ensure that the bill is renewed and enacted in the current legislative period.

[122] The Authority is financed by a 0.04% levy on the capital and capital increases of certain companies, budgetary transfers from the Ministry of Customs and Trade, and revenue *inter alia* from its publications.

[123] For example, in 2010 the Board issued communiqués clarifying the principles and procedures of hearings, right of access to files and the protection of trade secrets, and simplifying the notification rules for mergers and acquisitions by providing for a turnover threshold instead of the system based on thresholds and market share. In 2011, the Board issued guidelines on mergers and acquisitions regarding the undertakings concerned, turnover, and ancillary restraints.

[124] The Law does not apply to mergers and acquisitions where the sectoral share of the total assets of the banks involved is below 20%.

[125] The Authority has also signed a protocol with the Turkish International Cooperation and Development Agency to deliver technical assistance within the framework of Turkey's aid policy.

Table III.21
Cases handled by the Competition Authority, 2000-10

	2000-10	2005	2006	2007	2008	2009	2010
Competition infringements							
Files opened	**1,174**	84	108	131	166	395	..
Files concluded	**1,193**	97	108	148	132	178	252
Mergers/acquisitions							
Files opened	**1,543**	164	199	238	249	169	..
Files concluded	**1,782**	170	186	232	255	146	276
Negative clearance/exemption							
Files opened	**403**	45	36	34	65	40	..
Files concluded	**497**	50	33	39	57	46	96
Total							
Files opened	**3,120**	293	343	403	480	604	..
Files concluded	**3,472**	317	327	419	444	370	624

.. Not available.

Source: Information provided by the Turkish authorities.

(x) Price controls

128. Prices for goods and services are generally determined freely by the market in Turkey. However, price controls exist for electricity, natural gas, pharmaceuticals, telecommunication services, and transport (in particular rail transport). The Board of the Energy Market Regulatory Authority (EMRA) approves the tariff for electricity transmission and distribution, the wholesale price of the state-owned wholesale company, and retail sales to "non-eligible" consumers. The EMRA Board also approves the retail, transmission, storage, and city distribution tariffs for natural gas.

129. For pharmaceuticals, a reference price system is used to control ex-factory prices. Mandatory discounts on sales of pharmaceuticals to the public health system were increased in December 2009. A decree was issued in December 2010 outlining price reductions of 9.5% to be implemented during 2011. The Telecommunication Authority introduced price-cap mechanisms for services provided by Turk Telekom in 2002.

(xi) Trade-related intellectual property regime

130. The principal legislation constituting Turkey's legal framework for the protection of intellectual property rights includes the Law on Intellectual and Artistic Works (No. 5846), as amended; the Law on Evaluation, Classification and Support of Films (No. 5224); the Trade Mark Protection Decree (No. 556); the Geographical Indications Decree (No. 555); the Industrial Design Decree (No. 554); the Patent Rights Protection Decree (No. 551); the Law on the Protection of Plant Breeder's Rights for New Plant Varieties (No. 5042); the Seed Law (No. 5553); the Law on the Protection of Integrated Circuit Topographies (No. 5147); the Amending Law of Patent, Design, Geographical Indications and Trade Mark Decree (No. 4128); the Law Amending the Decree-Laws on the Protection of Patent, Industrial Designs, Geographical Indications and Trade Mark (No. 5194); the Law for the Establishment and Functions of the Turkish Patent Institute (Law No. 5000); and the Turkish Criminal Code (Articles 334/1 and 336/1), the new Commercial Code (Articles 55/1(b-3) and (d), and 56), and the Human Medicinal Products Licensing Regulation (Article 28), for ensuring the protection of undisclosed information. Turkey's intellectual property legislation was reviewed by the

WTO TRIPS Council in November 2000.[126] Turkey is a signatory to various IPR conventions and treaties (Table III.22). As intellectual property law is one of the negotiating chapters in the EU accession process, an EU-Turkey Working Group on Intellectual Property Rights has been established.[127]

Table III.22
Membership in international agreements, conventions, and treaties, 2010

Name	Date of membership
Paris Convention on the Protection of Industrial Property (1883)	10 October 1925
Berne Convention for the Protection of Literary and Artistic Works (1886)	1 January 1952
Convention establishing WIPO (1967)	12 May 1976
Rome Convention for the Protection of Performers, Producers of Phonograms and Broadcasting Organizations (1961)	8 April 2004
Nice Agreement concerning the International Classification of Goods and Services for the purpose of Registration of Marks (1957)	1 January 1996
Patent Co-operation Treaty (1970)	1 January 1996
Vienna Agreement Establishing an International Classification of the Figurative Elements of Marks (1973)	1 January 1996
Strasbourg Agreement Concerning the International Patent Classification (1971)	1 October 1996
Budapest Treaty on the International Recognition of the Deposit of Micro-Organisms for the Purpose of Patent Procedure (1977)	30 November 1998
Protocol relating to Madrid Agreement (1996)	1 January 1999
Locarno Agreement Establishing an International Classification for Industrial Designs (1968)	30 November 1998
Patent Law Treaty	2 June 2000
European Patent Convention (1973)	1 November 2000
Hague Agreement (International Deposit of Industrial Designs)	1 January 2005
Trademark Law Treaty	1 January 2005
Singapore Treaty on the Law of Trademarks	28 March 2006
WIPO Copyright Treaty	28 November 2008
WIPO Performances and Phonogram Treaty	28 November 2008

Source: Information provided by the Turkish authorities.

131. The main institutions responsible for intellectual property matters are the Directorate General of Copyrights and Cinema in the Ministry of Culture and Tourism for copyright and related rights; the Turkish Patent Institute for patents, trade marks, geographical indications, designs, and chip topographies; the Ministry of Food, Agriculture and Livestock for plant breeders' rights; the Directorate General of Customs in the Ministry of Customs and Trade for border measures; and the Ministry of Justice for enforcement before the courts.[128] The Intellectual and Industrial Property Coordination Board, set up in 2008, is convened twice a year to develop strategies for the implementation of the IPR regime and improve coordination between the relevant institutions.[129]

[126] WTO document IP/Q-Q4/TUR/1, 12 April 2001 contains the introductory statement made by Turkey, as well as the questions posed and answers given during the review. For an overview of the main substantive provisions of Turkey's IPR legislation see WTO (2003) and WTO (2007).

[127] The working group met for the first time in Ankara on 18 May 2011.

[128] See WTO (1998).

[129] The Board is composed of high-level representatives from the ministries of Justice, Interior, Health, Food, Agriculture and Livestock, Customs and Trade, and Economy; the Deputy Undersecretary of the Ministry of Development, the Director General of Copyright and Cinema; the President of the Turkish Patent Institute; TUBITAK; and the European Union Secretariat General.

Enforcement agencies include the Justice Academy, IPR police units, and the Anti-piracy Commission.

132. Since its last TPR, Turkey has amended the Law on Intellectual and Artistic Works to harmonize its provisions with the new Turkish Criminal Code and the Criminal Procedure Code (in 2008) and launched studies to amend the law further to eliminate remaining discrepancies with the EU *acquis*. Regulations have also been issued regarding the establishment of a joint IPR database, amending the banderole implementation system; and amending the certification system for enterprises' dissemination and distribution of intellectual and artistic works.[130] A circular on the use of licensed software in public institutions has also been issued.[131]

133. In the area of enforcement, Turkey has 22 specialized IPR courts (11 civil courts and 11 criminal courts).[132] In addition, general civil and criminal courts are competent to deal with IRP cases in cities where there are no specialized IPR courts. In November 2008, the General Directorate for Criminal Affairs at the Ministry of Justice announced that public prosecutors' offices handling more than 500 IPR investigations annually should establish a special bureau responsible for such investigations. Special bureaus have now been set up in seven cities (Adana, Bakirkoy, Beyoglu, Kadiköy, Kartal, Istanbul, and Izmir). In 234 of the 707 public prosecutors' offices in Turkey, one or more prosecutors have been assigned for IPR investigations. The specialized IPR courts are being linked to the Turkish Judiciary Information System (UYAP) network.

134. A copyright automation system (TEHAKSIS) has been established to provide online access to the Non-periodical Banderole Automation System[133], the Certification System, the Producers Certificate System, and the Optional Registration System, to facilitate the exchange of information between related institutions. Authority to grant online access has been delegated to the (81) provincial Cultural Directorates and the National Police to accelerate the inspections of the provincial Inspection Commissions. Furthermore, the Ministry of Justice and the Ministry of Culture and Tourism signed a protocol to integrate the UYAP and TEHAKSIS information systems in December 2010. After completion of the integration, the trial processes in cases involving intellectual property rights are expected to be shortened.

135. In 2008, Turkey's specialized criminal IPR courts concluded 7,762 cases. The average time span from receipt of a case until the rendering of a decision was 500 days. The specialized civil IPR courts concluded 2,765 cases in 2009, of which 1,279 were either fully or partially accepted. The average trial span in the specialized civil IPR courts was 613 days, ranging from 286 days in the

---

[130] The Regulation on Intellectual Property Joint Database, published in the *Official Gazette* on 6 November 2010; Regulation on the Amendment of the Regulation on the Procedures and Principles Related to Banderole Implementation (*Official Gazette*, 1 November 2010); and Regulation on the Amendment of the Regulation on Procedures and Principles Regarding the Certification of the Enterprises Performing the Record, Copying, Selling or Disseminating of the Materials on which Intellectual and Artistic Works are Fixed (*Official Gazette*, 4 March 2011). Banderoles are sold by collection societies. The Ministry of Culture and the Federation of Publisher Collecting Societies (YAYFED) signed a protocol on 6 April 2011 to activate the sale of non-periodicals banderole through the Federation.

[131] Circular on Use of Licensed Software at Public Institutions No. 2008/17, published in the *Official Gazette* on 16 July 2008.

[132] After the first specialized IPR courts were established in Istanbul in 2001, the number of such courts rose steadily to reach 23 in 2008. The Beyoglu court house was merged with the Istanbul court house in July 2011. Thus, the civil cases were transferred to the existing 4th civil IPR court of Istanbul, and the criminal cases to the 4th criminal IPR court of Istanbul, established by the same decision of the Supreme Council for Judges and Prosecutors.

[133] A banderole is a security strip, such as those found on cassette tapes or cigarette packets.

Bakirköy civil court to 1,137 days in the Istanbul 2nd civil court. The Turkish enforcement authorities normally conduct some 3,000-4,000 operations per year involving infringements of intellectual property rights. The volume of confiscated pirated materials was about 24-25 million pieces in 2009 and 2010.

136. Mechanisms for the collective management of rights have been further developed. Four collecting societies in the music sector signed a cooperation agreement in February 2007, and subsequently concluded collective agreements with professional associations representing the users for the licensing of musical works in hotels (March 2008) and in broadcasts (November 2008). The United Actors Collecting Society (BIROY) was formed in October 2009. Seven collecting societies operating in the cinema business founded the Headquarter of Collecting Societies of Cinema in January 2011.

137. Recognizing that Turkey has made progress in the fight against abuse of intellectual property rights, Turkey was moved from the U.S. Special 301 Priority Watch List to the Watch List in 2008. However, noting that counterfeiting and piracy remains widespread, Turkey is being urged to make further efforts.[134] The European Commission notes that further work is required, including the adoption of legislative amendments to provide deterrent criminal sanctions, a law on IPR enforcement procedures in line with the EU Enforcement Directive, and that the civil, criminal and administrative IPR procedures, including *ex-officio* measures to combat piracy and counterfeiting, should be strengthened.[135]

[134] USTR (2011).
[135] EU (2011).

IV. TRADE POLICIES BY SECTOR

(1) AGRICULTURE

(i) Main features

1. Agriculture remains a key sector in Turkey, although its share in the economy has been declining as a result of structural change towards services and industry.[1] Primary agriculture contributed 8.4% to GDP and 25.2% to employment in 2010, which implies that labour productivity was considerably lower than in the rest of the economy. Turkish agriculture is still dominated by small-scale and semi-subsistence family farms[2], which is why labour productivity has been lagging (the lowest among OECD countries).[3] Further integration of the large informal sector (i.e. much of Turkish agriculture) into the market economy requires substantial agricultural policy reform, and modernization of the agriculture sector.

2. Turkey ranks amongst the largest agricultural producers in the world. The main crop is wheat. In the period under review, the country has been a net-importer of wheat (over 90% self-sufficient) and corn (about 80% self-sufficient), and a net-exporter of barley.[4] Other major crops include fruit and vegetables, nuts, tobacco, cotton, and sugar. Irrigation is used for about half of Turkey's crop land, and agriculture accounts for about 75% of total water consumption. It is likely that agriculture will have to bear the main burden of adjusting to increasing water scarcity.[5] Turkey is one of the major milk producers in the world, predominantly for domestic consumption of cheese and yoghurt. While Turkey has specialized feedlots and dairy farms, and large-scale commercial poultry farms, livestock production is mainly extensive and small-scale. For livestock products, Turkey is more or less self-sufficient. Foot-and-mouth disease is endemic in parts of Turkey. The last outbreak occurred in 2009, according to the authorities, and the Trace region has been recognized by OIE as an FMD-free region, with vaccination in May 2010.

3. Turkey remains a net-exporter of agricultural products. Since its last Review, the share of agricultural trade (both imports and exports) in Turkey's trade in goods has increased (Tables AI.1 and AI.3). The main traditional exports include hazelnuts (largest exporter in the world), fruit and vegetables, and oriental tobacco. Turkey's main market for agricultural products is the EU, followed by the United States. Turkey uses export subsidies for a number of agricultural products.

(ii) Policy framework

4. As part of the structural reforms of the economy, following the Turkish financial crisis in 2001, the Government launched the Agricultural Reform Implementation Project (ARIP), which marked a significant policy shift towards liberalization and increased market-orientation of the agriculture sector. Steps were taken to abolish traditional instruments of support (administered prices for agricultural commodities, credit, and other input subsidies) and replace them with direct income support, cushioned by some transitional assistance.[6] The ARIP was phased out in 2008.

---

[1] The structural adjustment of the agriculture sector has been quite remarkable over the past decades; in 1980 agriculture's shares in Turkey's GDP and employment were at 23% and 50%, respectively.

[2] The average size of Turkey's 3 million farms is 5 hectares, and holdings are often split up into small parcels because of Turkish inheritance laws (OECD, 2011b).

[3] Ministry of Agriculture and Rural Affairs (undated), p. 13.

[4] Turkish Grain Board (2011).

[5] OECD (2010a).

[6] WTO (2003) and (2007).

5. Turkish agricultural policy is governed by the Agricultural Strategy 2006-10, the Agricultural Law (No. 5488) of 2006, and the Strategic Plan (2010-14), which were adopted with a view, *inter alia*, to aligning Turkey's agricultural policy more closely with the EU Common Agricultural Policy. Turkey's main policy objectives are food security and food safety, and raising the self-sufficiency level for selected net-imported products; improving productivity and competitiveness; ensuring sustainable farm incomes; rural development; and improving institutional capacity. The Agricultural Law provides for the continuation of the direct income support policy initiated under ARIP (45%), and specifies complementary instrument to support agriculture: deficiency payments (13%); compensatory and transitional payments (5%); livestock support (12%); crop insurance support (5%); rural development support (10%); environmental payments (5%); and other (5%).[7] Actual payments have diverged considerably from these targets since Turkey has moved away from direct income support towards deficiency payments and other instruments of support, mainly area-based payments. Agricultural support budget allocations for 2010 were: area-based support (38%)[8], deficiency payments (32%), livestock support (22%), rural development support (3%), agriculture insurance support (1.25%), compensatory payments (1.35%) and other (2.4%).

6. Since its last Review, Turkey has modified its rural development strategy. Beyond its traditional focus on infrastructure projects, rural development now embraces objectives such as income diversification (e.g. rural tourism), development of human resources, and the preservation of the environment. Rural development is crucial in Turkey, given that most of the rural labour force is employed in agriculture, and education and skills are lacking. As part of the accession partnership between Turkey and the EU, an IPARD framework was established (Pre-Accession Assistance Rural Development Programme), which sets out Turkey's measures for 2007-13 to achieve consistency with EU's rural development policy and the CAP.[9] The IPARD programme identifies the key sectors requiring further assistance to comply with EU regulations (dairy and meat, fruit and vegetables, and fisheries). IPARD measures (co-financed by the EU) include investment aid to modernize agricultural production, processing and marketing; capacity-building and support for producer groups; environmental measures, and diversification measures. In 2010, Turkey adopted a new national Rural Development Plan (2010-13), which focuses on rural employment, human resources and poverty, settlement and infrastructure, environment and natural resources. Projects involve co-financing the beneficiaries to mobilize private-sector resources.

7. Turkey's institutional and regulatory framework in agriculture is complex. A large number of institutions are involved in implementing agricultural policy, some of which have authority in regulating agricultural markets (including agricultural state-owned enterprises, the Turkish Sugar Authority; and the Tobacco and Alcoholic Market Regulatory Authority). In addition to the restructured Ministry of Food, Agriculture and Livestock, various agencies are responsible for channelling support payments or subsidized credit to farmers, including the Agricultural Bank of Turkey (Ziraat Bank), agricultural credit cooperatives, and agricultural sales cooperatives unions. A feature of Turkish agriculture is its widespread cooperative organization, ranging from production cooperatives (e.g. irrigation and sugar beet cooperatives) to credit and marketing cooperatives.

(iii) Border measures

8. Turkey's applied MFN tariffs on agricultural products, averaging 46.5% in 2011, are generally quite high compared with tariffs on non-agricultural products (WTO definition) (Table III.1). Applied tariffs are highest for meat and live animals, followed by dairy products (Chart III.2). SPS-related

---

[7] The numbers in parentheses indicate the Agricultural Strategy's targeted budget allocations for 2010.

[8] Area-based support encompasses a number of measures, including input subsidies, support for hazelnuts, support for organic farming, and soil analysis.

[9] Ministry of Agriculture and Rural Affairs (undated).

import restrictions on meat and live animals maintained since 1996 were relaxed in 2010 (Chapter III(3)(iii)). In 2010-11, Turkey allowed tariff-quota imports of beef and slaughter cattle.[10] Applied tariffs are comparatively low on production inputs and raw materials such as cotton, oilseeds, or seeds and breeding animals. Applied tariffs on some commodities such as wheat, rice, and red meat, have been adjusted temporarily to respond to supply and demand conditions on the domestic market. Turkey has some latitude in this regard, given the considerable gap between applied and bound tariffs (Chart III.2).

9. Applied MFN tariffs on processed agricultural products comprise an agricultural component and an industrial component: the latter is subject to the applicable EU common external tariff. For imports from the EU, the industrial component is duty free, while the agricultural component is subject to preferential tariffs. In addition, duty-free tariff quotas apply for imports of certain processed agricultural products from the EU.

10. Turkey has no WTO tariff-quota commitments but maintains numerous tariff quotas under preferential agreements (Table AIII.5). The Government has also been using unilateral tariff quotas as a trade policy instrument to facilitate imports. The Ministry of Economy is responsible for tariff quota licensing procedures. Tariff quotas are generally allocated on the basis of first-come-first-served and/or past-performance criteria, as published through communiqués in the *Official Gazette*. Under the past-performance method, part of the tariff quota is allocated equally to applicants and the remainder is allocated taking into consideration, *inter alia,* the import performance and the production and consumption rates of the importer/producers. There no charges or fees for tariff-quota applications.

(iv) Domestic programmes

(a) Direct income support

11. Direct income support was first introduced in 2001 to align Turkey's system of agricultural support with the "single payment scheme" under the EU reformed CAP. The payments to Turkish farmers were to partially compensate their income losses arising from the removal of administered prices (i.e. guaranteed minimum prices). Payments were set at a uniform rate, up to a ceiling of 50 ha, with no requirement to produce anything in order to receive the payment. Such schemes can help reduce the distortions in the agriculture sector since they are not linked to the type of crop or the volume of production. The DIS scheme covered about two thirds of Turkey's agricultural area in 2008 but was phased out in 2009. The National Farmer Registration System was established to implement the direct income support scheme. The OECD notes that "an accurate, reliable and transparent" registry is critical for the functioning of direct payments and other area-based payments.[11] It appears, however, that a lack of familiarity with decoupled payments, payments delays, and other concerns made the direct income support scheme unpopular among farmers. The authorities note that Turkish agricultural policy is in a process of transition and that the Government plans to provide direct payments in the future, while the agricultural support model applied in the EU will be adopted after full membership. Turkey is taking steps in this direction. The authorities expect that the Strategy on the Identification of Agricultural Lands, and the National Farmer Registration System will enable

[10] Tariff quotas were opened for 7,500 tonnes of beef at an in-quota tariff of 25% and for 16,000 tonnes of live slaughter cattle at 10% import duty. A duty-free tariff quota equivalent to 100,000 tonnes of live bovine animals (excluding for pure-bred breeding) has been allocated for the usage of the Meat and Fish Board until end 2011.

[11] OECD (2011b).

Turkey to meet the EU Land Parcel Identification System (LPIS) standards and enhance its capacity for implementing decoupled supports.[12]

12. Most of Turkey's domestic agricultural programmes provide incentives to producers through instruments such as deficiency payments or input subsidies, to stimulate production of selected net-imported crops and livestock products. For surplus crops, the Government tends to favour supply management through production controls or incentive payments encouraging farmers to switch to alternatives. There are also intervention purchase programmes implemented by state-owned enterprises (see next section).

(b) Deficiency payments

13. The effect of a deficiency payments scheme on production is similar to that of an administered price system as it guarantees producers a minimum price. During the review period, deficiency payments were granted mainly for wheat, cotton, sunflowers, maize, tea, barley, and milk (Table AIV.1). The deficiency payments are made in the form of premium payments per unit of output, and have varied considerably from year to year. The payment rates are determined on the basis of production costs, market conditions, and budgetary considerations. Sunflower seed, soybean, rapeseed, safflower, olive oil, cotton seed, and tea are the commodities eligible for deficiency payments in 2011. In 2010, a novel deficiency payment scheme was introduced, whereby payments per kg or head of livestock are differentiated between Turkey's 30 agricultural regions (basin-based support programme). The related legislation requires the Cabinet to determine "the agricultural basins where agricultural production is to be concentrated, supported, organized and specialized according to the regions' ecological conditions". The objective of the programme is to increase productivity, with crops to be produced based on the most suitable ecological conditions. The boundaries of these 30 agricultural basins were established in 2009, based on a model developed by the Ministry of Food, Agriculture and Livestock.

(c) Input subsidies

14. Input subsidies include concessional loans and support for livestock (see below) (Table AIV.1). Concessional loans carry a subsidy element ranging from 25% to 100%.[13] Diesel and fertilizer subsidies were introduced in 2007 to recipients of direct income support. While direct income support payments have been terminated, diesel and fertilizer subsidies continue. The subsidies are paid on a per-hectare basis and vary by crop. Diesel payments range from TL 2 to 5/ha for fruit and vegetables, to TL 60/ha for industrial crops; the respective fertilizer payments range from TL 3 to 5/ha to TL 60/ha. Insurance for crops and livestock against natural disasters was introduced in 2006; 50% of the premiums are subsidized (Agriculture Insurance Law No. 5363 of 2005).

(d) Livestock support

15. Domestic support for livestock includes milk incentive premiums for milk delivered to dairies (deficiency payments), support for imported breeding cattle for "livestock improvement" (Table AIV.1), support for artificial insemination, and feed crop premiums. Under the Investment

[12] The Government also plans to establish an Integrated Administration and Control System (IACS), a tool used by the EU for managing the system of payments to agricultural land and other instruments of the Common Agricultural Policy.

[13] Activities eligible for concessional loans include good agricultural practices, organic farming, production of certified seeds, agricultural research and development, breeding dairy cattle, irrigation, mechanization (except tractors and harvestors), greenhouse horticulture, medicinal crops, milking units, and cooling tanks.

Encouragement Programme (Chapter III(1)(iv) and (3)(i)), which has regional and horizontal objectives for the Turkish economy as a whole, certain investments in primary agriculture qualify for incentives (tariff and tax exemptions, interest rate subsidies). Eligible investments include dairy farms with at least 150 cattle and dairy product manufacturing, integrated with fodder production and/or cold storage warehouse; feedlots (with at least 150 cattle per fattening period) integrated with a slaughterhouse and cold storage warehouse and/or fodder production unit and/or meat production unit; greenhouse production; and mushroom cultivation.[14]

(e) Production controls

16. Under ARIP, one-off transitional payments were made to producers of hazelnuts and tobacco to address structural surpluses and to encourage farmers to grow alternative (deficit) crops, such as oilseeds, feed crops, and corn. The deadline for production control measures in tea with income compensation payments expired in August 2011 (i.e. payments for pruning, after which tea leaf output drops). As previous measures to control hazelnut production have proved ineffective, according to the OECD, hazelnut producers have received payments since 2009 based on a fixed area (TL 1,500/ha per year).[15] Sugar beet production is restricted through a national sugar quota (2.2 million tonnes in 2011). The quota is fixed annually by the Sugar Board and allocated to sugar factories.

(f) Environmental measures

17. Environmental issues, particularly soil erosion and overuse of water resources because of poor water management, have become a concern in Turkish agriculture, as reflected in Turkey's Agricultural Strategy and the Rural Development Strategy. Since 2005, environmental payments have been made under the Environmentally Based Agricultural Land Protection Programme (ÇATAK), to compensate farmers for setting aside land and using soil conservation techniques in environmentally vulnerable areas (see "land compensation" in Table AIV.1).[16] Area-based payments range from TL 300 to TL 1,350 per ha. Organic farming and "good agricultural practices", aimed, *inter alia,* at protecting natural resources, traceability, and food safety, are also supported. Support under good agricultural practices is at TL 200/ha for fruits and vegetables, TL 800/ha for greenhouses, and TL 250/ha for organic farming.

(v) Agricultural state-owned enterprises

18. Some agricultural state-owned enterprises (SOEs) continue to play a role in production, processing, and marketing of agricultural products, and in supporting and regulating designated agricultural commodity markets on behalf of the Government but, overall, the significance of SOEs has diminished. SOEs include the Turkish Grain Board (TMO), the Turkish Sugar Factories Corporation (TŞFAŞ), the Tobacco, Tobacco Products, Salt and Alcohol Enterprise Corporation (TTA), the Meat and Fish Board (EBK), and ÇAYKUR (tea) (Table III.19). Budgetary transfers to cover the debts and "duty losses" of SOEs have been substantial (Table AIV.1). The TTA[17] and the TŞFAŞ are in the process of privatization, while the TMO (for cereals) and EBK (meat processing) are to be restructured as paying agencies in accordance with the EU harmonization programme.

[14] WTO document G/SCM/N/186/TUR, 2 March 2010.
[15] OECD (2011b).
[16] Soil Conservation and Land Use Law No. 5403. See WTO (2007).
[17] Formerly named TEKEL; the tobacco production unit of TEKEL was privatized in 2008 (OECD, 2011b).

19. Most administered prices, including for cereals and paddy rice, have been abolished since 2002. However, some of the SOEs, such as the TMO, continue to set purchase/intervention prices, which, according to the authorities, are fixed by the respective board of directors in line with market conditions. With the exception of opium, the SOEs do not operate as the sole buyer or seller in the domestic market nor do they hold an export monopoly.[18] The TMO had a maximum market share of 18% in 2007-10 in terms of purchases of Turkey's annual wheat production (17% for barley, and 19% for corn).[19]

20. The OECD notes that agricultural SOEs have systematically benefited from payments from the Treasury to bridge the gap between purchase/intervention prices and export prices (duty loss) (Table AIV.1).[20] Article 35 of Decree law No. 233 provides that a "duty loss" may occur (i) when SOEs are assigned a task (duty) related to their activities by the Council of Ministers and a loss occurs or profit is forgone due to this task; and (ii) when prices of the goods and services produced by SOEs are determined by the Council of Ministers and these prices are below cost. The authorities claim that no export subsidies are being implemented by state-owned enterprises. They note that SOE losses arise from various "duties", including hazelnut purchases and sales.

21. The TMO sells domestic wheat at world market prices to domestic manufacturers of flour and pasta in volumes that are related to their exports of flour and pasta; and exports surplus stocks through international competitive tenders (in accordance with the Turkish Grain Board Tender Regulation).[21] TMO is also responsible for holding emergency stocks (Decree Law 2006/10506). These activities have involved duty losses, as domestic wheat prices have been substantially higher than world market prices.[22]

22. In tobacco, the export share of TEKEL/TTA (compared with the private sector) varied between 29% and 68% in volume terms in 2007-10. The TTA does not enter into contracts for tobacco production nor does it purchase tobacco from other firms. ÇAYKUR export prices for tea are determined by its Board of Directors on the basis of world market prices. Manufacturers that use sugar as a raw material are eligible to purchase domestic sugar production at world market prices (C sugar).

(vi) Export measures

23. Turkey maintains an export subsidy programme for agricultural products with the aim of developing its export potential in value-added processed agricultural products.[23] Sixteen product groups are eligible to receive export subsidies (Table AIV.2). Turkey's WTO export subsidy reduction commitments cover 44 product groups (at the HS four-digit level).[24] Export subsidies are

[18] The TMO is responsible for purchasing and exporting all of Turkey's opium production at prices announced by Council of Ministers' Decision.

[19] The TMO's purchase (intervention) prices and sales prices are determined, taking into account "production costs, inflation rate, production quantity, developments in the world markets, prices of previous year and sustainability of the production". See Turkish Grain Board (2011).

[20] OECD (2011b), p. 43.

[21] In the Committee on Agriculture, Turkey responded to questions regarding implementation of its commitments for exports of wheat flour (WTO document G/AG/R/51, 6 June 2008).

[22] Directorate General of State Owned Enterprises (2008), p. 84. See also Undersecretariat of Treasury online information, "State Owned Enterprises Statistics". Viewed at: http://www.treasury.gov.tr/irj/portal/anonymous?NavigationTarget=navurl://263c93ab665e5050055e7fe7606 abf8f &LightDTNKnobID=-1969438794.

[23] WTO document G/SCM/N/186/TUR, 2 March 2010.

[24] WTO online information. Viewed at: http://www.wto.org/english/thewto_e/countries_e/turkey_e.htm.

granted in the form of reductions of the exporters' debts *vis-à-vis* public corporations (for example, deduction of taxes, telecommunications or energy bills). Export refunds are specified through annual decree and administered by the Ministry of Economy; goods must be of Turkish origin and of marketable quality. All destinations are eligible, including to the EU.

24. Exporters of agricultural products are eligible for generally available export credits (Chapter III(2)(iv)). Export taxes are levied on hazelnuts and raw skins (Chapter III(2)(ii)). Turkey prohibits exports of a number of agricultural products (Table III.14). Export licensing applies to sugar and feedstuffs for monitoring purposes (Table III.15).

(vii) Evolution of support and protection

25. This overview of support and protection of Turkish agriculture relies to a large extent on OECD data and analysis, since Turkey has not provided any domestic support and export subsidy notifications to the WTO since 2002. Members have expressed concern about Turkey's outstanding notifications in the Committee on Agriculture.[25] Since its last Review, Turkey has abandoned its direct income support policy and increased considerably the level of market price support, deficiency payments, and other production-stimulating instruments of support, in particular on net-imported products.[26]

26. Market price support remains the main instrument of support to Turkish agriculture: it encompasses all policy measures that raise the domestic price relative to the border price of the commodity concerned, including border measures (tariffs, tariff quotas, and other import restrictions); intervention prices, and export subsidies. In the period under review, about 80% of Turkey's Producer Support Estimate (PSE)[27] has been production-stimulating market price support, pushing domestic commodity prices above international prices and "taxing" Turkey's consumers in a manner that is not transparent for them (the remaining 20% has been budgetary payments under domestic programmes). Turkey's market price support has increased in recent years, mainly due to higher domestic prices rather than lower world market prices. However, market price support tends to be capitalized in the value of agricultural land, as a result of which only a small fraction of the support ends up as farmers' income; it also impedes expansion in farm size and growth in productivity. Moreover, market price support distorts the price signals for farmers to respond to market demand and produce the products in which Turkey has a comparative advantage. Green Box measures have low priority in Turkey's agricultural budget, although experience from other countries shows that research, training, and extension have positive long-term effects for productivity and competitiveness.

27. The nominal protection coefficients (NPC) of some of the main commodities are generally higher than the OECD average, reflecting Turkey's high levels of market price support.[28] The average NPC was 1.23 in 2010, meaning that Turkey's average producer prices were about 23% higher than border prices (Chart IV.1).[29] The effective protection rates may be lower for products where negative tariff escalation exists, for example, processed dairy, meat and grain products.

[25] WTO document G/AG/R/60, 19 January 2011, p. 6.

[26] Turkey has no domestic support reduction (AMS) commitments under the Agreement on Agriculture. The applicable *de minimis* ceiling of support is 10% of the value of production.

[27] PSE is total annual monetary transfers to farmers individually (not agriculture generally) from: market price support mainly through border measures but also food aid, export subsidies (calculated by the price gap between domestic and border price); payments to farmers; and tax/fee reductions (revenue forgone).

[28] The average producer price includes payments based on current output, e.g. deficiency payments, which are not included in the estimate of market price support.

[29] OECD (2011a).

Chart IV.1
Nominal Protection Coefficients of selected agricultural commodities
2007-09 average

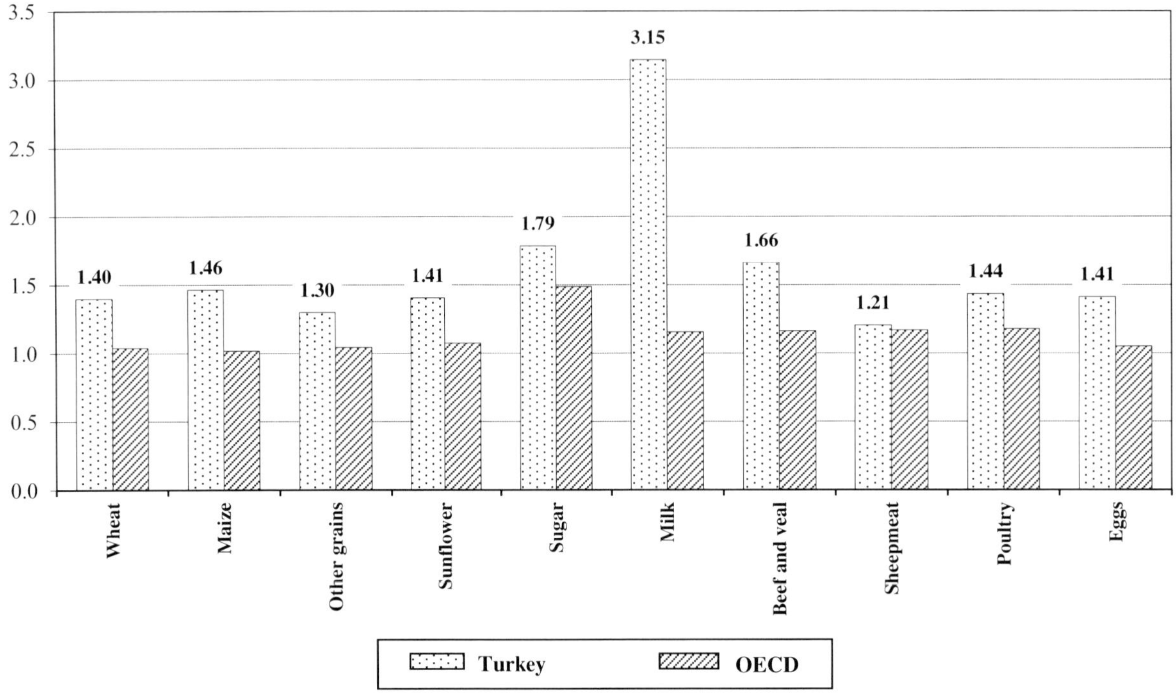

Source: OECD, PSE/CSE database, 2010.

28. Overall, thought substantial increases in support and protection for agriculture, Turkey's agriculture has become less market oriented. According to the OECD, the level of support (PSE) in Turkey, measured as a percentage of gross farm revenues, declined in relative terms from 38% in 2006 to 25% in 2008 rising to 28%, in 2010, meaning that 28% of farmers' revenues were due to support policies (financial support, tariff and other border protection).[30] While the long-term OECD trend has been declining levels of support (percentage PSE), Turkey has been moving in the opposite direction (Chart IV.2). Turkey's percentage PSE has long been lower than the OECD average, but now exceeds it. Moreover, contrary to the OECD trend, Turkey continues to deliver most of its support and protection in the potentially most trade-distorting manner (support tied to production or input use). Turkey has become an outlier in the OECD because (i) the value of its support to agricultural producers (in absolute terms and as a percentage of the agricultural production value) is increasing; and (ii) an increasing portion of its support is provided in the most trade-distorting ways.

[30] The percentage PSE is a useful indicator for comparisons over time and among countries, *inter alia*, because it eliminates the effect of inflation.

Chart IV.2
Turkey's level and composition of support to agricultural producers

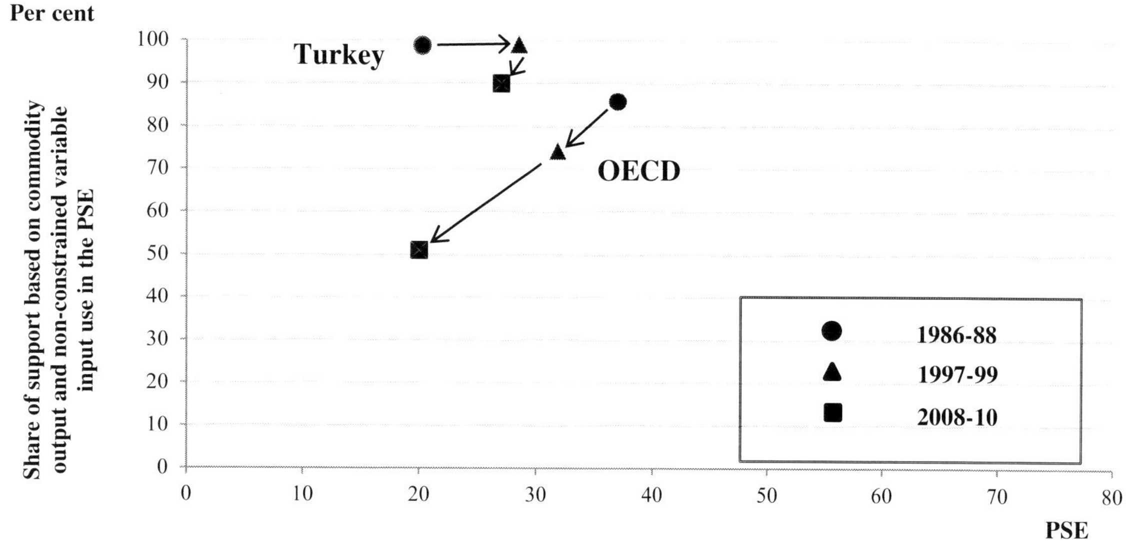

Note: The level of support is presented by the percentage PSE. The composition of support is presented by the share in gross farm receipts of market price support, payments based on output and payments based on non-constrained variable input use.

Source: OECD, PSE/CSE database, 2010.

(2) ENERGY

29. Turkey's primary energy consumption totalled 80.5 million tonnes of oil equivalent (toe) in 2009. Although consumption declined between 2007 and 2008 due to the slowdown of economic activity, on average Turkey's energy market has expanded by 4% annually over the past decade. Fossil fuels (coal, oil, natural gas) constitute almost 90% of the present energy supply. As Turkey has a young and urbanizing population and its per capita consumption is still below the average of industrialized countries, it is expected to experience the fastest medium- to long-term growth in energy demand among members of the International Energy Agency.[31] By 2020, Turkey's primary energy demand is expected to reach 222 million toe.

30. The projected increase in energy demand will require considerable investments to expand the energy infrastructure. As the private sector is expected to lead the way in financing these investments, the Turkish Government has taken steps to reduce its own involvement on the supply side, and provide a more transparent, predictable, liberalized and competitive framework for privately owned operators in the energy market. Between 2001 and 2007, Turkey passed new legislation to reform the energy sector, including the Electricity Market Law (2001), the Natural Gas Market Law (2001), the Petroleum Market Law (2003), the Liquefied Petroleum Gas (LPG) Market Law (2005), the Law on the Utilization of Renewable Energy Sources for the Purpose of Generating Electrical Energy (2005), the Energy Efficiency Law (2007), the Law on Geothermal Resources and Natural Mineral Waters (2007), and the Law on Construction and Operation of Nuclear Power Plants and Energy Sale (2007). The Energy Market Regulatory Authority (EMRA) was established in 2001 to perform independent regulation and supervision of the market and its operators. Despite the reform efforts, Turkey's market for petroleum and petroleum products is still dominated by large state-owned

[31] IEA (2009).

or former state-owned enterprises, i.e. the Turkish State Petroleum Company (TPAO), the Turkish Petroleum Refinery Corporation (TÜPRAŞ), and the Petroleum Pipeline Corporation (BOTAŞ).

(i) Oil and oil products

31. Turkey has its own resources of oil and natural gas, but domestic production covers no more than 8% of its needs. Turkey's oil resources are owned by the State, which grants licences for exploration and production. TPAO, which is wholly state-owned, accounts for almost 75% of domestic production, the remainder is extracted by smaller independent upstream companies. Imported crude oil (17.3 million tonnes in 2010) is predominantly sourced from Iran, the Russian Federation, Saudi Arabia, and Iraq.

32. TÜPRAŞ, which was privatized in stages in 2005 and 2006, controls nearly all the refining capacity in Turkey.[32] However, the EMRA has issued licences to two enterprises to build new refining capacity, as well as wholesale licences to 52 domestic and foreign companies. In 2010, the wholesale enterprises imported some 8.5 million tonnes of petroleum products. Turkey also imported 3.7 million tonnes of liquefied petroleum gas in 2010, supplementing domestic production of 650,000 tonnes.[33] The EMRA has licensed nearly 24,000 operators to engage in importation, refining, transportation, storage, wholesale or retail trade in petroleum products and LPG by the end of 2010. The pricing of petroleum products was liberalized on 1 January 2005.

33. The main objective of Turkey's energy policy is to ensure supply security. The stockholding capacity remains limited. On the other hand, Turkey has secured agreements with some of the world's major suppliers of oil and gas in its vicinity. The agreements have also enhanced Turkey's status as an important transit country. Two major international oil pipelines cross Turkey: the Iraq-Turkey pipeline with a throughput capacity of 1.4 million barrels/day and the Baku-Tbilisi-Ceyhan crude oil pipeline, which may transport 1.2 million barrels/day. Further pipeline projects are under consideration.

(ii) Natural gas

34. Turkey's consumption of natural gas has increased rapidly since it was introduced as a source of energy on a commercial scale in 1987. In 2008, natural gas overtook oil as the principal source of primary energy. Of the 37.4 billion cubic metres consumed in 2010, around half was used in gas-fired power plants; industrial and other commercial users took 32%, while households consumed the remaining 17% (district heating, cooking, etc.). As Turkey's domestic production of natural gas is now negligible, the gas is mostly imported on long-term (20 to 25-year) contracts. Turkey has concluded eight sales and purchase agreements with six supplying countries; the Russian Federation, Turkmenistan, Iran, Azerbaijan, Algeria, and Nigeria. The natural gas from the Russian Federation, Iran, and Azerbaijan arrives via pipelines, while gas from Algeria and Nigeria is shipped in the form of LNG.[34] Turkey has a connection with Greece for export purposes. Planned pipeline projects may further diversify Turkey's sources of imports and strengthen its role as a transit country. In particular, the Nabucco Pipeline Project, linking consumers in Central and Eastern Europe with gas from the Caspian Sea and possibly also suppliers in the Middle East, gives Turkey a key role in opening the fourth supply corridor for natural gas into Europe.

---

[32] TÜPRAŞ is currently a joint-venture between Koç (51%) and Shell (49%).

[33] A particular feature of the Turkish market is the use of LPG as an automotive fuel.

[34] Although the 30-year contract with Turkmenistan was signed in 1999, implementation still requires the establishment of transit regimes and the construction of pipelines.

35. The purpose of the 2001 Natural Gas Market Law was to harmonize Turkey's legislation with the EU *acquis*, reduce the role of the State in the sector, and establish a truly competitive gas market in Turkey, thus breaking up the monopoly of BOTAŞ. Unbundling its transmission, distribution, and trading activities (by 2011), the intention has been to privatize the storage and trading arms of BOTAŞ. The state-owned company will continue to operate a monopoly on the pipeline transmission grid, with private companies operating competitively in all other segments of the market.

36. The EMRA, the licensing, regulatory, and surveillance authority, began issuing licences to operators in the natural gas market in November 2002, and had issued a total of 198 licences by May 2010. However, even though the Law envisaged limiting the share of any importer or wholesaler to maximum 20% of the market by 2009, BOTAŞ still dominates the wholesale market for natural gas. BOTAŞ was given the option of reducing its share by contract transfer or volume transfers to private enterprises, but the implementation of the contract release programme has been slow. A tender for 4 billion cubic metres per year for 15 years (12% of the current import volume) was held in 2005. All four companies that won the tender had begun importing gas by April 2009. Nevertheless, as suppliers of gas have been reluctant to conclude contracts with companies other than BOTAŞ, its share of Turkey's gas imports remained at 84% in 2010.[35]

37. Turkey has been significantly more successful in its deregulation efforts on the distribution side. In order to stimulate the use of natural gas in district heating, Turkey has been divided into 60 distribution regions, with the EMRA awarding distribution licences through an auction system. Successful bidders have also undertaken commitments to invest in extensions of the local distribution networks. Except for two regions (Istanbul and Ankara), where privatization is currently under way, the distribution of natural gas in Turkey's cities is now in the hands of the private sector. As for power generation, the privatization process for the Hamitabat gas-based power plant, owned by the Electricity Generation Co. Inc. (EÜAŞ), commenced in 2011.

38. Third-party access to the distribution and transmission network is regulated and non-discriminatory. The operators must demonstrate to the EMRA that their operations are cost-efficient and reliable. The EMRA regulates and approves transmission and all retail tariffs, and will continue to regulate storage tariffs until the market has become more competitive. The tariffs set by the distribution companies comprise the city-gate gas price paid to the suppliers plus a service and depreciation charge, determined by their tender.

(iii) Coal

39. Turkey has significant proven reserves of coal, mostly lignite.[36] The domestic coal is primarily absorbed in electricity generation (87%), but locally mined coal is also used in industrial processes as well as for heating. Turkey's production of lignite rose by nearly 10 million tonnes from 2000 to 2010 due to the rising demand for electricity. Turkey is self-sufficient in lignite consumption, whereas it imports around 90% of hard coal demand. Hard coal is imported in the form of steam coal from the Russian Federation, and coking coal from the United States and other suppliers (e.g. Australia, Colombia, South Africa).

40. Of the 72 million tonnes of coal mined in Turkey in 2010, 92% was produced by three state-owned companies (the Turkish Coal Enterprises (TKI), the Electricity Generation Co. Inc. (EÜAŞ), and the Turkish Hardcoal Enterprises (TTK). However, as much as 35% of their reported production

[35] The Law was amended in 2008 to liberalize spot and long-term imports of LNG. By 2011, 26 companies (including BOTAŞ) had been granted import licences for LNG.

[36] The quality of Turkish lignite is generally poor.

is effectively mined by sub-contracted private-sector companies.[37] TKI and TTK determine their own prices for hard coal and lignite, taking into account world market prices, but the Turkish Government may also intervene in the price setting for economic or social reasons.

41. Large-scale surface operations allow lignite to be produced at relatively low cost in Turkey. TKI has therefore been able to establish prices that cover its costs, and the company has been profitable since 1995. By contrast, TTK's production costs are well above comparable world market prices for the end product.[38] TTK accumulated losses of some US$2.3 billion between 2000 and 2009, covered by capital injections from the Treasury. In 2010, TTK losses amounted to approximately TL 450 million, or nearly US$30,000 per employee. The Treasury and other related institutions have launched a study to restructure TTK to minimize the company's losses.

(iv) Electricity

42. The demand for electricity in Turkey has followed the same trend as the expansion in output over the last ten years, but at a faster pace.[39] Projections suggest that the consumption of electricity, which was 209 billion kWh in 2010, may rise to 370-390 billion kWh by 2019. At present, roughly half of Turkey's electricity is generated in gas-fired power stations, one quarter is derived from the burning of coal, and the remaining quarter consists of hydropower and other renewable sources of energy. Turkey's power grid is linked to its neighbours, and some exchanges of electricity take place in the course of the year; however, the volumes are modest.[40]

43. The 2001 Electricity Market Law, amended in 2008, and secondary legislation pertaining to licensing, tariffs, grids, distribution, imports and exports, and balancing and settlement, constitutes the legal framework regulating the sector. The 2001 Law unbundled the vertically integrated state-owned electricity company (TEAŞ) into three separate entities responsible for generation (EÜAŞ), transmission (TEIAŞ), and wholesale trade (TETAŞ). The Turkish Electricity Distribution Company (TEDAŞ) was also restructured in 2005, and regional distribution companies were formed and prepared for privatization. Private-sector participation in power generation and distribution has been allowed since the mid 1990s, and the EMRA has become the regulator and licensing authority for all operators engaged in generation, transmission, distribution, wholesale, retail, importation, and exportation.[41] The regime foresees the dominance of private enterprises in all activities, except transmission. Licences are granted for minimum 10 years and maximum 49 years.[42] Further plans for reforms, including a road map for a new wholesale market regime, are outlined in the Electricity Market and Security of Supply Strategy Paper of May 2009. A major step was taken in early 2011 as customers purchasing more than 30,000 kWh per year were allowed to enter the wholesale market and

[37] TKI has leased or sold some of its mines to the private sector. EÜAŞ tendered a contract to produce and supply lignite to one of its power stations in 2007. A subsequent tender for another two power stations was eventually cancelled after evaluation of the bids. Pursuant to the Mining Law (2004), the TTK has used an option to transfer some of its rights to private undertakings on a royalty payment basis.

[38] Due to the geological conditions at the existing sites, the mining of hard coal is very labour intensive in Turkey. In 2008, TTK's production costs averaged US$289 per ton, whereas the price per ton obtained in the domestic market ranged from US$50-55 in power generation to US$180 in iron and steel production.

[39] On average, the demand for electricity outpaced the growth in GDP by 1.4% annually between 2000 and 2010.

[40] On average, Turkey has exported 2 billion kWh per year and imported 1 billion kWh.

[41] A separate licence is required for each activity and each facility.

[42] BOT and similar arrangements concluded prior to the 2001 Law remain valid until their expiry.

thus negotiate directly with their supplier of choice.[43] The strategy foresees that all consumers, including households, should be able to choose their suppliers by 2015.

44. Retail tariffs (i.e. for "non-eligible" customers), network tariffs and the wholesale prices of TETAŞ are regulated. The wholesale tariffs are now fully cost-based. Artificially low end-user tariffs, at times below production costs, have contributed to occasional supply shortages in the past.[44] A new retail pricing mechanism was introduced in July 2008, involving automatic quarterly tariff adjustments based on changes in input prices (coal and natural gas), inflation, and movements in exchange rates. All distribution companies are being subject to a uniform national retail tariff, approved by the EMRA, until the end of 2012. The present system involves a certain amount of cross-subsidization due to cost differences between regions. From 2013 onwards, the distribution companies will establish individual price caps, subject to the approval of the EMRA.[45]

45. Private investment accounted for 75% of the new installed power-generation capacity between 2002 and 2009. So far, private-sector operators have favoured gas-fired generation because of the short lead times. Further new capacity to meet the projected rise in demand is likely to come from coal, hydropower, wind, and nuclear energy rather than natural gas. Turkey has no nuclear reactors at present, but signed an intergovernmental agreement with the Russian Federation for the construction and operation of a nuclear power plant at Akkuyu on the Mediterranean coast, in May 2010. Sinop (on the Black Sea) has been identified as the site for the construction of a second nuclear power plant.

(v) Renewable energy

46. Although Turkey has steadily added new hydropower stations to its generation network, the share of renewables in Turkey's total primary energy supply declined from 17% in the mid 1990s to 9.4% in 2009. The decline reflects the growing use of natural gas in power generation, but also a massive shift from traditional use of biomass (fuelwood) to more modern forms of heating. The share of renewables rose in 2010 as new hydro and wind power plants were coming on stream. As of 2011, Turkey had an estimated 16,160 MW of installed hydropower capacity in operation and a further 14,600 MW under construction; wind-power capacity in operation amounted to 1,360 MW with an additional 2,130 MW under construction Turkey has established an overall target for renewable energy to constitute 30% of its electricity supply by 2023, including capacity targets for wind (20,000 MW) and geothermal energy (600 MW). The Turkish authorities also see some potential in solar energy and biomass.

47. The legal framework, i.e. the Law on the Utilization of Renewable Energy Sources for the Purpose of Generating Electrical Energy (2005) together with the Electricity Market Law and the Energy Efficiency Law, includes several instruments to promote electricity generation from renewable sources of energy including feed-in tariffs and purchase obligations, connection priority, reduced licence fees, and reduced fees for project preparation and land acquisition. Furthermore, the 2005 Law was amended in January 2011 to introduce bonus tariffs for licence holders using locally manufactured mechanical or electro-mechanical components. Under an implementing regulation issued on 19 June 2011, the beneficiaries must obtain a manufacturing certificate attesting

[43] The eligibility threshold was 9 GWh per year when the wholesale market was first opened in March 2003, and was reduced to 3 GWh per year in 2007.

[44] Low tariffs, *inter alia*, caused TEDAŞ to accumulate TL 4.5 billion in operating losses between 2006 and 2008, and payment arrears affecting its suppliers of coal (TKI) and natural gas (BOTAŞ).

[45] The transition period contracts mandating the electricity trade between TETAŞ and the distribution companies will expire by 2013.

that the components comply with international or Turkish standards, as well as a "manufacture status document" certifying that the components are manufactured in Turkey.

(vi) Energy efficiency

48. According to the International Energy Agency, Turkey has significant potential to improve the efficient use of energy in all sectors. A more sustainable transport system could save energy, avoid congestion, and improve air quality. Buildings, which represent 37% of the final energy consumption, appear to offer the largest gains at low cost. Turkey's Energy Performance Regulation (2009), which sets the rules for policies indicated in the Energy Efficiency Law (2007), harmonizes Turkey's requirements with those of the Energy Performance of Buildings Directive No. 2002/91/EC. The regulation covers the energy performance of heating, cooling, thermal insulation, hot water, and electrical and lighting systems in dwellings as well as in commercial and services facilities, and provides an energy-savings potential of 30-50% in buildings. Efficiency-enhancing projects may also be viable for industrial users.

49. The distribution system for electricity is prone to significant losses and theft, although estimated losses and theft fell from 25% in 2002 to 14% in 2009. The tariff system is designed to encourage distributors to pursue such leakages. From 2013, distribution tariffs will include a "loss-theft" adjustment component, rewarding distribution companies that beat their target loss-theft ratio.

50. Turkey's per capita carbon emissions are increasing. Turkey became a party to the Kyoto Convention in 2009, but has preferred not to set an overall quantitative target to limit CO_2 emissions or a national emission target for 2020.

(3) MANUFACTURING

51. Turkey's transformation from an agrarian economy to manufacturing on a significant scale began in earnest in the early 1980s. Turkey is now a major producer and exporter of a wide range of machinery, appliances, and other industrial goods, as well as jewellery and furniture. Three of the most prominent manufacturing sectors are highlighted below. The most notable trend over the years has been the relative decline in the share of textiles and clothing in total exports, as the sector played a key role in the earlier part of Turkey's export-oriented industrialization phase.

(i) Automotive sector

52. Turkey was the world's 16th largest manufacturer of motor vehicles in 2010. In Europe, Turkey is the leading manufacturer of commercial and light commercial vehicles, and the second most important manufacturer of buses. Turkey's motor-vehicle industry consists of 15 assemblers and manufacturers, and some 800 suppliers of components. The components subsector employs approximately 150,000 workers, while more than 40,000 people are employed in the assembly and manufacture of vehicles. Annual production capacity exceeds 500,000 units of commercial vehicles and 800,000 passenger cars.[46] Turkey exported motor vehicles and spare parts worth almost US$17 billion in 2010. About 73% of the production is exported to the EU, mainly to France, Germany, Italy, and the UK.[47]

[46] The industry's objective is to raise its production capacity to 2 million units per year in the short-term, and to 4 million units by 2023.

[47] At the same time, about 60% of all motor vehicles sold in Turkey are imported. For passenger cars, the import share is close to 70%.

53. The industry is mostly foreign owned, joint ventures, or operating under foreign licence. Turkey has five passenger-cars manufacturers; Oyak-Renault, Tofaş (a Fiat S.p.A. and Koç Holding partnership), Toyota, Hyundai Assan, and Honda Turkey. Ford Otosan and Tofaş are the principal producers of commercial vehicles, followed by seven other manufacturers. Turkey also has two manufacturers of tractors. Although the Turkish industry has been expanding rapidly, Otoyol and Askam (commercial vehicles) as well as Uzel Makine (tractors) have left the sector since 2007. The global financial crisis also had a negative impact on many of Turkey's smaller component makers.

54. Investment in Turkey's automotive industry has been attracted by relatively low labour costs, duty-free access to the EU market, and the good quality of the local components industry. Although Turkey does not host its own automobile brand, many of the cars produced in Turkey are currently designed domestically. In February 2011, the special consumption tax on motor vehicles was reduced from the ordinary rate of 37% to 3-15% for comparable cars with electric engines to stimulate mass production of electric automobiles in Turkey.

(ii) Iron and steel

55. The iron and steel industry has been the backbone of industrialization in Turkey, commencing with the production of raw steel in Karabük in 1940. The sector currently employs around 200,000 people. The industry is now operated entirely by the private sector. The privatization process, which began with the transfer of the loss-making Karabük Steel Mill (Kardemir) in 1994, culminated with the privatization of the Erdemir Group in 2006.[48]

56. Accounting for just over 2% of global production, Turkey is the 10th largest producer of crude steel.[49] Production capacity more than doubled from 2002 to 2010, and annual production rose from 16.5 million tonnes to 29.1 million tonnes.[50] According to the Turkish Steel Manufacturers' Association DÇÜD, annual output is projected to reach 42 million tonnes in 2012. The Turkish industry's output consists of long steel (75%) and flat steel products (25%). Turkey is a major importer of scrap iron, and 72% of its steel production is currently made from recycled materials. Turkey imported iron and steel worth US$6.5 billion in 2009 (pipes not included); imports of scrap iron amounted to US$7.1 billion in 2010.

57. Exports from Turkey of iron and steel, including steel products, exceeded US$13 billion in 2010.[51] Turkey's principal export markets for iron and steel are located in the EU, the Middle East and in North Africa. Although the Turkish steel industry produces most types of steel, the dominant output is lower value-added long steel used in construction. Turkish producers meet 38% of the world's demand for long products.[52] On the other hand, the needs for flat steel by Turkish manufacturers of motor vehicles, household appliances, and consumer electronics are mostly met through imports. Accordingly, the Turkish steel industry is channelling its investments into modernization and adding new capacity for flat steel to reduce the imbalance between the local production and consumption of long and flat steel.

---

48 Erdemir is Turkey's largest producer of steel with 26% of total output. The group is now owned by Ataer Holding, a subsidiary of the Armed Forces Pension Fund (Oyak).

49 Over the last ten years, the growth in Turkey's steel production has been surpassed only by China and India.

50 Driven by the construction boom, domestic consumption of finished steel rose almost three-fold over the same period to reach 23.6 million tonnes in 2010.

51 In volume terms, Turkey's exports amounted to 17.6 million tonnes of iron and steel.

52 According to data from the Turkish Steel Manufacturers' Association, Turkey produced 19.7 million tonnes of long steel products in 2010, of which 11.6 million tonnes were consumed domestically and 8.1 million tonnes were exported.

(iii) Textiles and clothing

58. Since the elimination of quotas under the Agreement on Textiles and Clothing at the end of 2004, Turkey's industry has been facing increasing competition from low-cost producers in Asia, both at home and in its major export markets (EU, the United States and the Russian Federation). Turkey's textiles and clothing sector is dominated by privately owned small and medium-sized businesses. Turkey has more than 40,000 textile and clothing manufacturers producing for export. The industry has responded to the competitive challenges by switching to higher value-added finished products and ready-made clothing, necessitating product innovation as well as brand-building. In Europe, Turkish exporters continue to capitalize on duty-free access and logistical advantages stemming from geographical proximity to their customers.

59. The textiles and clothing sector still accounts for nearly 10% of Turkey's GDP and more than 11% of the manufacturing labour force. Traditionally relying on an ample supply of local cotton, the industry has become increasingly dependent on imported cotton as domestic production has been in decline since the 2004-05 marketing year. However, the focus on value added has also implied a shift away from basic cotton products. According to the Turkish industry, its main challenges at present stem from high cotton prices caused by short supply and protective trade measures applied by cotton producing countries, high electricity prices by international standards, and rising wage costs.[53]

60. Initiatives taken by the industry include establishing a textile research and development centre in Istanbul, the Istanbul Fashion Academy, organizing the Istanbul Fashion Week, and using stylist and designer competitions to stimulate new talent. Many textiles and clothing companies have trademarked their own brands, and sought IPR protection for special designs. World-famous branded goods are also produced for export in Turkey under licence from the foreign right holders.

61. In 2010, Turkey ranked 5th among the world's exporters of apparel and 8th among the exporter of textiles. Turkey is the second-largest supplier to the EU market, which accounts for 80% of Turkey's exports of clothing. In textiles, the principal export markets are the Russian Federation, Italy, Germany, Romania, and the United States.

62. As shown in Table AIII.1, the textiles and clothing sector is subject to higher tariff protection than most other industrial activities. Anti-dumping measures also affect the importation of yarn and textile fabrics (Table III.11). In response to complaints from domestic producers, an investigation was launched on 13 January 2011 regarding a possible increase in import duties on a broad range of textile and clothing accessories. On 15 September 2011, Turkey began applying additional rates of duty ranging from 11% to 20% on textiles and 17% to 30% on clothing products within fixed *ad valorem* limits expressed in US$/kg depending on the origin (LDCs, developing, or other countries). Turkey does not have bound tariff rates for most of the products subject to the additional duties. However, for goods with bound tariff rates, the duty increases are capped by the bound level. The additional import duties are applied to all countries, except the European Union and Turkey's free-trade partners. For goods shipped from third countries, Turkey takes into account their preferential origin under its GSP scheme.

(4) SERVICES

63. Although agriculture and manufacturing remain important, Turkey has become an economy dominated by services. In terms of number of people employed, and excluding governmental services, the main sectors are wholesale and retail trade; transport, storage, and communication; real

[53] According to the Turkish authorities, Turkey is now striving to increase its cotton production and attain a sustainable level of domestic production regardless of global prices and other exogenous factors.

estate, renting, and business activities; construction; architecture; engineering; and hotels and restaurants. The highest value added (per employee) is in electricity, gas, and water supply. The evolution of Turkey's foreign trade in services over the last five years is detailed in Tables IV.1 and IV.2.

Table IV.1
Exports of commercial services, 2006-10
(US$ million at current prices)

	2006	2007	2008	2009	2010
Commercial services (excluding government services)	**25,275**	**28,624**	**34,783**	**33,195**	**33,878**
Transportation	4,972	6,541	7,793	7,825	9,026
Sea transport	418	747	843	661	1,213
Air transport	3,395	4,401	5,196	5,361	6,018
Other transport (road transport)	1,159	1,393	1,754	1,803	1,795
Travel	16,853	18,487	21,951	21,250	20,807
Business travel	1,885	1,820	2,837	2,732	2,673
Personal travel	14,968	16,667	19,114	18,518	18,134
Other commercial services (commercial services - travel & transport)	3,450	3,596	5,039	4,120	4,045
Communications services	416	506	725	633	463
Construction (abroad)	936	856	1,146	1,279	1,120
Insurance services	522	645	752	676	719
Financial services	277	395	841	464	482
Computer and information services	12	15	13	12	16
Royalties and licence fees	..	..	..	..	..
Other business services	289	208	338	282	333
Personal, cultural and recreational services	998	971	1,224	774	912

.. Not available.

Source: IMF BOP statistics.

Table IV.2
Imports of commercial services, 2006-10
(US$ million at current prices)

	2006	2007	2008	2009	2010
Commercial services (excluding government services)	**10,800**	**14,608**	**16,694**	**15,600**	**18,309**
Transportation	4,662	6,966	7,984	6,535	8,291
Sea transport	2,571	4,640	5,444	3,824	4,994
Air transport	1,853	2,054	2,242	2353	2,833
Other transport	238	272	298	358	464
of which Road transport	201	237	261	333	420
Travel	2,743	3,260	3,506	4,147	4,826
Business travel	1,020	1,207	1,300	1,539	1,789
Personal travel	1,723	2,053	2,206	2,608	3,037
Other commercial services (commercial services - travel & transport)	3,395	4,382	5,204	4,918	5,192
Communications services	299	305	298	247	246
Construction (abroad)	57	97	172	189	261
Insurance services	1,140	1,544	1,436	1,203	1,188
Financial services	524	623	978	826	724
Computer and information services	15	26	32	30	38
Royalties and license fees	531	647	729	648	816
Other business services	723	1,029	1,378	1,568	1,673
Personal, cultural and recreational services	106	111	181	207	246

Source: IMF BOP statistics.

64. Services are not covered by the customs union agreement between Turkey and the EU. However, in the context of Turkey's accession negotiations, work has been initiated on alignment with the EU *acquis* on the right of establishment and freedom to provide cross-border services. The process will require Turkey's alignment with the EU Directive on Services in the Internal Market, including the establishment of a Point of Single Contact and competent authorities. Turkey will need to amend some of its nationality and language requirements, and extend the scope for mutual recognition of professional qualifications. Moreover, Turkey's current requirements for the granting of work and residence permits to service providers established in EU member states are not compatible with the EU *acquis*.

(i) Banking

65. Turkey has 48 banks, including 31 deposit banks, 13 development and investment banks, and 4 (Islamic) participation banks (as at September 2011). Nine of these banks are state-owned, and 23 are wholly owned by foreign banks, branches of foreign banks, or have majority stakes held by non-resident investors.[54] At the end of June 2011, the assets of the Turkish banking sector totalled TL 1,146 billion, or the equivalent of 95% of Turkey's GDP. The four largest banks are similar in size as their balance sheets each represent 10-14% of the sector's total assets.

66. Except for underwriting services, which may only be provided by development and investment banks, Turkish banks are universal banks. Most insurance and leasing companies are either owned by, or affiliated with, the banks. Banks may engage in equity intermediation through their subsidiaries. Foreign and domestic banks are subject to the same rules in terms of establishment, operation, and supervision. Cross-border supply of banking services is not legally restricted. The Turkish banking sector owned 38 financial subsidiaries, 78 branches, and 11 representation offices abroad as of December 2011.

67. At the peak of its crisis, in November 2000 and February 2001, Turkey had a fragile banking system vulnerable to reversals in capital flows and a rising stock of non-performing loans.[55] Although action had been taken prior to the twin crisis, further measures were considered necessary. The economic reform programme launched in May 2001 included measures specifically directed at the banking system, notably enhancing the powers of the Banking Regulation and Supervision Authority (BRSA), the strengthening of private banks, and restructuring of state-owned banks with the aim of privatization.[56] The Savings Deposit Insurance Fund (SDIF) was given a key role in the protection of public rights and the management and disposal of assets of banks entering into administration or liquidation procedures (Box IV.1). The overhaul of the Turkish banking system, including the restructuring of public banks, is estimated to have cost the Government some US$53.6 billion.

---

[54] Foreign banks have 41 representative offices in Turkey (as at September 2011).

[55] The banks' vulnerability was enhanced by a high public sector borrowing requirement, reliant on continuing demand for government securities, and rising interest rates under the Government's crawling-peg disinflation programme.

[56] The BRSA was established pursuant to the Banks Act No. 4389 in June 1999 and began operations in August 2000.

Box IV.1: Turkey's Savings Deposit Insurance Fund

Established in 1983 to ensure deposits, and granted an additional role to strengthen and restructure banks (in 1994), the SDIF originally reported to the Central Bank of Turkey. The Banking Law adopted in 1999 transferred the representation and administration of the SDIF to the newly founded BRSA. The SDIF became a separate legal entity in 2003.

In all, 25 banks were taken over by the SDIF between 1994 and 2003. The banks were resolved through merger, sale, or direct liquidation. Among the 25 banks, 6 were under direct liquidation, 4 were sold directly, 6 were disposed of through mergers, 1 was merged with a public bank, and 8 were transferred to the "Joint Fund Bank Inc.", which is limited to operations directly related to asset liquidation as a "transition bank".

The average settlement process for the banks taken over by the SDIF was 14 months, except for the 6 banks in the process of liquidation and the Joint Fund Bank Inc. The losses of the banks transferred to the SDIF totalled US$23.2 billion, and the resources transferred to the banks by the SDIF amounted to US$30.2 billion, including nearly US$6.6 billion in depositor compensation following the collapse of a major bank in 2003. The balance sheet of the Joint Fund Bank Inc. has been scaled down significantly since 2006. At the end of 2009, the bank's loan portfolio had been reduced to TL 193 million, including TL 61 million in non-performing loans. As of the end of 2010, the SDIF had collected US$19.7 billion from the resolved banks.

The SDIF guarantees deposits up to TL 50,000 per customer (per bank) in lira, foreign currency or gold. Membership in the scheme is compulsory for all banks accepting deposits in Turkey. The SDIF is funded by a risk-based premium collected quarterly from the participating banks. If necessary, the SDIF may also borrow government securities from the Treasury, receive advances from the Central Bank, or collect insurance premiums in advance. At the end of 2010, the 36 member banks held deposits totalling US$401.5 billion, of which US$99.5 billion was insured. The SDIF reserve amounted to US$5.4 billion.

Source: BRSA (2010), *From Crisis to Financial Stability Turkey Experience*, Working Paper (Revised Third edition), 3 September. Viewed at: http://www.bddk.org.tr/WebSitesi/english/Reports/Working_Papers/8675from_crisis_to_financial_stability_turkey_experience_3rd_ed.pdf; and the SDIF.

68. The global financial crisis in 2008-09 led to a surge in non-performing loans in the Turkish banking sector, but no intervention was needed to rescue individual banks.[57] At the end of September 2011, the deposit, development and investment banks had non-performing loans totalling TL 17.3 billion, representing 2.8% of their total loans.[58] At the same time, the banks had made specific provisions against loan losses totalling more than TL 14.2 billion. The Turkish banking system reported an average return on equity of 18.1% in 2009, 16.4% in 2010, and 13.9% as of September 2011. Only two banks recorded losses for the year 2010.

69. The numbers of bank branches/offices and staff have been rising since 2003, reaching more than 10,000 branches/offices and 190,000 employees in September 2011.[59] Among the 7.8 million active users of internet banking services (as of September 2011), 90% are individual users and 10% are corporate customers. Almost 78 million debit and 50 million credit cards have been issued (end-September 2011).

[57] The guarantee of deposits was unlimited between 1994 and 2000, and the unlimited coverage was reintroduced during the crisis in 2001. The present guaranteed amount (TL 50,000) has remained unchanged since 2003. However, as a precautionary step, authority to determine the coverage and amount was transferred from the SDIF to the Council of Ministers in November 2008 for a period of two years. Temporary relaxed rules on loan provisioning and restructuring were ended on 1 March 2011.

[58] Including participation banks, the ratio of non-performing loans to total loans in the Turkish banking sector amounted to 3.6% in 2008, 5.2% in 2009, and 3.5% in 2010. The rise in defaults and the subsequent recovery was particularly marked for credit cards and car loans.

[59] The closure and restructuring of Turkish banks in response to the earlier crisis had a profound effect on employment in the banking system, which fall from 175,000 in 2000 to 126,000 in 2002.

70. The banking sector is regulated pursuant to Banking Law No. 5411, which entered into force on 1 November 2005, and Law No. 5464 on Bank Cards and Credit Cards. The banking legislation was introduced and amended to align with the EU *acquis* and to improve the administrative capacity for the effective implementation of new regulations. The BRSA has issued secondary legislation, such as regulations on the establishment and operation of banks, corporate governance, protective provisions, financial reporting, and non-bank financial institutions, as well as communiqués on capital adequacy, financial reporting, and the operation of branches of foreign banks established outside of Turkey.

71. The BRSA became a member of the Basel Committee on Banking Supervision in May 2009, and of the Islamic Financial Services Board in December 2010. Turkey is also a member of the Financial Stability Board. The BRSA has begun implementation of the Basel II rules, requesting banks to use these standards for reporting and review purposes during a transition period from 1 July 2011 until 30 June 2012. However, the Basel II rules are not used to sanction non-compliance at this stage.

72. A project to make Istanbul a regional and global financial centre was launched in 2009. The centre would be fully integrated in Turkey's legislation and tax system. The plan calls for upgrading Turkey's legal system, increasing the diversity of financial products and services, a simple and more effective tax system, an improved regulatory and supervisory framework, and a stronger physical and technological infrastructure. Nine working groups have been established pursuant to the Strategy and Action Plan.[60] In response to these plans, banks located in Ankara have begun the process of moving their headquarters to Istanbul.

(ii) Telecommunications

73. The Electronic Communications Law No. 5809, which entered into force on 10 November 2008, provides the legal basis for the current regulatory framework for telecommunication services in Turkey.[61] The Act updated Turkey's legislation in this area and brought it closer to the EU *acquis*, i.e. Directive 2002/21/EC of 7 March 2002 and the specific directives relating to access, authorization, universal service, and privacy.[62] The Law designates the Ministry of Transport, Maritime and Communications and the Information and Communication Technologies Authority (ICTA) as the competent authorities in this sector.[63]

74. The role of the Ministry is primarily to develop the general policy with respect to electronic communication services and to maintain an alternative communications network in case of emergency or natural disaster. The ICTA (formerly the Telecommunications Authority) has been given a wide range of responsibilities spanning from granting authorizations, supervision, and the elaboration of secondary legislation on issues such as spectrum management, access and interconnection, numbering, number portability, tariffs, and consumer protection.

---

[60] See State Planning Organization (2009).

[61] The Law replaced the legal framework based on Telegram and Telephone Law No. 406 of 21 February 1924, except for the provisions relating to authorization, which entered into force on 10 May 2009. Law No. 5369 on universal services in electronic communication (of 2005) remains in force, as does Wireless Law No. 2813, although the title of the latter is now the Law on Establishment of ICTA.

[62] According to the European Commission, the Law is not fully aligned with the EU *acquis*, notably with respect to definitions and scope, authorization, universal service obligations, retail tariff regulation, spectrum management, access and interconnection, and market analysis (EU, 2011).

[63] The ICTA is a member of the Independent Regulators Group (IRG) and participates in Body of European Regulators for Electronic Communications (BEREC) as an observer.

75. Suppliers of electronic communications services require authorization from the ICTA. If the service does not require allocation of scarce resources (such as frequency or satellite slots), the service is considered authorized upon notification to the ICTA. When allocation of resources is required, the ICTA may grant a right of usage valid for up to 25 years. Unless the number of rights has been limited, e.g. for reasons of efficiency, rights of usage are granted within 30 days from the date of application. In addition to an annual administrative fee, the Council of Ministers sets minimum right of usage fees based on proposals by the Ministry of Transport, Maritime and Communications taking into account suggestions from the ICTA.

76. The pricing of electronic communication services is, in principle, determined by the operators themselves.[64] However, the ICTA may intervene in the tariff setting of enterprises deemed to possess significant power in the relevant market.[65] Further to its supervisory functions, the ICTA may impose monetary fines on enterprises found to be in breach of the legislation or the terms of its authorization or usage rights. ICTA may also obligate an operator to accept requests from other operators for access or interconnection with its network. As the powers of the ICTA and the Competition Authority overlap in the telecommunications sector, the Law aims at establishing a cooperative relationship between the two agencies. To enhance their coordination, the ICTA and the Competition Authority signed a protocol on 2 November 2011 to increase the exchange of information, mutual cooperation, and collaboration between the agencies' experts.

77. As at 31 October 2011, 558 authorizations have been granted to operators in the electronic communications market in Turkey.[66] Since the abolition of Türk Telekom's monopoly rights on fixed line, domestic long-distance, and international telephony on 31 December 2003, 166 authorizations have been issued for fixed telephony services. Nevertheless, the incumbent Türk Telekom continues to dominate the market for fixed-line telephony, holding a 90-93% market share (measured by revenue) in mid-2011. However, the number of fixed-line subscribers has been in steady decline over the years and currently totals around 15.5 million.

78. Introduced in 1986, mobile telephony now dominates over fixed-line calls and accounts for roughly 84% of the total traffic.[67] The nearly 64.8 million mobile subscriptions in Turkey are divided among three operators; Turkcell (34 million), Vodafone (17.8 million), and Avea (12.5 million).[68] After a long period of uninterrupted growth, the number of mobile subscriptions decreased by nearly 10% from 2008 to early 2011. The decline has been attributed to the introduction of number portability and flat-rate tariffs, leading to the cancellation of second mobile subscriptions. At the

[64] In addition to value-added tax, all types of installation, transfer, and telecommunication services provided by mobile telephone operators are subject to a Special Communication Tax. The tax rate is 5% for fixed-line and mobile internet services, 25% for other mobile communications services, and 15% for other fixed-line communications services.

[65] More generally, the Law also contains provisions regulating subscription contacts, i.e. minimum content, equal access to services, quality and transparency, and other consumer rights. The ICTA has issued further regulations with respect to customer rights and the quality of services.

[66] The number of service providers may be lower as some services may not yet have been launched.

[67] Mobile calls rose from 20.3 billion minutes in 2004 to 125.8 billion minutes in 2010. Fixed-line calls declined from 65.2 to 23.6 billion minutes during the same period.

[68] Shares in Turkcell were floated in an initial public offering in 2000. Its principal shareholder at present is Turkcell Holding (51%), whilst 33.48% of the shares are tradeable on the stock exchange. Vodafone Group Plc acquired the mobile operator Telsim for US$4.5 billion at a public auction in 2005. Avea is owned by Türk Telekom (81.13%) and Türkiye Iş Bankasi (14.03%). In 2005, the Turkish Government sold 55% of Türk Telekom to a consortium (Ojer Telekomünikasyon AS) at a public auction for US$6.55 billion. The Government shed another 15% of Türk Telekom in a public offering to local and foreign investors in 2008, raising an additional US$1.9 billion (see Chapter III(3)(viii)).

same time, the operators have also seen a shift from pre-paid subscriptions to more lucrative post-paid tariff schemes.

79. Turkey had approximately 28 million internet users at the end of 2010, corresponding to some 9 million internet subscriptions, primarily in the form of fixed-line (xDSL), mobile broadband, and cable modem or fibre internet access. As of November 2011, the ICTA had authorized 141 internet service providers by notification. At end-June 2011, TTNet (the fixed-line incumbent's subsidiary) held a 55.6% share of all broadband internet subscriptions, including all types of broadband internet subscriptions via fixed-line, mobile, cable, fibre or other types of access. However, competition is intensifying as mobile operators are offering mobile broadband services. 3G services were launched in July 2009, and 30.8 million mobile subscribers are 3G users.

80. Türk Telekom and the three mobile operators generated net sales worth TL 21.2 billion in 2010. The revenue of the other operators amounted to nearly TL 1.1 billion, including the combined income of smaller internet providers of TL 754 million. Since 2006, Türk Telekom and Turkcell have each generated net profits in the order of TL 2-3 billion annually, while Vodafone and Avea are still operating at a loss. In terms of employment, two thirds of the 38,000 people working in the sector are employed by Türk Telekom, against 7,500 in the mobile operators, and 4,600 in other communication operators.

(iii) Transport

81. Turkey's transport policy falls within the scope of the Ministry of Transport, Maritime and Communications. The Ministry carries out transport infrastructure operations and regulation of all modes of transport as well as the communications sector. The Directorate General of Coastal Safety, the General Directorate of State Airports Authority, the Turkish State Railways, and the General Directorate of Post and Telegraph Organization are related bodies of the Ministry; and the Information and Communication Technologies Authority and TURKSAT A.S. are affiliated bodies. Under the Ninth Development Plan (2007-2013), Turkey aims, *inter alia,* to create an efficient transport subsector, giving priority to environmental aspects; and to increase traffic safety in all modes of transport.

(a) Maritime transport

82. Surrounded by sea on three sides, and with four of its major industrial centres (Istanbul-Izmit, Izmir, Bursa, and Adana) located on or near the sea, it is not surprising that approximately 85% of Turkey's foreign trade is carried by maritime transport. The volume of seaborne trade rose steadily between 2001 and 2008, to reach almost 225 million tonnes, but declined in 2009 due to a fall in import shipments of 12 million tonnes. Turkish ports unloaded an additional 58 million tonnes of transit cargo in 2009, and a further 18 million tonnes of merchandise was shipped between Turkish ports that year.[69]

83. Maritime activities are administered pursuant to Turkish Commercial Law No. 6762, Cabotage Law No. 815, Ports Law No. 618, and the International Convention on Standards of Training, Certification and Watchkeeping for Seafarers of 1978. Turkey has a two-register system; the Turkish National Ship Registry and the Turkish International Ship Registry. At the end of 2010, the Turkish merchant fleet registered in Turkey consisted of 701 ships (1,000 gross tonnes and over) with a total capacity of 8.6 million deadweight tonnes (dwt). In tonnage terms, more than 90% of this fleet is registered in the Turkish International Ship Registry. However, including Turkish-owned

[69] In 2010, Turkish ports handled 247 million tonnes of cargo, including 64 million tonnes of transit cargo.

ships bearing flags of convenience (e.g. Malta, the Marshall Islands, Panama), the Turkish-owned merchant fleet totals over 2,500 ships with a combined capacity of almost 19 million dwt.

84. The National Ship Register is reserved for vessels owned by Turkish citizens and companies majority-owned (51% or more) by Turkish nationals. First mates and masters of ships must be of Turkish nationality, but up to 40% of the officers of ships engaged in international seaborne transportation (i.e. excluding cabotage) may be foreign nationals. Turkey's International Ship Register, established in 1999, is also open to ships and yachts owned by foreign persons resident in Turkey and foreign-owned companies incorporated pursuant to Turkish legislation. In addition to the special tax incentives offered through the international register, flying the Turkish flag allows the vessels to perform cabotage operations in Turkish waters and a 10% price preference in bidding for the transport of public cargoes or strategic raw materials.[70] Nevertheless, almost 80% of Turkey's seaborne foreign trade is performed by vessels registered elsewhere in the world.

85. In order to deal with congestion and inefficiencies at Turkish ports, the operational rights of 13 public ports operated by the General Directorate of the Turkish Maritime Organization were privatized several years ago. Turkey has also established 36-year concessions for three of its major ports operated until recently by the Turkish State Railways (TCDD); Mersin (in 2007), Samsun (2010), and Bandirma (2010). The privatization process of other ports owned by the TCDD (i.e. Derince, Iskenderun, Galataport, Izmir) is on-going. In addition, a major port is under construction at Çandarli, and is expected to handle its first cargo in 2013. Plans to build a 50-km canal west of Istanbul to alleviate traffic through the Bosporus straight are still at an early stage.

86. At the end of 2009, Turkey had 65 shipyards and a further 60 shipyards were under construction. The main shipyards are located in Tuzla and Yalova (east of Istanbul). Turkey's shipyards were operating at less than 50% capacity during the recent crisis, and employment in the industry fell from 33,500 in August 2008 to 8,000 in January 2010. However, the industry began to recover in 2011. Turkey also has a thriving boat-building industry, producing a full range of boats from skiffs to large (90 m+) yachts. Turkey exported ships and yachts worth US$1.1 billion in 2010.

(b) Road transport

87. The Ministry of Transport, Maritime and Communications regulates road transport in Turkey, including road-safety issues and the conditions applied to cargo operators, carrier agents, brokers, and warehouses.[71] Moreover, the Ministry establishes the qualifications, rights and duties of persons employed in the sector. Road transport services are provided by private companies; an operating licence issued by the Ministry is obligatory. Cross-border transportation of goods and passengers is subject to bilateral or multilateral agreements or permits issued by the Council of Ministers. Vehicles registered in a foreign country may not transport goods or passengers between two points within Turkey. Turkey's road transport fleet (45,000 vehicles) is among the largest and most modern in Europe. According to the authorities, transit quota limitations applied by partner countries continue to prevent the efficient use of Turkish trucks.

88. The General Directorate of Highways is responsible for the construction, maintenance, and operation of roads. The road network of the General Directorate of Highways consists of 2,236 km of motorways, 31,383 km of state roads, and 31,459 km of provincial roads. The General Directorate

[70] Pursuant to the Cabotage Law, merchant maritime transport and passenger services, pilotage, and all other port services may only be provided by Turkish-flag ships. For further details regarding the incentives and privileges, see WTO (2003) and WTO (2007).

[71] Turkey became a party to the European Agreement on the international carriage of dangerous goods by road (ADR) on 22 February 2010. A regulation on transport of dangerous goods has entered into force.

also administers Turkey's toll plazas, collecting tolls manually or automatically on a number of roads and bridges. Road transport is the preferred mode of domestic transport, accounting for more than 90% of the volume of both freight and passengers.[72]

89. The General Directorate began a programme in 2003 to upgrade highways in Turkey from single to dual carriageway. At present, 33% of the Turkish road network is dual carriageway. Several major projects have been launched recently to upgrade the road infrastructure further, including a 420-km highway linking Istanbul and Izmir, the North Marmara Motorway Project (including a third suspension bridge across the Istanbul strait), as well as a tunnel under the Bosporus. Private entrepreneurs are invited to tender for the projects, to be constructed on a build-operate-transfer (BOT) basis. Planned motorway projects until 2023 total 5,550 km. The intention is to finance many of these projects through private-public partnerships.

(c) Rail transport

90. The Turkish State Railways (TCDD) has a *de jure* monopoly in providing rail passenger and freight transport services in Turkey. The TCDD owns and operates the entire railway system. The reorganization and restructuring of the loss-making TCDD has been a key area of reform under the Ninth Development Plan (2007-2013). As noted above, the management of several ports owned by TCDD have been turned into concession agreements with private operators, and other ports are in the process of privatization.

91. Turkey's railway system consists of 11,940 km of track. Major investments have been undertaken in recent years to build high-speed lines between some of Turkey's major cities. The high-speed lines linking Ankara with Eskisehir and Konya have opened, and further projects are either under construction or on the agenda. The Turkish railway system is connected to the networks of neighbouring countries via seven border crossings. Completion of the Marmaray Project, a 76-km commuter railway and sub-sea rail tube crossing of the Bosporus straight, would allow Turkey to connect to the Trans-European Transport Network and potentially become a hub for railway freight between Europe, Central Asia, and the Middle East.

92. Although ambitious targets have been set for 2023, the contribution of Turkish railways in the transportation of passengers and freight is still modest.[73] Continuing investments in infrastructure and new rolling stock is designed to make rail travel and rail cargo more attractive. Turkey is also planning to open the sector to competition, although the infrastructure would remain state-owned. Draft legislation to reform the railway sector is currently before the Ministry of Transport, Maritime and Communications.

(d) Air transport

93. The national flag-carrier Turkish Airlines, 49% state-owned, continues to dominate Turkey's air transport sector. As of September 2011, Turkish Airlines controlled a fleet of 177 aircraft, including six freight planes operated by its subsidiary Turkish Cargo. Turkish Airlines formally joined the global Star Alliance in April 2008. Private air carriers have been allowed to establish since 1983. In addition to Turkish Airlines, Turkey currently has 19 air carriers, 4 of which (Onur Air, Pegasus Airlines, SunExpress, and AnadoluJet) operate a fleet of 20 aircraft or more. Low-cost carriers have gradually been increasing their presence in Turkey.

---

[72] The share of road transport in the carriage of Turkey's foreign trade has been around 10-12% in recent years.

[73] The share of rail transport in total transport is about 5% for freight and 2% for passengers. Only around 1% of Turkey's foreign trade is carried by rail.

94. Turkey has a total of 67 airports, 47 of these are civil airports, of which 35 are open to international flights. Several new regional airports are under construction. The General Directorate of State Airports Authority (DHMI) is in charge of airport management and the provision of air navigation services throughout Turkey's airspace. However, private enterprises have been granted concessions to run the terminal operations at some of Turkey's busiest airports (i.e. the Istanbul Atatürk Airport, Antalya, Esenboga (Ankara), Izmir Adnan Menderes, and Dalaman).

95. Airport access is regulated by the Turkish Civil Aviation Authority pursuant to the General and Aerodrome sections of the *Turkish Aeronautical Information Publication,* while slot allocation has been the responsibility of the DHMI since May 2010. Air carriers operating scheduled flights to Turkey are authorized on the basis of reciprocity within the framework of bilateral aviation agreements. Charter services are authorized on the basis of reciprocity under the rules of the European Civil Aviation Commission. Turkey has signed bilateral air transport agreements with 121 partners. Turkey concluded an Open Skies Air Transport Agreement with the United States in 2000. Since its last TPR, Turkey has concluded a bilateral air transport agreement with Canada (in 2009), and initialled a civil aviation agreement with the EU (25 March 2010). The new "horizontal" agreement does not replace existing bilateral agreements between Turkey and individual EU member states, but aligns them with EU law.[74]

(iv) Tourism

96. Turkey is one of the world's major tourist destinations; it ranked 7th in international tourist arrivals (28.6 million) in 2010, and 10th in receipts from tourism (US$20.8 billion). It is targeting revenue of US$60 billion from 60 million tourist arrivals annually by 2023. Whereas Turkey was widely regarded as a low-cost destination in the early stages of the industry's development, it is increasingly focusing on the higher end of the market and all-year tourism. As the bulk of Turkey's visitors from the EU, the Russian Federation, and Ukraine choose Turkey for their summer holidays, much of the industry has a distinct seasonal character. Projects to extend the tourism season, particularly in the Antalya region, include investments in golf courses, health clinics, shopping, and entertainment facilities. Istanbul maintains its importance as an international hub throughout the year. As a cultural centre and congress venue, Istanbul hosted nearly 7 million foreign visitors in 2010, and is expecting to host some 8 million visitors in 2011.

97. Turkey is becoming a popular destination for health tourism. According to the Turkish Statistical Institute, 115,223 people visited Turkey for medical purposes in 2010. Since 2007, the Ministry of Culture and Tourism has been backing initiatives to promote Turkey's spas, thermal waters, and health centres. At present, Turkey has about 270 spas and thermal springs, and some 385 hotels offer spa and wellness facilities. However, as more than 1,300 thermal sources have been identified across Turkey, the thermal resources could cater to a much larger number of visitors. The Turkish Government is accordingly prepared to provide funding for the promotion and development of existing and new sites.

98. As Turkey has been the home of numerous civilizations in the past, the country has an estimated 20,000 monuments and sites of archaeological significance. The Anatolia region also includes many holy sites of early Christianity and Judaism; and religious and cultural tourism is being recognized as an area of significant potential. Funds have been made available for the restoration and preservation of some 150 historical assets across Turkey since 2007.

[74] Notably, due to the large Turkish population living in Germany, the air transport agreement between the two countries is a *de facto* open skies agreement.

99. Although a fairly new concept in Turkey, winter tourism is being regarded as a potentially profitable industry in the mountainous and less developed provinces of Eastern Turkey. Two existing ski resorts (Palandöken and Sarikamis) are popular among ski tourists from the Russian Federation and other CIS countries. However, as these parts of Turkey are sparsely populated, further development of winter tourism would not only require investment in ski lifts, ice rinks, snowboard ramps, toboggan trails, etc. but also in basic infrastructure such as airports, roads, and hotels. Mountaineering and adventure tourism is also being considered as complementary activities to extend the tourist season.

100. The Government provides a number of incentives for investments in tourist facilities, including the allocation of public land on 49-year leases, the provision of water and electricity at low rates, tax exemptions on imported goods, as well as exemptions from VAT and other taxes on purchases of local products. Many tourism projects are being contemplated as public-private-sector partnerships, constructed on a build-operate-transfer or similar basis.

(v) Construction

101. The Turkish construction sector, originally domestically oriented and focused on the construction of residential property, began its development in the 1980s as major infrastructure projects were being undertaken in Turkey in joint-ventures with foreign constructors. At present, the industry provides employment for some 1.5 million people. The sector spans from a large number of small, mostly family-owned businesses to some 150 large contractors working internationally. The construction industry accounts for more than 5% of Turkey's GDP directly, but its indirect effects on the economy are thought to be significantly larger. Turkey is among the world's top 12 manufacturers of building materials, such as cement, glass, steel, and ceramic tiles.

102. Turkey has an estimated 200,000 contractors in the construction sector. No licence is required to operate a construction company in Turkey, except for construction licences granted by the Ministry of Environment and Urbanism for on-going construction projects subject to Law No. 2886; construction works of institutions not subject to Law No. 4743; construction procurements of municipalities in the form of building with flat compensation, and the construction works of private cooperatives. Pursuant to Regulation No. 27787 On the Registry of Building Contractors, Field Supervisors and Licensed Craftsmen, all contractors will need to obtain a competence number from 1 January 2012 onwards. The regulation also stipulates that all projects subject to a construction permit must be built under the responsibility of a building contractor. National building standards were tightened in the wake of the earthquake in 1999.

103. Domestically, the performance of the construction sector mirrors closely the path of the overall economy, but with much higher volatility (Chart IV.3). After the crisis in 2001, the sector benefited from a stable investment climate and reduced interest rates. The demand for housing was also stimulated by the availability of long-term financing on attractive terms.[75] The economic downturn in 2008-09 affected the sector severely, but the subsequent rebound has been similarly spectacular. In commercial real estate, a temporary oversupply of office and retail space in the Istanbul area appears to have disappeared rapidly with the renewed strength of the Turkish economy.

[75] The volume of housing loans provided by the banking sector rose from €400 million in 2003 to €18 billion in 2008. BRSA (2009). Turkish banks require minimum 25% equity put up by the homeowner in order to extend a mortgage loan (DEIK, 2011).

Chart IV.3
(a) Turkey's construction sector, 1999-2011

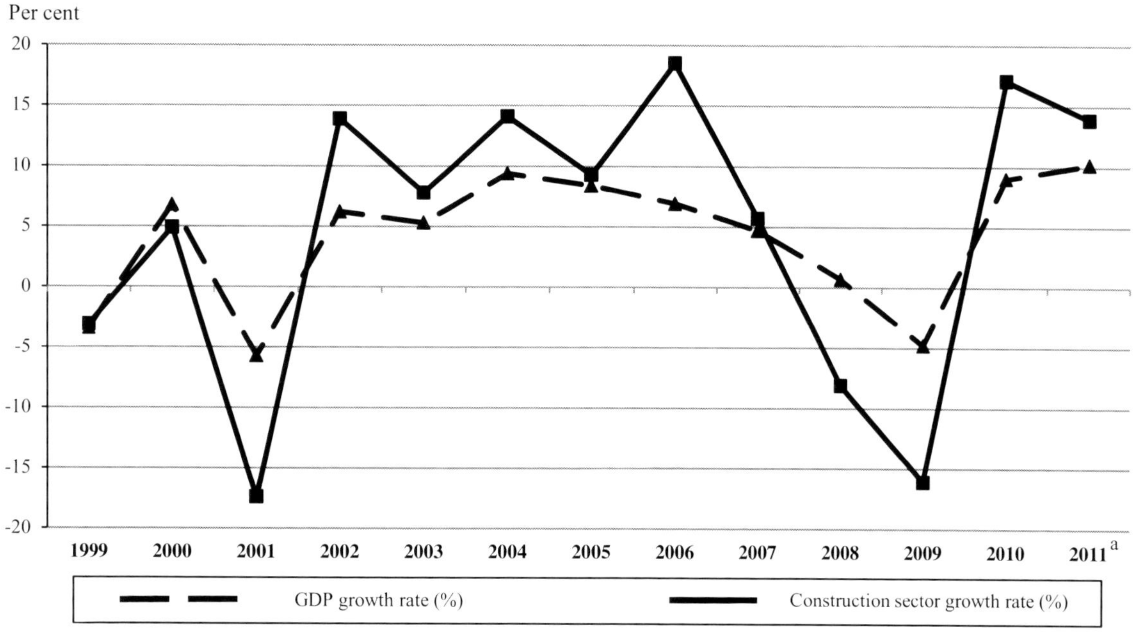

a First six months.

Source: Turkish Contractors Association online information. Viewed at: http://www.tmb.org.tr/doc/Turk_Yurtdisi_Muteahhitlik_Hizmetleri_en.doc.

(b) International activity of Turkish contractors, 2001-10

Annual project value

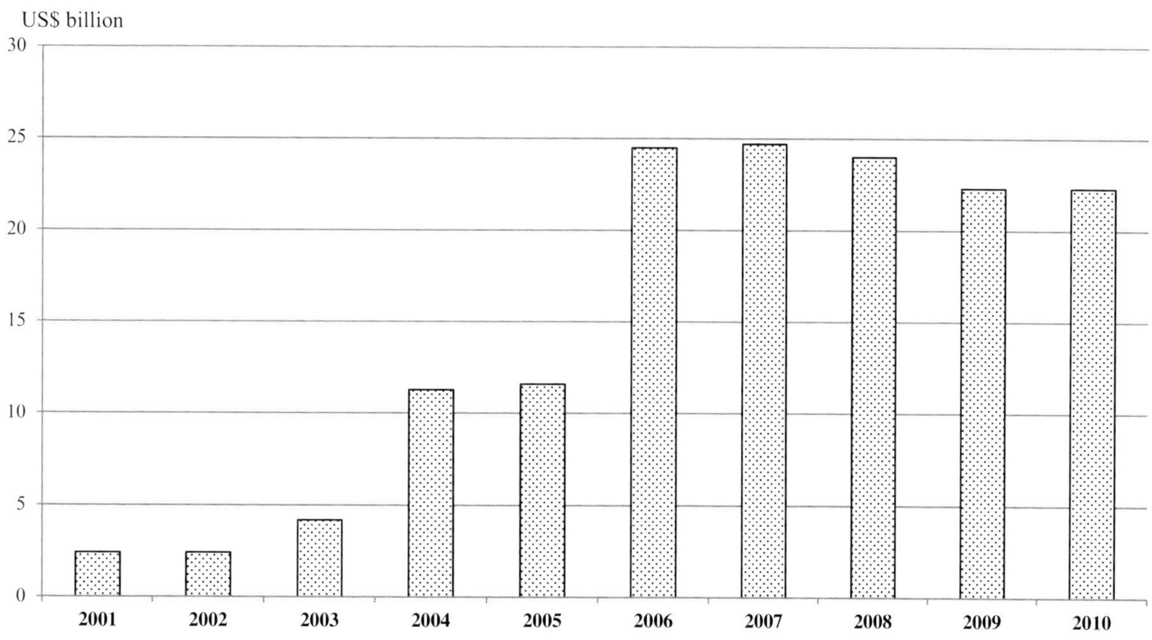

Source: Turkish Contractors Association.

104. Outside of Turkey, Turkish contractors have undertaken about 6,500 projects for a total value of US$205 billion over the last 40 years. The annual project volume has risen from US$2.4 billion in 2001 and 2002 to exceed US$22 billion every year since 2006. The internationally oriented segment of the Turkish construction industry has become increasingly diversified in terms of markets, products, and business models. In 2010, Turkish contractors undertook 577 projects in 50 countries, ranging from infrastructure projects (roads, bridges, tunnels), residential housing, sports facilities, energy projects, tourism establishments, etc. Geographically, the Russian Federation, Libya, Turkmenistan, Kazakhstan, and Iraq have been the leading markets, representing around 50% of the business volume.

105. According to the *Overseas Contracting Communication* (Communication No. TAU/2007/001), an "Overseas Contracting Certificate" valid for three years may be issued to overseas contractors within four categories: (i) civil engineering structures, plants, maintenance, and repair works; (ii) industrial and technological manufacturing, installation, and assembly works; (iii) operation, management, and maintenance works; and (iv) design, engineering, and consultancy works. A "Temporary Overseas Contracting Certificate", granted for a maximum of one year (but renewable under certain conditions), may be provided to natural and juridical persons who do not meet the value thresholds stipulated for such works, but who are aiming to complete their overseas construction commitments. Since 2003, contractors have been provided 330 overseas contracting certificates and 526 temporary certificates.

106. Some Turkish contractors have specialized in the construction of particular types of infrastructure such as international airports, railways, and urban transport systems.[76] Another trend has been a growing interest in direct investment and property management abroad among Turkish construction companies.

[76] The companies are being classified by affiliated chambers of the Union of Chambers and Commodity Exchanges of Turkey according to EU NACE codes.

REFERENCES

BRSA (2009), *Structural developments in banking*, Issue 4, December. Viewed at: http://www.bddk.org.tr/WebSitesi/english/Reports/Structural_Developments/8938strdevinban09.pdf.

DEIK (2011), *Turkish Business Outlook*, 18 September.

Directorate General of State Owned Enterprises (2008), *2007 Public Enterprises Report*. Viewed at: http://www.treasury.gov.tr/irj/go/km/docs/documents/Treasury%20Web/Research&Data/Reports/State%20Owned%20Enterprises%20Reports/2007_Public_Enterprises_Report.pdf.

EU (2010), *Turkey 2010 Progress Report*, Commission Staff Working Document, SEC(2010) 1327 - Accompanying the Communication from the Commission to the European Parliament and the Council, Enlargement Strategy and Main Challenges 2010-2011, EN, COM(2010) 660, November, Brussels.

EU (2011), *Turkey 2011 Progress Report,* Commission Staff Working Document, SEC(2011) 1201 - Accompanying the Communication from the Commission to the European Parliament and the Council, Enlargement Strategy and Main Challenges 2011-2012, EN, COM(2011) 666, October, Brussels.

IEA, Energy Policies of IEA Countries, Turkey 2009 Review. Viewed at: http://www.iea.org/publications/free_new_Desc.asp?PUBS_ID=2276.

Ministry of Agriculture and Rural Affairs (undated), *Instrument for Pre-Accession Assistance Rural Development (IPARD) Programme*. European Commission online information. Viewed at: http://ec.europa.eu/enlargement/pdf/turkey/ipa/tk5_tk_ipard_programme _2007_en.pdf.

OECD (2010a), *Agricultural Water Pricing: Turkey,* Cakmak, Erol H. Viewed at: http://www.oecd.org/dataoecd/26/21/45016347.pdf.

OECD (2010b), *Economic Surveys: Turkey,* September. Viewed at: http://www.oecd.org/dataoecd/23/10/ 45951718.pdf.

OECD (2011a), *Agricultural Policies in OECD Countries and Emerging Economies,* Part II, Paris. Viewed at: http://www.oecd-ilibrary.org/docserver/download/fulltext/5111031ec020.pdf?expires=1317980850&id=id&accname=ocid195767&checksum=7E96407D145A076DAD284F2A7B9F4ECF

OECD (2011b), *Evaluation of Agricultural Policy Reforms in Turkey,* Paris. Viewed at: http://dx.doi.org/10.1787/9789264113220-en.

State Planning Organization (2009), *Strategy and Action Plan for Istanbul Financial Center* (IFC-Istanbul), Ankara, October. Viewed at www.ifm.gov.tr/Shared%20Documents/Strategy%20and%20Action%20Plan%20for%20IFC%20Istanbul.pdf.

Turkish Grain Board (2011), *Grain Report for the Year 2010*. Viewed at: http://www.tmo.gov.tr/Upload/Document/yayinlar/2010_Hububat_Raporu_ING.pdf.

UNCTAD (2011), *World Investment Report 2011*, July, Geneva. Viewed at: http://www.unctad.org.

Undersecretariat of Treasury, *State Owned Enterprises Statistics.* Viewed at: http://www.treasury.gov.tr/irj/portal/anonymous? NavigationTarget=navurl://263c93ab665e5050055 7fe7606abf8f&Light DTNKnobID=1969438794.

U.S. Commercial Service (2011), *Doing Business in Turkey: 2011 Country Commercial Guide for US Companies.* Viewed at http://export.gov/turkey/doingbusinessinturkey/index.asp.

USDA Foreign Agricultural Service (2011), *Turkey Exporter Guide 2010,* April. Viewed at: http://gain.fas.usda.gov/Recent%20GAIN%20Publications/Exporter%20Guide_Ankara_Turkey_2-4-2011.pdf.

USTR (2011), *2011 National Trade Estimate Report on Foreign Trade Barriers: Turkey.* Viewed at: http://www.ustr.gov/about-us/press-office/reports-and-publications/2011-0.

WTO (1998), *Trade Policy Review: Turkey,* Geneva.

WTO (2003), *Trade Policy Review: Turkey,* Geneva.

WTO (2007), *Trade Policy Review: Turkey,* Geneva.

WTO (2009), *Statistics Database, Trade Profiles: Country Profile: Turkey*, Geneva. Viewed at: http://stat.wto.org/countryprofile/wsdbcountrypfview.aspx?languageturkey=e&country=tr.

APPENDIX TABLES

Table AI.1
Structure of exports, 2006-10
(US$ million and %)

	2006	2007	2008	2009	2010
Total (US$ million)	85,534.7	107,271.7	132,027.2	102,142.6	113,883.2
			(%)		
Total primary products	17.7	17.5	17.8	18.0	19.5
Agriculture	10.1	9.1	8.7	11.0	11.1
Food	9.3	8.4	8.1	10.4	10.4
Agricultural raw material	0.8	0.7	0.6	0.6	0.7
Mining	7.6	8.4	9.2	7.0	8.4
Ores and other minerals	1.8	1.9	1.9	1.8	2.6
Non-ferrous metals	1.7	1.7	1.6	1.3	1.9
6842 Aluminium and aluminium alloys, worked	0.9	1.0	0.8	0.8	1.0
Fuels	4.2	4.8	5.7	3.8	3.9
Manufactures	81.0	81.1	79.0	76.9	78.3
Iron and steel	8.5	8.9	12.8	8.9	9.0
6762 Bars/rods (not 676.1) iron/steel, hot-rolled, etc.	0.1	0.1	0.1	0.0	0.1
6726 Semi-finished iron/steel products <0.25% carbon	0.4	0.5	1.2	0.9	1.4
6794 Other tubes, pipes, and hollow profiles, iron/steel	1.1	1.0	1.1	1.0	1.0
Chemicals	4.6	4.4	4.6	5.2	6.0
Other semi-manufactures	8.9	9.0	9.3	10.2	10.4
6612 Portland cement and similar hydraulic cements	0.5	0.5	0.9	1.2	1.0
Machinery and transport equipment	30.8	31.9	29.7	28.2	27.9
Power generating machines	0.8	0.8	0.8	0.6	0.6
Other non-electrical machinery	4.0	4.4	4.2	3.8	4.0
Agricultural machinery and tractors	0.3	0.3	0.3	0.3	0.3
Office machines & telecommunication equipment	3.7	2.7	1.8	2.0	1.8
7611 Color television receivers	3.4	2.2	1.4	1.7	1.5
Other electrical machines	5.2	5.7	5.3	6.1	6.3
7731 Insulated wire, cable, etc.; optical fibre cables	1.3	1.6	1.6	1.4	1.6
7752 Household fridges and freezers	1.1	1.1	0.8	1.0	1.0
Automotive products	13.7	14.5	13.5	11.7	12.1
7812 Motor vehicles for the transport of persons, n.e.s.	6.6	6.4	5.7	6.0	5.5
7821 Goods vehicles	3.5	3.9	3.9	2.3	2.9
7843 Other motor vehicle parts and accessories of 722, 781 to 783	2.1	2.4	2.2	2.0	2.3
Other transport equipment	3.6	3.9	3.7	3.6	3.0
7139 Parts, n.e.s., for piston engines of 713.2, 713.3, 713.8	1.2	1.2	1.0	0.8	1.0
Textiles	8.9	8.3	7.1	7.6	7.9
6552 Other knitted/crocheted fabrics, not impregnated/coated, etc.	0.8	0.9	0.8	0.9	1.0
Clothing	14.1	12.9	10.3	11.3	11.2
8454 T-shirts, singlets and other vests, knitted or crocheted	3.4	2.9	2.2	2.3	2.4
8453 Jerseys, pullovers, cardigans, etc., knitted/crocheted	1.4	1.2	0.9	1.1	1.1
8426 Trousers, breeches, etc., women's/girls', not knitted/crocheted	1.7	1.5	1.1	1.1	1.0
8414 Trousers, bib and brace overalls, breeches and shorts	1.1	1.0	0.9	1.0	0.9
Other consumer goods	5.3	5.5	5.2	5.6	5.9
8973 Jewellery of gold, silver or platinum metals (except watches)	1.3	1.5	1.3	1.1	1.3
Other	1.2	1.4	3.2	5.1	2.2
Gold	0.7	0.9	2.8	4.5	1.8
9710 Gold, non-monetary (excl. gold ores and concentrates)	0.7	0.9	2.8	4.5	1.8

Source: UNSD, Comtrade database (SITC Rev.3); and data provided by the Turkish authorities.

Table AI.2
Destinations of exports, 2006-10
(US$ million and %)

	2006	2007	2008	2009	2010
Total (US$ million)	85,534.7	107,271.7	132,027.2	102,142.6	113,883.2
			(%)		
America	7.4	5.2	5.0	4.8	5.3
United States	5.9	3.9	3.3	3.2	3.3
Other America	1.5	1.3	1.7	1.6	2.0
Europe	60.1	60.4	53.1	52.8	50.8
EU(27)	56.0	56.3	48.0	46.0	46.3
Germany	11.3	11.2	9.8	9.6	10.1
United Kingdom	8.0	8.0	6.2	5.8	6.4
Italy	7.9	7.0	5.9	5.8	5.7
France	5.4	5.6	5.0	6.1	5.3
Spain	4.3	4.3	3.1	2.8	3.1
Romania	2.7	3.4	3.0	2.2	2.3
The Netherlands	3.0	2.8	2.4	2.1	2.2
Belgium	1.6	1.6	1.6	1.8	1.7
EFTA	1.4	1.2	2.5	4.2	2.1
Switzerland	1.1	0.9	2.2	3.9	1.8
Other	2.6	2.9	2.6	2.5	2.4
Commonwealth of Independent States (CIS)	7.7	8.8	9.8	7.8	9.0
Russian Federation	3.8	4.4	4.9	3.1	4.1
Azerbaijan	0.8	1.0	1.3	1.4	1.4
Africa	5.3	5.6	6.9	9.9	8.2
Egypt	0.8	0.8	1.1	2.5	2.0
Libya	0.6	0.6	0.8	1.8	1.7
Middle East	11.9	12.5	17.2	16.7	18.4
Iraq	3.0	2.7	3.0	5.0	5.3
United Arab Emirates	2.3	3.0	6.0	2.8	2.9
Iran Islamic Rep.	1.2	1.3	1.5	2.0	2.7
Saudi Arabia	1.1	1.4	1.7	1.7	1.9
Israel	1.8	1.5	1.5	1.5	1.8
Syrian Arab Republic	0.7	0.7	0.8	1.4	1.6
Asia	3.5	3.6	4.2	4.9	5.8
China	0.8	1.0	1.1	1.6	2.0
Japan	0.3	0.2	0.3	0.2	0.2
Six East Asian Traders	1.0	0.9	1.2	1.2	1.5
Other Asia	1.4	1.5	1.7	2.0	2.0
Other	4.1	3.9	3.8	3.1	2.5
Free zones	3.5	2.7	2.3	1.9	1.8

Source: UNSD, Comtrade database (SITC Rev.3); and data provided by the Turkish authorities.

Table AI.3
Structure of imports, 2006-10
(US$ million and %)

	2006	2007	2008	2009	2010
Total (US$ million)	139,576.2	170,062.7	201,963.6	140,928.4	185,544.3
			(%)		
Total primary products	32.9	33.4	38.7	34.7	35.7
Agriculture	5.2	5.8	6.5	6.8	6.9
Food	2.5	3.0	4.2	4.3	4.0
Agricultural raw material	2.7	2.7	2.2	2.5	2.9
2631 Cotton (other than linters), not carded or combed	0.7	0.8	0.5	0.7	0.9
Mining	27.7	27.6	32.2	27.9	28.8
Ores and other minerals	3.5	3.9	5.1	3.9	4.6
2823 Other ferrous waste and scrap	2.8	3.3	4.4	3.0	3.8
Non-ferrous metals	3.5	3.7	3.2	2.8	3.4
6821 Copper anodes; alloys; unwrought	1.3	1.4	1.2	1.1	1.4
6841 Aluminium and aluminium alloys, unwrought	0.9	1.0	0.8	0.8	0.9
Fuels	20.7	19.9	23.9	21.2	20.7
3330 Crude oils of petroleum and bituminous minerals	7.7	6.9	7.7	4.6	0.0
3212 Other coal, whether or pulverized, not agglomerated	1.4	1.5	1.6	2.1	0.5
3442 Gaseous hydrocarbons, liquefied, n.e.s.	1.1	1.0	1.1	1.1	1.2
Manufactures	63.9	63.1	58.5	63.7	62.7
Iron and steel	5.8	6.7	7.4	5.4	5.2
Chemicals	13.2	13.0	12.6	14.4	13.7
5429 Medicaments, n.e.s.	1.3	1.2	1.3	1.8	1.4
5751 Propylene polymers or of other olefins	1.1	1.1	1.0	1.0	1.2
5711 Polyethylene	0.7	0.8	0.7	0.8	0.8
Other semi-manufactures	5.1	4.9	4.5	4.8	4.9
Machinery and transport equipment	30.8	29.3	25.5	29.1	29.0
Power generating machines	0.7	0.8	1.2	2.2	1.9
7165 Generating sets	0.1	0.2	0.4	0.6	0.6
Other non-electrical machinery	9.2	9.0	7.3	7.3	7.1
Agricultural machinery and tractors	0.4	0.2	0.2	0.2	0.2
Office machines & telecommunication equipment	5.5	5.1	4.0	5.1	4.6
7643 Radio or television transmission apparatus	1.1	1.1	0.8	0.9	0.8
7522 Data processing machines, with at least processing, input, and output units	0.5	0.5	0.4	0.7	0.6
Other electrical machines	3.7	3.7	3.4	4.2	3.9
7788 Electrical machinery and equipment, n.e.s.	1.0	0.9	0.8	1.1	1.1
Automotive products	9.3	8.6	7.5	7.5	8.3
7812 Motor vehicles for the transport of persons, n.e.s.	3.1	2.8	2.3	3.0	3.7
7843 Other motor vehicle parts and accessories of 722, 781 to 783	3.0	2.9	2.6	2.4	2.4
7132 Internal combustion engines for vehicles of 78; 744.14, 744.15, 891.11	1.5	1.5	1.3	1.1	1.2
Other transport equipment	2.4	2.0	2.1	2.9	3.2
7924 Aeroplanes, etc. (excluding helicopters), >15,000 kg unladen	0.9	0.4	0.6	0.4	1.2
Textiles	3.4	3.6	2.9	3.5	3.6
Clothing	0.8	0.9	1.1	1.5	1.5
Other consumer goods	4.8	4.7	4.4	4.9	4.7
Other	3.2	3.5	2.8	1.6	1.6
Gold	2.9	3.1	2.5	1.2	1.4
9710 Gold, non-monetary (excluding gold ores and concentrates)	2.9	3.1	2.5	1.2	1.4

Source: UNSD, Comtrade database (SITC Rev.3); and data provided by the Turkish authorities.

Table AI.4
Origins of imports, 2006-10
(US$ million and %)

	2006	2007	2008	2009	2010
Total (US$ million)	139,576.2	170,062.7	201,963.6	140,928.4	185,544.3
			(%)		
America	6.7	7.1	8.5	8.7	9.1
United States	4.5	4.8	5.9	6.1	6.6
Other America	2.2	2.3	2.6	2.6	2.4
Europe	46.0	43.9	40.3	42.4	41.4
EU(27)	42.6	40.3	37.0	40.2	38.9
Germany	10.6	10.3	9.3	10.0	9.5
Italy	6.2	5.9	5.5	5.4	5.5
France	5.2	4.6	4.5	5.0	4.4
Spain	2.7	2.6	2.3	2.7	2.6
United Kingdom	3.7	3.2	2.6	2.5	2.5
Romania	1.9	1.8	1.8	1.6	1.9
Belgium	1.8	1.7	1.6	1.7	1.7
Netherlands	1.5	1.6	1.5	1.8	1.7
Poland	1.0	1.0	1.0	1.3	1.4
Sweden	1.1	1.0	0.9	1.3	1.0
EFTA	3.2	3.4	3.1	2.0	2.2
Switzerland	2.9	3.1	2.8	1.4	1.7
Other	0.2	0.2	0.2	0.2	0.3
Commonwealth of Independent States (CIS)	16.5	18.2	20.8	18.3	16.5
Russian Federation	12.8	13.8	15.5	13.8	11.6
Ukraine	2.2	2.7	3.0	2.2	2.1
Kazakhstan	0.7	0.8	1.2	1.0	1.3
Africa	5.3	4.0	3.8	4.0	3.5
Algeria	1.3	1.2	1.6	1.4	1.2
Middle East	7.1	7.1	8.0	6.1	8.0
Iran Islamic Rep.	4.0	3.9	4.1	2.4	4.1
Saudi Arabia	1.6	1.4	1.6	1.2	1.3
Asia	17.4	18.7	17.6	19.5	20.4
China	6.9	7.8	7.8	9.0	9.3
Japan	2.3	2.2	2.0	2.0	1.8
Six East Asian Traders	5.4	5.4	4.6	4.7	5.0
Korea, Rep. of	2.5	2.6	2.0	2.2	2.6
Chinese Taipei	1.2	1.1	0.8	1.0	1.0
Other Asia	2.8	3.4	3.3	3.8	4.3
India	1.1	1.4	1.2	1.4	1.8
Other	1.0	1.0	1.0	1.0	1.1

Source: UNSD, Comtrade database (SITC Rev.3); and data provided by the Turkish authorities.

Table AII.1
Trade-related legislation, 2011

Area	Legislation	Entry into force
Foreign trade; including export promotion, and "additional financial obligations" on foreign trade transactions	Foreign Trade Regulations Law (No. 2976 of 1984)	1984
Customs	Customs Law (No. 4458 of 2000)	2000
Import regulations	Import Regime Decree (No. 7606 of 1995)	1995
	Quota and Tariff Quota Administration Decree (No. 339 of 2010)	2010
Export regulations	Law on Measures to be taken by the Government Relating to Taxes for the Purpose of Promoting Exports (No. 261 of 1963)	1963
	Export Regime Decree (No. 7623 of 1995)	1996
	Export Regulation (*Official Gazette* No. 26190 of 2006)	2006
	Inward Processing Regime Decree (No. 8391 of 2005)	2005
	Outward Processing Regime Decree (No. 11864 of 2007)	2007
Government procurement	Public Procurement Law (No. 4734 of 2002)	2002
	Public Procurement Contracts Law (No. 4735 of 2002)	2002
State aid	Decree Concerning State Aid to Investments (No. 15199 of 2009)	2009
	Communiqué Regarding the implementation of the Decree Concerning State Aid to Investments (No. 1 of 2009)	2002 2006
	State Aid on Exports Decree (No. 6401 of 1994)	1994
	Procedures for Collection of Public Claims Law (No. 6183 of 1953)	1995
Fiscal	Personal Taxes Law (No. 5479 of 2006)	2006
	Corporate Tax Law (No. 5520 of 2006, amending Law No. 5422)	2006
	Income Tax Law (No. 5479 of 2006)	2006
	Law No. 4842 of 2003, amending Law No. 4369 of 1998,	2003
	Special Consumption Tax (SCT) Law (No. 4760 of 2002)	2002
Privatization	Privatization Law No. 4046 of 1994, amended by Law No. 4971 of 2003	2003
	Law No. 4446 of 1999 (amendment of Articles 47 and 155 of the Constitution)	1999
Land ownership	Land Registry Law No. 2644 (Article 35 and 36)	2005
	Law on Soil Conservation and Land Use (No. 5403)	
Employment	Labour Law (No. 4857 of 2003)	2003
	Employment of Foreign Personnel Law (No. 4817 of 2003)	2003
	Maritime Labour Law (No. 854)	1967
	Press Labour Law (No. 5953)	1952
	Draft amendments to legislation on the employment of foreigners, presented to the Parliament in May 2006	
	Turkish Employment Agency Law (No. 4904 of 2003)	2003
Regional investment incentives	Organized Industrial Zones Law (No. 4562 of 2000)	2000
	Industrial Zones Law (No. 4737 of 2002)	2002
	Law on the Encouragement of Investment and Employment and Amendment of Certain Laws (No. 5084 of 2004)	2004
	Law (No. 5350 of 2005), and Law (No. 5615 of 2007) amending Law No. 5084	2005, 2007
	Communiqué No. 2007/1 regarding the implementation of Energy Support Measures (*Official Gazette* No. 26572 of 2007)	2007
Subsidies	Adopting the Agreement on Interpretation and Application of Articles IV, XVI, and XXIII of the GATT (subsidies code) Decree (No. 9155 of 1985)	1985
Free zones	Free Zones Law (No. 3218 of 1985)	1985
	Law on the Encouragement of Investment and Employment and Amendment of Certain Laws (No. 5084 of 2004)	2004
Technical regulations and standards	The Law Relating to the Preparation And Implementation Of Technical Legislation On Products (No. 4703)	2002
	Ministerial Decree on the Regime Regarding Technical Regulations and Standardization for Foreign Trade (No. 9454 of 2005)	2005
Sanitary and phytosanitary measures	Sanitary Law (No. 1593 of 1930)	1930
	Turkish Foods Codex Regulation (*Official Gazette* No. 23172 (bis) of 1997)	1997
	Fisheries Law (No. 1380 of 1971); amended by Law No. 3288/1986	1986
	Fisheries Regulation (No. 22223 of 1995)	1995
	Law on Veterinary Services, Plant Health, Food, and Feed No. 5996	2010

Table AII.1 (cont'd)

Area	Legislation	Entry into force
Anti-dumping and countervailing measures	Law on the Prevention of Unfair Competition on Imports (No. 4412 of 1999)	1999
	Decree on the Prevention of Unfair Competition on Imports (No. 23861 of 1999 and Amendment 9840 of 2005)	1999
	Regulation on the Prevention of Unfair Competition on Imports (No. 23861 of 1999 and Amendment No. 24743 of 2002 and Addendum No. 26061 of 2006)	1999
Safeguard measures	Decree No. 7305 (*Official Gazette* No. 25476 of 29 May 2004) Regulation on Safeguard Measures for Imports (*Official Gazette* No. 25486 of 8 June 2004)	2004 2004
Competition	The Act on the Protection of Competition (No. 4054 of 1994)	1994
	Communiqué 1997/1 on Mergers and Acquisitions of 1997	1997
	Communiqué No. 1997/5 on the conclusion of the organization of the competition	1997
	Communiqué 1998/4 on Methods and Principles to be pursued during the course of Pre-Notifications and Applications for Authorization Made on the Competition Authority in order to Acquisitions via Privatization to judicially be valid	1998
	Block Exemption Communiqué No. 2002/2 regarding Vertical Agreements	2002
	Block Exemption Communiqué No. 2003/2 on Research and Development Agreements	2003
	Block Exemption Communiqué No. 2005/4 on Vertical Agreements and Concerted Practices in the Motor Vehicle Sector	2006
	Communiqué No. 2006/2 on an amendment to the Communiqué No. 1997/1 on mergers and acquisitions calling for the authorization of the Competition Board, and on the abolition of Communiqués No. 1997/2 and 1997/6	2006
	Communiqué No. 2007/1 on the announcement of an increase in administrative fines, valid until 31 December 2007	2007
	Guidelines on the explanation of block exemption Communiqué No. 2002/2 regarding vertical agreements	2003
	Guidelines in respect of the voluntary notification of agreement, concerted practices and decisions of associations of undertakings	2006
	Guidelines on the explanation of the block exemption Communiqué No. 2005/4 on vertical agreements and concerted practices in the motor vehicle sector	2006
Intellectual property rights	Law No. 5000 relating to the establishment and the functions of the Turkish Patent Institute	2003
	Protection of Patent Rights Decree (No. 551 of 1995), as amended	1995
	Protection of Trade Mark Rights Decree (No. 556 of 1995), amended by the Directive on Trade and Services Marks (*Official Gazette* No. 24)	1995
	Protection of Industrial Designs Decree (No. 554 of 1995)	1995
	Protection of Geographical Indications Decree (No. 555 of 1995)	1995
	Intellectual and Artistic Works Law (No. 5846 of 1951; amended by Law No. 2936 of 1983, No. 4110 of 1995, Law No. 4630 of 2001, Law No. 5101 of 2004, Law No. 5571 of 2006, and Law No. 5728 of 2008)	1951 1995
	Additional Penalty Provisions to the Decrees No. 551, 554, 555, and 556 (Law No. 4128 of 1995)	1995
	Amendment of the Transition Period of Patent Protection of Pharmaceutical and Veterinary Products and Processes Decree (No. 566 of 1995)	2004
	Law on the Amendment of Various IPRs Laws (No. 5101of 2004)	2004
	Law on the Protection of Integrated Circuit Topographies (No. 5147 of 2004)	2004
	Law No. 5194 amending Decree Laws No. 551; 554 of 1995, and on Trademarks	
	Law on ratification of participation in WIPO Copyright Treaty	2008
	Law on ratification of participation in WIPO Performances and Phonogram Treaty	2008
	Law No. 5042 on protection of breeders' rights on new plant varieties	2004
	Law No. 5833 Amending the Decree Law on Protection of Trademarks	2009
Consumer protection	Law on the Protection of Consumers (No. 4077 of 1995)	1995
	Law (No. 4822 of 2003, amending Law No. 4077)	2003

Table AII.1 (cont'd)

Area	Legislation	Entry into force
Foreign investment	Foreign Direct Investment (FDI) Law (No. 4875 of 2003)	2003
	Regulation for the Implementation of the FDI Law (*Official Gazette* No. 25205 of 20 August 2003	
Company establishment	Turkish Commercial Code No. 6762	1957
	Law amending the Turkish Commercial Code, Tax Procedure Law, Stamp Tax Law, Labour Law and Social Insurance Law (No. 4884 of 2003)	2003
	New Turkish Commercial Code (No. 6102 of 2011)	2012
Agriculture	Agriculture Law (No. 5488 of 2006)	2006
	Seed Law (No. 5553 of 2006)	2006
	Agricultural Products Licensed Warehousing Law (No. 5300)	2005
	The Law About the Regulation of Trade of Vegetable and Fruit and Other Commodities that has Sufficient Intense in Demand and Supply (No. 5957 of 2010)	2012
	Decree on Seed Imports (No. 8231 of 1984)	1984
	Decree on Customs Tax Exemption On Seed Imports (No. 4190 of 1993)	1993
	Regulation on Chemical Fertilizers Used in Agriculture (No. 25406 of 2004), amended by *Official Gazette* No. 26243 of 2006	2004
	Regulation on Production, Import, Export, Marketing, and Control of Organic, Orgonomineral and Microbial Fertilizers and Soil Regulators Used in Agriculture (No. 25452 of 2004), amended by Nos. 26048 and 26290 of 2006, and No. 26449 of 2007	2004 2005
	Regulation No. 25841 of 2005 on Principles and Applications of Organic Farming, amended by No. 26322 of 2006	2005
	Regulation No. 25577 of 2004 on Good Agricultural Practices, amended by No. 25806 of 2005 and No. 26169 of 2006	2004
	Agricultural Insurance Law (No. 5363 of 2005)	2005
	Organic Farming Law (No. 5262 of 2004)	2004
	Law on Agricultural Producer Unions (No. 5200 of 2004)	2004
	Regulation on aquaculture (*Official Gazette* No. 25507 of 2004), amended by *Official Gazette* Nos. 25901 and 25967 of 2005, and No. 26556 of 2007	2004
	Agriculture Strategy Paper 2006-10 (No. 2004/92 of 2004)	2004
Mining and energy	Mining Law (No. 3213 of 1985)	1985
	Mining Law (No. 5177 of 2004)	2004
	Mining Law (No. 5995 of 2010)	2010
	Electricity Market Law (No. 4628 of 2001)	2001
	Petroleum Market Law (No. 5015 of 2003)	2003
	Natural Gas Market Law (No. 4646 of 2001)	2001
	LPG Market Law (No. 5307 of 2005)	2005
	Law on the Use of Renewable Energy Resources for Electricity Production Purposes (No. 5346 of 2005)	2005
	Petroleum Law (No. 6326 of 1954)	1954
Telecommunications	Telegraph and Telephone Law (No. 406 of 1924)	1924
	Law Amending Telegraph and Telephone Law (No. 4000 of 1994)	1994
	Law Amending Telegraph and Telephone Law (No. 4107 of 1995)	1995
	Law Amending Telegraph and Telephone Law (No. 4161 of 1996)	1996
	Telecommunications Law Amending Telegraph and Telephone Law (No. 4502 of 2000)	2000
	Law Amending Telegraph and Telephone Law (No. 4673 of 2001)	2001
	By-Law on Authorization for Electronic Communications Sector	2009
	By-Law on Tenders Concerning Authorization in the Electronic Communications Sector	2010
	By-Law on Number Portability	2009
	Regulation on Procedures and Principles Regarding the Provision of Trial Permission in the Electronic Communications Sector	2004
	By-Law on Numbering	2009
	By-Law on Rights of Way Regarding Provision of Electronic Communication Services	2010
	Law Amending Establishment and Broadcast of Radio TVs Law (No. 4756 of 2002)	..
	Law on "Establishment of Radio and Television Enterprises and Their Media Services"	2011
	Law No. 6112; Date: 15.02.2011	2011

Table AII.1 (cont'd)

Area	Legislation	Entry into force
Financial services	Banking Law (No. 5411 of 2005)	2005
	Capital Market Law (No. 2499 of 1981), amended in 1992 by Law No. 3794, and in 1999 by Law No. 4487	1999
	Insurance Supervision Law (No. 5684 of 2007)	2007
	Public Financial Management and Control Law (No. 5018)	2003
	Bank Cards and Credit Cards Law (No. 5464 of 2006)	2006
	Law on Financial Restructuring of SMEs' Debts to the Financial Sector (No. 5569 of 2006)	2006
	Financial Leasing Law (No. 3226 of 1985)	1985
Transport	Turkish Commercial Law (No. 6762 of 1956)	1956
	Cabotage Law (No. 815 of 1926)	1926
	Public Law on Turkish Civil Aviation (No. 2920 of 1983; Article 25 was changed on 19.04.2001 by Law No. 4647)	1983
	Ports Law (No. 168 of 1925)	1925
	Turkish International Ship Register (No. 4490 of 1999)	1999
	Regulation on Commercial Air Transport Operations (No. SHY-6A of 1984), amended by Regulation No. 24362 of 03.04.2001)	2001
	Regulation on Airport Construction, Operation and Certification (SHY-14 A), issued by Regulation No. 24755 of 14.05.2002	2002
	Regulation on Airport Ground-handling (SHY-22), issued by Regulation No. 22741 of 28.08.1996 was amended on 19.09.1999	1999
	Law No. 4925 on Road Transport	2003
	Law on training for professional competence in road transport operations (*Official Gazette* No. 25572 of 2004)	2004
	Law on Road Traffic (*Official Gazette* No. *2918* of 1983), amended by (*Official Gazette* No. *54952* of 2006)	2006
	General Directorate of Civil Aviation Law (No. 5431 of 2005)	2005
Tourism	Tourism Encouragement Law (No. 2634 of 1982)	1982
	Law on Travel Agencies and Association of Travel Agencies (No. 1618 of 1972)	1972

.. Not available.

Source: Information provided by the Turkish authorities.

Table AIII.1
Textiles and clothing products subject to registration

HS code	Descriptions
3204.11.00.00.00	- - Disperse dyes and preparations based thereon
3204.12.00.00.11	- - Acid dyes, whether or not premetallized, and preparations based thereon; mordant dyes and preparations based thereon: acid dyes
3204.12.00.00.19	- - Acid dyes, whether or not premetallized, and preparations based thereon; mordant dyes and preparations based thereon: other
3204.13.00.00.00	- - Basic dyes and preparations based thereon
3204.14.00.00.00	- - Direct dyes and preparations based thereon
4203.10	- Articles of apparel
4203.21	- Gloves, mittens and mitts: specially designed for use in sports
4203.29	- Gloves, mittens and mitts: other
4203.30	- Belts and bandoliers
4303.10	- Articles of apparel and clothing accessories
43.04	Artificial fur and articles thereof
Chapter 50	Silk
Chapter 51	Wool, fine or coarse animal hair; horsehair yarn and woven fabric
Chapter 52	Cotton
Chapter 53	Other vegetable textile fibres; paper yarn and woven fabrics of paper yarn
Chapter 54 (excluded 5407.20)	Man- Made filaments (excluding woven fabrics obtained from strip or the like (HS 540720)
Chapter 55	Man- Made staple fibres
Chapter 56	Wadding, felt and nonwovens; special yarns; twine, cordage, ropes and cables and articles thereof
Chapter 57 (excluded 57.01 and 57.02)	Carpets and other textile floor coverings [excluding carpets and other textile floor coverings, knotted (HS 5701) and carpets and other textile floor coverings, woven, not tufted or flocked, including "Kelem", "Schumacks", "Karamanie" and similar hand-woven rugs (HS 5702)
Chapter 58 (excluded 58.05)	Special woven fabrics; tufted textile fabrics; lace; tapestries; trimmings; embroidery (excluding hand-woven tapestries of the type gobelins, flanders, aubusson, beauvais and the like, and needle-worked tapestries (HS 5805)
Chapter 59	Impregnated, coated, covered or laminated textile fabrics; textile articles of a kind suitable for industrial use
Chapter 60	Knitted or crocheted fabrics
Chapter 61	Articles of apparel and clothing accessories, knitted or crocheted
Chapter 62	Articles of apparel and clothing accessories, not Knitted or crocheted
Chapter 63 (excluded 6305.32 and 6305.33)	Other made up textile articles; sets; worn clothing and worn textile articles; rags (excluding man-made textile materials: flexible intermediate bulk containers (HS 630532) and other, of polyethylene or polypropylene strip (HS 630533)
65.05	Hats and other headgear, knitted or crocheted, or made up from lace, felt or other textile fabric, in the piece (but not in strips), whether or not lined or trimmed; hair-nets of any Material, whether or not lined or trimmed
9404.21	- Mattresses: of cellular rubber or plastics, whether or not covered
9404.29	- Mattresses: of other materials
9404.30	- Sleeping bags
9404.90	- Other articles of bedding and similar furnishing

Source: Information provided by the Turkish authorities.

Table AIII.2
Products subject to non-*ad valorem* tariffs, 2011

HS code	Duty	*Ad Valorem* equivalent (%)	Bound duty (%)
Compound duties:			
0403.10.51.10.00	€140.9/100 kg/net+8.3%	n.a.	180
0403.10.51.90.00	€140.9/100 kg/net+8.3%	n.a.	180
0403.10.53.10.00	€142.31/100 kg/net+8.3%	n.a.	180
0403.10.53.90.00	€142.31/100 kg/net+8.3%	n.a.	180
0403.10.59.10.00	€176.24/100 kg/net+8.3%	n.a.	180
0403.10.59.90.00	€176.24/100 kg/net+8.3%	n.a.	180
0403.10.91.10.00	€21.05/100 kg/net+8.3%	n.a.	180
0403.10.91.90.00	€21.05/100 kg/net+8.3%	n.a.	180
0403.10.93.10.00	€26.21/100 kg/net+8.3%	n.a.	180
0403.10.93.90.00	€26.21/100 kg/net+8.3%	n.a.	180
0403.10.99.10.00	€34.82/100 kg/net+8.3%	n.a.	180
0403.10.99.90.00	€34.82/100 kg/net+8.3%	n.a.	180
0403.90.71.10.00	€140.9/100 kg/net+8.3%	n.a.	180
0403.90.71.90.00	€140.9/100 kg/net+8.3%	n.a.	180
0403.90.73.10.00	€142.31/100 kg/net+8.3%	n.a.	180
0403.90.73.90.00	€142.31/100 kg/net+8.3%	n.a.	180
0403.90.79.10.00	€176.24/100 kg/net+8.3%	n.a.	180
0403.90.79.90.00	€176.24/100 kg/net+8.3%	n.a.	180
0403.90.91.10.00	€21.05/100 kg/net+8.3%	n.a.	180
0403.90.91.90.00	€21.05/100 kg/net+8.3%	n.a.	180
0403.90.93.10.00	€26.21/100 kg/net+8.3%	n.a.	180
0403.90.93.90.00	€26.21/100 kg/net+8.3%	n.a.	180
0403.90.99.10.00	€34.82/100 kg/net+8.3%	n.a.	180
0403.90.99.90.00	€34,82/100 kg/net+8.3%	10.0	180
0710.40.00.00.00	€2.91/100 kg/net+5.1%	8.7	59
0711.90.30.00.00	€2.91/100 kg/net+5.1%	5.2	59
1517.10.10.00.00	€25.82/100 kg/net+8.3%	21.0	59
1517.90.10.00.00	€25.82/100 kg/net+8.3%	n.a.	59
1702.50.00.00.00	€19.5/100 kg/net+16%	28.0	29
1704.10.10.00.11	€72.74/100 kg/net+6.2%	15.1	135
1704.10.10.00.19	€94.3/100 kg/net+6.2%	28.6	135
1704.10.90.00.11	€79.81/100 kg/net+6.3%	23.8	135
1704.10.90.00.19	€72.99/100 kg/net+6.3%	28.7	135
1704.90.30.00.00	€89.67/100 kg/net+9.1%	33.0	135
1806.10.20.00.00	€68.4/100 kg/net+8%	28.3	90
1806.10.30.00.00	€71.71/100 kg/net+8%	23.2	90
1806.10.90.00.00	€106.68/100 kg/net+8%	n.a.	90
1901.90.11.00.00	€35.45/100 kg/net+5.1%	28.7	63
1901.90.19.00.00	€21.85/100 kg/net+5.1%	25.6	63
1902.11.00.00.11	€10.67/100 kg/net+7.7%	16.2	45
1902.11.00.00.19	€10.67/100 kg/net+7.7%	12.1	45
1902.19.10.00.00	€10.67/100 kg/net+7.7%	15.0	45
1902.19.90.00.11	€11.37/100 kg/net+7.7%	12.9	45
1902.19.90.00.12	€11.37/100 kg/net+7.7%	15.6	45
1902.19.90.00.19	€11.37/100 kg/net+7.7%	17.3	45
1902.20.91.00.00	€50.89/100 kg/net+8.3%	24.0	45
1902.20.99.00.00	€48.89/100 kg/net+8.3%	20.6	45
1902.30.10.00.00	€40.27/100 kg/net+6.4%	24.0	45
1902.30.90.00.00	€39.01/100 kg/net+6.4%	38.8	45
1902.40.10.00.00	€10.67/100 kg/net+7.7%	14.8	45
1902.40.90.00.00	€30.21/100 kg/net+6.4%	16.7	45

Table AIII.2 (cont'd)

HS code	Duty	*Ad Valorem* equivalent (%)	Bound duty (%)
1903.00.00.00.00	€18.88/100 kg/net+6.4%	22.4	39
1904.10.10.10.00	€55.63/100 kg/net+3.8%	38.5	68
1904.10.10.90.00	€55.63/100 kg/net+3.8%	37.8	45
1904.10.30.10.00	€44.21/100 kg/net+5.1%	25.7	68
1904.10.30.90.00	€44.21/100 kg/net+5.1%	21.1	45
1904.10.90.10.00	€62.62/100 kg/net+5.1%	39.6	68
1904.10.90.90.00	€62.62/100 kg/net+5.1%	29.6	45
1904.20.91.10.00	€55.63/100 kg/net+3.8%	53.5	68
1904.20.91.90.00	€55.63/100 kg/net+3.8%	36.5	45
1904.20.95.10.00	€44.21/100 kg/net+5.1%	n.a.	68
1904.20.95.90.00	€44.21/100 kg/net+5.1%	9.2	45
1904.20.99.10.00	€62.62/100 kg/net+5.1%	17.5	68
1904.20.99.90.00	€62.62/100 kg/net+5.1%	20.6	45
1904.30.00.00.00	€22.33/100 kg/net+8.3%	50.1	68
1904.90.10.10.00	€59/100 kg/net+8.3%	n.a.	90
1904.90.10.90.00	€53.3/100 kg/net+8.3%	35.1	68
1904.90.80.10.00	€22.33/100 kg/net+8.3%	n.a.	90
1904.90.80.90.00	€22.33/100 kg/net+8.3%	11.5	68
1905.10.00.00.00	€37.91/100 kg/net+5.8%	23.4	45
1905.20.10.00.00	€85.45/100 kg/net+9.4%	33.7	68
1905.20.30.00.00	€79.82/100 kg/net+9.8%	30.6	68
1905.20.90.00.00	€93.89/100 kg/net+10.1%	40.9	68
1905.90.10.00.00	€62.17/100 kg/net+3.8%	33.5	45
1905.90.20.00.11	€49.1/100 kg/net+4.5%	n.a.	45
1905.90.20.00.12	€49.1/100 kg/net+4.5%	5.5	45
1905.90.20.00.13	€49.1/100 kg/net+4.5%	n.a.	45
1905.90.20.00.14	€49.1/100 kg/net+4.5%	10.4	45
1905.90.20.00.19	€49.1/100 kg/net+4.5%	7.2	45
2001.90.30.00.00	€28.43/100 kg/net+5.1%	30.4	59
2001.90.40.00.00	€16.46/100 kg/net+8.3%	n.a.	59
2004.90.10.00.00	€24.69/100 kg/net+5.1%	24.1	59
2005.80.00.00.00	€22.9/100 kg/net+5.1%	27.3	59
2008.99.85.00.00	€49.77/100 kg/net+5.1%	34.8	59
2008.99.91.00.00	€37.37/100 kg/net+8.3%	n.a.	59
2101.30.19.00.00	€108.32/100 kg/net+5.1%	n.a.	75
2101.30.99.00.00	€92.5/100 kg/net+10.8%	55.3	75
2102.10.31.00.00	€59.4/100 kg/net+12%	30.5	32
2102.10.39.00.00	€12.47/100 kg/net+12%	23.1	32
2105.00.10.10.00	€64.3/100 kg/net+8.6%	37.8	75
2105.00.10.90.00	€64.3/100 kg/net+8.6%	38.1	59
2105.00.91.10.00	€90.46/100 kg/net+8%	25.8	75
2105.00.91.90.00	€90.46/100 kg/net+8%	25.5	59
2105.00.99.10.00	€57.13/100 kg/net+7.9%	21.2	75
2105.00.99.90.00	€57.13/100 kg/net+7.9%	19.9	59
2202.90.91.00.00	€51.23/100 kg/net+6.4%	40.6	43
2202.90.95.00.00	€40.79/100 kg/net+5.5%	41.1	43
2202.90.99.00.00	€47.44/100 kg/net+5.4%	41.5	43
3505.10.10.00.00	€1.76/100 kg/net+9%	10.3	39
3505.10.90.00.11	€4.3/100 kg/net+9%	15.8	39
3505.10.90.00.19	€3/100 kg/net+9%	12.4	39
3505.20.10.10.00	€1.39/100 kg/net+8.3%	..	39
3505.20.10.90.00	€1.39/100 kg/net+8.3%	9.7	39
3505.20.30.10.00	€2.76/100 kg/net+8.3%	..	39

Table AIII.2 (cont'd)

HS code	Duty	*Ad Valorem* equivalent (%)	Bound duty (%)
3505.20.30.90.00	€2.76/100 kg/net+8.3%	10.3	39
3505.20.50.10.00	€4.39/100 kg/net+8.3%	15.6	39
3505.20.50.90.00	€4.39/100 kg/net+8.3%	14.1	39
3505.20.90.10.00	€5.49/100 kg/net+8.3%	..	39
3505.20.90.90.00	€5.49/100 kg/net+8.3%	13.8	39
3809.10.10.00.00	€2.76/100 kg/net+8.3%	10.1	15
3809.10.30.00.00	€3.84/100 kg/net+8.3%	11.2	15
3809.10.50.00.00	€4.68/100 kg/net+8.3%	11.8	15
3809.10.90.00.00	€3.67/100 kg/net+8.3%	10.4	15
Mixed duties:			
2106.90.20.00.00	€17.3 min €1//% vol/hl	17.3	102
3302.10.10.00.00	€17.3 min €1/% vol/hl	17.3	102
5701.10.90.00.11	€8 max €2.8/m^2	5.6	Unbound
5701.10.90.00.12	€8 max €2.8/m^2	3.3	Unbound
5701.10.90.00.13	€8 max €2.8/m^2	2.6	Unbound
5701.10.90.00.14	€8 max €2.8/m^2	2.2	Unbound
5701.10.90.00.90	€8 max €2.8/m^2	3.5	Unbound
7003.12.99.10.00	€3.8 min €0.6/100 kg	3.8	Unbound
7003.12.99.90.00	€3.8 min €0.6/100 kg	3.8	Unbound
7003.19.90.10.11	€3.8 min €0.6/100 kg	2.8	Unbound
7003.19.90.10.12	€3.8 min €0.6/100 kg	1.7	Unbound
7003.19.90.10.19	€3.8 min €0.6/100 kg	7.7	Unbound
7003.19.90.90.00	€3.8 min €0.6/100 kg	21.1	Unbound
7003.20.00.10.00	€3.8 min €0.4/100 kg	12.2	Unbound
7003.20.00.90.00	€3.8 min €0.4/100 kg	4.6	Unbound
7004.20.99.10.00	€4.4 min €0.4/100 kg	10.8	Unbound
7004.20.99.90.11	€4.4 min €0.4/100 kg	11.0	Unbound
7004.20.99.90.12	€4.4 min €0.4/100 kg	0.6	Unbound
7004.20.99.90.13	€4.4 min €0.4/100 kg	12.8	Unbound
7004.20.99.90.14	€4.4 min €0.4/100 kg	2.7	Unbound
7004.90.80.10.00	€4.4 min €0.4/100 kg	2.0	Unbound
7004.90.80.90.00	€4.4 min €0.4/100 kg	0.9	Unbound
7016.90.40.00.00	€3 min €1.2/100 kg	..	Unbound
7016.90.70.00.11	€3 min €1.2/100 kg	..	Unbound
7016.90.70.00.12	€3 min €1.2/100 kg	..	Unbound
7016.90.70.00.13	€3 min €1.2/100 kg	..	Unbound
7016.90.70.00.19	€3 min €1.2/100 kg	..	Unbound
9101.11.00.00.00	€4.5 min €0.3 unit max €0.8 unit	3.1	Unbound
9101.19.00.00.00	€4.5 min €0.3 unit max €0.8 unit	0.5	Unbound
9101.21.00.00.00	€4.5 min €0.3 unit max €0.8 unit	0.2	Unbound
9101.29.00.00.00	€4.5 min €0.3 unit max €0.8 unit	0.3	Unbound
9101.91.00.00.11	€4.5 min €0.3 unit max11 €0.8 unit	4.5	Unbound
9101.91.00.00.12	€4.5 min €0.3 unit max €0.8 unit	6.3	Unbound
9101.91.00.00.19	€4.5 min €0.3 unit max €0.8 unit	4.5	Unbound
9101.99.00.00.11	€4.5 min €0.3 unit max €0.8 unit	1.2	Unbound
9101.99.00.00.12	€4.5 min €0.3 unit max €0.8 unit	4.5	Unbound
9101.99.00.00.19	€4.5 min €0.3 unit max €0.8 unit	4.5	Unbound
9102.11.00.00.00	€4.5 min €0.3 unit max €0.8 unit	4.5	Unbound
9102.12.00.00.00	€4.5 min €0.3 unit max €0.8 unit	8.2	Unbound
9102.19.00.00.00	€4.5 min €0.3 unit max €0.8 unit	4.7	Unbound
9102.21.00.00.00	€4.5 min €0.3 unit max €0.8 unit	0.4	Unbound
9102.29.00.00.00	€4.5 min €0.3 unit max €0.8 unit	1.3	Unbound
9102.91.00.00.11	€4.5 min €0.3 unit max €0.8 unit	7.8	Unbound
9102.91.00.00.12	€4.5 min €0.3 unit max €0.8 unit	7.7	Unbound

Table AIII.2 (cont'd)

HS code	Duty	*Ad Valorem* equivalent (%)	Bound duty (%)
9102.91.00.00.19	€4.5 min €0.3 unit max €0.8 unit	8.4	Unbound
9102.99.00.00.11	€4.5 min €0.3 unit max €0.8 unit	5.4	Unbound
9102.99.00.00.12	€4.5 min €0.3 unit max €0.8 unit	9.1	Unbound
9102.99.00.00.19	€4.5 min €0.3 unit max €0.8 unit	5.9	Unbound
9108.20.00.00.00	€5 min €0.17 unit	5.0	Unbound
9108.90.00.00.00	€5 min €0.17 unit	5.0	Unbound
9110.11.10.00.00	€5 min €0.17 unit	5.0	Unbound
9111.10.00.00.00	€0.5 unit min €2.7 max €4.6	4.4	Unbound
9111.20.00.00.00	€0.5 unit min €2.7 max €4.6	4.7	Unbound
9111.80.00.00.00	€0.5 unit min €2.7 max €4.6	4.8	Unbound
9111.90.00.00.00	€0.5 unit min €2.7 max €4.6	4.5	Unbound
Specific duties:			
2205.10.10.00.00	€10.9/hl	17.1	102
2205.10.90.00.11	€0.9/%vol/hl + €6.4/hl[a]	21.9	102
2205.10.90.00.12	€0.9/%vol/hl + €6.4/hl[a]	24.4	102
2205.90.10.00.00	€9/hl	n.a.	102
2205.90.90.00.11	€0.9/% vol/hl	18.0	102
2205.90.90.00.12	€0.9/% vol/hl	18.0	102
2207.10.00.90.11	€19.2/hl	n.a.	102
2207.10.00.90.12	€19.2/hl	n.a.	102
2207.20.00.90.13	€10.2/hl	n.a.	102
2207.20.00.90.14	€10.2/hl	n.a.	102
2207.20.00.90.15	€10.2/hl	n.a.	102
2208.40.11.00.00	€0.6/% vol/hl + €3.2/hl[a]	28.1	102
2208.40.39.00.11	€0.6/% vol/hl + €3.2/hl[a]	28.2	102
2208.40.39.00.12	€0.6/% vol/hl + €3.2/hl[a]	30.2	102
2208.40.51.00.00	€0.6/% vol/hl	27.0	102
2208.40.99.00.00	€0.6/% vol/hl	27.0	102
2208.90.91.90.00	€1/% vol/hl + €6.4/hl[a]	46.4	102
2208.90.99.90.00	€1/% vol/hl	40.0	102
2501.00.51.00.00	€1.7/1,000 kg/net	0.7	Unbound
2501.00.91.00.00	€2.6/1,000 kg/net	0.4	Unbound
2501.00.99.10.00	€2.6/1,000 kg/net	0.5	10
2501.00.99.90.00	€2.6/1,000 kg/net	11.7	Unbound
3706.10.99.10.00	€5/100 M	37.9	75 TL/kg
3706.10.99.20.00	€5/100 M	19.4	100 TL/kg
3706.90.99.10.00	€3.5/100 M	..	75 TL/kg
3706.90.99.20.00	€3.5/100 M	0.1	100 TL/kg
Variable duties:			
0405.20.10.00.00	9%+T1	35.8	59
0405.20.30.00.00	9%+T1	n.a.	59
1704.90.51.00.00	9%+T1	42.9	135
1704.90.55.00.00	9%+T1	29.4	135
1704.90.61.00.11	9%+T1	29.5	135
1704.90.61.00.19	9%+T1	57.8	135
1704.90.65.00.11	9%+T1	44.6	135
1704.90.65.00.12	9%+T1	47.0	135
1704.90.65.00.19	9%+T1	61.3	135
1704.90.71.00.00	9%+T1	43.5	135
1704.90.75.00.00	9%+T1	34.3	135
1704.90.81.00.00	9%+T1	54.3	135
1704.90.99.10.11	9%+T1	76.4	135
1704.90.99.10.19	9%+T1	45.2	135

Table AIII.2 (cont'd)

HS code	Duty	*Ad Valorem* equivalent (%)	Bound duty (%)
1704.90.99.20.00	9%+T1	114.6	135
1704.90.99.30.00	9%+T1	n.a.	135
1704.90.99.40.00	9%+T1	49.3	135
1704.90.99.90.11	9%+T1	55.6	135
1704.90.99.90.12	9%+T1	89.3	135
1704.90.99.90.19	9%+T1	45.6	135
1806.20.10.00.00	8.3%+T1	42.8	90
1806.20.30.00.00	8.3%+T1	53.4	90
1806.20.50.00.00	8.3%+T1	57.1	90
1806.20.70.00.00	15.4%+T1	52.8	90
1806.20.80.00.00	8.3%+T1	49.3	90
1806.20.95.00.00	8.3%+T1	61.3	90
1806.31.00.00.11	8.3%+T1	40.8	90
1806.31.00.00.19	8.3%+T1	29.3	90
1806.32.10.00.00	8.3%+T1	35.8	90
1806.32.90.00.00	8.3%+T1	30.3	90
1806.90.11.00.00	8.3%+T1	17.3	90
1806.90.19.00.00	8.3%+T1	23.7	90
1806.90.31.00.00	8.3%+T1	23.1	90
1806.90.39.00.00	8.3%+T1	19.7	90
1806.90.50.00.00	8.3%+T1	39.6	90
1806.90.60.00.00	8.3%+T1	51.0	90
1806.90.70.00.00	8.3%+T1	58.7	90
1806.90.90.00.00	8.3%+T1	55.8	90
1901.10.00.19.00	7.6%+T1	29.3	68
1901.10.00.20.00	7.6%+T1	62.4	90
1901.10.00.90.00	7.6%+T1	31.5	54
1901.20.00.10.00	7.6%+T1	63.4	68
1901.20.00.20.00	7.6%+T1	29.9	90
1901.20.00.90.00	7.6%+T1	50.9	54
1901.90.99.10.00	7.6%+T2	50.1	68
1901.90.99.20.00	7.6%+T2	n.a.	90
1901.90.99.90.19	7.6%+T2	52.9	54
1904.20.10.00.00	9%+T1	45.2	59
1905.31.11.00.00	9%+T1	52.6	68
1905.31.19.00.00	9%+T1	49.3	68
1905.31.30.00.00	9%+T1	29.8	68
1905.31.91.00.00	9%+T1	40.1	68
1905.31.99.00.19	9%+T1	53.8	68
1905.32.05.00.00	9%+T1	19.1	68
1905.32.11.00.00	9%+T1	43.6	68
1905.32.19.00.00	9%+T1	36.7	68
1905.32.91.00.00	9%+T1	n.a.	68
1905.32.99.00.19	9%+T1	62.8	68
1905.40.10.00.00	9.7%+T1	41.1	68
1905.40.90.00.00	9.7%+T1	44.6	45
1905.90.30.00.00	9.7%+T1	44.9	45
1905.90.45.00.00	9%+T1	30.6	68
1905.90.55.00.00	9%+T1	37.5	68
1905.90.60.00.11	9%+T1	25.3	68
1905.90.60.00.12	9%+T1	n.a.	68
1905.90.60.00.13	9%+T1	35.9	68
1905.90.60.00.14	9%+T1	37.3	68
1905.90.60.00.19	9%+T1	37.7	68

Table AIII.2 (cont'd)

HS code	Duty	*Ad Valorem* equivalent (%)	Bound duty (%)
1905.90.90.00.11	9%+T1	n.a.	45
1905.90.90.00.19	9%+T1	84.9	45
2004.10.91.10.00	7,6%+T1	n.a.	47
2004.10.91.20.00	7,6%+T1	n.a.	59
2005.20.10.10.00	8,8%+T1	46.0	47
2005.20.10.20.00	8,8%+T1	53.0	59
2101.12.98.10.00	9%+T2	18.4	52
2101.12.98.90.00	9%+T2	21.8	68
2101.20.98.00.00	6,5%+T2	24.6	68
2106.10.80.00.19	0%+T2	10.7	59
2106.90.98.00.12	9%+T1	n.a.	59
2106.90.98.00.13	9%+T1	34.4	59
2106.90.98.00.14	9%+T1	51.6	59
2106.90.98.00.15	9%+T1	38.6	59
2106.90.98.00.19	9%+T1	55.7	59
3302.10.29.00.00	9%+T2	19.4	Unbound

n.a. Not applicable. *Ad valorem* equivalents of specific duties cannot be calculated as there were no imports in 2007-10.

.. Not available.

Source: Information provided by the Turkish authorities.

Table AIII.3
Applied MFN tariff averages by HS2, 2011

Code	Description	No. of lines	Average tariff (%)	Range (%)	Standard deviation (%)	Imports 2010[a] (US$ million)
	Total	16,448	12.2	0-225	27.1	185,541
01	Live animals	83	33.2	0-135	41.9	333
02	Meat and edible meat offal	235	126.8	23.4-225	75.2	250
03	Fish and crustaceans, molluscs and other aquatic invertebrates	327	29.8	0-37.5	9.2	134
04	Dairy produce; birds' eggs; natural honey; edible products of animal origin, not elsewhere specified or included	209	103.6	0-180	64.1	128
05	Products of animal origin, not elsewhere specified or included	38	1.8	0-20	5.0	38
06	Live trees and other plants; bulbs, roots and the like; cut flowers and ornamental foliage	52	17.6	3.9-46.8	19.0	50
07	Edible vegetables and certain roots and tubers	166	20.5	0-49.5	10.2	315
08	Edible fruit and nuts; peel of citrus fruit or melons	148	41.8	15.4-145.8	22.8	315
09	Coffee, tea, maté and spices	57	38.4	0-145	32.8	103
10	Cereals	65	52.3	0-130	45.0	1,057
11	Products of the milling industry; malt; starches; inulin; wheat gluten	102	39.9	4-102.6	15.9	53
12	Oil seeds and oleaginous fruits; misc. grains, seeds and fruit; industrial or medicinal plants; straw and fodder	129	14.2	0-35	10.7	1,559
13	Lac; gums, resins and other vegetable saps and extracts	36	4.2	0-25	8.3	32
14	Vegetable plaiting materials; vegetable products not elsewhere specified or included	21	0.0	0	0.0	7
15	Animal or vegetable fats and oils and their cleavage products; prepared edible fats; animal or vegetable waxes	201	22.5	0-50	16.2	990
16	Preparations of meat, of fish or of crustaceans, molluscs or other aquatic invertebrates	134	100.8	54-121.5	25.0	4
17	Sugars and sugar confectionery	63	80.4	0-135	51.2	52
18	Cocoa and cocoa preparations	29	29.8	0-61.3	19.4	407
19	Preparations of cereals, flour, starch or milk; pastry cooks' products	88	27.4	4.5-84.9	17.3	169
20	Preparations of vegetables, fruit, nuts or other parts of plants	371	55.0	0-135.9	16.3	63
21	Miscellaneous edible preparations	63	17.6	0-58.5	16.7	376
22	Beverages, spirits and vinegar	208	40.9	0-70	32.0	139
23	Residues and waste from the food industries; prepared animal fodder	83	8.6	0-13.5	4.1	739
24	Tobacco and manufactured tobacco substitutes	28	38.8	10-74.9	22.3	368
25	Salt; sulphur; earths and stone; plastering materials, lime and cement	154	0.3	0-11.7	1.1	314
26	Ores, slag and ash	51	0.3	0-12.5	1.8	999
27	Mineral fuels, mineral oils and products of their distillation; bituminous substances; mineral waxes	216	2.0	0-8	1.7	26,704
28	Inorganic chemicals; organic or inorganic compounds of precious metals, of rare-earth metals, of radioactive elements or of isotopes	562	4.6	0-5.5	1.7	1,424
29	Organic chemicals	1,696	4.7	0-9.6	2.6	4,016
30	Pharmaceutical products	100	0.2	0-3.3	0.7	4,410
31	Fertilizers	56	4.5	0-6.5	2.8	1,017

Table AIII.3 (cont'd)

Code	Description	No. of lines	Average tariff (%)	Range (%)	Standard deviation (%)	Imports 2010[a] (US$ million)
32	Tanning or dyeing extracts; tannins and their derivatives; dyes, pigments and other colouring matter; paints and varnishes; putty and other mastics; inks	101	5.7	0-6.5	1.6	1,545
33	Essential oils and resinoids; perfumery, cosmetic or toilet preparations	72	2.9	0-19.4	3.9	984
34	Soap, organic surface-active agents, washing preparations, lubricating preparations, artificial waxes, prepared waxes, polishing or scouring preparations, candles and similar articles, modelling pastes, dental waxes and dental preparations with a basis	55	1.7	0-6.5	2.1	626
35	Albuminoidal substances; modified starches; glues; enzymes	53	9.0	0-15.8	4.4	429
36	Explosives; pyrotechnic products; matches; pyrophoric alloys; certain combustible preparations	25	6.3	5.7-6.5	0.3	36
37	Photographic or cinematographic goods	81	5.5	0-37.9	4.7	224
38	Miscellaneous chemical products	245	5.6	0-11.8	1.9	1,795
39	Plastics and articles thereof	272	5.7	0-6.5	2.1	9,730
40	Rubber and articles thereof	211	2.1	0-6.5	1.9	2,322
41	Raw hides and skins (other than furskins) and leather	98	2.4	0-6.5	2.7	473
42	Articles of animal gut (other than silk-worm gut)	75	4.4	1.7-9.7	2.2	409
43	Furskins and artificial fur; manufactures thereof	47	1.8	0-3.7	1.3	82
44	Wood and articles of wood; wood charcoal	279	1.7	0-10	2.6	1,098
45	Cork and articles of cork	14	3.8	0-4.7	1.7	6
46	Manufactures of straw, of esparto or of other plaiting materials; basketware and wickerwork	29	2.9	0-4.7	1.3	12
47	Pulp of wood or of other fibrous cellulosic material; recovered (waste and scrap) paper and paperboard	25	0.0	0	0.0	545
48	Paper and paperboard; articles of paper pulp, of paper or of paperboard	352	0.0	0	0.0	2,820
49	Printed books, newspapers, pictures and other products of the printing industry; manuscripts, typescripts and plans	64	0.0	0	0.0	138
50	Silk	34	4.6	0-7.5	2.5	40
51	Wool, fine or coarse animal hair; horsehair yarn and woven fabric	125	3.8	0-8	3.4	370
52	Cotton	382	6.7	0-8	2.1	3,386
53	Other vegetable textile fibres; paper yarn and woven fabrics of paper yarn	74	3.9	0-8	3.2	257
54	Man-made filaments	330	6.2	3.8-8	2.0	1,686
55	Man-made staple fibres	240	6.9	4-8	1.8	2,089
56	Wadding, felt and nonwovens; special yarns; twine, cordage, ropes and cables and articles thereof	90	5.8	3.2-12	2.2	420
57	Carpets and other textile floor coverings	71	7.0	2.2-8	1.9	181
58	Special woven fabrics; tufted textile fabrics; lace; tapestries; trimmings; embroidery	94	7.5	5-8	0.9	174
59	Impregnated, coated, covered or laminated textile fabrics; textile articles of a kind suitable for industrial use	78	6.5	4-8	1.2	285
60	Knitted or crocheted fabrics	68	8.0	6.5-8	0.3	372
61	Articles of apparel and clothing accessories, knitted or crocheted	228	11.6	8-12	1.1	1,007
62	Articles of apparel and clothing accessories, not knitted or crocheted	368	11.4	6.3-12	1.6	1,550

Table AIII.3 (cont'd)

Code	Description	No. of lines	Average tariff (%)	Range (%)	Standard deviation (%)	Imports 2010[a] (US$ million)
63	Other made up textile articles; sets; worn clothing and worn textile articles; rags	150	9.9	0-12	3.2	147
64	Footwear, gaiters and the like; parts of such articles	105	9.2	3-17	5.4	660
65	Headgear and parts thereof	23	2.6	0-5.7	1.3	42
66	Umbrellas, sun umbrellas, walking-sticks, seat-sticks, whips, riding-crops and parts thereof	9	4.4	2.7-5.2	1.0	42
67	Prepared feathers and down and articles made of feathers or of down; artificial flowers; articles of human hair	17	3.1	1.7-4.7	1.2	31
68	Articles of stone, plaster, cement, asbestos, mica or similar materials	89	1.3	0-3.7	1.2	428
69	Ceramic products	118	4.9	0-12	2.5	390
70	Glass and glassware	217	4.7	0-21.1	3.1	616
71	Natural or cultured pearls, precious or semi-precious stones, precious metals, metals clad with precious metal, and articles thereof; imitation jewellery; coin	94	1.1	0-4	1.6	3,037
72	Iron and steel	785	6.3	0-22.4	6.8	16,119
73	Articles of iron or steel	398	1.9	0-15	2.0	1,967
74	Copper and articles thereof	100	3.5	0-5.2	1.9	3,299
75	Nickel and articles thereof	35	0.8	0-3.3	1.4	168
76	Aluminium and articles thereof	96	6.3	0-10	2.1	2,488
78	Lead and articles thereof	11	2.0	0-5	2.2	180
79	Zinc and articles thereof	25	3.4	0-5	1.4	434
80	Tin and articles thereof	18	0.0	0	0.0	55
81	Other base metals; cermets; articles thereof	134	2.7	0-9	2.6	86
82	Tools, implements, cutlery, spoons and forks, of base metal; parts thereof of base metal	172	3.0	1.7-8.5	1.6	583
83	Miscellaneous articles of base metal	72	2.2	0-3.7	1.0	674
84	Nuclear reactors, boilers, machinery and mechanical appliances; parts thereof	1,434	1.6	0-9.7	1.4	21,266
85	Electrical machinery and equipment and parts thereof; sound recorders and reproducers, television image and sound recorders and reproducers, and parts and accessories of such articles	910	2.4	0-14	2.7	14,642
86	Railway or tramway locomotives, rolling-stock and parts thereof; railway or tramway track fixtures and fittings and parts thereof; mechanical (including electro-mechanical) traffic signalling equipment of all kinds	43	1.7	0-3.7	0.6	526
87	Vehicles other than railway or tramway rolling-stock, and parts and accessories thereof	310	6.7	0-22	4.9	13,408
88	Aircraft, spacecraft, and parts thereof	27	2.1	0.9-4.2	1.1	3,156
89	Ships, boats and floating structures	62	0.8	0-2.7	1.0	1,040
90	Optical, photographic, cinematographic, measuring, checking, precision, medical or surgical instruments and apparatus; parts and accessories thereof	473	1.7	0-6.7	1.8	3,438
91	Clocks and watches and parts thereof	70	4.4	0.2-9.1	1.8	253
92	Musical instruments; parts and accessories of such articles	30	3.2	1.7-4	0.5	37
93	Arms and ammunition; parts and accessories thereof	28	2.2	0-3.2	1.1	33
94	Furniture; bedding, mattresses, mattress supports, cushions and similar stuffed furnishings; lamps and lighting fittings, not elsewhere specified or included; illuminated signs, illuminated name-plates	172	2.4	0-5.7	1.5	1,081

Table AIII.3 (cont'd)

Code	Description	No. of lines	Average tariff (%)	Range (%)	Standard deviation (%)	Imports 2010[a] (US$ million)
95	Toys, games and sports requisites; parts and accessories thereof	66	2.1	0-4.7	1.7	472
96	Miscellaneous manufactured articles	90	3.3	0-7.7	1.4	387
97	Works of art, collectors' pieces and antiques	14	0.0	0	0.0	23

a The total of imports is higher than the sum of sub-items, as certain imports, to the value of US$12,672.8 million are not classified in the Harmonized System.

Note: 2011 tariff is based on HS07 nomenclature consisting of 16,448 tariff lines (at 12-digit tariff line level).
Calculations include AVEs provided by the authorities for non-*ad valorem* rates. In case of unavailability of AVEs, the *ad valorem* part is used for compound rates.

Source: WTO Secretariat estimates, based on data provided by the Turkish authorities; imports from UNSD, Comtrade database.

Table AIII.4
Preferential trading agreements, 2011

Agreement	Coverage by Turkey	Preferential margin
Customs Union with the EU	All industrial products and industrial components of processed agricultural products	Duty free on industrial products and on the industrial component of processed agricultural products
Agreement between Turkey and the EU on trade in agricultural products	Some agricultural products	Preferential tariff quotas, most with zero rate
Free Trade Agreement between Turkey and the EU on ECSC products	ECSC products	Duty free on ECSC products
Free-trade agreement with thepean Free Trade Association (EFTA)[a]	All industrial products Fish and fishery products Processed agricultural products	Duty free on industrial products and on the industrial components of processed agricultural products; duty free on fish and fishery products
Economic Cooperation Organization (ECO) (Iran, Pakistan, Turkey)	36 items at the HS four-digit level[b]	No preferential rates applied[c]
GSP	2,884 items at the HS 12-digit level Turkey has fully adopted the EU GSP regime, i.e. all sensitive and non-sensitive products within the scope of the EU GSP Regulation, all the duty rates of the products covered by Customs Union Agreement and countries (except Armenia, due to political reasons) have been totally aligned with those of the EU	2,174 duty-free items for developing countries and 2,884 for least developed countries Duty free on industrial and industrial components of processed agricultural products for least developed countries (LDCs) and special incentive countries (GSP+) and preferential duty rates for developing countries
Israel	All industrial products Some agricultural and processed agricultural products (5 items at the HS 4-digit level, 16 items at the HS 6-digit level, 37 items at the HS 8-digit level, 12 items at the HS 12-digit level)	Duty free on industrial products; preferential tariff quotas on agricultural and processed agricultural products
Macedonia (FYR)	All industrial products Some agricultural and processed agricultural products (4 items at the HS 4-digit level) (13 items at the HS 6-digit level) (12 items at the HS 8-digit level)	Duty free on industrial products; preferential tariff quotas on agricultural and processed agricultural products
Croatia	All industrial products Some agricultural and processed agricultural products (12 items at the HS 4-digit level) (5 items at the HS 6-digit level)	Duty free on industrial products; preferential tariff quotas on agricultural and processed agricultural products
Bosnia-Herzegovina[d]	All industrial products Most agricultural and processed agricultural products, with a few exceptions (194 items at the HS 4-digit level) (7 items at the HS 6-digit level) (22 items at the HS 8-digit level)	Duty free on industrial products, on basic agricultural products (except 8 items at the HS 4-digit level) and on the industrial components of processed agricultural products. Also, for 6 items at the HS 4-digit level, duty free on both agricultural and industrial components of processed agricultural products
Morocco	Most industrial products Some agricultural and processed agricultural products (4 items at the HS 4-digit level, 15 items at the HS 6-digit level, 2 items at the HS 8-digit level)	Duty free on industrial products; preferential tariff quotas on agricultural and processed agricultural products
Palestinian Authority	All industrial products	Duty free on industrial products

Table AIII.4 (cont'd)

Agreement	Coverage by Turkey	Preferential margin
Syria	All industrial products Some agricultural and processed agricultural products (5 items at the HS 4-digit level, 20 items at the HS 6-digit level,1 items at the HS 8-digit level)	Duty free on industrial products; preferential tariff quotas on agricultural and processed agricultural products
Tunisia	Most industrial products Some agricultural and processed agricultural products (2 items at the HS 4-digit level, 5 items at the HS 6-digit level)	Duty free on industrial products; preferential tariff quotas on agricultural and processed agricultural products
Egypt	All industrial products Some agricultural and processed agricultural products (1 item at the HS 2-digit level, 17 items at the HS 4-digit level, 9 items at the HS 6-digit level)	Duty free on industrial products; preferential tariff quotas on agricultural and processed agricultural products
Albania	All industrial products Some agricultural and processed agricultural products (25 items at the HS 4-digit level) (13 items at the HS 6-digit level)	Duty free on industrial products; preferential tariff quotas on agricultural and processed agricultural products
Georgia	All industrial products Most agricultural and processed agricultural products (except 11 chapters, 16 items at HS 4-digit level, 3 items at HS 6-digit level and 2 items at HS 8-digit level)	Duty free on industrial products; preferential tariff quotas or duty free on specific agricultural and processed agricultural products
Montenegro	All industrial products Some agricultural and processed agricultural products (3 items at the HS 4-digit level)	Duty free on industrial products; preferential tariff quotas on agricultural and processed agricultural products
Serbia	All industrial products Some agricultural and processed agricultural products (13 items at the HS 4-digit level) (24 items at the HS 6-digit level) (14 items at the HS 8-digit level)	Duty free on industrial products; preferential tariff quotas on agricultural and processed agricultural products
Chile	Almost all industrial products (except 3 items at HS 6-digit level, 1 item at HS 8-digit level and 2 items at 10-digit level) and some agricultural and processed agricultural products (51 items at HS 6-digit level, 152 items at HS 8-digit level, 16 items at 10-digit level, and 44 at HS 12-digit level)	Duty free on almost all industrial products; preferential tariff quotas or duty free on specific agricultural and processed agricultural products
Jordan	Most industrial products Some agricultural and processed agricultural products (9 items at the HS 4-digit level) (23 items at the HS 6-digit level) (7 items at the HS 12-digit level)	Duty free on most industrial products; preferential tariff quotas on agricultural and processed agricultural products

Table AIII.4 (cont'd)

Agreement	Coverage by Turkey	Preferential margin
Lebanon	Most industrial products Some agricultural and processed agricultural products (5 items at the HS 4-digit level) (6 items at the HS 6-digit level) (8 items at the HS 12-digit level)	Duty free on most industrial products; preferential tariff quotas on agricultural and processed agricultural products
Mauritius	All industrial products Some agricultural and processed agricultural products (31 items at the HS 6-digit level) (3 items at the HS 8-digit level) (1 item at the HS 10-digit level) (11 items at the HS 12-digit level)	Duty free on most industrial products; preferential tariff quotas on agricultural and processed agricultural products

a A number of agricultural goods are covered under bilateral agreements between Turkey and individual EFTA countries.

b Including certain marble, pharmaceuticals, detergents, leather products, paper and paperboard, canvas, centrifugal pumps for liquids, compressors, henna, and bentonite.

c Preferential margin is a 10% reduction in the statutory rates. As these rates are higher than MFN rates, preferential rates are not applied.

d Turkey did not grant Bosnia-Herzegovina concessions for live bovine animals, sheep, and goats, certain live poultry and meat, edible offal of bovine animals, sheep, goats, and meat and edible offal of certain poultry. Turkey applies the agricultural component for imports of processed agricultural products, and the MHF (housing fund) levy on imports of fishery products originating in Bosnia-Herzegovina.

Source: Information provided by the Turkish authorities.

Table AIII.5
Preferential tariff quotas on agricultural goods, processed agricultural products, and fish and fish products, 2011

Free-trade agreement partner	Number of items	Products affected
EU	108 items at the HS 6-digit level	Live bovine animals and their meat, milk powder, butter, cheese, egg yolks, flower bulbs, live plants, fresh cut flowers, foliage, mushrooms, frozen beans, pears, strawberries, potato seed, apple, peach, tamarinds, passion fruit, tea, wheat, rye, barley, rice, maize, oats, malt, sunflower seeds, sugar beet seed, cotton seed, crude and refined soya bean oil, sugar, crude sunflower oil, crude rape, colza and mustard oil, tomato paste, prepared vegetables, jams and jellies, fruit juices, sparkling wine, vinegar, flours, meals and pellets of meat or meat offal of fish or of crustaceans, oilcake and other solid residues, dog or cat food, and other animal feeds
EU (processed agricultural products)	8 items at the HS 4-digit level	Sugar confectionery, chocolate, malt extract, food preparations of flour, groats, meal, starch or malt extract, pasta, prepared foods obtained by the swelling or roasting of cereals, bread, pastry, cakes, biscuits, ice cream, and food preparations, n.e.s.
Israel	5 items at the HS 4-digit level, 16 items at the HS 6-digit level, 37 items at the HS 8-digit level, 12 items at the HS 12-digit level	Birds' eggs, bulbs, tubers, tuberous roots, corms, edible fruit or nut trees, dried vegetables and mixtures of vegetables, avocado, mango, carrot, sweet corn, citrus fruit, orange juice, coffee, kosher-brandy, and vodka
Macedonia (FYR)	(4 items at the HS 4-digit level), (13 items at the HS 6-digit level), (12 items at the HS 8-digit level)	Some fresh vegetables (tomato, onion, shallots, cucumber, etc.), beans, watermelons, apples, rice, canned vegetables, and sauces and preparations (mixed condiments and seasoning), soups and broths and preparations (wine of fresh grapes, undernatured ethyl alcohol of an alcoholic strength by volume of less than 80% volume)
Croatia	(12 items at the HS 4-digit level), (5 items at the HS 6-digit level)	Cheese and curd, apples, maize, sugar confectionery, chocolate and other food preparations containing cocoa, malt extract, pasta, prepared foods obtained by swelling or roasting of cereals or cereal products, bread, pastry, cakes, biscuits and other bakers' wares, fruit and vegetable juices, sauces and preparations therefore, mixed condiments and mixed seasoning, soups and broths and preparations therefore, waters, including mineral waters and aerated waters, containing added sugar or other sweetening matter or flavoured, beer made from malt, wine of fresh grapes, undernatured ethyl alcohol of an alcoholic strength by volume of 80% vol or higher, preparations of a kind used in animal feed
Bosnia-Herzegovina	(194 items at the HS 4-digit level), (7 items at the HS 6-digit level), (22 items at the HS 8-digit level)	All agricultural products classified under HS Code 1-24 with the exception of: live bovine animals; live sheep and goats; live poultry (exclusively fowl of the species *Gallus domesticus*); meat of bovine animals; meat of sheep or goats; edible offal of bovine animals, swine, sheep, goats, horses asses, mules or hinnies; meat and edible offal of poultry (exclusively fowl of the species *Gallus domesticus*)
Tunisia	2 items at the HS 4-digit level, 5 items at the HS 6-digit level	Dates, sardines, mackerel, shrimps and prawns, molluscs, harissa, and wine
Morocco	4 items at the HS 4-digit level, 15 items at the HS 6-digit level, 2 items at the HS 8-digit level	Live plants, orchids, cabbages, turnips, asparagus, mushrooms, sweet peppers, sweet corn, capers, cucumbers, preserved cucumber, broad beans, avocados, coriander seeds, ginger, saffron, turmeric, thyme, bay leaves, curry, locust beans, preserved apricots, coffee extracts, wine, and bran
Syria	5 items at the HS 4-digit level, 20 items at the HS 6-digit level, 1 item at the HS 8-digit level	Cut flowers, onions and shallots, garlic, capers, grapes, cherries, peaches, seeds of anise, seeds of cumin, ginseng roots, parts of plants spices, crude soya bean oil, crude sunflower seed oil, sugar confectionary, chocolates, preserved fruit, preserved pepper, jams and marmalades, apple juices, wine, and olive pulp
Egypt	1 item at the HS 2-digit level, 17 items at the HS 4-digit level, 9 items at the HS 6-digit level	Fish and crustaceans, molluscs, aquatic invertebrates, live plants, cut flowers, potatoes, garlic, lettuce, carrots, turnips, frozen vegetables, provisionally preserved vegetables, dried vegetables, dates, guavas, mangoes, strawberries, spices, rice, groundnuts, sugar confectionery, chocolate pasta, bakers' wares, preserved cucumbers, preserved fruit, fruit juices, and active yeasts

Table AIII.5 (cont'd)

Free-trade agreement partner	Number of items	Products affected
Albania	(25 items at the HS 4-digit level), (13 items at the HS 6-digit level)	Cheese and curd, eggs, honey, live plants, tomatoes, onions, cabbages, carrots, cucumber, beans, frozen vegetables, dried vegetables, peas, spices, melons, frozen fruits, plants and parts of plants, preserved fish, chocolates, bakers' wares, preserved cucumbers, preserved tomatoes, jams and jellies, preserved fruit, fruit juices, tomato paste, ice cream, mineral water, wine, vermouth, and ethyl alcohol
Georgia[a]	Most agricultural and processed agricultural products (except 11 chapters, 16 items at HS 4-digit level, 3 items at HS 6-digit level and 2 items at HS 8-digit level)	Anchovies, tomatoes, quail eggs, natural honey, pears and quinces, chocolate, extracts, essences and concentrates, of coffee, tea, melons, sunflower seeds, butter and other fats and oils derived from milk, cut flowers, apricots, preparations of cereals, flour, starch or milk, baker's yeast, flours of anchovies, jams, fruit jellies, marmalades, fruit, fruit juices, wine of fresh grapes
Montenegro	(3 items at the HS 4-digit level)	Pasta, couscous, jams, fruit jellies, marmalades, fruit or nut puree and fruit or nut pastes, wine of fresh grapes
Serbia	(13 items at the HS 4-digit level), (24 items at the HS 6-digit level), (14 items at the HS 8-digit level)	Roses, forest trees, cut flowers and flower buds, tomatoes, leeks and other alliaceous vegetables, white cabbages and red cabbages, carrots and turnips, peas, fruits of the genus capsicum or of the genus pimenta, beans, sweetcorn, strawberries, sour cherries, prunes, seeds of fennel, juniper berries, sugar beet, lucerne, vetch, forest-tree and Canary, margarine, pasta, wine of fresh grapes, fruit juices, soups, chocolate, ice cream, bread, pastry, cakes, cucumbers
Chile	Some agricultural and processed agricultural products (51 items at HS 6-digit level, 152 items at HS 8-digit level, 16 items at 10-digit level and 44 HS 12-digit level)	Salmon, toothfish, sardines, shrimps, oysters, hair, ossein, fish waste, bulbs, tubers, crowns, onions and shallots, garlic, peas, sweetcorn, mushrooms, coconut, avocados, apple, apricot, strawberry, cherry, vanilla, cinamon, malt, flake, sunflower seed, olive oil, anchovies, sweet biscuit, yams, peanut butter, culture yeast, soya sauce, water, grappa, cognac, calvados, tequila
Jordan	9 items at the HS 4-digit level, 23 items at the HS 6-digit level, 7 items at the HS 12-digit level	Eggs for hatching, edible products of animal origin, cut flowers and flower buds, potatoes, tomatoes, cabbage lettuce, carrots and turnips, cucumbers and gherkins, beans, asparagus, aubergines, fruits of the genus capsicum, oranges, mandarins, grapefruit, apples, pears and quinces, peaches, liquorice roots, lemons , melons, strawberries, ginseng roots, tomato ketchup, pasta, fresh grapes, chocolate, bread, pastry, cakes, biscuits, sugar confectionery
Lebanon (signed, not yet in force)	5 items at the HS 4-digit level, 6 items at the HS 6-digit level, 8 items at the HS 12-digit level	Cut flowers and flower buds, globe artichokes, avocados, apples, pears and quinces, loquat, sesame oil and its fractions, sugar confectionery, chocolate, bread, pastry, cakes, thyme biscuits and other bakers' wares, wine of fresh grapes, guavas, mangoes
EFTA	15 items at the HS 4-digit level, 128 items at the HS 6-digit level, 398 items at the HS 8-digit level, 397 items at the HS 12-digit level	Other meat and edible meat offal, fresh, chilled or frozen; live fish: Fish, fresh or chilled, excluding fish fillets and other fish meat of heading 0304; fish, frozen, excluding fish fillets and other fish meat of heading 0304; fish fillets and other fish meat (whether or not minced), fresh, chilled or frozen; fish, dried, salted or in brine; smoked fish, whether or not cooked before or during the smoking process; flours, meals and pellets of fish, fit for human consumption; crustaceans, whether in shell or not, live, fresh, chilled, frozen, dried, salted or in brine; crustaceans, in shell, cooked by steaming or by boiling in water, whether or not chilled, frozen, dried, salted or in brine; flours, meals and pellets of crustaceans, fit for human consumption; molluscs, whether in shell or not, live, fresh, chilled, frozen, dried, salted or in brine; aquatic invertebrates other than crustaceans and molluscs, live, fresh, chilled, frozen, dried, salted or in brine; flours, meals and pellets of aquatic invertebrates other than crustaceans, fit for human consumption; fats and oils and their fractions, of fish or marine mammals, whether or not refined, but not chemically modified; animal or vegetable fats and oils and their fractions, partly or wholly hydrogenated, inter-esterified, re-esterified or elaidinized, whether or not refined, but not further prepared; extracts and juices of meat, fish or crustaceans, molluscs or other aquatic invertebrates; prepared or preserved fish; caviar and caviar substitutes prepared from fish eggs; crustaceans, molluscs and other aquatic invertebrates, prepared or preserved; flours, meals and pellets, of meat or meat offal, of fish or of crustaceans, molluscs or other aquatic invertebrates, unfit for human consumption; greaves

Table AIII.5 (cont'd)

Free-trade agreement partner	Number of items	Products affected
Mauritius	31 items at the HS 6-digit level, 3 items at the HS 8-digit level, 1 item at the HS 10-digit level, 11 items at the HS 12-digit level	Yellowfin tunas, bigeye tunas, swordfish, bulbs, tubers, tuberous roots, corms, crowns and rhizomes, in growth or in flower; chicory plants and roots, cut flowers, palm hearts, pineapples, guavas, mangoes and mangosteens, lychee, curry, tunas, skipjack and bonito, containing eggs, pasta, sweet biscuits, waffles and wafers, mango chutney, jams, fruit jellies, marmalades, banana chips, hot pepper sauce, mineral waters and aerated waters, malt beer, dog or cat food

a In addition to the products under tariff quota, all agricultural products classified under HS Code 1-24 with the exception of: live animals, meat and edible meat, fish and crustaceans, dairy produce, lemons, grapes, kiwifruit, apricots, tea, cereals, starches, sugar beet, wheat, cereal flours, cane or beet sugar, animal or vegetable fats and oils, hazelnut paste, tomatoes, ice cream, unmanufactured tobacco, apples are subject to zero tariffs.

Source: Information provided by the Turkish authorities.

Table AIII.6
Excise duties or special consumption tax on petroleum products, 2011

HS Code	Product description	Unit	Tax (TL)
2710.11.11.00.00	(Light oils and its preparations) For undergoing a specific process	kg	0
2710.11.31.00.00	(Only naphtha) Aviation spirit	Litre	0
2710.11.41.00.00	(With a lead content not exceeding 0.013 g per litre) With an octane number less than (RON) of 95 (Unleaded normal gasoline)	Litre	1.8500
2710.11.45.00.11	(With a lead content not exceeding 0.013 g per litre) With an octane number (RON) of 95 or more but less than 98 (Unleaded gasoline 95 octane)	Litre	1.8915
2710.11.45.00.12	(With a lead content not exceeding 0.013 g per litre) With an octane number (RON) of 95 or more but less than 98 (Mixed unleaded gasoline 95 octane)	Litre	1.8915
2710.11.45.00.19	(With a lead content not exceeding 0.013 g per litre) With an octane number (RON) of 95 or more but less than 98 Others	Litre	1.8915
2710.11.49.00.11	(With a lead content not exceeding 0.013 g per litre) With an octane number (RON) of 98 or more (Unleaded gasoline 98 octane)	Litre	2.0135
2710.11.49.00.19	(With a lead content not exceeding 0.013 g per litre) With an octane number (RON) of 98 or more Others	Litre	2.0135
2710.11.51.00.00	(With a lead content exceeding 0.013 g per litre) With an octane number (RON) of less than 98 (Leaded normal gasoline) (Leaded superl gasoline)	Litre	1.8800
2710.11.59.00.00	(With a lead content exceeding 0.013 g per litre) With an octane number (RON) of 98 or more (Leaded super gasoline)	Litre	1.8800
2710.11.70.00.00	Spirit type jet fuel	Litre	0
2710.19.21.00.00	Jet fuel (Kerosene)	Litre	0
2710.19.41.00.11	(With a sulphur content not exceeding 0.05% by weight) Diesel oil	Litre	1.3045
2710.19.41.00.13	(With a sulphur content not exceeding 0.05% by weight) Rural diesel	Litre	1.3045
2710.19.41.00.29	(With a sulphur content not exceeding 0.05% by weight) Others	Litre	1.3045
2710.19.45.00.12	(With a sulphur content exceeding 0.05% by weight but not exceeding 0.2% by weight) Rural diesel	Litre	1.2345
2710.19.45.00.13	(With a sulphur content exceeding 0.05% by weight but not exceeding 0.2% by weight) Marine diesel (DMX)	Litre	1.2345
2710.19.45.00.14	(With a sulphur content exceeding 0.05% by weight but not exceeding 0.2% by weight) Marine diesel (DMA)	Litre	1.2345
2710.19.45.00.15	(With a sulphur content exceeding 0.05% by weight but not exceeding 0.2% by weight) Marine diesel (DMB)	Litre	1.2345
2710.19.45.00.16	(With a sulphur content exceeding 0.05% by weight but not exceeding 0.2% by weight) Marine diesel (DMC)	Litre	1.2345
2710.19.45.00.29	(With a sulphur content exceeding 0.05% by weight but not exceeding 0.2% by weight) Others	Litre	1.2345
2710.19.49.00.13	(With a sulphur content exceeding 0.2% by weight) Marine diesel (DMX)	Litre	1.2345
2710.19.49.00.14	(With a sulphur content exceeding 0.2% by weight) Marine diesel (DMA)	Litre	1.2345
2710.19.49.00.15	(With a sulphur content exceeding 0.2% by weight) Marine diesel (DMB)	Litre	1,2345

Table AIII.6 (cont'd)

HS Code	Product description	Unit	Tax (TL)
2710.19.49.00.16	(With a sulphur content exceeding 0.2% by weight) Marine diesel (DMC)	Litre	1.2345
2710.19.49.00.18	(With a sulphur content exceeding 0.2% by weight) Others	Litre	1.2345
2710.19.61.00.11	(Fuel oils) With a sulphur content not exceeding 1% by weight Fuel oil 3	kg	0.2370
2710.19.61.00.12	(Fuel oils) With a sulphur content not exceeding 1% by weight Marine diesel (RMA-30)	kg	0.2370
2710.19.61.00.13	(Fuel oils) With a sulphur content not exceeding 1% by weight Marine diesel (RMB-30)	kg	0.2370
2710.19.61.00.14	(Fuel oils) With a sulphur content not exceeding 1% by weight Marine diesel (RMD-80)	kg	0.2370
2710.19.61.00.15	(Fuel oils) With a sulphur content not exceeding 1% by weight Marine diesel (RME-180)	kg	0.2370
2710.19.61.00.16	(Fuel oils) With a sulphur content not exceeding 1% by weight Marine diesel (RMF-180)	kg	0.2370
2710.19.61.00.17	(Fuel oils) With a sulphur content not exceeding 1% by weight Marine diesel (RMG-380)	kg	0.2370
2710.19.61.00.18	(Fuel oils) With a sulphur content not exceeding 1% by weight Marine diesel (RMH-380)	kg	0.2370
2710.19.61.00.21	(Fuel oils) With a sulphur content not exceeding 1% by weight Marine diesel (RMK-380)	kg	0.2370
2710.19.61.00.22	(Fuel oils) With a sulphur content not exceeding 1% by weight Marine diesel (RMH-700)	kg	0.2370
2710.19.61.00.23	(Fuel oils) With a sulphur content not exceeding 1% by weight Marine diesel (RMK-700)	kg	0.2370
2710.19.61.00.29	(Fuel oils) With a sulphur content not exceeding 1% by weight Others	Kg	0.2370
2710.19.63.00.11	(Fuel oils) With a sulphur content exceeding 1% by weight but not exceeding 2% by weight Fuel oil 4 (heating fuel)	kg	0.4760
2710.19.63.00.12	(Fuel oils) With a sulphur content exceeding 1% by weight but not exceeding 2% by weight Marine diesel (RMA-30)	kg	0.4760
2710.19.63.00.13	(Fuel oils) With a sulphur content exceeding 1% by weight but not exceeding 2% by weight Marine diesel (RMB-30)	kg	0.4760
2710.19.63.00.14	(Fuel oils) With a sulphur content exceeding 1% by weight but not exceeding 2% by weight Marine diesel (RMD-80)	kg	0.4760
2710.19.63.00.15	(Fuel oils) With a sulphur content exceeding 1% by weight but not exceeding 2% by weigh Marine diesel (RME-180)	kg	0.4760

Table AIII.6 (cont'd)

HS Code	Product description	Unit	Tax (TL)
2710.19.63.00.16	(Fuel oils) With a sulphur content exceeding 1% by weight but not exceeding 2% by weigh Marine diesel (RMF-180)	kg	0.4760
2710.19.63.00.17	(Fuel oils) With a sulphur content exceeding 1% by weight but not exceeding 2% by weigh Marine diesel (RMG-380)	kg	0.4760
2710.19.63.00.18	(Fuel oils) With a sulphur content exceeding 1% by weight but not exceeding 2% by weigh Marine diesel (RMH-380)	kg	0.4760
2710.19.63.00.21	(Fuel oils) With a sulphur content exceeding 1% by weight but not exceeding 2% by weigh Marine diesel (RMK-380)	kg	0.4760
2710.19.63.00.22	(Fuel oils) With a sulphur content exceeding 1% by weight but not exceeding 2% by weigh Marine diesel (RMH-700)	kg	0.4760
2710.19.63.00.23	(Fuel oils) With a sulphur content exceeding 1% by weight but not exceeding 2% by weigh Marine diesel (RMK-700)	kg	0.4760
2710.19.63.00.29	(Fuel oils) With a sulphur content exceeding 1% by weight but not exceeding 2% by weight Others	kg	0.4760
2710.19.65.00.11	(Fuel oils) With a sulphur content exceeding 2% by weight but not exceeding 2.8% by weight Fuel oil 5	kg	0.2240
2710.19.65.00.12	(Fuel oils) With a sulphur content exceeding 2% by weight but not exceeding 2.8% by weight Marine diesel (RMA-30)	kg	0.2240
2710.19.65.00.13	(Fuel oils) With a sulphur content exceeding 2% by weight but not exceeding 2.8% by weight Marine diesel (RMB-30)	kg	0.2240
2710.19.65.00.14	(Fuel oils) With a sulphur content exceeding 2% by weight but not exceeding 2.8% by weight Marine diesel (RMD-80)	kg	0.2240
2710.19.65.00.15	(Fuel oils) With a sulphur content exceeding 2% by weight but not exceeding 2.8% by weight Marine diesel (RME-180)	kg	0.2240
2710.19.65.00.16	(Fuel oils) With a sulphur content exceeding 2% by weight but not exceeding 2.8% by weight Marine diesel (RMF-180)	kg	0.2240
2710.19.65.00.17	(Fuel oils) With a sulphur content exceeding 2% by weight but not exceeding 2.8% by weight Marine diesel (RMG-380)	kg	0.2240
2710.19.65.00.18	(Fuel oils) With a sulphur content exceeding 2% by weight but not exceeding 2.8% by weight Marine diesel (RMH-380)	kg	0.2240
2710.19.65.00.21	(Fuel oils) With a sulphur content exceeding 2% by weight but not exceeding 2.8% by weight Marine diesel (RMK-380)	kg	0.2240
2710.19.65.00.22	(Fuel oils) With a sulphur content exceeding 2% by weight but not exceeding 2.8% by weight Marine diesel (RMH-700)	kg	0.2240
2710.19.65.00.23	(Fuel oils) With a sulphur content exceeding 2% by weight but not exceeding 2.8% by weight Marine diesel (RMK-700)	kg	0.2240
2710.19.65.00.29	(Fuel oils) With a sulphur content exceeding 2% by weight but not exceeding 2.8% by weight Others	kg	0.2240

Table AIII.6 (cont'd)

HS Code	Product description	Unit	Tax (TL)
2710.19.69.00.11	(Fuel oils) With a sulphur content exceeding 2.8% by weight Fuel oil 6	kg	0.2240
2710.19.69.00.12	(Fuel oils) With a sulphur content exceeding 2.8% by weight Marine diesel (RMA-30)	kg	0.2240
2710.19.69.00.13	(Fuel oils) With a sulphur content exceeding 2.8% by weight Marine diesel (RMB-30)	kg	0.2240
2710.19.69.00.14	(Fuel oils) With a sulphur content exceeding 2.8% by weight Marine diesel (RMD-80))	kg	0.2240
2710.19.69.00.15	(Fuel oils) With a sulphur content exceeding 2.8% by weight Marine diesel (RME-180)	kg	0.2240
2710.19.69.00.16	(Fuel oils) With a sulphur content exceeding 2.8% by weight Marine diesel (RMF-180)	kg	0.2240
2710.19.69.00.17	(Fuel oils) With a sulphur content exceeding 2.8% by weight Marine diesel(RMG-380)	kg	0.2240
2710.19.69.00.18	(Fuel oils) With a sulphur content exceeding 2.8% by weight Marine diesel(RMH-380)	kg	0.2240
2710.19.69.00.21	(Fuel oils) With a sulphur content exceeding 2.8% by weight Marine diesel(RMK-380)	kg	0.2240
2710.19.69.00.22	(Fuel oils) With a sulphur content exceeding 2.8% by weight Marine diesel(RMH-700)	kg	0.2240
2710.19.69.00.23	(Fuel oils) With a sulphur content exceeding 2.8% by weight Marine diesel(RMK-700)	kg	0.2240
2710.19.69.00.99	(Fuel oils) With a sulphur content exceeding 2.8% by weight Others	kg	0.2240
27.11	Petroleum gases and other gaseous hydrocarbons (Other than 2711.11.00.00.00; 2711.12; 2711.13; 2711.19.00.00.11; 2711.21.00.00.00; 2711.29.00.00.11 and 2711.29.00.00.12)	kg	0
2711.11.00.00.00	(Liquefied) Natural gas Those used as fuel oil in motor vehicle Others	Standart M^3 Standart M^3	0.6964 0.0230
2711.12	(Liquefied) Propane	kg	1.2100
2711.13	(Liquefied) Butane	kg	1.2100
2711.19.00.00.11	Liquefied petroleum gas (LPG) Those to be used in motor vehicle (Auto gas) Others	kg	1.2780 1.2100
2711.21.00.00.00	(In gaseous state) Natural gas Those to be used in motor vehicle Others	Standart M^3 Standart M^3	0.6964 0.0230
2711.29.00.00.11	(In gaseous state) Propane	kg	1.2100

Table AIII.6 (cont'd)

HS Code	Product description	Unit	Tax (TL)
2711.29.00.00.12	(In gaseous state) Butane	kg	1.2100
27.13	Petroleum coke, petroleum bitumen and other residues of petroleum oils or of oils obtained from bituminous minerals (Other than 2713.11.00.00.00; 2713.12.00.00.00; 2713.20.00.00.19; 2713.90)	kg	0
2713.11.00.00.00	(Petroleum coke) Not calcined	kg	0
2713.12.00.00.00	(Petroleum coke) Calcined	kg	0
2713.20.00.00.19	(Petroleum bitumen) Others	kg	0
2713.90	Other residues of petroleum oils or of oils obtained from bituminous minerals (Other than for the carbon manufacture of the products of heading 28.03)	kg	0
2715.00.00.00.00	Bituminous mixtures based on natural asphalt, on natural bitumen, on petroleum bitumen,on mineral tar or on mineral tar pitch (for example, bituminous mastics, cut-backs)	kg	0
3824.90.97.90.54	Auto Biodiesel	Litre	0.9100
3824.90.97.90.55	Fuel Biodiesel	Litre	0.9100
2707.10	Benzol (Benzene)	kg	2.0135
2707.20	Toluol (toluene)	kg	2.0135
2707.50.90.00.11	Solvent naphtha	kg	2.0135
2710.11.21.00.00	White spirit	kg	2.0135
2710.11.25.00.00	Others	kg	2.0135
2710.11.90.00.11	Other solvents (Solvents) (Petroleum ether)	kg	2.0135
2710.11.90.00.19	Others (Petroleum ether)	kg	2.0135
2710.19.29.00.00	Others (Petroleum ether)	kg	2.0135
2901.10.00.90.11	Hekzane	kg	2.0135
2901.10.00.90.12	Heptane	kg	2.0135
2901.10.00.90.13	Pentane	kg	2.0135
2902.20.00.00.00	Benzene (Benzol)	kg	2.0135
2902.30.00.00.00	Toluen (Toluol)	kg	2.0135
2909.19.90.00.13	Methyl tersier butyl ether (MTBE)	kg	2.0135
3811.21.00.10.00	(Including petroleum oils or oils obtained from bituminous minerals) Mineral oils or other chemical alloys for other liquid oils used for the same purpose such as mineral oils	kg	2.0135
3811.29.00.10.00	(Unincluding petroleum oils or oils obtained from bituminous minerals) Mineral oils or other chemical alloys for other liquid oils used for the same purpose such as mineral oils	kg	2.0135
3811.90.00.10.12	Chemical alloys for light mineral oils	kg	2.0135
3814.00.90	Organic composite solvents and thinners, not elsewhere specified or included in tariff; chemicals to remove the paint or varnish Others (Other than based on butyl acetate)	kg	0.0650
3824.90.40.00.00	Inorganic composite solvents and thinners for varnish, etc.	kg	0.0650
2710.19.71.00.00	(Lubricating oils; other oils) For undergoing a specific process	kg	1.0560
2710.19.75.00.00	(Lubricating oils; other oils) For undergoing chemical transformation by a process other than those specified in respect of subheading 2710.19.71.00	kg	1.0560
2710.19.81.00.00	(Lubricating oils; other oils) Motor oils, compressor lube oils, turbine lube oils	kg	1.0560

Table III.6 (cont'd)

HS Code	Product description	Unit	Tax (TL)
2710.19.83.00.00	(Lubricating oils; other oils) Liquids for hydraulic purposes	kg	1.0560
2710.19.85.00.00	(Lubricating oils; other oils) White oils, liquid paraffine	kg	1.0560
2710.19.87.00.00	(Lubricating oils; other oils) Gears oils and reductor oils	kg	1.0560
2710.19.91.00.00	(Lubricating oils; other oils) Metal-working compounds, mould release oils, anti-corrosion oils	kg	1.0560
2710.19.93.00.00	(Lubricating oils; other oils) Electrical insulating oils	kg	1.0560
2710.19.99.00.25	(Lubricating oils; other oils) Other mineral oils	kg	1.0560
2710.19.99.00.21	(Lubricating oils; other oils) Spindle oil	kg	1.0560
2710.19.99.00.22	(Lubricating oils; other oils) Light neutral	kg	1.0560
2710.19.99.00.23	(Lubricating oils; other oils) Heavy neutral	kg	1.0560
2710.19.99.00.24	(Lubricating oils; other oils) Bright stock	kg	1.0560
2710.19.99.00.98	(Lubricating oils; other oils) Others (Only base oils)	kg	1.0560
2710.19.25.00.11	Gas oil	Litre	0.7605
2710.19.25.00.19	Others	Litre	0.7605
3403.11.00.00.00	(Lubricating preparations) Preparations specific for being processed of materials suitable for weaving, leather, the post and fur or the other substances	kg	0.3000
3403.19.10.00.00	(Lubricating preparations) On condition that it is not accepted as the main substance, chemical alloys containing oil obtained 70% or more from petroleum or bituminous minerals as of weight	kg	0.3000
3403.19.90.00.00	(Lubricating preparations) Others	kg	0.3000
3403.91.00.00.00	(Lubricating preparations) Preparations specific for being processed of materials suitable for weaving, leather, the post and fur or the other substances	kg	0.3000
3403.99.00.00.00	(Lubricating preparations) Others	kg	0.3000

Source: Information provided by the Turkish authorities.

Table AIII.7
Key features of the export credit and guarantee programmes, 2011

Scheme	Eligibility	Conditions	Year and amount of credit (US$ million)
Pre-Shipment Turkish Lira Export Credit Programme (PSEC TL)	Exporters, manufacturer-exporters	Interest rate is determined by Turk Eximbank in accordance with developments in money markets and varies according to repayment period and outstanding company risk. Intermediation charges are also added to the interest rates by commercial banks[a] Maturity maximum 540 days Maximum 100% of f.o.b. export commitments and Company limit is US$15 million per company including the sum of FX and TL credits	2007 1,904.5 2008 2,200.4 2009 1,465.2 2010 1,252.7 2011* 698.5
Pre-Shipment Small and Medium-Scale Enterprises Export Credit Programme[b]	SME manufacturer-exporters of up to 250 employees, with net sales revenue or total assets less than TL 25 million, and which do not have a partnership of more than 25%	Same as PSEC TL	2007 566.7 2008 604.8 2009 403.8 2010 308.8 2011* 152.1
PSEC-Priority Development Areas Export Credit Programme[b]	Priority development areas (mainly eastern and south-eastern provinces)	Interest rate equals to the rates applied for firms with an outstanding risk up to TL 500,000 in PSEC-TL program	2007 295.6 2008 322.9 2009 216.9 2010 262.8 2011* 132.9
Pre-Shipment Foreign Currency Export Credit Programme (PSEC FX)	Exporters, manufacturer-exporters	Interest rate varies in accordance with the repayment period together with outstanding company risk and it is linked to LIBOR/ EURIBOR/STG LIBOR/TIBOR. Intermediation charges are also added to the interest rates by commercial banks[c] Maturity maximum 540 days Maximum 100% of f.o.b. export commitments Company limit is US$15 million per company including the sum of FX and TL credits	2007 680.3 2008 845.3 2009 962.4 2010 853.3 2011* 474.9
Free Trade Zones Pre-Shipment Foreign Currency Export Credit Programme (FTZ-PSEC FX)	Manufacturers-manufacturer/exporters with operating license and located in FTZs	Same as PSEC-FX	2007 .. 2008 .. 2009 0.4 2010 2.5 2011* 1.0
Foreign Trade Companies (FTC) Short-Term Turkish Lira Export Credit Programme	All companies that qualify as foreign trade corporate companies (FTCC) or have been granted sectoral foreign trade companies (SFTC)[d] status by UFT	Interest rate is determined by Turk Eximbank in accordance with developments in money markets and varies according to repayment period Maturity maximum 360 days Maximum 100% of f.o.b. export commitments	2007 659.9 2008 666.9 2009 281.3 2010 230.8 2011* 71.8
Foreign Trade Companies Short-Term Foreign Currency Export Credit Programme	All companies that qualify for FTCC or SFTC[d] status by UFT	Interest rate varies in accordance with repayment period and is linked to LIBOR/ EURIBOR/ STG LIBOR/TIBOR Maturity maximum 360 days Maximum 100% of f.o.b. export commitments	2007 119.2 2008 120.2 2009 34.8 2010 2.0 2011[k] 11.5
Pre-Export Small and Medium Scale Enterprises (SMSEs) Credit Programme	Small and medium-scale manufacturer-exporters of up to 250 employees and with net sales revenue or total assets less than TL 25 million and which do not have partnership of more than 25%	Interest rate for TL credits determined by Turk Eximbank in accordance with developments in money markets and varies according to repayment period. Interest rate for foreign currency credits varies in accordance with repayment period and is linked to LIBOR/ EURIBOR/STG LIBOR/TIBOR Maturity maximum 540 days for TL credits and 360 days for FX credits Maximum 100% of f.o.b. export commitments Maximum US$200,000 per company	2007 1.5 2008 1.1 2009 1.3 2010 1.1 2011* 0.8

Table AIII.7 (cont'd)

Scheme	Eligibility	Conditions	Year and amount of credit (US$ million)	
Pre-export Turkish Lira Credit Programme	Export-oriented manufacturers, manufacturer-exporters and exporters, except FTCC and SFTC, that have exported more than US$200,000 of goods in the preceding 12 months or as simple average of last 3 years	Interest rate is determined by Turk Eximbank in accordance with developments in money markets and varies according to repayment period and outstanding company risk Maturity maximum 540 days Maximum 100% of f.o.b. export commitments Company limit is 100% of past export performance and the upper limit is US$15 million per company including the sum of FX and TL credits	2007 2008 2009 2010 2011[*]	217.2 253.7 183.6 111.1 55.5
Pre-export Foreign Currency Credit Programme	Export-oriented manufacturers, manufacturer-exporters and exporters, except FTCC and SFTC, that have exported more than US$200,000 of goods in the preceding 12 months or as simple average of last 3 years	Interest rate varies in accordance with the repayment period together with outstanding company risk and it is linked to LIBOR/ EURIBOR/STG LIBOR/TIBOR Maturity maximum 540 days Maximum 100% of f.o.b. export commitments Company limit is 100% of past export performance and the upper limit is US$15 million per company including the sum of FX and TL credits	2007 2008 2009 2010 2011[k]	109.1 154.5 204.3 173.2 91.5
Free Trade Zones (FTUs) Pre-Export Foreign Currency Credit Programme	Manufacturers-manufacturer/exporters with operating licence and located in FTZs	Same as Pre-Export Foreign Currency Credit Programme	2009 2010 2011[*]	.. .. ..
Tourism Credit Programme[e]	Travel agencies (member of TURSAB and with an "A" group certificate) and private airline companies resident in Turkey those attracting more than US$200,000 of foreign currency to Turkey annually and tourism companies which are accepted as exporters that attract US$1.000.000 of currency and mainly function in accommodation	Interest rate is determined by Turk Eximbank in accordance with developments in money markets and varies according to repayment period and outstanding company risk Interest rate for foreign currency credits is linked to LIBOR/EURIBOR/STG LIBOR/TIBOR Maximum maturity 540 days Company limit is 100% of past tourism service performance and the upper limit is US$8 million per company including the sum of FX and TL credits	2007 2008 2009 2010 2011[*]	2.2 2.5 10.3 6.0 7.9
International Transportation Marketing Credit Programme	International transportation companies with freight revenue of more than US$200.000 in the previous year or the last 12 months before the date of application	Interest rate is determined by Turk Eximbank in accordance with developments in money markets and varies according to repayment period and outstanding company risk. Interest rates for foreign currency credits linked to LIBOR/EURIBOR/STG LIBOR/TIBOR Maximum maturity 540 days Company limit is 100% of past freight revenue performance and the upper limit is US$6 million per company including the sum of FX and TL credits	2007 2008 2009 2010 2011[*]	1.4 4.3 23.3 9.3 2.6
Credit Programme For Participating to Overseas Trade Fairs[f]	Trade fair attending companies and organizers	Interest rate is determined by Turk Eximbank in accordance with developments in money markets and varies according to repayment period and outstanding company risk. Maximum maturity 540 days The amount of credit is limited to 80% of total expenditures of the proposed project for attending companies and 30% for organizers Company limit for attending companies is TL 100.000 and for organizers is maximum TL 1.000.000	2008 2009 2010 2011[*]	.. 1.2 0.9 ..
Short-Term Export Credit Discount Programme	Exporters, manufacturer-exporters	Discount rate: LIBOR + spread Maturity maximum 120 days	2007 2008 2009 2010 2011[*]	8.5 5.1 2.7 2.6 0.1

Table AIII.7 (cont'd)

Scheme	Eligibility	Conditions	Year and amount of credit (US$ million)	
Islamic Development Bank (IDB) Export Financing Scheme-Line[g]	Exports particularly to OIC[h] members and/or non-OIC members; minimum 50% domestic content	Mark-up rate: LIBOR + spread Maturity 12 to 60 months With financing rate as maximum 85% of export value	2007 2008 2009 2010 2011	.. ..
IDB Import Trade Financing Operations (ITFO Line)	Imports of raw materials, semi-capital and capital goods used in the production of export goods; export commitment is required	Mark-up rate is EURIBOR + 1.225% for imports from OIC members and EURIBOR + 1.4% from non-member countries Maturity maximum 30 months for capital goods and 9-24 months for other goods Maximum 80% of import amount	2007 2008 2009 2010 2011	.. ..
The International Islamic Trade Finance Corporation (ITFX) Backed Credit Programme[g]	Exporters, manufacturer-exporters, export commitment is required	Mark-up rate: LIBOR+2.50% Maturity maximum 12 months	2010 2011[*]	.. ..
Overseas Chain Stores Investment Credit Programme	Turkish entrepreneurs' overseas investments for the establishment of shopping malls and chain stores	Interest rates determined by Turk Eximbank specifically for each project Maturity maximum 7 years Maximum 85% of investment amount	2007 2008 2009 2010 2011[*]	.. ..
Specific Export Credit Programme	Exporters, manufacturer-exporters for their foreign currency generating projects in Turkey or abroad at preshipment stage	Terms (interest rate and maturity) are determined on project basis Average maturity 18 months	2007 2008 2009 2010 2011[k]	0.5 1.4 8.5 .. ..
Shipbuilding Finance and Guarantee Programme	Turkish firms involved in shipbuilding and/or the export of ships	Maximum maturity 2 years Direct loans and/or letters of guarantee so that they may obtain pre-financing either in advance or in instalments from the buyer or they can buy supplies and materials with payments having a fixed term	2007 2008 2009 2010 2011[*]	12.3 21.7 7.7 ..
Buyers' Credit & Guarantee Programme[h]	Foreign buyers of Turkish goods and services, min. 50% of Turkish content	Interest rate depends on the recipient countries' relative credit risk standing Maturity 2 years or more Deferred payments Maximum 85% of the goods and services provided from Turkey	2007 2008 2009 2010 2011[*]	16.5 2.3 26.6 6.5 12.3
Short-Term Pre-Shipment Rediscount Programme	Exporters, manufacturer-exporters	Discount rate: LIBOR + spread Maturity maximum 120 days	2007 2008 2009 2010 2011[*]	0.6 .. 1,443.7 1,141.4 658.5
Credit Programme for Foreign Currency Earning Services	Earning services and the export of services such as software projects, and consultancy services	Terms and conditions determined on transaction basis	2007 2008 2009 2010 2011[*]	3.8 .. 0.8 .. 0.3
Bridge Credit Programm for Overseas Contractor Services	Contractors in international markets	For foreign currency credits: Interest rate: LIBOR/EURIBOR+spread Maturity: maximum 360 days For TL credits: Interest rates: constant or TRLIBOR+spread Maturity maximum 2 years For both limit is US$25 million	2007 2008 2009 2010 2011[*]	.. .. 88.9 71.1 14.0
Letter of Guarantee Programme for Overseas Contractors' Services	Contractors in international markets	Guarantees and bonds are issued on behalf of Turkish contractors who participate in tenders abroad, under the counter-guarantee of Turkish commercial banks	2007 2008 2009 2010 2011[*]	.. ..

Table AIII.7 (cont'd)

Scheme	Eligibility	Conditions	Year and amount of credit (US$ million)	
Export Finance Intermediation Loan (EFIL-IV)[j]	Exporters, manufacturer-exporters	Finance with a World Bank credit line of US$246 million Interest rate is LIBOR+spread	2009 2010 2011*	65.9 25.3 3.7
European Investment Bank (EIB) Funded Loan[k]	The firms benefitting from the credit may be a main contractor, a subcontractor or a partner of a consortium.	In order to be eligible to benefit from this program the firms must be established in accordance with the Turkish Commercial Code and should be financially sound and experienced in their field of operation	2009 2010 2011*	2.3 6.5 16.5

.. Not available.

* As of 20 May 2011.

a Intermediation charges by commercial banks usually bring an additional one to two points to the interest charged, while commercial banks are permitted to add a maximum of one point to the interest rates determined by Turk Eximbank.

b These programmes are sub-programmes of PSEC TL. A minimum of 30% of the general limit allocated to commercial banks has to be extended to small and medium-scale enterprises, while intermediary banks are required to extend at least 5% of their general limit to credit demands for firms in priority development areas.

c Intermediation charges by commercial banks usually bring an additional one to two points to the interest charged, while commercial banks are permitted to add a maximum of 0.5 points to the interest rates determined by Turk Eximbank.

d Foreign trade companies established by export-oriented manufacturing firms operating in the same sector.

e Tourism Marketing Credit Programme was renamed as Tourism Credit Programme in June 2010.

f Credit Programme For Participating to Overseas Trade Fairs was put into practice on December 2008.

g Islamic Development Bank mandated all existing funds and facilities related to the trade finance to the International Islamic Trade Finance Corporation (ITFC) on January 2008.

h OIC = Organization of Islamic Cooperation.

i Projects undertaken by Turkish contractors abroad are mainly financed under this programme.

j The EFIL-IV Programme has started in 2008.

k EIB funded Credit Programme has started in 2009.

Note: Export credit insurance has been voluntary since 17 February 1997. However, if beneficiaries of the Pre-Shipment Export Credit Programmes, Foreign Trade Companies Export Credit Programmes and Pre-export Credit Programmes are also short-term export credit insurance policy holders, they receive discount on interest rates (0.5 point discount on TL credits and 0.25 point discount on foreign currency credits).

Source: Information provided by the Turkish authorities.

Table AIV.1
Main measures of support of Turkish agriculture, 2006-10
(TRY million)

	2006	2007	2008	2009	2010
Producer Support Estimate (PSE)	28,719	25,237	26,504	31,200	33,184
Percentage PSE (total PSE in % of total value of production)	38	31	25	29	28
Market price support, of which:	22,967	19,070	20,748	26,999	27,929
Milk	3,947	2,526	3,334	3,015	2,674
Grapes	1,091	1,525	647	2,052	2,455
Beef	1,690	1,379	1,443	850	1,816
Poultry	419	601	573	1,106	1,618
Apples	786	1,044	1,299	1,630	1,369
Potatoes	1,104	1,082	1,230	1,186	1,355
Barley	483	0	402	1,204	926
Eggs	277	100	761	581	831
Wheat	2,602	1,497	0	1,531	623
Maize	509	482	206	478	549
Deficiency payments, of which:	1,723	1,834	1,649	1,540	2,110
Wheat premium	472	300	673	478	888
Cotton premium	566	828	683	509	519
Sunflower premium	165	203	115	179	200
Maize premium	191	209	71	152	163
Tea leaf premium	82	88	102	112	126
Barley premium	53	0	0	32	114
Milk incentive premium	162	177	0	0	0
Input subsidies, of which:	1,269	1,342	1,289	910	656
Concessional loans	146	225	298	405	320
Livestock improvement	447	476	676	288	0
Livestock development project – Apiculture	517	526	116	24	26
Disaster payments – Crops	45	5	1	0	128
Interest concessions	0	0	74	101	80
Direct payments					
Direct income support	2,690	1,641	1,138	0	0
Cattle breed registration payment	0	18	59	326	596
Feed crops premium	0	404	676	288	583
Diesel payment	0	479	473	618	658
Fertilizer payment	0	342	342	447	532
Land compensation	1	2	5	4	10
Other					
Duty loss	186	232	614	483	775
Debt write off	195	172	121	0	0
Equity injections from Treasury to state-owned enterprises	1,556	60	545	2,022	677
Transfer to Agricultural Sales Co-operative Unions	215	213	0	0	0

Note: PSE: total annual monetary transfers to farmers individually (not agriculture generally) from: market price support mainly through border measures but also food aid, export subsidies (calculated by the price gap between domestic and border price); payments to farmers; and tax/fee reductions (revenue forgone).

Source: OECD, *PSE/CSE database*. Viewed at: http://www.oecd.org/document/59/0,3746,en_2649_37401_39551355_1_1_1_37401,00.html#country.

Table AIV.2
Export subsidy rates, 2011
(US$ and %)

Product	Rate (US$/tonne)	Share of exported quantity eligible for the subsidy (%)
Cut flowers (fresh)	205	40
Vegetables, frozen (excluding potatoes)	79	45
Vegetables (dehydrated)	370	40
Fruits (frozen)	78	45
Preserves, pastes	63	35
Honey	65	32
Homogenized fruit preparations	75	100
Fruit juices (concentrated)	150	15
Olive oil	40	100
Prepared or preserved fish	250	100
Poultry meat (excl. edible offals)	186	41
Eggs	15US$/1,000 pieces	65
Preserved poultry meat products	250	50
Chocolate and other food preparations containing chocolate	119	48
Biscuits, waffles	119	18
Macaroni, vermicelli	66	32

Source: Ministry of Economy.

PART C

REPORT BY TURKEY

CONTENTS

I. INTRODUCTION

(1) Overview

1. This Government Report of Turkey – which we believe would facilitate Turkey's Fifth Trade Policy Review under the Trade Policy Review Mechanism of the World Trade Organization – comes out at times of uncertainty and pessimism in the global economy.

2. Although the global economy exited the deepest recession of its history with record expansion of trade and the revival of economic activity in 2010, the post-crisis economy has not been free from some old and new challenges. Despite rebound, fragility of global economic recovery with serious downside risks remained.

3. As a result of timely and decisive economic policies, robust macroeconomic fundamentals, enduring capital inflows, lower interest rates and loan expansion; Turkish economy grew strongly after the global economic crisis in 2008. GDP growth rate was 9% in 2010 and 10.2% in the first half of 2011. Industrial sector achieved a notable growth rate of 12.6% in 2010, whereas the growth rate in services sector was recorded 8.5% in the same year, which assumed a significant role in high GDP growth. Thanks to all these positive developments, Turkish economy became one of the fastest growing economies in the world in 2010. In the first half of 2011, the pace of strong and stable growth continued through favourable domestic conditions, and the GDP growth rate has been 10.2% in this period. In accordance with the *Economic Intelligence Unit* data, in the first quarter of 2011 Turkey has been the fastest growing country in the world. In the second quarter of the same year, Turkey preserved its high growth rate. Industrial and services sectors' growth rates were very high in the first half of 2011, with 10.4% and 10.6% respectively. Especially, manufacturing, construction, retail and wholesale trade and transportation were key subsectors for high performance in GDP growth. Additionally, agricultural sector grew by 6.8% in this period. According to the Economic Intelligence Unit analysis, based on 2010 data, Turkey became the 6th country in the world that has a population larger than 70 million and a per capita income over US$10,000. Turkey's GDP per capita has increased to US$10,067 in 2010, from US$7,586 in 2006. Turkey became the 17th biggest economy in the world and 6th in Europe as of 2010. Thus, the growth targets of the 9th Development Plan for 2007-2013 have already been met.

4. Fiscal discipline has been one of the cornerstones of Turkey's ongoing economic program and played the leading role in maintaining macroeconomic stability by decreasing debt burden. Hence, the successful debt management strategy contributed to the impressive track record of the Turkish economy in the past ten years. The tenets underlying the economic program enabled the Turkish economy to deal with the negative effects of the global financial crisis of 2008 effectively.

5. Through durable fiscal adjustment, the risk premium and cost of public borrowing declined considerably. As the public debt fell as a share of GDP, at the same time its structure has improved. The average maturity of the debt increased and the foreign exchange denominated component of the debt decreased significantly.

6. Accelerating short-term capital inflows, the divergence between domestic and external demand growth and rapid credit expansion contributed to the widening of the current account deficit in the second half of 2010, necessitating a close monitoring of macro-prudential risks to Turkey. Therefore, the Central Bank of the Republic of Turkey (CBT) started to follow a monetary policy framework where price stability and financial stability complement each other. This involves pursuing a monetary policy with multiple tools. Thus, with the main objective of maintaining price stability in

addition to the duty to observe financial stability, the CBT adopted a new policy mix with policy rates, interest rate corridor and required reserve ratios in order to contain macro-prudential risks.

7. Having deepened during the final quarter of 2008, the global downturn began to weigh more heavily on the Turkish economy, which caused domestic demand to slump during 2009. Hence, exports and imports were markedly down year-on-year throughout 2009. However, as imports contracted at a faster pace than exports, the trade deficit and the current account deficit narrowed considerably year-on-year in 2009. Although external demand remained weak amid Europe's sovereign debt problems, domestic demand grew at a relatively steady pace, leading to a large increase in the foreign trade deficit during 2010. Moreover, due to the sharp rise in commodity prices during 2010, prices of imports increased at a faster pace than prices of exports. Total exports of goods increased by 11.5% to US$113.9 billion, while total imports of goods rose by 31.7% to US$185.5 billion. Net services revenues dropped by 12.7% year-on-year in 2010 due to the widening foreign trade deficit and the rapid increase in service expenditures, causing the current account deficit to expand, climbing to US$47.7 billion in 2010 from US$14.0 billion in 2009. In 2011, current account deficit continued to augment due to high energy and other commodity prices and continued increase in imports induced by domestic demand for investment goods and durables. However, through the measures taken by the government and expected relative slowdown in the economy in the second half of 2011 and 2012, the efforts of the Banking Regulation and Supervision Agency and the CBT are expected to pave the way in reducing the current account deficit. In accordance with the Medium-Term Program for 2012-2014 fiscal discipline will continue to be an important component of the fiscal policy with the aim of constraining the current-account deficit and maintaining a low level of public debt. The aim is to continue the private-sector-led growth of the economy.

8. The unfavorable effects on capital flows due to the global financial crisis that deepened in the last quarter of 2008, continued in the first quarter of 2009 as well and net outflows were observed in this period. Although the tightness in international credit markets persisted throughout 2009, and capital flows – especially to developing countries – slowed down, net inflows were observed in the second half of 2009. Long-term capital inflows, which reached high levels owing to the upsurge in private sector utilization of long-term credits in recent years, were replaced by outflows and both the private sector and the banking sector remained net re-payer of debt in 2009. In addition, direct investments and portfolio investments remained limited. However, in 2010, the widening discrepancies in interest rates and growth between advanced and emerging economies due to expansionary monetary and fiscal policies in advanced countries associated with their weak stimulating impact on economic activity in those countries, coupled with the rising risk appetite, have attracted more capital flows to emerging economies. As a result, Turkey experienced a net portfolio inflow of US$16.1 billion in 2010. Meanwhile, net foreign direct investment increased by 14% to US$7.8 billion. Moreover, the private sector became net creditor, while banking sector borrowing, especially short-term, increased. According to the balance of payments statistics of the CBT, total value of FDI inflow was US$22 billion in 2007; US$19.5 billion in 2008; US$8.4 billion in 2009; US$9.3 billion in 2010 and US$10.1 billion as of August 2011.

9. The Turkish financial sector, mostly composed of banks, has been on a sound growth path in the past decade. The Turkish banking sector, which has undergone a major restructuring process following the economic crisis in 2001, managed to overcome the recent global financial crisis with no apparent damage and verified its outstanding resilience.

10. The headwinds from the global crisis have remained relatively subdued thanks to the resilience of the financial system and prudent macro policies. Turkey was one of the few emerging

countries that ended up with higher credit rating than pre-crisis level and no rescue package was needed to support the banking system.

(2) Macroeconomic Policies and Development

(i) Fiscal policy

11. As a result of policies applied for increasing the fiscal discipline, transparency, accountability and effectiveness in debt management; for simplifying the tax system and lowering general tax rates by improving the tax base; for reforming the Social Security System[1] and public sector governance comprehensively, Turkish economy has undergone significant structural changes over the past ten years. Public debt stock ratios have lowered subsequently with an exception in year 2009. Due to the global financial crisis, there have been slight increases in debt stock ratios in 2009. Following this period, ratios turn into the regular decreasing trend again. The net public debt to GDP ratio fell from 66.4% in 2001 to 28.8% in 2010 with an average 4.2 point decrease each year. EU defined general government debt to GDP ratio decreased from 77.9% to 42.2% in the same period. In addition, this ratio is expected to decrease gradually and to become 32% by the end of 2014.

12. The adverse effects of the global economic crisis interrupted the public finance performance. The fiscal stimulus package, adopted to mitigate the effects of the crisis on the economy, raised the central government budget deficit to GDP ratio to 5.5% in 2009. Nevertheless, fiscal measures and the rapid economic recovery resulted in this ratio to decline 3.6% in 2010 and it is expected to be 1.7% in 2011.

13. The developments of the past ten years prove that reducing the public debt ratio and maintaining the economic growth primarily depends on strict control of public finance. In this respect, Medium Term Program of 2012-2014 envisages a gradual decrease in the central government budget deficit and sets a target of 1.0% by the end of 2014.

14. During the global economic crisis, decreasing borrowing costs together with stability of Turkish financial sector increased public confidence, improved the risk perception for Turkey and contributed to the extension of borrowing maturities. In order to achieve an extended yield curve, a 10 year fixed coupon bond was issued in January 2010 and a 10 year CPI indexed bond was issued in April 2010 in line with the strategic benchmarks. These two issues represent the longest auction maturities in local currency achieved in the history of the Republic of Turkey. The average maturity of cash-based domestic borrowing increased to 44.1 months in 2010 from its 2009 level of 31.3 months and reached 47.2 months as of September 2011. On the other hand, in 2010 the cost of TL denominated zero coupon bonds decreased from its early 2009 levels of 16% to the one-digit levels after August 2010, and to its historically lowest level of 7.1% in January 2011, parallel to the high demand from domestic markets and the CBT rate cuts. As of September 2011, the cost of TL denominated zero coupon bonds is 8.2%.

[1] "Social Security and General Health Insurance" Law was enacted in May 2008 with the aim of ensuring justice in social security system, reducing social security deficit and facilitating access to health care services. With this law fundamental institutional and parametric changes put in to practice. Thus, social security standards for workers, civil servants and the self employed brought to same level, a general health insurance scheme has been introduced, and retirement age has gradually been increased to 65. The reform aims to decrease the burden of the social security system from 4.5% of the GDP to 1% in the long-run via a new pension scheme and universal health insurance.

15. In line with the aim of sustaining transparency and predictability in debt management, the domestic borrowing strategy previously announced in monthly periods is disclosed for a rolling three months horizon, starting from January 2010.

16. With the aim of increasing domestic savings, diversifying borrowing instruments and broadening the investor base, Revenue Indexed Bonds, of which coupon payments are indexed to the transfers of State Owned Enterprises, were first issued in 2009 and have continued to be issued regularly in 2010 and 2011.

17. The main principles of public debt management are to maintain an accountable, transparent, sustainable borrowing policy which is compatible with the monetary and fiscal policies and to meet financing needs with the optimal cost possible in the medium and long term with the risk level determined by considering domestic and international market conditions. In this framework, strategic benchmarks are determined to guide borrowing policies since 2003. These policies mainly aim at reducing the interest rate, exchange rate and liquidity risks arising from public debt portfolio. According to the strategic benchmarks for the 2012-2014 period:

- The domestic cash borrowing will be made mainly in the TL,

- Fixed rate instruments will be used as a major source in TL borrowing and the share of debt which has interest rate re-fixing period less than 12 months will be reduced,

- The average maturity of domestic cash borrowing will be increased taking market conditions into consideration and the share of debt maturing within 12 months will be reduced,

- A certain level of cash reserve will be kept in order to reduce the liquidity risk associated with cash and debt management.

(ii) Inflation and monetary policy

18. The CBT continued to implement inflation targeting together with a floating exchange rate regime in 2008-2011 period so as to achieve and maintain price stability.

19. CPI inflation ended 2008 at 10.06%. Inflation in 2008 was largely determined by developments in the global economy. After sharp increases in energy and other commodity prices in the first three quarters, there was a dramatic shift in inflation dynamics in the last quarter of 2008 due to the challenging developments in the global economy.

20. Originating in the advanced economies, the financial crisis, as the deepest fall since the Great Depression of the 1930s, late in 2008 spread to the entire global system. Its effects were seen on economic and financial stability throughout 2009. Thanks to the experience gained from domestic crises in the recent past, the CBT was able to make prompt and effective decisions, thus played its part successfully to minimize the adverse impacts of the global crisis. The resilience of the financial system coupled with the relatively limited level of risk premium provided room for manoeuvre for monetary policy.

21. Pursuant to its projection that problems in international credit markets and the global economy following the deepening of the crisis would continue to restrain both domestic and foreign demand for an extended period, the CBT focused on containing the potential damage of the crisis to economic activity. Within this framework, the CBT launched the monetary expansion process in

November 2008 and became a pioneer in cutting policy rates among the central banks of emerging markets. Projecting that the probability of undershooting the inflation target would increase, the CBT adopted a front-loaded policy by cutting policy rates by 650 basis points in the December 2008-April 2009 period.

22. Policy implementations of the CBT are shaped in view of medium-term developments rather than short-term economic developments. Accordingly, despite signals of partial recovery in domestic economic activity as of the second half of 2009, judging that uncertainties pertaining to the strength and permanence of recovery in demand persisted, the CBT continued to ease policy rates, based on projections that recovery in economic activity and employment conditions would take a significant time. Within this framework, policy rates have been cut by totally 1,025 basis points since the Monetary Policy Committee meeting of November 2008. Thus, Turkey lowered policy rates more than any other emerging market operating within an inflation-targeting framework. Reduced concerns over inflation during the crisis prepared the ground for the CBT to focus on economic activity and financial stability.

23. Accordingly, though it is still adhered to its primary objective of achieving price stability, the CBT took some additional measures – besides policy rate cuts – that would alleviate liquidity shortage, help the credit market operate smoothly and support the corporate sector with the aim of preventing the adverse impacts of the global financial crisis on the Turkish economy and financial stability. To sum up, with its appropriate policy decisions, the CBT succeeded in containing damage caused by the global financial crisis on domestic economic activity and prevented inflation from deviating from the target by a significant margin.

24. With the economic slowdown due to global crisis and favorable outlook in cost-based factors, annual CPI inflation in 2009 was 3.5 points lower than the 2008 figure. CPI inflation ended 2009 at 6.53%. The sharp contraction in economic activity and the collapse of commodity prices brought down inflation rates in all major categories of the CPI basket, especially in the first half of 2009. In this respect, energy and processed food prices, which are particularly sensitive to commodity price developments, displayed a sharp decline. Inflation in core goods and services also slowed down owing mainly to weak domestic demand and temporary tax cuts implemented to stimulate economic activity. In the third quarter, despite the partial withdrawal of the said tax cuts, the underlying disinflation trend was strong enough to bring headline inflation downwards further. Fourth quarter of 2009 saw record high run-up in unprocessed food prices, the upsurge in oil and other commodity prices and the expiration of temporary tax incentives, which drove inflation higher.

25. While the global economy continued to gradually recover in 2010, the recovery in advanced economies presents a slow and vulnerable outlook in contrast to the faster recovery in emerging markets. In fact, production in many emerging economies, including Turkey, has exceeded the pre-crisis levels in 2010 and the improvement in the labour markets of these countries has been more stable. In this respect, the decoupling between the pace of recovery in advanced and emerging economies has become more pronounced.

26. Following the ease of the impact of the crisis on financial markets, the CBT, announced on 14 April 2010, its exit strategy, which entailed removal of liquidity measures taken during the crisis and normalization of the operational framework of monetary policy. Acting upon favorable developments in the credit market and the recovery in economic activity, the CBT withdrew the temporary liquidity measures it had introduced during the crisis and gradually mopped up excess liquidity provided for the market, and raised required reserve ratios. In this context, the CBT has

initiated the first step of the technical arrangement to facilitate a change in the operational structure of liquidity management in May by which the one week repo rate, became the new policy rate.

27. Besides the monetary policy exit strategy, the CBT accelerated reserve accumulation with an aim to contributing to financial stability and in order to be able to adapt to the rapidly changing structure of capital flows, adopted a more flexible method for foreign exchange buying auctions in October 2010. Moreover, with the aim of ensuring more effective use of alternative instruments towards curbing risks pertaining to financial stability, the CBT terminated the remuneration of Turkish Lira required reserves and changed the operational structure of liquidity management. In addition to these measures, the CBT introduced further measures to direct the capital inflows driven by global monetary expansion to investment instruments with longer maturities.

28. With the main objective of maintaining price stability in addition to the duty to observe financial stability, the CBT adopted a new policy mix with lower policy rates, wider interest rate corridor and higher required reserve ratios in order to contain macro-prudential risks in the fourth quarter of 2010.

29. In this context, in order to encourage long-term capital inflows and to maintain the stability of the Turkish Lira, the CBT reduced the one-week repo auction rate. Moreover, the CBT significantly widened the spread between overnight borrowing and lending rates. The CBT has taken important steps regarding reserve requirements, a key element of the CBT's policy mix serving to contain macro-prudential risks. In December, the CBT adopted a more comprehensive approach and decided to differentiate TL reserve requirement ratios by maturity in order to extend the maturity of the banking system's liabilities, thereby reducing maturity mismatches, and to encourage long-term capital inflows. Accordingly, the required reserve ratio on short-term liabilities was raised and the required reserve base was expanded by including repo transactions, except interbank and CBT transactions. In order to more effectively benefit from capital flows by boosting foreign exchange reserves while also enhancing the resilience against volatile capital flows, the CBT decided to change the method of foreign exchange buying auctions in October 2010.

30. Inflation continued to rise during the first four months of 2010, largely due to tax hikes in fuel, alcoholic beverages and tobacco products in January. In addition, as in the last quarter of 2009, the rate of change in unprocessed food prices displayed another historically high print in the first quarter of 2010. The upward trend in inflation due to these factors has continued until the last quarter of 2010. However, the determinant of the inflation developments throughout 2010 was the course of food prices. The annual energy inflation rose in the first half of the year, then declined gradually in the second half and the annual services inflation dropped down to the lowest level in its history in 2010. At the end of 2010, the annual rate of increase in the CPI was 6.4%.

31. Regarding the inflation developments in 2011, the downward trend in inflation, which became apparent particularly in the last quarter of 2010, continued during the first quarter and the annual rate of increase in CPI fell to a level as low as 3.99% as of March. However, the depreciation of the Turkish Lira and the increase in commodity prices started to affect the consumer prices from the first months of 2011. Core goods, on which the pressure of the aforementioned increases was more pronounced, had its annual inflation rising significantly. The rapid surge in oil and commodity prices in the subsequent period increased the upside risks to inflation, necessitating an additional tightening in order to limit the second round effects.

32. The CBT, continued to implement the policy mix of low policy rate, wide interest rate corridor and high reserve requirement ratios in the first quarter of 2011. Assessing that required

reserve ratios rather than policy rates would be more effective for containing macro financial risks driven by the divergence between domestic and external demand, the additional tightening was implemented through a substantial increase in the weighted average of the required reserve ratios. In order to balance domestic and external demand, and thus limit macro financial risks, TL and FX required reserve ratios were raised slightly and FX required reserve ratios were differentiated by maturity and raised slightly for short-term deposits on 21 April 2011.

33. The mounting concerns in the second quarter regarding sovereign debt problems across some European countries as well as global economic growth adversely affected the risk appetite and capital flows to emerging economies. In view of these developments, the daily amount to be purchased via FX auctions was reduced. Towards the end of July, FX buying auctions were suspended in order to monitor the effects of the decisions taken by the EU pertaining to solve the sovereign debt problems. Additionally, in July, in order to extend the maturity structure of the banking sector liabilities, foreign exchange required reserve ratios were decreased for long-term liabilities.

34. The policies implemented by the CBT since end-2010 aimed at gradually rebalancing the economy towards a healthier growth composition without hampering the medium-term inflation outlook. These involved necessary measures were taken in cooperation with other institutions, to ensure reasonable levels in loan growth rates.

35. As the risk perceptions deteriorated rapidly in early August 2011 and debt problems in the euro area further intensified, the CBT held an interim meeting on 4 August 2011 to contain the potential adverse effects of these developments on financial stability and economic activity, and announced a comprehensive package of measures. These measures laid the background for a timely, controlled and effective provision of liquidity to markets in the event of a financial turmoil that may be driven by the developments in the global economy. The CBT cut the policy rate by 0.50% points in order to contain the risk of a recession in economic activity that may be posed by the escalating global economic problems. During this period, upon the acceleration of capital outflows from emerging economies, a series of liquidity measures were taken to contain the fluctuations in the foreign exchange market.

36. Measures regarding Turkish Lira market in August-October period were built on two pillars. First is preventing extreme volatility in overnight interest rates by narrowing the interest rate corridor, which was previously used as an instrument to discourage short term capital flows as well. The second element of the measures regarding TL liquidity is to meet the TL liquidity requirement of the Turkish banking system in a more permanent way. Accordingly, the upper limit for FX reserves that may be held to meet Turkish Lira reserve requirements was raised to 40% of Lira liabilities. Required reserve ratios for certain Turkish Lira liabilities were reduced such that the weighted average TL required reserve ratio, has come down to 10.5%. Furthermore, in August-October period of 2011, some measures regarding foreign exchange markets were also taken to lay the background for a timely, controlled and effective provision of liquidity to markets in the event of a financial turmoil that may be driven by the developments in the global economy.

37. The ongoing deterioration in global risk appetite, which started in August, has led to an excessive depreciation of the Turkish Lira. Accumulated depreciation of 30% since November 2010 started to pose risks on the inflation outlook. Moreover, in October, the adjustments in administered prices were far beyond the assumptions of the CBT, which brought about a sizeable upward revision for the short-term inflation forecasts. Accordingly, in its October meeting, the CBT underlined that it would not tolerate the outlook for medium-term inflation expectations to be affected by these

developments, and decided to widen the overnight interest rate corridor by raising the lending rate from 9% to 12.5%.

38. At the Monetary Policy Committee meeting of 4 August 2011, the CBT agreed to closely monitor developments, and if necessary, take measures to provide foreign exchange liquidity via the appropriate methods and instruments. Accordingly, taking global developments into consideration, the CBT commenced supplying FX liquidity to the market via high-volume foreign exchange selling auctions as of 5 October 2011. Furthermore, as unhealthy price formations in exchange rates are being observed due to speculative behaviour stemming from a decrease in market depth, on 18 October 2011, the CBT directly intervened in the market through FX sales.

(iii) Labour market reforms

(a) Accelerating employment creation and jobs recovery

39. Significant political measures in terms of accelerating employment creation and jobs recovery have been taken in the last few years. These measures are:

- 25% of social security employer's contribution for pensions, disability and death insurance is paid by Central Government Budget.

- Social security employer premium of firms hiring young people (18-29) and women is paid by the unemployment insurance fund.

- To avoid dismissals in the case of a sectoral crisis, regional crisis or a general economic crisis short time working allowance is introduced.

(b) Active labour market programs

40. The financial resources of Active Labour Market programs, including for public works increased and vocational training, internship for youth and entrepreneurship education activities are expanded.

(c) Struggle with informal employment

41. To reduce the amount and the effects of shadow economy and especially unregistered employment, "Struggle Against Informal Economy Action Plan 2008 – 2010" has been put into force in 2008.

(iv) Private sector's role in the economy

(a) Improvement of the investment environment

42. Strengthening private sector's role in Turkish economy continues to be an integral part of Turkey's overall macroeconomic program. To this end, Turkey has put efforts for improving the investment climate among the top agenda items and initiated a comprehensive reform program – "the Reform Program for the Improvement of the Investment Environment" – in 2001 in order to streamline all investment-related procedures. The Coordination Council for the Improvement of Investment Environment (YOIKK) and the Investment Advisory Council (IAC) are the pioneer public private partnership platforms which have been formed within the Reform Program to lead investment environment studies.

43. YOIKK aims to solve the problems of both national and international investors through conciliating the responsible institutions and agencies. The effective information sharing process between the public and private sector representatives and the strong coordination between all the parties are the key success factors of the YOIKK platform.

44. Since its formation, YOIKK has established 12 specialized technical committees to work on developing concrete proposals and strategies in order to overcome all main obstacles in the following fields:

- Company registration
- Employment
- Sectoral licensing
- Investment Location
- Taxes and Incentives
- Foreign Trade and Customs
- Industrial and Intellectual Property Rights
- Foreign Direct Investments Legislation
- Investment Promotion
- Small and Medium Sized Enterprises
- Corporate Governance
- Research and Development.

45. So far, the activities of the YOIKK have been quite successful. YOIKK conducts its studies via annual Action Plans since 2007. The main developments achieved through these Action Plans since the last TPR (2007) are listed below.

46. The Law on the Amendment of the Income Tax Law and Some Laws entered into force on 4 April 2007 in order to lower the tax burden on the employees by the implementation of the minimum living allowance system. By this amendment, Turkey has moved on 5 steps on the ranking among OECD countries in terms of the tax burden on employees.

47. By the Law No. 5838 published on the Official Gazette on 18 February 2009:

- The requirements to benefit from short term employment allowance have been alleviated.
- Communication tax concerning wired, wireless and mobile internet services was reduced to 5% from the level of 15% as a result of the amended tax regulations.
- By the provisional Article No. 75 attached to Income Tax Law, firms are enabled to benefit from Research and Development incentives which are provided to individuals.
- Investments to be made in line with the new regional, sectoral and project based incentive system have been supported via reduced corporate tax rate.

48. "Law No. 5746 on Enhancing Research And Development Activities", which involves important incentives towards accelerating research and development activities and innovation, was published on the Official Gazette on 12 March 2008 and came into force in April 2008.

49. Prime Ministry Circular No. 2008/7 on The Establishment of Coordination Council for Intellectual and Industrial Property Rights was enacted on 21 May 2008.

50. The Employment Package aiming to decrease the bureaucratic and financial burden on labour force and increase the flexibility of the labour market was enacted on 26 May 2008.

51. "The Regulation on the Ex-Post Inspection and the Control of the Risky Operations" aiming at accelerating the work flow via the ex-post inspection of the customs operations, was enacted on 27 October 2008.

52. Law No. 5891 which enables firms operating in trade and services sectors, along side with the manufacturing firms, benefit from the supports provided by the Small and Medium Industry Development Organization (KOSGEB) was enacted on 5 May 2009.

53. Law No. 5909 amending the Law on Regulation of Public Finance and Debt Management was enacted on 24 June 2009 with the aim to improve the credit guarantee system.

54. A new scheme for government incentives for investment projects incorporating sectoral and regional development priorities was introduced with the Decree on Government Incentives for Investments dated 16 July 2009.

55. The Regulation on KOSGEB Support Programs was promulgated in the Official Gazette on 15 June 2010 in order to provide micro and small firms to access KOSGEB Support programs easier. In the context of regulation, principles that will enable micro and small firms to access support programs easier were identified, "SMEs Information System" which will provide online application was formed and work has started to form "KOSGEB call center".

56. In the context of "Work Permits Automation Project", work permit applications can be only made via electronic environment since 2 August 2010.

57. The Communiqué related to Turkey-EU Instrument for Pre-Accession Assistance issued by the then Undersecretariat of Customs (now the Ministry of Customs and Trade) was promulgated in the Official Gazette on 15 October 2010 with the aim to grant exemption to the products brought under the projects supported within the international bilateral and multilateral R&D programs.

58. While achieving quite positive results in improving the environment for business by means of national platforms like YOIKK, another structure with an international perspective, the Investment Advisory Council (IAC) for Turkey was established in 2004 with a view to raise the competitive position of Turkey in the world economy as an investment location. The high – level IAC meetings in 2004, 2005, 2006, 2007, 2008 and 2010 brought together the top executives of leading multinational companies, international organizations and the heads of Turkish private sector associations in İstanbul and every meeting was chaired by the Prime Minister Recep Tayyip Erdoğan.

(b) Privatization

59. Turkey continues to attach importance on privatization as a component in a well functioning, open and competitive market economy. Thus, privatizations continued since the last TPR in 2007.

60. Turkey initiated the privatization process of the seaports. Mersin port was privatized in 2007, followed by the privatization of ports in Bandırma and Samsun in 2010. In the same spirit, the tender processes of İskenderun, Derince and İzmir Ports were initiated. The tender for the transfer of management rights of İskenderun Port (located on the Mediterranean coast of Turkey), which is an asset of Turkish State Railways Administration, for a period of 36 years was held on 17 May 2010. The highest bid was given in an amount of US$372 million. The Concession Rights Agreement was signed and the privatization process of İskenderun Port will be finalized after confirmation of The Council of State.

61. The tender process for the transfer of operational rights of İzmir Port (located on the Aegean coast of Turkey), which is an asset of Turkish State Railways Administration, for a period of 49 years has been cancelled on 28 April 2010. The privatization is planned to take place in 2014 according to Medium Term Fiscal Plan.

62. Besides, the privatization of 24 sugar manufacturing companies and their related assets will be completed until 2014. The privatization studies of toll motorways, two Bosphorous bridges, the beltways (periferique) of Ankara and İzmir and the service units operated by Turkish Highways General Directorate is underway.

63. Overall privatization proceeds realized by Turkish Privatization Administration (PA) have reached to US$42 billion as of mid-2011. US$15.6 billion revenue have been generated from the privatization of blue chip companies, including Türk Telekom, Tüpraş, Erdemir and Petkim. Since inception of PA (1984) and as of 30 June 2011, the privatization implementations of Turkey have resulted in a net worth of approximately US$53.5 billion.[2]

(v) Financial sector reforms

(a) Banking sector

64. Since the last TPR in 2007, developing a financial system, which has a competitive scale, sufficient instrument diversity and depth to channel resources to investments, minimized intermediation costs and which is supervised and audited in line with international standards, has continued to be a main objective. With this goal in mind, the regulation and supervision of the financial sector has been improved in line with international standards and EU Acquis and amendments have been made to the legislation in accordance with the needs arise in practice. The amendments on sub regulations covered a wide range of issues, including the establishment and operations of banks, loan transactions, protective provisions, corporate governance, liquidity adequacy, financial reporting, non-bank financial institutions, bank and credit cards and other provisions.

65. There are also some recent measures supporting banking sector reforms in order to enhance Turkish banking sector resilience against the global economic and financial crisis. The CBRT has been actively using reserve requirement ratios and liquidity management tools, meanwhile the Banking Regulation and Supervision Agency (BRSA) has taken some measures related with general provisioning and loan to value ratios as part of macro-prudential policy in order to deal with the challenges emerged in the post crisis era.

66. The issues becoming prominent in the banking area within the scope of Harmonization Program of Turkey to EU Acquis and Turkey's National Program regarding Undertaking EU Acquis for 2008 are harmonization to Basel-II Capital Adequacy Directives, enhancement of corporate risk management and consolidated audit.

67. Recent main regulatory issues, aiming harmonization with international standards and to reduce effects of global financial crisis, are as follows:

- BRSA is conducting a study on Basel II requirements to provide implementation in Turkish banking sector. BRSA was accepted as a member to the Basel Committee on

[2] See Annexed Table 3: Privatization Implementations by Years and Table 4: Significant Privatization Implementations between 2008-30 September 2010.

Banking Supervision (BCBS) in 2009 and participates to the related working groups in various levels. Preparations on transition process of Turkish banking sector to Basel II has been continued and related draft legislation has been issued in March 2011. In order to ensure the adaptation of Basel II rules by the sector, banking regulation and Supervision Board has decided that the Basel II rules in Turkish banking legislation will be implemented only within the aim of reporting to the BRSA between 01 July 2011 and 30 June 2012.

- In line with the Financial Stability Board (FSB) membership of Turkey, the FSB studies are followed closely by the BRSA, studies are conducted in order to maintain the adaptation of banking legislation to the FSB principles and standards and active participation is ensured to the related topics such as international cooperation and information sharing. Within the frame of the adaptation obligation of member countries to the FSB standards, BRSA published supervisory guidance on compensation in June 2011. Banking Regulation and Supervision Board took a decision stipulating that the harmony levels of implementation of corporate governance principles including the ones regarding the compensation will be taken into account in calculation of banks' ratings conducted by the on-site supervisors. The ratings given by the supervisors are taken into account in the calculation of insurance premiums of the banks. Those ratings are also important in terms of the assessment of banks' situations in enforcement actions.

- On 30 September 2010, BRSA regulated the issuance of bills and bonds by banks. A dynamic function of equity, saving deposit, asset size and capital adequacy ratio has been developed to limit the amount of bonds to be issued by the banks.

- As of 1 January 2011, BRSA limited consumer loans mortgaged by the residential real estate to 75% of the value of the real estate subject to the mortgage and limits commercial loans extended for the purchase of commercial real estate to 50% of the value of such real estate.

- To reduce the economic impact of the global crisis, rules of provisioning and loan restructuring has been changed. BRSA has also issued sub regulations to encourage banks to keep high capital levels and profit distribution has been subject to BRSA's approval. Additionally, rules of managing and monitoring liquidity adequacy have been revised.

- Exemptions on preparation consolidated financial statements of banks are revised in light of related accounting standards. Besides, financial statements' formats have been revised in light of the latest accounting standards.

- Concerning the measurement and management of interest rate risk in the banking book, a regulation has been issued in August 2011 and the regulation will be fully in force in July 2012.

68. The credit intermediation role of the banking sector is improving with the support of the reforms in the sector and declining public sector borrowing need. The ratio of credits to assets has increased from 23% in 2002 to 54% as of August 2011 (52% in 2010). Although the amount and ratio of loans have increased, the total credit to GDP ratio in Turkey is still lower than many developed countries.

69. The Systemic Risk Coordination Committee formed within the scope of the Systemic Risk Cooperation Protocol on Financial System, which was signed among the Undersecretariat of Treasury, BRSA, SDIF and CBT for the management of risk and preparation of emergency action plan concerning a possible systematic risk that may occur in the sector, commenced its operations in 2010. Model based scenario analysis was developed in order to increase the capacity of stress test realization of the BRSA.

70. The implementation of "FINTURK – Turkey's Financial Map", which demonstrates the distribution of financial data of banking sector in Turkey geographically with the intermediation of an interactive map, was put into force with the aim of increasing transparency in sectoral data and contributing to the process of producing information in 2008.

71. Market structure of the Turkish banking sector has transformed considerably in the last 11 years within the framework of the fundamental developments that occurred. Within this process, the sector has reshaped with numerous banks going out of the system, re-structuring, mergers and transfers, share purchases, strategic investments, regulatory framework, risk management and contribution of global capital and market dynamics. Total assets of the Turkish banking sector increased by 20.8% in 2010 comparing to previous year-end and realized above TL 1 trillion. When this figure is compared with the average asset size of developed countries, it is seen that Turkey has a higher growth rate in banking sector assets. The ratio of total loans to GDP increased to 40% in 2010 by doubling from 19.1% in 2000 which gives Turkey in this field a net growth potential in face of developed countries having a ratio over 80%. The share of loans is 52.2% within total assets of the sector. It is observed that the intermediation which is the main function of the banking sector has developed during the period of 2002-2010, except 2009 during which the effects of the global economic crisis were intense.

72. The relatively high capital adequacy ratio of 16.7% and low gross non-performing loan ratio of 2.8% as of August 2011 are two indicators of the high asset quality in the Turkish banking system. Additionally, the net foreign exchange open position of the banking sector is relatively low. There exists a target capital adequacy ratio equivalent to 12% for banks which desire to open new branches. Currently, the NPL ratio is 3.66% and the special reserves is 83.6% as of 2010.

73. In parallel with the improvements in the banking business, there have been significant changes in the ownership structure of the banking sector in terms of increased foreign participation and declining state ownership. With strong growth potential of the economy and the sector, Turkish banks have become more attractive for foreign investors. Total share of foreign participation in the banking sector capital has increased from 22.4% in 2006 to 25.2% as of June 2011 through mergers and acquisitions in the last decade. On the other hand, due to the steps to further reduce the public sector's share in the banking sector, the public share in banks has declined to 27% as of June 2011. As of 2010, in 75% of 49 banks operating in the Turkish banking sector there are shares of global capital. Global capital is mostly present in deposit banks. They are followed by public banks and banks under the control of holding companies.

74. With the regulation dealing with the preparation of financial reports in capital markets, which has been prepared in accordance with EU Acquis and came into force at April 2008, corporations listed on the ISE, financial intermediaries, portfolio management companies, and subsidiaries, affiliates and partnerships of those corporations will be implementing International Accounting Standards and International Financial Reporting Standards as accepted by the EU as of 1 January 2008.

75. Also, in the context of the Financial Restructuring Programme for the SME's, a total number of 115 firms have been taken under the scope of restructuring in 2008. Besides, the improvement of legal infrastructure of factoring and leasing sectors has been aimed.

76. In order to develop new capital instruments and functionality of existing markets and instruments Emerging Companies Market has been established following İstanbul Stock Exchange Emerging Companies Market Communiqué has been published in Official Gazette on 18 August 2009 and entered into force.

77. Principles regarding real estate investment trusts, venture capital investment trusts and investment funds were rearranged in the last 3 years. In order to promote effectiveness and competition in financial markets, principles on establishment and activities of pension mutual funds and portfolio management were reorganized. To ensure instrument diversity in Turkish capital markets and to increase market depth, the principles regarding public offering and sale of foreign capital market instruments and deposit certificates were rearranged.

(b) Insurance sector

78. The economic crisis also affected the insurance sector in Turkey negatively. In the last two years, Turkish insurance sector experienced a real shrinkage in terms of premium production because of the fierce price competition in additional to the economic crisis. However, total premium with TL 14.1 billion volume displayed an increase 6.8% growth in 2010 in real terms, compensated the previous two years' shrinkage and came into growing period again.

79. As of 2010, number of companies carrying out insurance and pension activities are 58. Out of these companies, 34 of them are licensed in non-life insurance, 10 in only life insurance, 13 in pension and life business and only 1 licensed reinsurance company in the domestic market.

80. Total premium amount generated by the Insurance Sector in 2010 was TL 14.1 billion of which TL 11.9 billion in non-life and TL 2.2 billion in life branches. Compared to the end of 2009, with 13.4% increase direct premium written by insurance companies also reached to TL 13.8 billion at the end of 2010. In real terms, direct premium growth rate increased by 6.5% after contraction in 2008 and 2009.

81. The growth potential continues to draw attention of foreign insurance companies to the Turkish insurance market. As of 2010 year-end, the share of foreign partners is above 50% in 37 of insurance companies. In addition to this, the share of foreign investment reached to 59% in total paid-in capital in the sector.

82. Turkey, as a country located in a high risk area, compulsory earthquake insurance put in application in order to reduce burden of government and citizens. As of 2010 year-end, the Marmara region has 33.4% of insured ratio. Total claims of TL 20.9 million losses were paid for 302 earthquakes occurred up-until the end of 2010, by Turkish Catastrophe Insurance Pool.

83. Private pension sector in Turkey tends to grow rapidly. As a result of this, total number of participants reached to 2,281,478 as of the end of 2010. Also, accumulation funds have increased by 31.5% reaching TL 12 billion. According to 2012 Annual Program, priority 18, Private Pension Savings System will be promoted to provide long term funds for the economy.

(c) İstanbul International Financial Center Project

84. Policy on making İstanbul an international financial center was firstly appeared in the 9th Development Plan covering the period of 2007-2013 and then in the 2008 Medium Term Programme (2009-2011). Efforts on this Project accelerated after a priority is given to implementing the İstanbul International Financial Center (IFC) Project in the 2009 Annual Programme under the title of "Developing Financial System." The "Strategy and Action Plan for IFC-İstanbul" entered into force after being published on the Official Gazette on 2 October 2009.

85. İstanbul Strategy and Action Plan envisages İstanbul to turn into a regional financial center and ultimately a global financial center. In order to achieve this vision, the priorities and actions were determined for forming a legal infrastructure that operates in international standards, increasing diversity of financial products and services, building a simple and effective tax system, improving regulatory and supervisory framework, enhancing physical and technological infrastructure, providing an education infrastructure which will satisfy the need for qualified human resource and establishing an organizational structure to carry out promotion and monitoring at world scale.

II. TRADE POLICIES

86. There has been a re-organization of the institutional structures of the ministries and some other public institutions as of July 2011 with the aim at increasing the effectiveness and efficiency of these institutions. Within this framework, the present Cabinet consists of the Prime Minister, four Deputy Prime Ministers and 21 Ministers. Accordingly, the Ministry of Economy is responsible with the formulation, administration, implementation and coordination of Turkey's foreign trade and foreign direct investment policies, in consultation with the related ministries and agencies where necessary.

87. Bearing in mind that it is one of the main pillars for the establishment of a fair and balanced global economic system, which can foster welfare and mitigate poverty worldwide, Turkey regards the priority of the multilateral trading system in its foreign trade policy. Free and fair trade principles as upholded in World Trade Organization (WTO) guide the formulation and conduct of Turkey's foreign trade policies.

88. Besides, Customs Union established with the European Community (EC) in 1995 and the process of full membership to the EU are also the main determinants of Turkey's trade policies.

89. Turkey as one of the active members of "Friends of the System" in the WTO Doha Development Round is committed to the conclusion of the multilateral trade negotiations on an ambitious yet balanced outcome. It has become more important than ever to conclude negotiations as it is believed that trade as one of the most outstanding sources of growth for the international economic system has vital role to play in terms of attenuating the impact of crisis through the expansion of world trade, thus supporting global economic growth in such extra-ordinary conditions contrary to the persisting protectionist sentiments.

90. Turkey also makes efforts to achieve more liberal trading conditions in its region. To this end, an ambitious trade agenda, which would also contribute to the economic and political stability in the region is pursued in the framework of those regional organizations including the Economic Cooperation Organization (ECO), Black Sea Economic Cooperation (BSEC), Organization of Islamic Conference (OIC) and Developing-8 (D-8). Besides that, Turkey is pursuing bilateral, plurilateral and regional initiatives with Jordan, Iraq, Syria, Lebanon, Bulgaria, Azerbaijan and other neighbouring countries in the form of strategic economic partnerships.

91. Representing 80% of the world trade volume, 90% of production and the two-thirds of the world's population, G-20 has become one of the main fora to deal with the insisting problems of today's global economy. As a member of the G-20 and an acceding country to the EU, Turkey has been undertaking major initiatives for the sustainability of open global trade contrary to the current phase of protectionist motives.

92. Turkey attributes great importance to the existence of the Least Developed Countries (LDCs) in the global trade with sufficient resources. Turkey reaffirms that negotiations for the accession of the LDCs to the WTO be facilitated and accelerated through simplified and streamlined accession procedures with a view to concluding these negotiations as quickly as possible. In this regard, Turkey acts in accordance with the guidelines for accession for the LDCs adopted by the Decision of the WTO General Council of 10 December 2002.

93. In 2007, Turkey hosted the United Nations Ministerial Conference on the LDCs. In May 2011, 4th United Nations Conference on the Least Developed Countries was also organized in İstanbul, for the first time in a developing country.

94. A comprehensive İstanbul Program of Action was agreed upon as a result of the Conference. It is a detailed document targeting the 48 LDCs with the ultimate aim of eradicating extreme poverty and hunger.

95. In guiding the development of such a program of action, Turkey prioritized the LDC-related topics and that these topics remain high on the agenda of international community.

96. In this regard, Turkey is committed to doing its part in assisting the development process of the LDCs. Turkey pledged to make available total of 200 million USD annually to LDCs, starting by 2012. This will be used for technical cooperation projects and programs as well as scholarships. Moreover, Turkey's current investments in the LDCs have reached to almost US$2 billion. Turkey also declared its aim to increase the level of direct investments to LDCs to US$5 billion by 2015.

97. Furthermore, Turkey is prepared to host an "International Science, Technology and Innovation Center" and an "International Agriculture Center" dedicated solely to the LDCs.

98. As one of the G-20 countries, Turkey actively participates to the work of G-20 on various grounds. Among others, Turkey gives due consideration to the work undertaken by G-20 with regard to providing a balanced and resilient growth in LDCs and to efforts to integrate these countries more into the multilateral trade system. Also, taking the positive linkage between trade and development into consideration, Turkey has always provided its utter support for the efforts within G-20 in adopting an encouraging attitude to successfully conclude the Doha Development Round on an ambitious yet balanced outcome.

99. Turkey was one of the 4 sponsor countries of the G-20 High-Level Trade Experts Group's Report[3] in which the costs of a failure in the Doha Round was dealt with elaborately.

100. At their last Summit held in Cannes on 3-5 November 2011, G-20 Leaders agreed upon that the Chairmanship of G-20 will be held by Turkey in 2015.

[3] 24 May 2011.

(1) TRADE IN GOODS

101. The Import Regime of Turkey reflects national economic needs and Turkey's rights and obligations arising from the WTO Agreements, the Customs Union with the EU and other bilateral, regional and multilateral agreements including the free trade agreements (FTAs).

102. Within the scope of the Turkish Import Regime, imports of goods are in line with Turkey's WTO commitments and obligations arising there upon.

103. The Turkish tariff structure is transparent and simple. With respect to taxes and fiscal charges, Turkey's import regime has been totally simplified.

104. The clarity of the Import Regime is ensured by indicating the rates of customs duties separately for countries and country groups; and by classifying the products under six lists; namely, agricultural products (List I), industrial products (List II), processed agricultural products (List III), fish and fishery products (List IV), the suspension list (List V), and list of goods used in civil aircraft eligible to relief from customs duties (List VI).

105. These lists are made available to the public in the Official Gazette in the beginning of each year. They are also released in the official website of the Ministry of Economy (www.ekonomi.gov.tr).

106. The most recent changes in the import regime were introduced with the Import Regime Decree for the year 2011, which was published in the Official Gazette (No. 27802 bis) on 31 December 2010. The Import Regime Decree of 2011 was prepared by taking into consideration the Agreement Establishing the WTO, the Turkey-EU Customs Union Decision (CUD), the free trade agreements with various countries, the preferential treatments granted under the Generalized System of Preferences (GSP) to developing, least developed and special incentive arrangement countries, and also the needs and demands of the agricultural and industrial sectors in accordance with the objectives determined by the development plans and annual programs.

(i) Non-agricultural products

107. As a participant to the Uruguay Round negotiations and a signatory to the Agreements as annexed to the Agreement Establishing the WTO, Turkey undertook tariff reductions on industrial and agricultural products to be implemented gradually. In addition, as a result of the Customs Union with the EC, Turkey began to apply the Community's Common Customs Tariff (CCT) on the imports of industrial goods from third countries, which is far below its Uruguay Round bound rates. Thus, with the Customs Union, Turkey's simple average protection rate for the third countries declined in the process from pre-Customs Union rate of approximately 15% to 4.2% as of 2011. This rate is zero for the EU and EFTA countries since 1996. Hence, despite its developing country status in the WTO, Turkey is one of the countries applying the lowest tariffs in non-agricultural goods among member countries.

108. CUD establishing the Customs Union between Turkey and the EC foresees Turkey align its Generalized System of Preferences with that of the EC's. Accordingly, duties on products under the CUD are entirely eliminated for the LDCs in line with the Everything But Arms (EBA) Initiative of the EC GSP Scheme. In compliance with the agreement with the EC, Turkey also grants further preferences to selected 15 countries under the Special Incentive Arrangements for Sustainable Development and Good Governance. Beneficiary countries are announced annually in the Annexes of Turkey's Import Regime.

(ii) Agricultural products

109. Within the framework of WTO Agreement on Agriculture, Turkey has bound all of its tariffs for the agricultural products in 1995. As reflected in Turkey's Schedule of Commitment List (Schedule XXXVII) to the WTO, Turkey has made 10% minimum cut per product and 24% average cut for all agricultural products between the period 1995 and 2004. The average customs duty for agricultural products by 2011 is 58.9%.

110. Turkish agricultural policy has been shaped via four main tools: the Agricultural Strategy 2006-10, the Agricultural Law (No. 5488) of 2006, the Strategic Plan (2010-14) and the Ninth Development Plan of Turkey. This policy framework was adopted with an aim of aligning Turkey's agricultural policy with the Common Agricultural Policy (CAP) of the EU. Turkey's main policy objectives are food security and food safety, and raising the self-sufficiency level for selected net-imported products; as well as improving productivity and competitiveness; ensuring sustainable farm incomes, rural development, and improving institutional capacity, in the agricultural sector.

111. Turkey has enriched the rural development policy alternatives very recently. Other than infrastructure projects, income diversification, development of human resources, and the preservation of the environment are taken into consideration during policy implementation. As part of the accession partnership between Turkey and the EU, Instrument for Pre-Accession Assistance-Rural Development Programme (IPARD) started in 2011 considering 2007-13 period to achieve consistency with EU's rural development policies.

112. Agriculture is one of the dominant sectors in the Turkish economy with its 25.2% share within the total employment in 2010. However, in comparison to the other sectors with respect to employment, the income of those employed in the agricultural sector remains extremely low. Therefore, the results of the WTO Agricultural Negotiations would be highly critical for Turkey with not only economic but also social-adjustment impacts. In case of the market access, as tariffs are the only instruments to sustain agricultural production in Turkey like most developing countries, a gradual liberalization process and some complementary instruments to minimize the possible negative impacts of liberalization are being sought within the WTO Agricultural Negotiations. In that sense, Turkey attaches the utmost importance to the flexibilities to be extended to developing countries including the Special Products (SP) and Special Safeguard Mechanism (SSM).

(iii) Safeguards

113. Decree No. 2007/12850 of 12 November 2007 on Amendment of the Decree on Safeguard Measures for Imports was published in Official Gazette No. 26721 of 5 December 2007. The Decree amending the existing safeguard legislation was entered into force on 4 January 2008 and circulated to the WTO members with the Document No. G/SG/N/1/TUR/3/Suppl.1 dated 3 March 2008. The aim of the amendment in the safeguard legislation is to prevent the activities eliminating the effects of a safeguard measure by disassembling the product subject to measure.

(iv) Technical barriers to trade

114. As being the national enquiry point of Turkey under the TBT Agreement, Directorate General of Product Safety and Inspection under the Ministry of Economy in July 2011, designed a website, www.teknikengel.gov.tr, to facilitate the access to TBT notifications of other countries by private and public sector and to get the business opinion on the relevant field. The website allows its subscribers to provide suggestions on the draft legislation of other countries and also to prepare themselves for future technical requirements. The system also allows them to give feedback on the implementations

of the administration as well as to acquaint them with most up-to-date information in the field of technical regulations through reports, announcements and notifications. Viewers and subscribers are also encouraged to submit their opinion on policy options to facilitate access to markets and to notify unnecessary obstacles they encounter in entering foreign markets.

115. The web service has also created a unique opportunity for the administration to get sound knowledge of reactions to the impediments to trade, to generate statistical analysis, to be familiar with market access failures, to overcome the impediments and to build a bilateral and multilateral understanding of common rules in international trade.

116. With rules and guidelines of the WTO system and our experience from the Customs Union with the EC, Turkey concludes that elimination of bilateral barriers would generate no less advantage than they can be achieved by international approach, tough it needs more concentration and more elaborated work. Turkey has initiated joint actions, within the context of cooperation building, with China's General Administration of Quality Supervision, Inspection and Quarantine (AQSIQ) to ensure that the quality and safety conditions are matched in bilateral trade.

117. Turkey and Ukraine declared a memorandum of intent on cooperation in the fields of standardization, metrology, conformity assessment and consumer's rights protection. Relations with Israel continue under FTA Joint Committee meetings. Turkey also signed agreements with Bulgaria, Lebanon, Jordan and Iran in the fields of technical legislation, standardization, accreditation, metrology and conformity assessment procedures which will be in force after the completion of internal approval procedures.

(2) INVESTMENT

118. Turkey has attributed considerable importance to the foreign investment and pursued liberal foreign policies since 1980's in parallel to the advances in the global economy. The new foreign direct investment regime became effective on 17 June 2003 by the publication of "Foreign Direct Investment Law No. 4875" in the Official Gazette. The law not only provides foreign capital the best international standards, such as equal treatment, guarantee to transfer proceeds, right to resort to international arbitration and right to employ key expatriate personnel, but also repeals prior approval procedures for foreign investors and minimum capital requirements to invest in Turkey. This favourable investment climate is also strengthened by Bilateral Investment Agreements which Turkey signed with 73 countries.

119. The Turkish Investment Encouragement System, which is currently in force, takes into account the recent changes in the global economic and social circumstances. This new system which has been in force since July 2009 has three main targets; reducing the inter regional development discrepancies, supporting large scale, technology and R&D intensive investments for increasing competitiveness and supporting sectoral clustering.

120. The new investment incentive system is based on three main pillars; large scale investments, regional incentives and a general incentive system. Large scale investments require advanced technology and high capital, which will contribute to the technological and R&D capacity of the country and develop Turkey's production base. Regional incentives aim to eliminate inter regional discrepancies and support an investment environment to encourage sectoral clustering. The provinces of Turkey have been categorized in four groups according to their level of development. As far as the mechanism is concerned, domestic and foreign investors are equally treated; the companies having foreign capital can benefit from all encouragement measures granted to domestic companies with the

same conditions. Within the objectives and the scope of the Program, eligible investment projects can benefit from tax based encouragement measures (namely, customs duty exemption, VAT Exemption, reduced corporate/income tax rate), support for employer's contribution for social security and land allocation where possible. Additionally, "interest rate support" provides for the compensation of certain percentage points of the interest rate for credits obtained in commercial terms by investors for the investments in the less developed regions.

121. In all legal measures and programs introduced, Turkey is very rigorous to observe its commitments to the WTO TRIMs Agreement. Today, Turkey's FDI regime is in full compliance with the rules set forth in the Agreement.

(3) SERVICES

122. In scope of the 2012 Annual Program, it is estimated that the annual real growth rate of the services sector would be 7.8% in 2011, while the share of services in GDP is expected to reach 72.5% in 2011. The current share of services is 72.4% of the GDP as of 2010. Services sector represented approximately 55% of the employment in Turkey in 2010.

123. With the aim of further liberalizing the services sector, Turkey has made commitments in several services categories under the General Agreement on Trade in Services (GATS). Turkey has also been actively and constructively engaged in trade in services negotiations (both bilaterally and plurilaterally) on the basis of GATS, since 2000. In World Economic Forum's Financial Development Report 2010, Turkey is listed as the best performer in terms of the commitments to the GATS. With this understanding, Turkey has joined in the efforts for the revival and the successful completion of Doha Round negotiations. Turkey was one of the members participated in signalling conference in 2008, stock-taking exercise in 2010, and plurilateral negotiations in 2011 in this regard.

124. In the Doha Round services negotiations, Turkey's objective is to improve the number and quality of market access and trade-related commitments. In this context, Turkey has submitted its initial conditional services offer to the WTO on 15 August 2003 and its revised conditional offer on 12 September 2005. They were circulated on 3 September 2003 (TN/S/O/TUR) and on 29 September 2005 (TN/S/O/TUR/Rev.1), respectively. Turkey is now in the process of drafting its second revised offer in accordance with the requests and the economic liberalization program of the government.

125. Turkey, on the way of full membership to the EU, has continued its regulatory reforms in services since its last TPR in 2007. Türk Telekom (TT), having been a state monopoly, was privatized as of 14 November 2005 and in 2008 after public offering Treasury share in TT decreased to 31.68%. The new Electronic Communications Law, which was prepared in line with the EU legislation, came into force in 2008. It introduced a general authorization regime that considerably simplifies market entry. Several secondary legislation has been put into force since the enactment of this Law.

(4) TRADE-RELATED INTELLECTUAL PROPERTY RIGHTS

126. In line with its commitments under the WTO TRIPS Agreement and in scope of its efforts to align laws and regulations with the EU legislation, Turkey has introduced certain changes to its intellectual property regime since the last TPR.

(i) Copyright

127. The Law of Intellectual and Artistic Works No. 5846 was amended by the Law No. 5728 (promulgated on the Official Gazette dated 8 February 2008) in order to harmonize the Copyright Law with the new Turkish Criminal Code and Turkish Criminal Procedure Code.

128. With the aim of accomplishing full harmonization with the EU Acquis and eliminating discrepancies in the implementation of intellectual property rights, the Law No. 5846 on Intellectual and Artistic Works is decided to be amended. Therefore the Draft Law was sent to the related institutions, organizations and collecting societies. Currently the views of these institutions are being evaluated.

129. Intellectual and Industrial Property Coordination Board has been established by Prime Minister Circular on Establishment of the Coordination Board (Official Gazette dated 21 May 2008 and No. 26882) with the aim of creating short, medium and long term strategies for the implementation of intellectual and industrial property rights in Turkey and improving the coordination between the relevant institutions. Within the context of Prime Minister Circular, Coordination Board convenes twice a year under the co-presidency of Ministry of Culture and Tourism and Ministry of Science, Industry and Technology with the participation of high level representatives of related institutions (Ministry of Justice, Ministry of Economy, Ministry of Interior, Ministry of Health, Ministry of Food, Agriculture and Livestock, Ministry of Customs and Trade, Ministry of Development, Directorate General of Copyright and Cinema, Turkish Patent Institute, The Scientific and Technological Research Council of Turkey and The Union of Chambers and Commodity Exchanges of Turkey).

130. As it is stated in last report, according to Law on Intellectual and Artistic Works the local administrative authorities may form an "inspection commission" in provinces by the provincial administrative authorities to mandate the control of the banderole implementation. Representatives of the Ministry and the collective societies can also take part in these commissions. With the amendment of Law No. 5846 by the Law No. 5571 (13 January 2007), a rewarding system was established for the public officers of inspection commissions responsible for combating piracy by taking into consideration the quantity of the seized material entered into force. Additionally a Cooperation Protocol was signed on 25 February 2010 between Ministry of Culture and Tourism and Ministry of Interior with the aim of fixing the procedures and principles of the inspections of Provincial Inspection Commissions. Within the context of the Protocol, the number of the Provincial Inspection Commissions has been increased from 65 to 81 and the presidency of the Commissions was delegated to the National Police by taking into consideration of their important role regarding fighting against piracy.

131. Copyright Automation System (TEHAKSIS) which is designed with a view to diminish bureaucratic transactions; strengthen inter-institutional coordination; ensure easy access to reliable information for pursuing the intellectual property rights and to shorten work flow process conducted between the Ministry of Culture and Tourism and other related institutions, has been considerably completed. Within the context of TEHAKSIS, following the non-periodicals banderole and certification applications; voluntary registration applications are currently available via internet through TEHAKSIS as of 22 November 2010. In April 2010, the authority of online access for using automation system was delegated to the Provincial Culture Directorates and National Police in order to accelerate the inspections of Provincial Inspection Commissions (in 81 Province) within the framework of fighting against piracy activities.

132. On the other hand, on 3 December 2010, a Protocol on Principles of Reciprocal Access, Sharing and Use of Data in the Field of Intellectual Property Rights was signed between Ministry of Justice and Ministry of Culture and Tourism with a view to provide the electronic access to the information and documents in the judicial process and to strengthen the fight against violation of the rights. The Protocol envisages establishing the integration of two automation systems by providing the data-communication between National Judiciary Informatics System (UYAP) and TEHAKSIS and thus the trial process will be shortened.

133. In order to overcome the problems regarding tariffs and license agreements, four collecting societies functioning in music sector (MÜYAP, MSG, MESAM, MÜYORBIR) signed a cooperation agreement in February 2007. Subsequently, collective agreements were signed between these collecting societies and professional associations representing users, regarding licensing of musical works used in hotels (on 26 March 2008) and in broadcasts (on 22 November 2008).

134. On 7 October 2009, BİROY (United Actors Collecting Society) was established with the participation of 300 audiovisual performers. With the establishment of BİROY, the new initiative was set out in the collective management of rights in cinema sector. The collective societies functioning in cinema came together on 14 October 2009 to sign common action protocol on tariffs and licensing like music collecting societies.

135. On the other hand, in order to ensure effective implementation of the licensing activities of the cinematographic works, 7 collecting societies (SETEM, TESİYAP, SEYAP, FİYAB, SİNEBİR, BİROY, BSB) operating in the field of cinema have been subsidized by Ministry of Culture and Tourism. Within the context of this financial support, "Headquarter of Collecting Societies of Cinema" was founded on 20 January 2011.

136. Moreover, "Publisher Collecting Societies Federation" (YAYFED) was founded on 14 February 2011, by collecting societies operating in the field of publishing (YAYBİR, BASYAYBİR). In order to effectively operate the banderol system through involvement of rights holders in the process of combating piracy, a protocol was signed between YAYFED and Ministry of Culture and Tourism, regarding the selling of non-periodicals banderol through the Federation on 06 April 2011.

137. Turkey became party to WIPO Copyright Treaty and the WIPO Performances and Phonograms Treaty by the enactment of "Law on Ratification of Participation in WIPO Copyright Treaty" and "Law on Ratification of Participation in WIPO Performances and Phonograms Treaty" by 28 November 2008.

138. As part to the process of Turkey's full membership to the EU, following the fulfillment of opening benchmarks, Chapter 7 on "Intellectual Property Rights" is opened for negotiation on 17 June 2008. In the context of the Chapter, five closing benchmarks are notified for the provisional closure of the negotiations. In order to meet the first closing benchmark of the Intellectual Property Law Chapter, Working Group on Intellectual Property Rights between European Union and the Republic of Turkey was established with the approval of Terms of Reference for the Working Group which was prepared in the consequence of negotiations between EU and Turkey by the Turkish Intellectual and Industrial Property Coordination Board. Additionally, Ministry of Culture and Tourism was appointed as coordinating authority of Working Group on behalf of Turkey.

139. The first meeting of the Working Group was held in Ankara, in 18 May 2011 with the participation of the representatives of Directorate General of Enlargement, the Directorate General of

Commerce of European Commission and Delegation of European Commission to Turkey as well as the representatives of Ministry of Culture and Tourism, Turkish Patent Institute, Ministry of Justice, Ministry of Interior, Ministry of Customs and Trade, Ministry of Economy, Ministry of European Union Affairs, Ministry of Food, Agriculture and Livestock and Ministry of Development. In the meeting, the legal regulations regarding the recent developments on intellectual property rights and administrative implementations have been discussed. The negotiations on draft operational conclusion of Working Group meeting are continuing.

(ii) Industrial property rights

140. A new law (the Law No. 5833), regulating the criminal provisions for the protection of trademark rights, has been adopted on 21 January 2009 and came into force on 28 January 2009. This Law has replaced the criminal provisions of the Decree Law No. 556 for the protection of trademark rights and it meets the requirements of the TRIPS Agreement and even goes beyond it in some penalties introduced for the infringers of trademark rights.

141. The Implementing Regulations of the Decree Law No. 554 on Protection of Industrial Designs, Decree Law No: 551 on Protection of Patents, and Decree Law No. 555 on Geographical Indications were simplified in accordance with the reduction of bureaucracy and simplification study conducted by the Prime Ministry. The amended regulations were published in the Official Gazette on 21 April 2009 and has become effective.

142. In order to increase the coordination among the administrative and policy making bodies/institutions in IPR field in Turkey, "The Intellectual and Industrial Property Rights Coordination Board" (IIPRCB) was established on 21 May 2008 with the power of the communiqué of the Prime Minister. The Board was mandated, inter alia, to develop short, medium and long term strategies in IPR field, to secure coordination and enhance cooperation among the relevant institutions, thus, ultimately to increase the effectiveness of applications in reaching the targets determined in the Government Action Plan (2008-2012) and in the Turkey's Programme for alignment with the EU Acquis (2007-2013). The Board is co-chaired by the Undersecretaries of Ministry of Science, Industry and Technology and the Ministry of Culture and Tourism. The Members of the Board are comprised of relevant Ministries and Undersecretaries that shall be represented at least at the level of Deputy Undersecretaries. Also the private sector representation has been secured through accepting the representation of the Union of Chambers and Commodity Exchanges of Turkey, which is the highest legal entity representing the private sector in Turkey. IIPRCB's members are to convene at least 2 times in a year and 6 meetings have been done so far.

143. With reference to the closing benchmark of one of the chapters of the ongoing negotiations between the EU and the Republic of Turkey, a "Working Group on Intellectual Property Rights" was established on 28 May 2010. The Working Group aims to discuss institutional, legislative, and enforcement related issues and to increase public awareness of consumers and right-holders in accordance with the agreed "Terms of Reference". The 1st meeting of the working group was held in Ankara, Turkey on 18 May 2011 with the participation of the EU Commission Representatives and the Turkish Representatives.

144. The EU sponsored Twinning project entitled "Supporting Turkey for Enhancing Implementation and Enforcement of Industrial Property Rights" which aimed to strengthen the enforcement capacity of Turkey in industrial property rights has been finalized with success in the last week of September 2011. With the twinning partner Federal Republic of Germany and its related organs, 114 activities were organized during 13 months period to which 80 experts from 11 different

countries were attended and over 5,000 stakeholders participated in the various activities offered. Guidelines for the use of patent and trademark experts have been prepared in order to streamline their work and to increase the transparency for the applicants.

145. Turkish Patent Institute co-chairs one of the committees of the "The Coordination Council for the Improvement of the Investment Environment" (CCIIE). CCIIE aims, inter alia, to rationalize bureaucratic procedures and reduce red tape, and in order to do so, a comprehensive reform program was launched in 2001 by Council of Ministers Leading Decision.

146. The Coordination Council for the Improvement of the Investment Environment (CCIIE) has become a key structure where private sector makes contributions in the process of improving investment climate. The Council conducts its agenda with the help of 12 Technical Committees working on specific issues with participation of both public and private institutions. TPI, as the co-chair of the "Industrial and Intellectual Property Rights Committee" has actively involved in the works of the council where the business needs and concerns determine the work and agenda of the committee.

(iii) IPR-related courts

147. For the first time, Specialized IPR Courts (one civil and one criminal IPR court) were established on January 2001 in İstanbul. Since then, the total number of the Specialized IPR Courts reached to 22, which are distributed as follows:

- İstanbul: 6 IPR civil courts, 7 IPR criminal courts
- Ankara: 4 IPR civil courts, 2 IPR criminal courts
- İzmir: 1 IPR civil court, 2 IPR criminal courts

148. General civil and general criminal courts are competent to deal with IPR cases where specialised IPR courts do not exist. (If there is one or two general civil or criminal courts, the first one is competent to deal with IPR cases. If there are three or more than three general civil or criminal courts, the third one is competent to deal with IPR cases.)

149. The Circular on the loss of tax revenues stemming from actions of piracy and counterfeiting was updated on 18 October 2011 by the High Council of Judges and Prosecutors. According to the Circular, the Offices of Public Prosecutors shall inform the Heads of Tax Administration on the final decisions of the criminal courts regarding conviction of piracy and counterfeiting to prevent tax evasion. The Circular also includes a provision on the specialization of public prosecutors on IPR infringement. If the number of investigation on IPR crimes is more than 500, chief public prosecutors shall establish a special "IPR bureau" responsible for investigate IPR crimes in accordance with the Circular. If the number of investigation on IPR crimes is not enough to establish a special "IPR bureau", the authority for investigation of IPR crimes shall give to one of the existing bureaus or to certain prosecutors.

(5) TURKEY'S ACCESSION PROCESS TO THE EU

(i) Recent developments in Turkey-EU relations

150. Since the EU Council adopted the European Commission's Accession Negotiations Framework for Turkey on 3 October 2005, Turkey has been working on adopting EU policies.

151. However, on 29 November 2006, the European Commission recommended that "full implementation of the Additional Protocol to the Association Agreement to all member states" is opening benchmark in 8 chapters (Free Movement of Goods, Right of Establishment and Freedom to Provide Services, Financial Services, Agriculture and Rural Development, Fisheries, Transport Policy, Customs Union and External Relations) and closing benchmark in all chapters. On 11 December 2006, the EU General Affairs and External Relations Council agreed with the recommendation of the Commission and it was confirmed by Brussels European Council of 14-15 December 2006. Moreover, due to the unilateral decisions of certain member states of the EU some other chapters are also blocked which makes 17 chapters out of 33 politically blocked in total.

152. Within this framework, as of October 2011, 13 chapters have been opened to negotiations, one of which was provisionally closed. These Chapters are "Science and Research"(provisionally closed), "Free Movement of Capital", "Company Law", "Intellectual Property Law", "Information Society and Media", "Statistics", "Enterprise and Industrial Policy", "Trans-European Networks", "Consumer and Health Protection", "Financial Control", "Taxation", "Environment", "Food Safety, Veterinary and Phytosanitary". There are only 3 chapters left that can be technically opened. These are "Competition Policy", "Public Procurement", "Social Policy and Employment".

153. Turkey is determined to continue its accession process. In 2010, Turkey prepared "EU Strategy for Turkey's Accession Process", which includes four pillars for accelerating negotiations and increasing the public awareness and support. The first pillar is the ongoing official negotiation process. In the second pillar, regardless of whether the chapters have been opened, suspended or blocked, Turkey aims to revive the commitments laid down for alignment of legislation with the EU Acquis. The third pillar is about providing the persistence of political criteria. Lastly, the fourth pillar is the communication strategy.

(ii) Developments in harmonization with the EU policies

(a) Harmonization in commercial policies

154. Harmonization with the basic mechanisms and principles of the EU's Common Commercial Policy constitutes a substantial part of Turkey's obligations in scope of the Decision No. 1/95 of the EC-Turkey Association Council establishing the Customs Union between Turkey and the European Union.

Generalized system of preferences

155. As of August 2004, all industrial products covered by the EC's GSP Regime are included into Turkey's GSP. Finally, by including processed agricultural products into the system as of 1 January 2010, Turkey's GSP system covers all the products under the Customs Union, in full harmony with that of the EU.

Free-trade agreements

156. The Customs Union between Turkey and the EU constitutes a legal basis for Turkey's free trade agreements.

157. The tariff concessions for the industrial and agricultural products, quantitative restrictions on imports and exports, customs duties or measures having equivalent effect, basic duties, safeguard measures, internal taxation, technical barriers to trade, sanitary and phytosanitary measures, rules of origin, services and investment, general exceptions, security exceptions, state monopolies, payments,

rules of competition, public procurement, intellectual property rights, dumping and subsidy, re-export and serious shortage and balance of payments difficulties are governed by FTAs. Moreover, rules of origin are a major component of the FTAs.

Turkey's free trade agreements

	Europe	Asia and Caucasus	Africa and Middle East	Americas
Signed Agreements (*)	European Free Trade Association (EFTA) Macedonia Croatia Bosnia and Herzegovina Albania Serbia Montenegro	Georgia	Israel Egypt Morocco Tunisia Palestine Authority Syria Jordan Lebanon (**) Mauritius (**)	Chile
Ongoing Negotiations	Moldova Faroe Islands	Malaysia South Korea	Cameroon Seychelles Libya Gulf Cooperation Council (GCC) Dem. Rep. of Congo	Ecuador Colombia Southern Common Market (MERCOSUR)
Exploratory Talks	Ukraine	Association of Southeast Asian Nations (ASEAN) India Indonesia	South Africa Customs Union (SACU) African Caribbean and Pacific (ACP) Countries Algeria	Mexico Canada Peru Central America

(*) FTAs with Lithuania, Hungary, Estonia, Latvia, Slovakia, Poland, Slovenia, Romania, Czech Republic and Bulgaria are not mentioned since all these countries became full member to the EU.

(**) Turkey-Lebanon FTA was signed on 24 November 2010 and Turkey-Mauritius FTA was signed on 9 September 2011. These Agreements will enter into force once the internal ratification procedures are completed by both countries.

158. Since the last TPR of Turkey in 2007, FTAs with Albania (May 2008), Georgia (November 2008), Montenegro (March 2010), Serbia (September 2010), Chile (March 2011), and Jordan (2011) have entered into force.

159. Turkey signed an FTA with Lebanon on 24 November 2010, which is still subject to internal ratification process of both countries.

160. In addition to these, Turkey's FTA negotiations with African, Caribbean and Pacific (ACP) countries were started in 2009. In this regard, the FTA between Turkey and Mauritius was signed on 9 September 2011, while the FTA negotiations with Seychelles, Cameroon and Democratic Republic of Congo are continuing. Moreover, the exploratory talks with CARICOM Secretariat were held in 2009.

161. The first round of FTA negotiations with Moldova was held in Chisinau in May 2011.

162. In the case of India and Indonesia, Joint Study Groups were established in January and March 2010 respectively to explore the feasibility of concluding comprehensive FTAs and to assess the potential outcomes of such agreements. Reports of the Joint Study Groups (completed in February and March 2011 respectively) indicate that such FTAs will contribute to improve the bilateral trade relations. The FTA negotiations are expected to start following the completion of relevant signature/ratification process of these reports.

163. Moreover, Turkey has also initiated FTA process with some other Asian countries. In accordance with the Customs Union with the EU as well as willingness to enhance and deepen our trade relations with those countries, Turkey is conducting FTA negotiations with South Korea and Malaysia. Besides, exploratory talks are held with Vietnam to start FTA negotiations.

164. Turkey's FTA negotiations with the Gulf Cooperation Council (GCC) countries[4] are under way. The exploratory talks with South African Customs Union (SACU), and Mexico were held in May 2005, and May 2007 respectively. Also, there have been three rounds of exploratory talks with Ukraine last of which was held in May 2009.

165. In the scope of Turkey's trade policy with Latin American countries in parallel with the EU, Turkey has started FTA negotiations with Colombia and negotiations on Trade Agreement for Development with Ecuador in 2011 and FTA exploratory talks with Peru and Panama are planned to be started in late 2011 or early 2012.

(b) Harmonization in technical legislation

166. Turkey has been harmonizing the technical legislation of the European Union for more than a decade within the framework of the Turkey – EU Association Council Decision (ACD) No. 1/95 that established a Customs Union and ACD No. 2/97 that determined the rules and scope of harmonization of technical legislation and is updating its regulations in accordance with the changes in the EU's horizontal legislation.

167. Moreover, in accordance with Article 6.3 of the TBT Agreement and in order to prevent any possible trade diversion between Turkey and the EU, Turkey is planning to conclude bilateral agreements parallel to EU's mutual recognition agreements. To this aim, The Decision on Mutual Recognition of Conformity Assessment of Products – Protocol E has been adopted during the Joint Committee Meeting held on 3 December 2009 between Turkey and EFTA. The internal procedures for the ratification of the Protocol have been concluded by both sides and it entered into force on 5 July 2011.

168. In order to create an accreditation system which is equivalent to that of the EU and functions according to internationally recognized principles, Turkish Accreditation Body (TURKAK) was established in 1999. It started accreditation activities in 2001 after completing its organizational structure. To enhance international cooperation, TURKAK applied to European Cooperation for Accreditation (EA) and was admitted to the membership of EA in late 2002. TURKAK signed 4 of the 7 MLAs (Multilateral Agreements) in 2006 and 3 of the 7 MLAs in 2008 for the recognition of its accreditation activities and finalizing the international acceptance. After being a member of ILAC in 2004 and ensuring mutual recognition with ILAC, TURKAK became a member of IAF at the end of 2006 and certificates given by TURKAK are recognized almost globally.

169. TURKAK has contributed to the assignment of notified bodies and as of today, there are 19 Turkish notified bodies under 13 new approach directives, such as lifts, machinery, medical devices and construction materials etc. There is also an approval body under Construction Products Directive (89/106/EEC; 93/68/EEC) named as Board of Technical and Scientific Research on Construction.

170. Turkish Standards Institute (TSE) as a full member of the International Organization for Standardization (ISO), the International Electrotechnical Commission (IEC) and an affiliate member

[4] GCC countries are Bahrein, Kuwait, Oman, Qatar, Saudi Arabia and United Arab Emirates.

of CEN and CENELEC since 1991, is the national standards body and it has been active in this area since 1950s. TSE applied for the full membership of CEN and CENELEC in August 2010 and TSE is expecting that this process will be concluded in 2011. Having almost 99% of CEN/CENELEC standards in Turkish system, it is certain that TSE will be an active stakeholder in the European system in the near future.

171. Within the context of the transposition of the EU technical legislation, By-Law on Construction Products (89/106/EEC) prepared based on Council Directive on the approximation of laws, regulations and administrative provisions of the Member States relating to construction products (89/106/EEC), lays down the essential requirements for any construction products, which is produced for incorporation in a permanent manner in construction works including both buildings and other civil engineering works and the conformity assessment procedures applicable to these products and the principles and procedures relating to market surveillance and inspection. By-Law on Construction Products (89/106/EEC) is mandatory as of 1 July 2007. In the framework of By-Law on Construction Products, 11 notified bodies are designated to perform conformity assessment activities on the basis of 185 technical specifications.

III. DEVELOPMENTS IN TURKISH FOREIGN TRADE

172. Since 1980s Turkey's foreign trade policy has been shaped by an export-led, outward-oriented economic growth approach. Thus, in this process, Turkey established an open market economy integrated into the global economic system. As a result of Turkey's Customs Union with the EC, although being an emerging economy, Turkey adopted more liberal policies in trade compared to its counterparts. The openness rate of Turkey, as the share of total trade volume in GDP, increased considerably to 40.7% in 2010 from 30.6% in 1994.

173. Turkey continues to put emphasis on diversifying its trade partners and lessen its market dependencies. Export strategies applied with this aim paved their way creating a favourable global environment for Turkish exports and Turkey's bilateral trade with almost all regions increased substantially in the last five years, reaching US$113.9 billion in 2010. Moreover, high growth rates in the Turkish economy increased the demand for imports due to higher income and additional investments. Turkey imports a large amount of intermediate goods, which constitutes almost 70% of its total imports. Consequently, integration of the Turkish economy to global markets accelerated with a dazzling performance in recent years.

174. Thus, Turkey's trade volume increased to US$299.4 billion by the end of 2010 from US$243 billion in 2009. The crisis in the global markets affected Turkey's trade volume in 2009 negatively and both exports and imports decreased, by 22.6% and 30.2% respectively. However, the impacts of the crisis were parried rapidly in 2010 and the pre-crisis trade volume of US$334 billion will be regained quickly. Over the past five years, while exports reached US$113.9 billion with an overall increase of 33%, imports surged to US$185.5 billion with a cumulative rise of 32%. In 2010, the ratio of exports to imports was 61.4%. As of September 2011 trade volume became US$281.2 billion with US$99.5 billion exports and US$181.7 billion imports.[5]

[5] See Annexed Table 5-A: Foreign Trade by Years.

(1) Trade Developments by Regions and Countries[6]

(i) The European Union (EU)

175. The EU is clearly the biggest trade partner of Turkey. In 2010, the EU accounts for 46.3% of total exports and 38.9% of total imports. Turkey is an important trade partner for the EU as well. The foreign trade statistics of the EU for the year 2010 demonstrate that Turkey ranks seventh at imports of the EU with a share of 2.8% and fifth at exports of the EU with a share of 4.5%.

176. The Customs Union has strengthened the traditionally comprehensive trade relations. The volume of trade between Turkey and the EU reached to US$124.9 billion in 2010 from US$27.9 billion in 1995. The trade volume in 2011 has been US$116 billion as of September, US$47 billion of which constitutes Turkey's exports whereas US$69 billion represents its imports.

177. Even though imports from the EU has fluctuated in parallel with internal and external macro economic developments, during the 1995-2010 period, exports recorded a higher rate of increase than imports. Although exports to the EU dropped by 26% to 47 billion dollars in 2009 due to the global economic crisis, the trend has been quite contrary in 2010. Our exports to and imports from the EU grew by annual 12.1% and 27.7% in 2010.

(ii) Other Europe & CIS countries

178. Compared to the EU, the growth rate of trade volume with other European countries transcended between 2002 and 2010. With the impetus stemming from the FTAs with the non-EU countries (such as Macedonia, Albania, Bosnia and Herzegovina, Serbia and Montenegro), jumping by nearly three fold since 2002, trade volume with this group of countries reached US$1.3 billion in 2010. Exports to other Europe in 2010 consists mostly of pearls, precious stone and metal products, coins, motor vehicles, fruits and mineral fuels and mineral oils. Imports from Other Europe consist mostly of raw materials, intermediate goods and energy.

179. On the other hand, The Commonwealth of Independent States (CIS), besides its cultural ties with Turkey, plays an important role in Turkey's foreign policy as well as in its external trade and economic strategies. The trade volume reached US$41.9 billion in 2010 with 35% increase compared to the year 2006. As of September 2011, Turkey's trade volume with these countries has been US$33.5 billion.

180. As of 2010, trade volume with Russian Federation, the first country in the ranking of Turkey's imports, totalled US$26.2 billion with a bilateral trade deficit of US$16.9 billion.

181. Thanks to the successful policies followed since 2006, the trade volume between Turkey and the Central Asian – Caucasian Republics attained US$10 billion in 2010 whereas it totalled only US$4.8 billion in 2006.

(iii) Asia-Pacific countries

182. Today, almost 30% of the global trade movements occur over Asia-Pacific countries. In 2009, despite the global crisis, the world trade volume was realized as US$25 billion and US$8 billion of this trade, which correspond to the 32% of the total, belonged to Asia-Pacific region. Considering these promising indicators, in order to facilitate trade and economic relations with the region, a trade

[6] See Annexed Table 5-B: Exports by Country Groups and 5-C: Imports by Country Groups.

development strategy was put into action by Turkey in 2005. By this strategy, a solid trade and investment infrastructure and an increase in the interaction with those growing markets are expected to be established.

183. Before the implementation of the regional strategy, in 2004, the total trade volume between Turkey and Asia Pacific countries were realized as US$17 billion. In 2010 the trade volume reached to US$44.4 billion with an increase of 162% compared to 2004. Turkey's exports to the Asia-Pacific countries were US$2 billion in 2004 and it increased to US$6.6 billion in 2010. This statement refers to the point that, exports of Turkey to the region has gained at least 20% increase almost every year from 2004 to 2010. Between 2005 and 2010 the share of Asia-Pacific countries in Turkish exports climbed from 3.3% to 5.7%. Imports from Asia-Pacific countries have reached to US$37.8 billion in 2010 with an increase of 152% compared to the volume of US$15 billion in 2004. As of September 2011, Turkey's trade volume with these countries has been US$47.8 billion, US$7.5 billion of this is Turkey's exports and US$40.3 of it is Turkey's imports. In 2010, the first five countries in Turkey's exports to Asia-Pacific region were China, India, Singapore, Australia and South Korea whereas China, South Korea, India, Japan and Taiwan were the leading five suppliers in Turkey's imports from the region.

(iv) Middle East

184. Over the last decade, the Middle East countries have become a crucial country group within the scope of Turkey's trade strategy. As a result of the steady increase in both imports and exports after 2003, Turkey's total trade volume with the region has increased from US$9.5 billion in 2003 to US$35.9 billion in 2010. The increase in trade volume between 2006 and 2010 is 80%. As of September 2011, Turkey's trade volume with these countries has been US$35.7 billion, US$20.2 billion of this is Turkey's exports and US$15.5 of it is Turkey's imports.

185. For five years since 2006, export of Turkish goods to this region has exceeded imports. However, trade surplus has gradually decreased from US$8 billion in 2009 to US$6 billion in 2010. The foremost reason of this decline is the increase in oil and natural gas imports. Exports of Turkey to the region totaled US$21 billion (18.4% of the total export of Turkey) in 2010.

(v) Africa

186. Having a 5.2% share in Turkey's total trade in 2010, African countries have gained particular significance in trade figures of Turkey starting especially with the contribution of African Countries Strategy in 2003. The results obtained so far in terms of the development of trade seem to be much promising. The total trade volume augmented to US$15.7 billion in 2010 with 31% cumulative increase between 2006 and 2010. Of the total trade with Africa, 67.1% of imports and 75.7% of exports in 2010 were realized with five North African countries, namely, Morocco, Algeria, Tunisia, Libya and Egypt. In the first three quarters of 2011, Turkey's trade volume with Africa reached US$12.6 billion.

(vi) Americas

187. Turkey's trade with the Americas approached US$23 billion in 2010. As of September 2011, trade volume has already exceeded 2010 level and has been realized as US$23.2 billion. Of the total trade volume with this group in 2010, 70.3% was realized only with the USA. Turkish exports to the USA declined to US$3.76 billion in 2010, with a share of 3.3% in Turkey's total exports. Having almost US$2 billion trade volume with Brazil and US$1.4 billion with Canada are the other biggest

trading partners of Turkey in the Americas. In 2010, Turkey's exports to Brazil reached US$614.6 million, while imports from Brazil amounted to US$1,347.5 million. In the same year, Turkey's exports to Canada were US$479.5 million, while imports from this country amounted to US$915.3 million.

188. In 2009, Turkey and the USA decided to raise the U.S.-Turkish bilateral economic partnership to the strategic level. As follow up to this commitment, a senior level U.S.-Turkish consultative body was set up and the new process named as the "Framework for Strategic Economic and Commercial Cooperation" (FSECC). Since, strong involvement of the private sector in both countries is critical to increasing bilateral trade and investment, a joint U.S.-Turkish, public-private Business Council was also created.

189. On the other hand, The Latin American and the Caribbean countries with strong economic capacity and trade potentials are among the priority regions with whom Turkey wishes to increase its trade. Due to the success of policies followed since 2006, in 2010, Turkey's export to Latin America and the Caribbean region reached to US$1.8 billion, and its import from these countries approached to US$3.6 billion. Turkey aims to sustain the increasing trend of its trade volume to the region and to MERCOSUR in particular. This aim is to be complemented by prospective FTAs with MERCOSUR, Andean and Central American Countries in addition to the existing one with Chile.

(2) TRADE DEVELOPMENTS BY REGIONAL ORGANIZATIONS

(i) Economic Cooperation Organization (ECO)[7]

190. Turkey's trade volume with the Economic Cooperation Organization (ECO) region reached US$20.9 billion by 2010, resulting in US$5.6 billion deficit. The value of Turkish exports to this region in 2010 reached US$7.6 billion, which represents a share of 6.7% in total exports. As of September 2011, Turkey's trade volume with ECO countries has been US$20.2 billion, US$6.8 billion of which has been Turkey's exports whereas US$17.4 billion has been Turkey's imports. Once the ECO Trade Agreement (ECOTA) becomes fully operational, it is expected that the steady increase in Turkish exports to the region will gain further momentum. ECOTA will also bring about deepening trade relations among ECO member countries.

(ii) Black Sea Economic Cooperation (BSEC)[8]

191. As for the Black Sea Economic Cooperation (BSEC), Turkey's trade with the region accelerated at spectacular rates in each year over the past four years. Having nearly 16 % share in Turkey's total trade volume, in 2010, the proportion of imports in the total trade volume with the BSEC countries was nearly 70% causing more than US$19.1 billion deficits. The value of Turkish exports to the BSEC region in 2010 reached US$14.5 billion (12.7% in total exports). As of September 2011, Turkey's exports to BSEC countries has been US$12.9 billion and its imports has been US$28.2 billion.

[7] Members of the ECO are: Afghanistan, Azerbaijan, Iran, Kazakhstan, Kyrgyz Republic, Pakistan, Tajikistan, Turkmenistan and Uzbekistan alongside Turkey.

[8] Members of the BSEC are: Albania, Armenia, Azerbaijan, Bulgaria, Georgia, Hellenic Republic, Republic of Moldova, Romania, Russian Federation, Serbia, and Ukraine alongside Turkey.

(iii) Organization of Islamic Conference (OIC)[9]

192. Turkey is a founding member of the Organization of Islamic Conference (OIC). In 2010, while Turkey's exports to OIC countries reached US$32.5 billion with a 13.6% annual increase, its imports from those countries showed a remarkable increase by 55.8% and reached US$27.9 billion mostly due to recovery of world economy in 2010. As of September 2011, Turkey's exports to OIC countries have been US$27 billion and its imports have been US$24.1 billion. Overall, the legal basis of the Trade Preferential System among the OIC countries (TPS-OIC) has been completed by 9 August 2011. TPS-OIC is expected to become fully operational once 10 OIC members which have completed the signature and ratification of three legal instruments of the Agreement, submit their tariff concessions lists. Fully operational TPS-OIC will have positive effects on Turkey's trade volume with these countries.

(iv) Developing 8 (D-8)[10]

193. Trade volume with Developing 8 (D-8) countries surged to US$19.8 billion in 2010 by 48.3% annual increase. While Turkey's exports to the member countries reached to US$6.4 billion with a 15.4% annual increase, imports from those countries reached US$13.4 billion with a considerable increase (72%) mainly due to a huge jump of imports from Iran. Preferential Trade Agreement (PTA) legally entered into force on 25 August 2011 between Turkey, Malaysia, Iran and Nigeria, members which completed internal ratification process. D-8 PTA is expected to be fully operational after the completion of the exchange of tariff concessions lists. Once the PTA becomes full operational, it is expected that these developments will further stimulate Turkey's trade with D-8 countries.

(3) TRADE DEVELOPMENTS BY SECTORS[11]

194. Sectoral composition of Turkey's exports has been changing towards more capital and technology intensive products in accordance with the developments in global trends in world trade. The share of medium and high-tech products in Turkish exports moved up from 28.9% with a value of US$25 billion in 2006 to 29.8% with a value of US$34 billion in 2010, increasing by 37%.

195. In the period between 2006 and 2010, with the exception of 2009 during which the negative impacts of the global economic crisis were heavily felt, imports also increased significantly due to various reasons. First of all, the economic growth fed the need for intermediary and capital goods. Also, energy prices rose dramatically pushing the cost of energy imports up in the world. US$46 billion of the rise in imports between 2006 and 2010 is due to intermediary and capital goods and US$9.6 billion of this increase is completely attributable to fuels and oil. Meanwhile, energy imports increased from US$28.9 billion to US$38.5 billion and constituted more than one fifth of total imports in 2010. In 2010, 15.5% of imports were capital goods, 70.8% were intermediary goods and 13.3% were consumption goods. Due to the import dependency in industrial production, growth in

[9] Members of the OIC are: Afghanistan, Albania, Algeria, Azerbaijan, Bahrain, Bangladesh, Benin, Brunei, Burkina Faso, Cameroon, Chad, Comoros, Cote D'Ivoire, Djibouti, Egypt, Gabon, Gambia, Guinea, Guinea-Bissau, Guyana, Indonesia, Iran, Iraq, Jordan, Kazakhstan, Kuwait, Kyrgyz Republic, Lebanon, Libya, Malaysia, Maldives, Mali, Mauritania, Morocco, Mozambique, Niger, Nigeria, Oman, Pakistan, Palestine, Qatar, Saudi Arabia, Senegal, Sierra Leone, Somalia, Sudan, Suriname, Syria, Tajikistan, Togo, Tunisia, Turkmenistan, Uganda, United Arab Emirates, Uzbekistan and Yemen alongside Turkey.

[10] Members of the D-8 are: Bangladesh, Egypt, Indonesia, Iran, Malaysia, Nigeria, Pakistan and Turkey.

[11] See Annexed Table 5-D: Exports by SITC and 5-E: Imports by SITC.

production triggers growth in imports. In 2010, intermediary, consumption and capital goods marked 32.1%, 28.2% and 34.3% annual increases, respectively.

196. The value of "machinery and transport equipment" export, a product group dominated by high value added and high-tech products, in 2010 reached US$31.8 billion, which represents a share of 28% in total exports. Particularly the "automotive industry products" played the most significant role in increasing the share of this relatively high capital-intensive product group in Turkey's exports. Although exports of "automotive products" and "electrical machinery" dropped by 33% and 12% in 2009 due to the global economic crisis, the trend has been quite contrary in 2010. Our exports in these product groups grew by annual 14.8% and 15.3% respectively in 2010.

197. The total share of "automotive industry products", "office machines and telecommunications equipment" and "chemicals" increased 17.3% in 2010 after the global economic crisis. Clothing, automotive products, iron and steel are the products with the largest weight in the exports of industrial products. The shares of these sectors in exports were 11.2%, 12.1% and 8.9% in 2010.

198. The Turkish apparel sector is one of the most critical sectors in Turkey in terms of contribution to GDP, employment generation and net exports. Currently, the Turkish textile and clothing industry focuses on value added products. The local clothing industry emphasizes on new designs and fashion collections for the top end international apparel market. Furthermore, İstanbul Fashion Week is getting increasingly more attractive for the fashion world and it is Turkey's aim to make İstanbul one of the top five fashion centers of the world as of 2023.

(4) Trade in Free Zones

199. Turkey has 19 free zones, which provide incentives for companies operating within them. The aim is to promote foreign direct investment and joint-ventures in export-oriented enterprises, provide easy access to imported raw materials and equipment on favourable terms, and to increase employment.

200. A mix of government and private partnership (often realized within the framework of "build, operate, transfer" schemes) is being utilized for the foundation and operation of the free zones. Office space, workshops and warehouses are made available for rent on attractive terms, but investors can also construct their own premises in the free zones.

201. High-technology products, leather goods, and storage facilities are among a wide range of areas that enterprises established in the free zones are active in. According to Article 10 of the Free Zones Regulation, all types of industrial, commercial and service operations deemed appropriate by the Supreme Planning Board may be conducted in the free zones.

202. In 2010, a total of US$18.6 billion trade was realized in free zones, the distribution of which is US$5.3 billion from free zones to the domestic market, US$4.4 billion from free zones to other countries, US$2.3 billion from domestic market to free zones and US$6.6 billion from other countries to free zones.

IV. FUTURE ECONOMIC AND TRADE POLICY GOALS

203. Starting in October 2009, a strategy has been prepared to develop the infrastructure necessary for Turkey to become one of the top 10 economies in the world. Thus, Turkey aims to achieve US$500 billion of exports by 2023 which is the centenary of Turkish Republic. Following the

successful implementation of Three Year (2007-09) Export Strategy Plan, Turkey's 2023 Export Strategy Project (2023 ESP) has been prepared in order to increase its current and potential market share in total world export through providing vision and leadership to the exporters in the field of science, technology and innovation. The long term policy objective of the 2023 ESP is to transform Turkey's export composition from low-tech to high-tech products.

204. In accordance with this export-oriented production strategy, the legal and intellectual infrastructure has been prepared in 2010, and the aim for 2011-2013 is to enable the necessary technological transformation. 2014-2023 is determined as the implementation period.

205. Within the framework of the strategy, the target markets and sectors for exports will be further diversified, the number of exporters will be increased, and raw-material necessary for exports will be produced in Turkey to the extent possible. Turkey will follow a pro-active policy in both goods and services exports. Ensuring the sustainable growth of exports is the main target of this strategy since exports are the main locomotive of the economic growth in Turkey. With sustainable growth in the economy, unemployment rate is expected to decrease, gaps between the regions be closed and the competitive power of Turkish industries be increased.

206. The targeted export levels for lead sectors and sub-sectors have been determined with this strategy in order to be able to have an export volume of US$500 billion by 2023. This means that Turkey targets to get a share of 1.2% by 2013, 1.3% by 2018, and 1.5% by 2023 from world trade.

207. In the process of meeting these targets Turkey, which is the 17th largest economy in the world as of 2010, aims to become the 15th largest economy in the world in 2013, 12th in 2018 and 10th in 2023.

208. Finally, it should be noted that, concluding the Doha Development Agenda Negotiations with its potential to deliver substantial new trade opportunities would facilitate to achieve this goal.

209. With this in mind, Turkey will continue to work constructively in the DDA throughout 2012 and onwards.

APPENDIX TABLES

Table 1
FDI inflows and their distribution by components between 2000-10
(US$ million)

	2000-05	2006	2007	2008	2009	2010
Foreign direct investment (net)	16,100	19,261	19,941	16,955	6,858	7,816
Foreign direct capital	19,934	20,185	22,047	19,504	8,411	9,280
Capital (net)	14,814	16,982	18,394	14,712	6,170	6,477
Inflow	16,073	17,639	19,137	14,747	6,252	6,512
Outflow	-1,259	-657	-743	-35	-82	-35
Other capital	938	281	727	1,855	459	309
Real estate (net)	4,182	2,922	2,926	2,937	1,782	2,494

Table 2
The number of companies established with foreign capital

Year	Number of companies
1954-2000 (cumulative)	4,588
2001	477
2002	495
2003	1,105
2004	2,095
2005	2,845
2006	3,350
2007	3,304
2008	3,171
2009	2,936
2010	3,344
Total number	25,948

Table 3
Privatization implementations by years

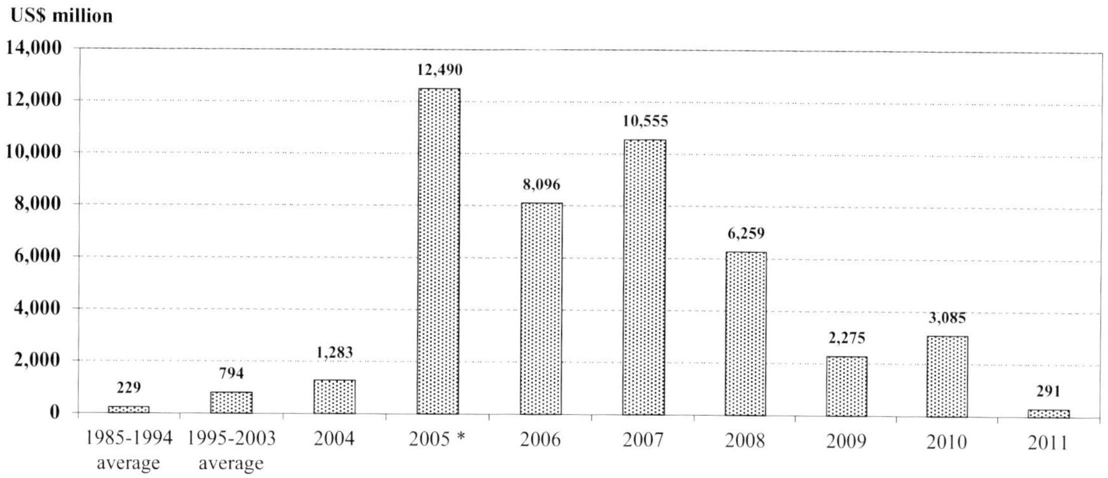

Note: (*) The Transfer of Operating Rights (TOR) of Ataturk Airport for 15.5 years in 2005 (USD 3 billion), Antalya Airport for 17 years in 2007 (USD 3.1 billion), Sabiha Gökçen Airport for 20 years in 2007 (USD 3 billion), TOR of İstanbul Sea Bus Co. and the Initial Public Offering (IPO) of Vakıflar Bank's 25.18% share in 2005 (USD 1.3 billion), are included.

Table 4
Significant privatization implementations between 2008 - 30 September 2010

Name of the privatized companies (2008-2009)	Area of activity	Date of privatization	Total (notional) market value of the company on the basis of its privatization price (million US$)	Percentage of equity sold to the new controlling investor (%)	Percentage of equity issued on or already in the stock market (%)	Percentage of the equity still owned by the Government (%)
Turk Telekom	Telecommunications	2008	1,911	IPO	15	40
Petkim Holding	Petrochemicals	2008	2,040	51	49	-
ADUAS	Electricity Production	2008	510	100		-
Tekel	Tobacco	2008	1,720	100-	-	-
Baskent El. Distribution	Electricity Distribution	2009	1,225	100	-	-
Sakarya El. Distribution	Electricity Distribution	2009	600	100	-	-
Meram El. Distribution	Electricity Distribution	2009	440	100		
Samsun Port	Shipping	2010	125.2	TOR	-	-
Bandırma Port	Shipping	2010	175.5	TOR	-	-
Osmangazi Elec. Dist.	Electricity Distribution	2010	485	100	-	-
Uludağ Elec. Dist.	Electricity Distribution	2010	940	100	-	-
Çamlıbel Elec. Dist.	Electricity Distribution	2010	258.5	100	-	-
Çoruh Elec. Dist.	Electricity Distribution	2010	227	100		

Table 5-A
Foreign trade by years
(Value 000 $)

Year	Exports		Imports		Balance		Volume of trade		Imports covered by exports
	Value	Change (%)	Value	Change (%)	Value	Change (%)	Value	Change (%)	(%)
2006	85,534,676	16.4	139,576,174	19.5	-54,041,499	24.8	225.,110,850	18.3	61.3
2007	107,271,750	25.4	170,062,715	21.8	-62,790,965	16.2	277,334,464	23.2	63.1
2008	132,027,196	23.1	201,963,574	18.8	-69,936,378	11.4	333,990,770	20.4	65.4
2009	102,142,613	-22.6	140,928,421	-30.2	-38,785,809	-44.5	243,071,034	-27.2	72.5
2010	113,883,219	11.5	185,544,332	31.7	-71,661,113	84.8	299,427,551	23.2	61.4

Table 5-B
Exports by country groups
(Value 000 $)

	2006	2007	2008	2009	2010
Total	**85,534,676**	**107,271,750**	**132,027,196**	**102,142,613**	**113,883,219**
A-EU COUNTRIES (27)	**47,934,746**	**60,398,502**	**63,390,419**	**47,013,415**	**52,685,304**
B-FREE ZONES IN TURKEY	**2,967,219**	**2,942,876**	**3,008,061**	**1,957,066**	**2,083,788**
C-OTHER COUNTRIES	**34,632,711**	**43,930,087**	**65,622,092**	**53,172,132**	**59,114,127**
1-Other European Countries	7,961,672	10,842,681	15,678,083	11,317,994	11,373,372
2-North African Countries	3,096,665	4,029,683	5,850,262	7,415,776	7,025,168
3-Other African Countries	1,469,127	1,946,661	3,212,341	2,738,866	2,257,898
4-North American Countries	5,439,399	4,540,601	4,801,535	3,578,829	4,242,435
5-Central America and Caribbean	548,451	548,835	828,687	621,826	597,975
6-South America Countries	340,598	513,719	901,401	677,599	1,237,356
7-Near and Middle Eastern	11,315,751	15,081,322	25,430,395	19,192,808	23,294,873
8-Other Asian Countries	3,941,556	5,227,250	7,074,123	6,705,544	8,580,833
9-Australia and New Zealand	327,020	342,812	435,326	361,640	402,591
10-Other Countries	192,474	856,524	1,416,562	561,251	101,627
Selected country groups					
OECD Countries	54,480,970	65,674,811	70,471,749	55,832,408	61,491,606
EFTA Countries	1,189,267	1,327,977	3,261,728	4,335,560	2,416,381
Organization of Black Sea Economic Co-operation	11,583,697	16,784,102	20,867,277	12,272,591	14,456,173
Organization for Economic Co-operation	3,340,996	4,700,072	6,247,706	5,948,111	7,617,077
New Independent States	6,992,529	10,088,336	13,938,226	7,957,492	10,288,272
Turkish Republics	1,981,603	2,874,467	3,749,451	3,399,485	3,921,072
Organization of Islamic Conference	15,007,499	20,310,574	32,596,965	28,626,586	32,469,556
Asia-Pacific Countries	3,013,944	3,846,208	5,535,084	5,045,113	6,558,584
Middle East Countries	10,212,502	13,387,571	22,765,082	17,042,483	20,975,107
Africa	4,564,707	5,976,110	9,062,590	10,179,965	9,283,024
Neighbouring and Surrounding Countries	29,380,904	40,381,302	56,648,561	42,979,736	49,120,660
D-8	2,225,732	2,953,763	4,343,981	5,589,255	6,438,640

Table 5-C
Imports by country groups
(Value 000 $)

	2006	2007	2008	2009	2010
Total	**139,576,174**	**170,062,715**	**201,963,574**	**140,928,421**	**185,544,332**
A-EU COUNTRIES (27)	**59,400,922**	**68,611,562**	**74,802, 380**	**56,587,647**	**72,243,512**
B-FREE ZONES IN TURKEY	**944,142**	**1,223,729**	**1,334,250**	**965,287**	**878,447**
C-OTHER COUNTRIES	**79,231,111**	**100,227,423**	**125,826,945**	**83,375,488**	**112,422,373**
1-Other European Countries	25,695,361	34,253,510	44,196,490	25,886,494	30,312,449
2-North African Countries	4,878,401	3,616,397	5,267,239	3,541,963	4,305,729
3-Other African Countries	2,526,126	3,167,700	2,503,214	2,158,010	2,107,927
4-North American Countries	6,935,690	9,032,926	13,404,016	9,513,149	13,234,069

Table 5-C (cont'd)

	2006	2007	2008	2009	2010
5-Central America and Caribbean	334,966	448,291	560,444	475,745	622,763
6-South America Countries	2,130,616	2,671,179	3,259,762	2,286,192	2,942,329
7-Near and Middle Eastern	10,568,063	12,641,279	17,627,603	9,595,220	16,091,252
8-Other Asian Countries	25,657,979	33,658,278	38,087,261	29,138,197	41,421,873
9-Australia and New Zealand	398,688	671,742	876,169	647,843	493,033
10-Other Countries	105,221	66,122	44,747	132,675	890,948
Selected country groups					
OECD Countries	77, 812,573	91,856,829	102,901,962	75,143,524	99,378,587
EFTA Countries	4,522,434	5,774,587	6,217,519	2,780,569	4,002,407
Organization of Black Sea Economic Cooperation	27,021,455	34,808,872	45,632,225	28,299,103	33,592,312
Organization for Economic Co-operation	8,101,662	9,972,107	13,220,660	7,010,888	13,298,439
New Independent States	23,372,924	31,262,659	42,613,879	26,044,568	30,599,779
Turkish Republics	1,967,429	2,669,249	4,278,503	2,873,767	4,614,713
Organization of Islamic Conference	19,110,794	21,524,428	29,178,544	17,969,867	27,949,043
Asia-Pacific Countries	24,311,765	31,851,317	35,466,523	27,561,662	37,881,747
Middle East Countries	9,882,728	12,022,007	16,172,653	8,555,903	14,932,769
Africa	7,404,523	6,784,092	7,770,443	5,699,967	6,413,592
Neighbouring and Surrounding Countries	45,823,039	55,728,240	73,531,501	45,394,550	60,752,117
D-8	8,912,940	11,179,601	13,619,621	7,773,834	13,369,328

Table 5-D
Exports by SITC, Rev.3
(Value 000 $)

	2006	2007	2008	2009	2010
Total	85,534,676	107,271,750	132,027,196	102,142,613	113,883,219
1- Agricultural products	8,633,253	9,769,025	11,473,866	11,189,510	12,663,950
i- Food	7,931,559	9,007,165	10,705,380	10,581,837	11,868,544
(0) Food and live animals	6,594,517	7,821,739	9,155,020	9,125,955	10,498,628
(00) Live animals	8,515	7,078	12,922	24,366	7,322
(04) Cereals and cereal preparations	876,054	1,036,754	1,385,466	1,481,627	1,782,194
(05) Fruits and vegetables	4,260,922	4,901,711	5,308,045	5,353,787	6,152,501
(06) Sugar, sugar preparations and honey	282,690	304,116	352,240	301,242	395,561
(08) Feeding stuff for animals	10,361	12,400	68,181	74,809	31,111
(01, 02, 03, 07, 08, 09) Others	1,155,975	1,559,680	2,028,166	1,890,123	2,129,909
(1) Beverages and tobacco	819,962	804,555	890,691	933,390	898,053
(11) Beverages	135,072	160,756	186,142	175,891	201,026
(12) Tobacco and tobacco manufactures	684,890	643,799	704,550	757,499	697,027
(4) Animal and vegetable oils, fats and waxes	437,581	290,073	570,268	427,121	345,917
(22) Oil seeds and oleaginous fruits	79,498	90,799	89,400	95,371	125,946
ii-Agricultural raw materials	701,694	761,859	768,486	607,673	795,406
(21) Hides, skins and furskins, raw	18,912	16,407	10,702	6,034	5,496
(23) Crude rubber (including synthetic, reclaimed)	13,248	15,272	30,861	20,622	35,215
(24) Cork and wood	28,841	32,914	30,617	37,433	41,331
(25) Pulp and waste paper	1,191	1,470	7,407	5,745	14,612
(26) Textile fibres (other than wool tops) and their wastes	540,787	587,569	571,334	423,381	566,391
(29) Crude animal and vegetable materials, n.e.s.	98,715	108,227	117,565	114,458	132,362

Table 5-D (cont'd)

	2006	2007	2008	2009	2010
2-Mining products	6,511,296	9,004,524	12,089,010	7,152,921	9,569,916
i-(27, 28) Metalliferous ores and metal scrap	1,497,428	2,078,264	2,462,893	1,853,884	2,948,914
ii-Minerals fuels, lubricants and related materials (3)	3,566,212	5,147,843	7,531,525	3,921,178	4,469,433
(32) Coal, coke and briquettes	2,605	12,688	32,397	1,883	6,999
(33) Petroleum, petroleum products and related materials	3,260,126	4,836,171	7,167,113	3,577,867	4,026,263
(34) Gas, natural and manufactured	179,910	130,180	258,716	201,746	255,033
(35) Electric current	123,570	168,804	73,300	139,681	181,138
ii-Non-ferrous metals (68)	1,447,656	1,778,416	2,094,592	1,377,859	2,151,569
3-Manufactures	69,325,372	87,007,336	104,255,769	78,563,009	89,126,928
i-Iron and steel (67)	7,239,269	9,585,832	16,841,632	9,081,057	10,199,467
ii-Chemicals	3,923,133	4,739,369	6,121,809	5,292,959	6,805,800
(57, 58) Plastics	1,443,695	1,861,901	2,365,570	1,983,395	2,428,061
(54) Pharmaceutical products	354,483	401,930	469,238	473,244	610,563
(51, 52, 53, 55, 56, 59) Other chemicals	2,124,956	2,475,538	3,287,000	2,836,319	3,767,175
iii-Other semi-manufactures	7,583,234	9,668,565	12,252,185	10,407,674	11,860,865
(61) Leather, leather manufactures, n.e.s. and dressed	144,311	164,865	150,821	116,315	159,183
(62) Rubber manufactures, n.e.s.	1,178,082	1,572,399	1,775,168	1,445,985	1,858,178
(63) Cork and wood manufactures (excluding furniture)	307,076	423,327	504,725	473,051	532,202
(64) Paper, paperboard and articles of paper pulp, of paper	600,235	823,662	1,035,584	965,291	1,169,250
(66) Non-metallic mineral manufactures, n.e.s.	2,477,208	3,064,214	3,987,814	3,512,343	3,708,419
(661) Lime, cement and fabricated construction	1,219,328	1,499,721	2,121,734	1,990,215	2,001,440
(664, 665) Glass and glassware	631,242	781,060	959,718	796,966	854,824
(66- (661+664+665)) Others	626,638	783,433	906,362	725,162	852,154
(69) Manufactures of metals, n.e.s.	2,876,323	3,620,098	4,798,073	3,894,689	4,433,634
iv-Machinery and transport equipment	26,385,878	34,250,969	39,147,395	28,788,981	31,811,230
(781, 782, 783, 784, 7132, 7783) Automotive products	11,688,733	15,581,880	17,872,796	11,985,061	13,753,084
(75, 76, 776) Office machines and telecommunications	3,165,320	2,870,741	2,399,886	2,011,498	2,074,348
(71-713) Power generating machinery	666,511	848,917	1,020,095	652,073	685,975
(72, 73, 74) Other non-electrical machinery	3,448,639	4,776,684	6,095,418	4,669,586	5,391,595
(79, 785, 786, 7131, 7138, 7139) Other transport	2,990,445	4,057,944	4,698,483	3,282,191	2,773,827
(77- (776+7783)) Electrical machinery and aparatus	4,426,230	6,114,803	7,060,785	6,188,572	7,132,401
v- Textiles (65)	7,584,693	8,950,041	9,406,905	7,733,300	8,969,554
vi- Clothing (84)	12,051,922	13,886,333	13,589,400	11,553,511	12,745,641
(848.1, 848.3) Articles of apparels, clothing accessories & other	386,414	398,827	411,097	314,707	355,992
(84- (848.1, 848.3)) Other cloting apparels	11,665,508	13,487,507	13,178,303	11,238,804	12,389,649
vii-Other consumer goods (81, 82, 83, 85, 87, 88, 89 (-891))	4,557,242	5,926,226	6,896,442	5,705,528	6,734,372
(81) Prefabricated buldings; sanitary, plumbing, heating and	1,003,119	1,223,910	1,387,990	1,129,126	1,183,487
(82) Furniture, bedding, mattress supports and cushions	788,154	1,067,523	1,367,084	1,180,728	1,393,205
(83) Travel goods, handbags and similar containers	96,320	121,498	141,144	111,130	140,653
(85) Footwear	237,069	316,740	344,890	289,473	395,624
(87) Professional, scientific and controlling instruments	195 402	271,749	327,506	287,377	319,572
(88, 89- (891)) Other manufactured articles	2,237,179	2,924,806	3,327,828	2,707,695	3,301,831
4- Other products (9+891)	1,064,744	1,490,865	4,208,551	5,237,173	2,522,425

Table 5-E
Imports by SITC, Rev.3
(Value 000 $)

	2006	2007	2008	2009	2010
Total	139,576,174	170,062,715	201,963,574	140,928,421	185,544,332
1- Agricultural products	7,286,159	9,812,753	13,037,582	9,630,588	12,879,646
i- Food	3,486,191	5,167,474	8,502,792	6,107,516	7,412,723
(0) Food and live animals	1,729,774	3,083,604	5,024,155	3,591,494	4,504,882
(00) Live animals	15,546	23,921	41,448	33,664	333,080
(04) Cereals and cereal preparations	211,783	1,023,694	2,207,585	1,284,854	1,169,797
(05) Fruits and vegetables	347,838	456,384	805,763	673,110	757,297
(06) Sugar, sugar preparations and honey	40,361	57,186	92,129	56,751	52,891
(08) Feeding stuff for animals	316,518	550,234	772,975	556,398	741,318
(01, 02, 03, 07, 08, 09) Others	797,728	972,186	1,104,256	986,717	1,450,499
(1) Beverages and tobacco	295,909	353,112	456,269	479,296	450,007
(11) Beverages	39,647	50,986	64,575	79,172	81,733
(12) Tobacco and tobacco manufactures	256,263	302,125	391,694	400,124	368,274
(4) Animal and vegetable oils, fats and waxes	932,701	828,962	1,702,286	1,122,449	1,047,127
(22) Oil seeds and oleaginous fruits	527,806	901,797	1,320,081	914,277	1,410,707
ii-Agricultural raw materials	3,799,969	4,645,279	4,534,790	3,523,072	5,466,923
(21) Hides, skins and furskins, raw	336,802	327,346	236,213	123,258	225,910
(23) Crude rubber (including synthetic, reclaimed)	614,554	723,491	945,314	568,753	1,016,126
(24) Cork and wood	475,729	540,392	548,540	359,767	462,119
(25) Pulp and waste paper	346,338	411,184	472,991	342,629	544,956
(26) Textile fibres (other than wool tops) and their wastes	1,835,552	2,421,004	2,074,340	1,895,158	2,948,806
(29) Crude animal and vegetable materials, n.e.s.	190,993	221,862	257,390	233,507	269,006
2-Mining products	38,601,438	46,932,435	65,011,388	39,334,811	53,353,881
i-(27, 28) Metalliferous ores and metal scrap	4,863,067	6,693,117	10,344,582	5,498,747	8,516,922
ii-Minerals fuels, lubricants and related materials (3)	28,858,774	33,882,782	48,280,963	29,905,148	38,496,980
(32) Coal, coke and briquettes	2,054,506	2,665,445	3,411,773	3,113,386	3,280,316
(33) Petroleum, petroleum products and related materials	16,608,314	19,339,366	27,034 429	15,171,831	21,037,562
(34) Gas, natural and manufactured	10,177,750	11,856,452	17,819,273	11,602,685	14,158,646
(35) Electric current	18,204	21,519	15,488	17,245	20,455
ii-Non-ferrous metals (68)	4,879,598	6,356,537	6,385,842	3,930,916	6,339,979
3-Manufactures	89,253,691	107,394,250	118,229,351	89,667,421	116,258,544
i-Iron and steel (67)	8,140,677	11,341,045	15,033,712	7,680,338	9,720,695
ii-Chemicals	18,407,548	22,106,761	25,541,690	20,265,674	25,446,320
(57, 58) Plastics	6,221,473	7,870,109	8,485,949	6,246,789	8,871,694
(54) Pharmaceutical products	3,343,087	3,838,377	4,738,445	4,418,944	4,777,741
(51, 52, 53, 55, 56, 59) Other chemicals	8,842,987	10,398,275	12,317,296	9,599,942	11,796,885
iii-Other semi-manufactures	7,177,461	8,313,408	9,073,931	6,695,610	9,039,774
(61) Leather, leather manufactures, n.e.s. and dressed	346,258	410,563	392,462	231,913	334,117
(62) Rubber manufactures, n.e.s.	910,175	1,103,071	1,225,733	931,708	1,228,795
(63) Cork and wood manufactures (excluding furniture)	464,867	624,904	617,662	377,089	642,710
(64) Paper, paperboard and articles of paper pulp, of paper	2,011,897	2,285,628	2,409,405	2,019,978	2,618,615
(66) Non-metallic mineral manufactures, n.e.s.	1,364,578	1,455,527	1,430,750	1,056,460	1,426,000
(661) Lime, cement and fabricated construction	287,261	250,795	209, 144	173,013	205,678
(664, 665) Glass and glassware	490,674	544,080	515,664	411,584	535,630
(66- (661+664+665)) Others	586,643	660,651	705,943	471,863	684,691
(69) Manufactures of metals, n.e.s.	2,079,687	2,433,716	2,997,919	2,078,463	2,789,538

Table 5-E (cont'd)

	2006	2007	2008	2009	2010
iv-Machinery and transport equipment	43,036,631	49,858,008	51,594,786	41,055,103	53,875,756
(781, 782, 783, 784, 7132, 7783) Automotive products	12,917,414	14,683,563	15,154,913	10,507,093	15,461,965
(75, 76, 776) Office machines and telecommunications	7,634,356	8,723,915	8,119,395	7,224,104	8,462,423
(71-713) Power generating machinery	989,600	1,375,628	2,352,967	3,097,896	3,540,769
(72, 73, 74) Other non-electrical machinery	12,841,462	15,262,601	14,769,596	10,308,840	13,151,924
(79, 785, 786, 7131, 7138, 7139) Other transport	3,443,948	3,457,886	4,326,805	4,041,391	6,030,799
(77- (776+7783)) Electrical machinery and aparatus	5,209,851	6,354,416	6,871,110	5,875,779	7,227,876
v- Textiles (65)	4,686,040	6,152,229	5,801,498	4,879,692	6,701,821
vi- Clothing (84)	1,097,719	1,566,561	2,216,248	2,147,857	2,835,239
(848.1, 848.3) Articles of apparels, clothing accessories & other	63,211	71,083	123,088	135,959	138,791
(84- (848.1, 848.3)) Other cloting apparels	1,034,508	1,495,478	2,093,160	2,011,898	2,696,448
vii-Other consumer goods (81, 82, 83, 85, 87, 88, 89 (-891))	6,707,615	8,056,237	8,967,486	6,943,147	8,638,939
(81) Prefabricated buldings; sanitary, plumbing, heating and	523,069	567,549	644,595	406,601	560,156
(82) Furniture, bedding, mattress supports and cushions	514,164	680,846	733,848	548,190	711,278
(83) Travel goods, handbags and similar containers	296,367	390,640	405,626	222 699	264,748
(85) Footwear	514,970	569,929	672,917	539,468	659,674
(87) Professional, scientific and controlling instruments	1,800,485	2,099,733	2,406,629	1,985,453	2,453,476
(88, 89- (891)) Other manufactured articles	3,058,560	3,747,540	4,103,871	3,240,736	3,989,607
4- Other products (9+891)	4,434,885	5,923,276	5,685,254	2,295,602	3,052,262